W9-AHC-721

The Complete Guide to the TOEFL® Test

HEINLE & HEINLE'S Complete Guide to the TOEFL® Test

Second Edition

Bruce Rogers
English Program, Economics Institute
University of Colorado
Boulder, Colorado

HEINLE & HEINLE PUBLISHERS

I(T)P AN INTERNATIONAL THOMSON PUBLISHING COMPANY

BOSTON, MASSACHUSETTS 02116 U.S.A.

"TOEFL" and "TWE" are registered trademarks of Educational Testing Service.

The test questions and any other testing information are provided in their entirety by Heinle & Heinle Publishers. No endorsement of this publication by Educational Testing Service should be inferred.

The publication of *The Complete Guide to the TOEFL Test, Second Edition* was directed by the members of the Newbury House ESL/EFL team at Heinle & Heinle:

Erik Gundersen, Editorial Director
Bruno Paul, Market Development Director
Kristin Thalheimer, Production Service Coordinator
Maryellen Eschmann Killeen, Production Editor

Also participating in the publication of this program were:

Stanley J. Galek, Vice President & Publisher
Ken Pratt, Associate Editor
Mary Sutton, Associate Market Development Director
Mary Beth Hennebury, Manufacturing Coordinator
Pre-Press Company, Inc., Interior Designer
Mark Caleb, Cover Designer

Library of Congress Catologing in Publication Data
Rogers, Bruce, 1949–
    Heinle & Heinle's Complete Guide to the TOEFL Test/Bruce Rogers 2nd.
    p. cm.
    ISBN 0-8384-6789-x
    1. Test of English as a Foreign Language—Study Guides.
2. English language—textbooks for foreign speakers. 3. English
language—Examinations—Study guides. I. Title.
P.E128.P6344 1997   97-29654
428'.0076—dc20   CIP

Copyright 1998 by Heinle & Heinle Publishers
All rights reserved, no parts of this publication may be reproduced or transmitted in any form or by any means, electronic or mechanical, including photocopy, recording, or any information storage and retrieval system, without permission in writing from the publisher.

Manufactured in the United states of America

Heinle & Heinle
An International Thomson Publishing Company
Boston, Massachusetts 02116 U.S.A.

ISBN 0-8384-6789-x

10 9 8 7 6

▲
CONTENTS

▼
PREFACE

About This Book

If you are preparing for TOEFL, you are not alone. Over three-quarters of a million people all over the world took the test in 1995-1996. A high score on this test is an essential step in being admitted to graduate or undergraduate programs at almost all colleges and universities in North America. But preparing for this test can be a difficult, frustrating experience. Perhaps you haven't taken many standardized, multiple choice tests such as TOEFL. Perhaps you are not familiar with the format of TOEFL. Maybe you've taken TOEFL once but were not satisfied with your score, or maybe you've taken the test several times but can't seem to improve your score beyond a certain point.

In any of these cases, you need a guide. That's why this book was written—to help students preparing for this important exam to maximize their scores.

This is the most complete, accurate, and up-to-date TOEFL preparation book now available. It is based on twelve years of classroom experience teaching TOEFL preparation classes in the United States and abroad, and on several years of research on the test. *The Complete Guide to the TOEFL Test* is simply written and clearly organized and is suitable for any intermediate or advanced student of English as a second or foreign language.

The Complete Guide to the TOEFL Test offers a step-by-step program that teaches you critical test-taking techniques, helps you polish the language skills needed for the exam, and generally makes you a smarter test-taker. And the *Guide* is an efficient way to prepare for TOEFL; by concentrating only on the points that are actually tested in TOEFL, it lets you make the most of your preparation period and never wastes your time.

Good luck on TOEFL!

What's New About the Second Edition

The Second Edition of *The Complete Guide to TOEFL* involves many changes. The Sample Test Sections and the Practice Tests have been modified to reflect the new (July 1995) test format. The strategies and tactics for Section 1 and Section 3 have similarly been altered to reflect the changes in those sections of the test. Material about "new" question types (such as the vocabulary-in-context items in Section 3) has been added and material about item types that are no longer used (such as location questions in Section 1, Part A or separate vocabulary questions in Section 3) has been deleted.

However, not all changes were made in response to the changes in the format of TOEFL. Since the first edition was published in 1993, users of the text have offered valuable insights and comments at conferences and through letters, faxes, and e-mail messages. My own students in TOEFL prep classes have provided a constant source of feedback. I've used much of this information in revising the text. For example, several items have been added to each exercise in Section 2 that do NOT focus on the target structure for that lesson. Adding these items makes these exercises considerably more challenging. Another change has been to add a third practice test. And, in general, key exercises and explanations have been expanded.

These and many other changes in the text came from suggestions of teachers and students who have used the first edition in the classrooom.

All in all, I believe that *The Complete Guide to TOEFL* continues to be the most complete, accurate, and up-to-date TOEFL preparation book available.

If you have comments about the Second Edition of this book, or about any aspect of TOEFL, I welcome your ideas, questions, and suggestions. Please feel free to contact me at the address, fax number, or e-mail address below.

And, as always, good luck on TOEFL!

Bruce Rogers
October 1996

Address: c/o Heinle & Heinle Publishers
20 Park Plaza
Boston, Massachusetts 02116

Fax: (303) 492-3006
E-mail: brogers@colorado.edu

Organization of this Book

Getting Started, the first section of the book, serves as an introduction to the exam. The opening portion of this section, **Questions and Answers about TOEFL,** provides you with information about the format of the test, guides you through the process of registering for the exam, and helps you understand your scores. The next portion of this section, **Keys to High Scores,** presents the "secrets" of being a good test-taker—picking the right test date, arranging your preparation time, using the process of elimination, coping with test anxiety, pacing yourself during the test, and other important techniques.

The main body of the book is divided into three parts, reflecting the three main sections of the test: Listening Comprehension, Structure and Written Expression, and Reading Comprehension. Each of these sections consists of the following components:

- An introduction containing basic strategies for that section of the test.

- A full-length sample test to give you a feel for each part of the test and to provide a basis for understanding the lessons.

- An introduction to each subsection of the test, with specific tactics for approaching the items in each portion of the test.

- Lessons that break down the knowledge and skills needed for each part of the test into comprehensible "bites" of information. Each of the forty-eight lessons in the book contains sample items that illustrate exactly how the point brought up in that lesson is tested in TOEFL. Furthermore, each lesson contains one or more exercises for practicing the relevant points. Some of these items follow TOEFL format, others follow formats appropriate for the particular point being taught, but all of them have the same "feel" as actual TOEFL items. There are around 125 of these exercises in the *Guide*—totaling over 2,500 practice items!

- Mini-tests that review the points brought up in the previous lessons. These tests put together the points practiced in isolation in the lessons and allow you to chart your progress. All the items on the mini-tests are identical in form to items on actual tests.

- Mini-lessons covering important testing points which require more time to master than points brought up in the lessons. You should begin studying and working the exercises in the mini-lessons as soon as you begin each section of the guide.

- **Section 1: Listening Comprehension** This section is subdivided into three parts, each one designed to familiarize you with the problems commonly encountered on the three parts of the revised Section 1: Dialogues, Extended Conversations, and Mini-Talks. The exercises and tests in this part of the book are intended to be used with the tapes that accompany the *Guide*. The mini-lessons for this section teach common idioms and figurative expressions that are often heard in Part A.

- **Section 2: Structure and Written Expression** The first part of this section categorizes common grammatical points tested in Structure problems and suggests ways to solve these problems. The second part lists the usual errors that must be identified in Written Expression problems and offers ways to identify these mistakes. The mini-lessons for this section cover preposition usage.

- **Section 3: Reading Comprehension** This section of the book prepares you for the revised third section of TOEFL. The Reading Comprehension portion of the book suggests reading attack skills, lists the various types of questions asked about the passages, and offers suggestions for answering each type of question. There are in-depth reading exercises to practice these techniques. The mini-lessons for this section involve vocabulary building.

- **The Test of Written English** This part of the book introduces the TWE and presents the best methods for planning, writing, and checking the essay you must write if you take this portion of the exam. There are two models of strong TWE essays and there are three practice TWE exams.

- **Three Complete Practice Tests** Practice tests provide one of the best ways to get ready for TOEFL because they draw together all the points you have studied. These tests duplicate the format, content, and level of difficulty of the actual exam. You may want to take one of these tests as a diagnostic when you begin your studies. To get the most out of these exams, follow the recommendations in the section titled **About Taking the Practice Tests.** Scoring information is also included here.

Suggestions for Using This Book

The Complete Guide to the TOEFL test is designed to be used either as a textbook for TOEFL preparation classes or as a tool for individuals preparing for the exam by themselves. If you are working alone, you will need the tapes to accompany the textbook as well as the answer keys and tapescripts.

Whether working alone or in a group, you should begin your preparation for TOEFL by reading the introductory chapters titled **Getting Started.** You can then work through the book in the order in which it is written or begin with the section in which you are weakest (or in which the majority of the students in a class are weakest.) Generally, you can make the fastest progress by working in your weakest area. You can determine which area is your weakest by looking at the scores from a previous test or by using one of the practice tests as a diagnostic test.

The amounts of time required to cover each segment of the *Guide* are given below. Keep in mind that these times are VERY approximate and do not include review sessions.

Getting Started	1–3 hours
Guide to Listening Comprehension	12–16 hours
Guide to Structure and Written Expression	20–25 hours
Guide to Reading Comprehension	15–20 hours
Guide to the Test of Written English	3–5 hours
Three Complete Practice Tests	6–8 hours

Acknowledgements

I would like to thank the following professionals for their comments and suggestions during the development of the first edition of this text:

Steven A. Stupak	Korea International Human Resources Development Center
Virginia Hamori	American Language Institute, American University of Paris
Jim Price	International Language Center, Bangkok
Stephen Thewlis	San Francisco State University
Connie Monroe	Queens College, The City University of New York
Steven Horowitz	Central Washington University
Dan Douglas	Iowa State University
Frederick O'Connor	Washington State University
Claire Bradin	Michigan State University

I would like to thank Donald Pharr for his expert proofreading.

Special thanks to all of the students in my TOEFL Preparation Classes at the Economics Institute.

Acknowledgements for the Second Edition

First, I would like to thank the many subscribers to the Material Writers branch of TESOL-L (an electronic bulletin board for teachers of English as a Second Language) who responded when I asked for suggestions on revising this text.

I would also like to thank the following for their reviews of an outline or an early draft of the manuscript:

Karin Avila-John	University of Dayton
James Beaton	Boston University
Debra Dean	University of Akron
Glenn Hawkes	University of Georgia
Thomas Leverett	Southern Illinois University
John Levis	North Carolina State University
Maryann O'Brien	Interlink Language Center, Colorado School of Mines
Ian Palmer	LASPAU, Harvard University
Ellen Polsky	Intensive English Center, University of Colorado
May Kay Purcell	University of Evansville
Antonina N. Rodgers	North Virginia Community College
Seth Sicroff	University of California at Davis
Ayse Gürsel Stromsdorfer	St. Louis University
Ted Tucker	China Institute of Technology, Taiwan
Nelleke Van Deusen-Scholl	University of California, Berkeley

Thanks also to the following their painstaking reviews and proofreading of the "final" draft of the manuscript:

Ian Palmer	LASPAU, Harvard University
Seth Sycroft	University of California, Davis

Domo arigato to Kayoko Otani, translator of the Japanese edition of *The Complete Guide to the TOEFL Test,* for suggesting some of the vocabulary-in-context items in Section 3, and to Satoshi Saito, editor of the Japanese edition, for numerous acts of kindness.

Thanks to Sandra Tompson, Anne Edmonson, and again to Donald Pharr for their proof-editing, and to Frank Weaver for his work on the answer key.

Thanks to my editors at Heinle & Heinle, David Lee, and Erik Gundersen, and of course to Ken Mattsson for keeping the project on track and to production editor Maryellen Killeen for making it happen.

And again, special thanks to the students in my TOEFL preparation courses at the Economics Institute.

Getting Started

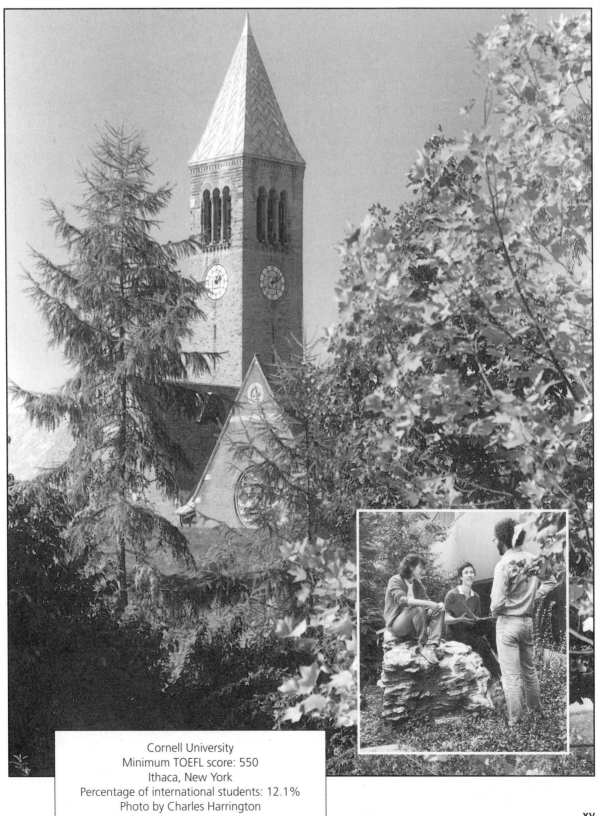

Cornell University
Minimum TOEFL score: 550
Ithaca, New York
Percentage of international students: 12.1%
Photo by Charles Harrington

Questions and Answers about TOEFL

Q: What is TOEFL?

A: TOEFL stands for *Test of English as a Foreign Language*. It is a test designed to measure the English-language ability of people who do not speak English as their first language and who plan to study at colleges and universities in North America either as undergraduate or graduate students.

Educational Testing Service (ETS) of Princeton, New Jersey, prepares and administers TOEFL. This organization produces many other standardized tests, such as the Test of English for International Communication (TOEIC), the Scholastic Aptitude Test (SAT), the Graduate Management Admission Test (GMAT), and the Graduate Record Exam (GRE).

Although there are other standardized tests of English, TOEFL is by far the most important in North America. ETS has offered this exam since 1965. Each year, almost 850,000 people take TOEFL at more than 1,250 testing centers all over the world. About 2,500 colleges and universities in the United States and Canada require students from non-English speaking countries to supply TOEFL scores as part of their application process.

Q: What format does TOEFL follow? How long does it take to complete?

A: All the questions on TOEFL are multiple choice questions with four answer choices. The test is divided into three sections, each with its own time limit. These sections are always given in the same order.

TOEFL Format		
	Standard Form	**Long Form**
Listening Comprehension	50 items 30 minutes (approximately)	80 items 45 minutes (approximately)
Structure and Written Expression	40 items 25 minutes	60 items 40 minutes
Reading Comprehension	50 items 55 minutes	75 items 80 minutes
Totals	140 items 1 hour 50 minutes	215 items 2 hours 45 minutes

The long form of TOEFL is sometimes given in the U.S. and Canada. The exact number of items and time limits varies somewhat from test to test on the long form. Only 140 out of the total number of items are scored. (The rest will appear on future TOEFL tests.) Unfortunately, there is no way to know which items are scored. You may see some "experimental" item types on the long form, especially in the Reading Comprehension section.

Because of the time it takes to check identification, show people to their seats, give directions, and pass out and collect exams, you will actually be in the testing room for about two and a half hours for the standard form of the test, and about three hours for the long form.

Q: How has TOEFL changed?

A: In July 1995, ETS began giving a slightly different form of TOEFL. In the Listening Section, the old Part A, called Statements, was eliminated. This part was replaced by a greater number of the old Part B Dialogs (short conversations). This became the new Part A. The old Part C, Extended Conversation and Mini-Talks, was divided into two parts. The new Part B consists of Extended Conversations; the new Part C consists of Mini-Talks (short lectures). The new Listening Comprehension section lasts about as long as the old one did (30 minutes). There are no new types of items.

There were no changes in Part 2, Structure and Written Expression.

Section 3, Vocabulary and Reading Comprehension, became Reading Comprehension. The thirty separate Vocabulary items that formerly began this section were eliminated. Twenty more Reading Comprehension questions were added, including many more vocabulary-in-context items that ask about words in the Reading passages. There are five or six passages, and the passages tend to be slightly longer than before. The new Section 3 takes 10 minutes longer to complete than did the old version. There are no new item types.

There are no changes in the means of calculating scores.

The overall changes are summarized in the following chart:

Old TOEFL Format	New TOEFL Format
Section 1: Listening Comprehension	**Section 1: Listening Comprehension**
Part A: Statements	Part A: Dialogs
20 items	30 items
Part B: Dialogs	Part B: Extended Conversations
15 items	2 conversations
Part C: Extended Conversations and Mini-Talks	7–8 items
4 conversations/talks	Part C: Mini-Talks
15 items	3 talks
	12–13 items
±30 minutes	±30 minutes
Section 2: Structure and Written Expression	**Section 2: Structure and Written Expression**
Structure (Sentence Completion)	Structure (Sentence Completion)
15 items	15 items
Written Expression (Error Identification)	Written Expression (Error Identification)
25 items	25 items
25 minutes	25 minutes
	(No changes in Section 2)
Section 3: Vocabulary and Reading Comprehension	**Section 3: Reading Comprehension**
Vocabulary	5–6 passages
30 items	50 items (including an increased number
Reading Comprehension	of vocabulary-in-context questions)
5 passages	
30 items	
45 minutes	55 minutes

More information is given about specific changes in the TOEFL in the introductions to the Listening Comprehension and Reading Comprehension sections of the *Guide*.

Q: What is an Institutional TOEFL?

A: Institutional TOEFL tests are given by English language schools and other institutions. Sometimes they are used for placement in a school's English program or for testing a student's progress. Institutional tests are made up of items that previously appeared on tests administered by ETS.

Because ETS does not supervise these tests, some universities won't accept the results. However, many other universities WILL. You should check with the admissions offices of universities to see what their policy is. You must arrange for the institute where you took the exam to send the scores to the university.

Q: Has the format of the Institutional TOEFL also changed?

A: According to ETS, Institutional TOEFL tests will continue to follow the old format until January 1997. At that time, they will begin to follow the new format as well.

Q: What is TWE?

A: TWE (*Test of Written English*) tests your ability to communicate in written English by requiring you to write a short essay on a specified topic. You have twenty-five minutes to complete your essay. TWE is given before the main part of TOEFL five times a year. There is no additional fee for taking TWE.

The format for TWE has not changed.

Some universities require both TOEFL and TWE scores, but many universities do not require TWE.

Q: What is TSE?

A: TSE (*Test of Spoken English*) tests your ability to communicate in spoken English. All of your responses are recorded on audio tape so that they can be evaluated later. The test takes about twenty minutes to complete and is given twelve times a year at various test centers. On TSE, you must answer questions about pictures or graphs, complete sentences, express your opinions on various topics, give short presentations, and so on. TSE is administered separately from TOEFL and must be paid for separately.

TSE is generally required only for students who are applying for positions as teaching assistants or for special programs or certificates.

Q: How do I register for TOEFL?

A: The first step is to obtain a current copy of the ETS publication, *Bulletin of Information for TOEFL and TSE*. In North America, these are usually available at English language centers and at the international student offices or admission offices of universities. You may also request one directly from ETS.

Address: TOEFL/TSE Services
             P.O. Box 6151
             Princeton, NJ 08541-6151
             U.S.A.

Telephone: 609/771-7100
Fax Number: 609/771-7500
E-mail: toefl@ets.org

If you are going to take TOEFL outside North America, you will probably need to obtain a *Bulletin* prepared specifically for your country or region. These are available from many U.S. cultural or educational facilities, English-language programs, bi-national centers and libraries, U.S. Information Service offices, and many other locations.

The *Bulletin* contains a schedule of tests, a registration form, and an envelope for sending it to ETS. Follow the directions in the *Bulletin* for completing the registration form. Payment for taking TOEFL in the United States must be in the form of a money order (in U.S. dollars) or a check from a U.S. bank. In the past, different fees were charged for tests given on Friday and tests given on Saturday (because it costs more to rent testing sites on Friday), but beginning in the 1997–1998 testing year, the fee for taking TOEFL on either day will be the same (U.S.$45).

Q: When should I register for TOEFL?

A: The deadline for applying for TOEFL is approximately one month before the testing date in the U.S. and Canada, and six weeks before in other countries. To get the location and testing date that you want, apply as early as possible. You might be assigned to an alternate site if your first choice of location is full.

Q: After I've registered for the test, when will I receive my admission ticket?

A: You should receive it about two weeks before the exam. The admission ticket will tell you exactly when and where to take the test. It's not possible to change the date and location. If you haven't received this form five days before the test date, call ETS at 609/771-7100 and inform them.

When you receive your admission ticket, fill it out according to the directions. Be sure you correctly copy the codes for the institutes that will receive your score. (These codes are listed in the *Bulletin*.)

Keep your admission ticket in a safe place. You'll need it to be admitted to the test center and later, if you correspond with ETS about the test, you'll need the registration number that appears on the ticket.

Q: What should I bring with me to the exam site?

A: You should bring the following:

- Your passport or other appropriate identification document (The *Bulletin* explains what forms of identification are acceptable.)
- Your admission ticket
- A watch
- Several pencils
- Your photo file record, with a recent $2\frac{1}{4}$ inch by $2\frac{1}{2}$ inch photograph attached (see the *Bulletin*)

If you take a disclosed test admission and want to receive a copy of the test, you will also need to bring a self-addressed, stamped envelope (See Key #4, page xxiii for more information.)

Don't bring any reference books, such as dictionaries. You are not permitted to smoke, eat, or drink in the test center.

Q: When will I receive the results of the test?

A: ETS sends scores to you and to the institutions that you request about four weeks after you have taken the test. ETS will not send your scores early or give out scores over the telephone.

Results for Institutional TOEFL tests are available sooner, often in a week or two.

Q: How does ETS calculate my TOEFL score?

A: There is a total score and three sub-scores, one for each section of the test. Each section counts equally toward the total score. To obtain these scores, ETS's computers count the number of correct answers in each section. The results are called raw scores. The raw scores are then converted into scaled scores. By means of a statistical process called test equating, a score from one TOEFL test is equivalent to the same score on another TOEFL, even if one of the tests is slightly simpler or more difficult than the other.

The scaled scores from each section are added together, multiplied by 10, and divided by 3 to arrive at a total score, as shown:

Scaled	Part 1		Part 2		Part 3		
scores	49	+	58	+	55	=	162

							Total Score
(162×10)	=	1620	÷	3	=		540

Total scores range from a high of 670 to a low of 200, although scores below 320 are rare. (Even if you don't open the test book and you fill in the blanks on your answer sheet at random, your score should be around 320.) You must answer at least 25% of the questions in all three sections to receive a test score.

Q: Is every item on the test scored?

A: No, there is usually at least one unscored item in each part of the test. This is generally the last item in each part. For example, in Section 2, items 15 (the last item in Structure) and item 40 (the last item in Written Expression) is usually not scored. However, it's not recommended that you skip these items—ETS could always change its system!

Q: What is a passing score on TOEFL?

A: There isn't any. Each university has its own standards for admission, so you should check the catalogs of universities you are interested in, or contact their admissions offices. Most undergraduate programs require scores between 500 and 550, and most graduate programs ask for scores between 525 and 600. In recent years, there has been a tendency for universities to raise their minimum TOEFL requirements. Of course, the higher your score, the better your chance of admission.

A chart in the Bulletin allows you to compare your TOEFL scores with those of other people who have taken the test in the last year. For example, the chart tells you that, if your total score was 540, 60% of all test-takers had lower scores than you did.

Q: How are universities informed of my scores?

A: ETS reports your score to three institutions for free. For a charge, ETS will send your scores to additional institutions. There is a form for requesting this service in the *Bulletin.* Some universities will also accept photocopies of the test results that were mailed directly to you.

Q: If I feel I haven't done well on TOEFL, can I have my scores canceled?

A: Yes, but only for a certain period of time. At the end of the test, you can fill in the Score Cancellation section of the answer sheet. You may also fax ETS at 609/771-7500 within a week of taking a test; write "Attention, TOEFL Score Cancellation" at the top of your fax message. Include your name, test date, number of your testing center, and registration number (from your admission test), and sign the fax.

You can't cancel your scores after you have seen the results, and you can't cancel TOEFL and TWE scores separately.

It is generally NOT a good idea to cancel scores. You may have done better on the test that you thought you did.

Q: Is it possible to improve one's score by cheating?

A: Don't try. Test-takers are seated carefully; it is very difficult for them to see anyone else's answer sheet. Even if a test-taker can see someone else's answers, there are different forms of the same exam. In other words, the items in one person's test book do not appear in the same order as they do in another person's. ETS also runs computer checks to detect patterns of cheating.

It is also very difficult to have someone else take the exam for you. You must bring an official identification document with your picture on it. You are also required to bring a photo file record with a recent photo of yourself. ETS copies this photo and sends it with your scores to universities. If the person in the photo is not the same person who enrolls, that person may not be admitted.

The following are also considered cheating:

- Taking notes during the Listening section
- Talking to or signalling any other test-takers
- Copying any test material
- Working on one section during the time allotted for another section
- Continuing to work on a section after time is called

Persons who are believed to be cheating will receive a warning for minor acts of cheating. For more serious matters, a person's scores will be canceled.

Q: How many times may I take TOEFL?

A: As often as you want; there is no limit. ETS will send only your most recent scores to institutions. It is not uncommon for people to take the test three, four, or more times before they obtain satisfactory scores.

Q: Will there be other changes in TOEFL in the near future?

A: Probably. ETS has announced that it will begin offering a computer-based version (TOEFL CBT) within the next few years. It will only be offered in North America at first, but will eventually be available at many testing sites overseas. Until it is available at all locations, some sites will still administer the pencil-and-paper version.

When you take the computer-based version of TOEFL, you will no longer have to sign up far in advance and you will take the test alone, not with hundreds of other people. You will receive your scores much faster. For test-takers who are not familiar with computers, there will be a tutorial program designed to teach you the basic skills you need to take the test on a computer. ETS is currently conducting research to make sure that computer skills, or a lack of them, do not affect TOEFL scores.

Q: Will the computer-based test be different from the current form of TOEFL?

A: At the time of this writing (1996), the exact format of the computer-based version of TOEFL has not been decided on. However, ETS has made some preliminary announcements:

- TOEFL CBT will probably have fewer items.
- A new system for scoring the test will be employed.
- The TWE may become part of Section 2, Structure and Written Expression. Test-takers may either enter their essay on a keyboard or write it out by hand.
- New types of items may appear.

Q: How can I get more information about TOEFL?

A: You now can contact ETS via the Internet or get updated information about the test from its home page on the World Wide Web:

E-Mail: toefl@ets.org
Web Site: http//www.toefl.org

Twelve Keys to High Scores on TOEFL

Key #1: Increase your general knowledge of English.

There are two types of knowledge that will lead to high TOEFL scores:

- A knowledge of the tactics used by good test takers and of the "tricks" of the test (which you will learn by using this *Guide*)
- A general command of English (which must be built up over a long period)

Following a step-by-step TOEFL preparation program, such as that presented in *The Complete Guide to the TOEFL Test,* will familiarize you with the tactics you need to raise your scores. The practice tests in this book will help you polish these techniques

The best way to increase your general knowledge of English is simply to use English as much as possible. Classes in English will be useful, and so will opportunities to speak, read, write, or listen to English.

Some people who are preparing for TOEFL think that conversation classes and practice are a waste of time because speaking skills are not tested on the exam. In fact, one of the best ways to get ready for the exam is to converse in English whenever you can. Not only will you improve your ability to listen to everyday English, but you'll also learn to think in English. If you are living in an English-speaking country, don't spend all your time with people from your own country. If you are living in your home country, try to arrange opportunities for conversations in English.

You can improve your listening comprehension skills by going to English language lectures and movies. Listening to news and informational broadcasts on the radio is especially useful. Reading books, magazines, and newspapers in English can help you prepare for the Reading Comprehension part of the test.

One of your most important jobs is to systematically improve your vocabulary. Vocabulary building will help you, not just in the Reading Comprehension section, but throughout the exam. You may want to keep a personal vocabulary list. When you come across an unfamiliar word, look it up in a dictionary and write the word and its definition in your personal vocabulary list. Keep this list with you and study it when riding buses, eating lunch, taking coffee breaks, or whenever else you have a free moment.

Key #2: Make the most of your preparation time.

You need to train for TOEFL just as you would train for any important competitive event. Obviously, the sooner you can start training, the better, but no matter when you begin, you need to get the most out of your preparation time.

Make a time management chart. Draw up an hour-by-hour schedule of your week's activities. Block out those hours when you are busy with classes, work, social activities, and other responsibilities. Then pencil in times for TOEFL preparation. You will remember more of what you study if you schedule a few hours every day or several times weekly instead of scheduling all your study time in large blocks on weekends. After following this schedule for a week, make whatever adjustments are necessary. After that, try to keep to this schedule until the week before the testing date. During that last week, reduce your study time and begin to relax.

If possible, reserve a special place where you do nothing but work on TOEFL preparation, separate from where you do your regular homework or other work. This place should be as free of distractions as possible.

A good method of studying for TOEFL is the "30-5-5" method:

- Study for thirty minutes.
- Take a five-minute break—leave your desk and do something completely different.

■ When you return, take five minutes to review what you studied before the break and preview what you are going to study next.

Incidentally, it's an excellent idea to meet regularly with a small group of people who are also preparing for TOEFL. Research has shown that this study-group approach to test preparation is very effective.

Key #3: Be in good physical condition when you take the exam.

When you make out your time management schedule, don't forget to leave time for physical activities—sports, aerobics, jogging, bicycling, or whatever else you prefer.

The most important physical concern is that you not become exhausted during your preparation time. If you aren't getting enough sleep, you'll need to reduce your study time or another activity. This is especially important in the last few days before the exam.

Key #4: Choose your test date carefully.

If you need test scores quickly, you should sign up for the earliest test date available. But if it's possible, sign up to take TOEFL on one of the Disclosed Test Administration dates. These dates are marked with an asterisk (*) on the ETS schedule of exams on the cover of the *Bulletin*. They are generally given on Fridays in July and September and on Saturdays in May, August, and October.

There are two advantages to taking tests on these dates:

■ You can keep the test book, which can be a valuable tool for study if you take the exam again.
■ The tests given on these dates are always standard (140-item) forms. Taking the shorter form of the test is less tiring and stressful than taking the long form.

To receive a copy of the test, you must bring a 6 inch by 9 inch (15.3 centimeters by 22.8 centimeters) envelope that you have addressed to yourself. You'll need enough postage on the envelope for a package weighing 1.5 ounces (43 grams). If your mailing address is in the United States, two first-class U.S. stamps will be sufficient.

Key #5: Be familiar with the format and directions.

You should have a clear "map" of the TOEFL test in your mind. Then, as you're taking the exam, you'll know exactly where you are and what's coming next. You can familiarize yourself with the basic TOEFL format by looking over the chart on page xvi.

The directions for each part of the TOEFL test are always the same; even the same examples are used. If you're familiar with the directions, you won't have to waste time reading them during the test. You can become familiar with these directions by studying the directions for the practice tests in this book.

Key #6: Organize your pre-exam time.

You shouldn't try to "cram" (study intensively) during the last few days before the exam. Last-minute studying can leave you exhausted, and you need to be alert for the test. The night before the exam, don't study at all. Get together the materials you'll need in the morning, then go to a movie, take a long walk, or do something else to take your mind off the test. Go to bed when you usually do.

If the exam is in the morning, have breakfast before you leave. Wear comfortable clothes because you'll be sitting in the same position for a long time. Give yourself plenty of time to get to the test site, keeping in mind traffic, weather, and parking problems. If you have to rush, that will only add to your stress.

Key #7: Use time wisely during the test.

TOEFL would be a far easier test if you could spend an unlimited amount of time working on it. However, there are strict time limits. Doing well on TOEFL means that you must find a balance between speed and accuracy. You don't want to rush through any section, but you do want to finish with a few minutes remaining so that you can go back to questions that you found difficult. (The timing on Section 1 is controlled by the tape and you can't go back and check your answers after completing this section.)

The questions on TOEFL are not equally difficult. Items can be classified as easy, medium, and difficult. The approximate distribution of items on a typical TOEFL are as follows: easy—30%; medium—40%; difficult—30%.

Easy items are usually found at the beginning of each part of the test, medium items are usually found in the middle of each part, and difficult items are usually found at the end of each part. You may be tempted to rush through the easy items to save time for the difficult ones at the end of each part. This is not a good strategy. Your goal is to get as many right answers as possible. Therefore, you want to concentrate on the items that give you the best chance of a correct answer—in other words, the easiest ones.

Hint: Remember, you don't get any extra points for answering difficult questions.

Work steadily. Never spend too much time on any one problem. If you are unable to decide on an answer, guess and go on. Answer each question as you come to it, even if you are not sure of the answer. You can mark difficult items on your answer sheet with check marks (as shown in Key #8). Then, if you have time at the end of the section, you can return to these problems. Sometimes when you come back to an item, you will find it easier. (Be sure to erase all of these check marks before you hand in your answer sheet.)

The most important tool for timing yourself is a watch, preferably one with a "count down" feature that you can set at the beginning of Sections 2 and 3. (Watches with alarms are not permitted.)

Key #8: Know how to mark your answer sheet.

One of the worst surprises you can have during a test is to suddenly discover that the number of the item that you are working on doesn't correspond to the number of the answer you are marking for that item. You have to go back to find where you first got off track, then change all the answers after that number. You can avoid this problem by using the test book itself as a marker. Cover all the unanswered items in each column on your answer sheet. Then uncover one item at a time as you advance. Every five items or so, quickly glance at the number of the question that you are working on and the number of the answer to make sure they are the same.

Mark answers by filling in the oval so that the letter cannot be seen. Don't mark answers any other way.

Bring several #2 black lead pencils. Make sure each has a functioning eraser. **Do not** use a pen, a liquid lead pencil, or any other kind of marker.

By the way, you may see either of two types of answer sheets. On one the answer choices are displayed horizontally, while on the other they are displayed vertically.

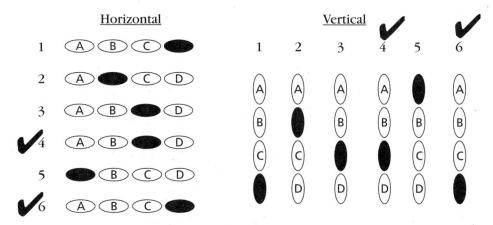

Always be sure you have filled in a circle completely and have filled in only one answer per item. If you have to erase an answer, erase it completely.

Notice the check marks by numbers 4 and 6. The test taker found these items difficult. He or she guessed at the answers, and then used the marks as a reminder to come back to these items if time allowed. These marks should be erased before the end of the test.

Incidentally, if you mark the same answer four times in a row, you'll know one of those four answers is wrong. The same correct answer will occur at most three times in a row on TOEFL.

> **Hint:** Don't sharpen your pencils too much before the exam. You can fill in circles more quickly if your pencil is not too sharp.

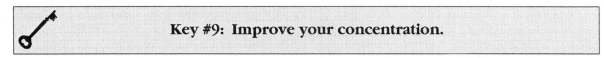

Key #9: Improve your concentration.

The ability to focus your attention on each item is an important factor in scoring high. Two and a half hours or more, after all, is a long time to spend in deep concentration. However, if your concentration is broken, it could cost you points. When an outside concern comes into your mind, just say to yourself, "I'll think about this after the test."

Like any skill, the ability to concentrate can be improved with practice. Work on it while you are taking the practice tests in this book.

Key #10: Use the process of elimination to make the best guess.

Unlike some standardized exams, TOEFL has no penalty for guessing. In other words, incorrect answers aren't subtracted from your total score. Even if you are not sure which answer is correct, you should always, always, always guess. But you want to make an educated guess, not a blind guess. To do so, use the process of elimination.

To understand the process of elimination, it may be helpful to look at the basic structure of a multiple-choice item. On TOEFL, multiple choice items consist of a **stem** and four **answer choices**. (The stem in the Listening section is spoken; in the other two sections, it is written.) One answer choice, called the **key,** is correct. The three incorrect choices are called **distractors** because their function is to distract (take away) your attention from the right answer.

STEM...........................
- (A) distractor
- (B) distractor
- (C) key
- (D) distractor

The three distractors, however, are usually not equally attractive. One is usually "almost correct." This choice is called the **main distractor**. Most people who answer an item incorrectly will choose this answer.

STEM......................
- (A) distractor
- (B) key
- (C) distractor
- (D) main distractor

To see how this works in practice, look at this simple Structure item:

Winter wheat _____ planted in the fall.
- (A) because
- (B) is
- (C) which
- (D) has

If you are sure of the answer, you should mark your choice immediately and go on. If not, you should use the process of elimination. In this item, choices (A) and (C) are fairly easy to eliminate. Because this sentence consists of a single clause, connecting words such as *because* and *which* are not needed. It may be a little more difficult to choose between choices (B) and (D) because both form correct verb phrases. Even if you are unable to decide between these two choices, you have a 50% chance of guessing correctly. That's twice as good as the 25% chance you would have if you had guessed blindly. (Choice (B) is the key, of course; a passive verb, not a present perfect verb, is required to complete the sentence correctly.) Choice (D) is the main distractor.

What if you eliminate one or two answers but can't decide which of the remaining choices is correct? If you have a "hunch" (an intuitive feeling) that one choice is better that the others, choose it. If not, just pick any remaining answer and go on.

If you have no idea which of the four answers is correct, it's better to use a standard "guess letter," such as (C), than to guess at random.

You should NEVER leave any items unanswered. Even if you don't have time to read an item, you have a 25% chance of guessing the key. If you are unable to finish a section, fill in all the unanswered ovals on your answer sheet with your guess letter in the last few seconds before time is called. Remember: Use the same guess letter all the time so that you can fill in the ovals quickly.

Key #11: Learn to control test anxiety.

A little nervousness before an important test is normal. After all, these tests can have an important effect on your plans for your education and career. If you were going to participate in a big athletic contest or give an important business presentation, you would feel the same way. There is an expression in English that describes this feeling quite well: "butterflies in the stomach." These "butterflies" will mostly disappear once the test starts. And a little nervousness can actually help by making you more alert and focused. However, too much nervousness can slow you down and cause you to make mistakes.

You may become anxious during the test because it seems very hard, and it seems that you are making many mistakes. Try not to panic. The test seems hard because it *is* hard. You can miss quite a few items and still get a high score.

One way to avoid stress on the day of the test is to give yourself plenty to time to get to the test center. If you have to rush, you'll be even more nervous during the exam.

If you begin to feel extremely anxious during the test, try taking a short break—a "ten-second vacation." Close your eyes and put down your pencil. Take a few deep breaths, shake out your hands, roll your head on your neck, relax—then go back to work.

Of course, you can't take a break during the Listening Comprehension section when the items are being read. However, if you're familiar with the directions, you can relax during the times when the directions are being read.

A positive, confident attitude toward the exam can help you overcome anxiety. Think of TOEFL not as a test of your knowledge or of you as a person but as an intellectual challenge, a series of puzzles to be solved.

 Key #12: Learn from taking practice tests and official TOEFL exams.

One of the most important steps in preparing for TOEFL is taking realistic, complete practice tests. There are now three tests in this book.

In addition, you may take the official TOEFL test several times. Each time you take a test, either a practice test or a real one, you should learn from it. Immediately after the exam, write down your reactions: Which section seemed difficult? Did you have problems finishing any sections? When you look at your results, is the score for one section significantly lower or higher than the scores for the other two sections? You can use this information to focus your studies for the next time you take the test.

> **Hint:** Whenever you take a practice test, pretend that you are taking an actual TOEFL exam. Whenever you take an actual exam, pretend you are taking a practice test.

Guide to Listening Comprehension

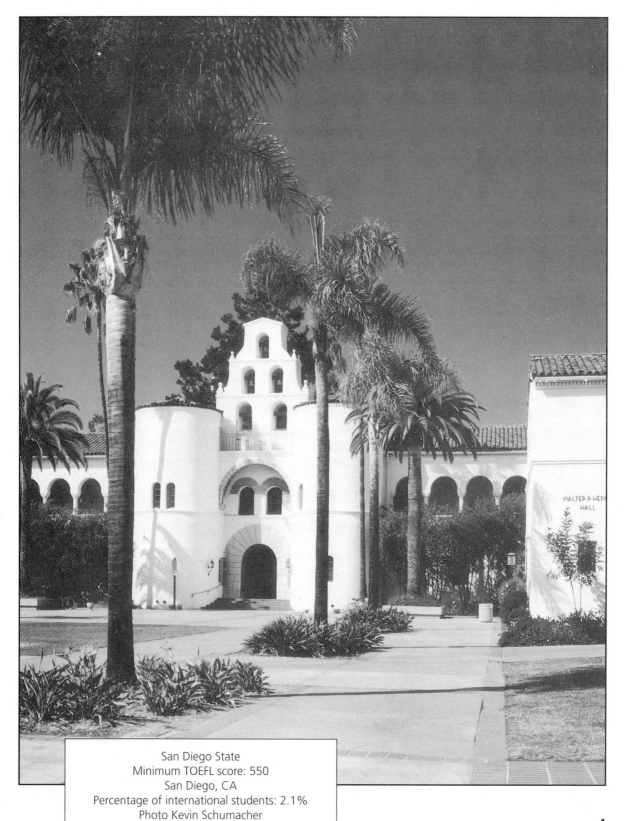

San Diego State
Minimum TOEFL score: 550
San Diego, CA
Percentage of international students: 2.1%
Photo Kevin Schumacher

About Listening Comprehension

The Listening Comprehension section of TOEFL is always given first. The purpose of this section is to test your understanding of spoken English.

The directions for this section are given on the tape as well as printed in your test book. There are four speakers, two men and two women. The speakers read the items at a normal speed. All four have standard North American accents. The tone of the items is conversational, much less formal than the items in the two other test sections.

Section 1 is divided into three parts, each with a different format and different directions. Since July 1995, it has followed this format:

Listening Comprehension Format		
	Standard Form	**Long Form**
Part A: Dialogs	30 items	45 items
Part B: Extended Conversations	2 conversations 7–8 items	3 conversations 10–12 items
Part C: Mini-Talks	3 talks 12–13 items	5 talks 13–15 items
Totals:	50 items +30 minutes	80 items +45 minutes

Listening Comprehension actually tests both your listening ability and your reading skills since you must understand both the material on the tape and the answer choices written in your test book.

Many test takers find the Listening Comprehension section the most difficult. Because it is given first, you may be more nervous during this part of the test. Furthermore, it is difficult to understand voices on tape (just as it is on the telephone or radio) because you can't see the speakers' gestures, facial expressions, or lip movements as you can during "live" listening. Finally, the test writers at ETS employ a number of "tricks" that make choosing the correct answer more difficult.

The exercises and tests in the Listening Comprehension section of this text are designed to help you overcome these difficulties. You will become more comfortable listening to taped materials in general and to TOEFL items in particular. You'll also become alert to many of the test writers' tricks.

Strategies for Section 1

- Familiarize yourself with the directions for each part before the exam. But remember, you are not permitted to turn the page to look over answer choices while the directions are being read. (No answer choices appear on the same page as the directions for Section 1.)

- If you have any difficulties hearing the tape, inform one of the proctors during the introductory section. Once the test has begun, the proctors cannot stop the tape.

- Never skip any items. If you're not sure of an answer, guess.

- Answer each item as quickly as you can; then preview the answer choices for the next item. Try to guess what the next item will be by the form of the answer choices.

- Concentration is very important in this part of the test. Once you choose an answer, don't think about the last item—start thinking about the next one. Don't daydream. Focus your attention on the tape and on the choices in your test book.

Begin your preparation for Section 1 by taking the Sample Listening Comprehension Test on the following pages. This will familiarize you with the first section of the exam.

Sample Listening Comprehension Test

This section tests your ability to comprehend spoken English. It is divided into three parts, each with its own directions. You are *not* permitted to turn the page during the reading of the directions or to take notes at any time.

Part A

Directions: Each item in this part consists of a brief conversation involving two speakers. Following each conversation, a third voice will ask a question. You will hear the conversations and questions only once, and they will *not* be written out.

When you have heard each conversation and question, read the four answer choices and select the *one*—(A), (B), (C), or (D)—that best answers the question based on what is directly stated or on what can be inferred. Then fill in the space on your answer sheet that matches the letter of the answer that you have selected.

Here is an example.

You will hear:

Sample Answer

You will read: (A) Open the window.
                (B) Move the chair.
                (C) Leave the room.
                (D) Take a seat.

From the conversation you find out that the woman thinks the man should put the chair over by the window. The best answer to the question "What does the woman think the man should do?" is (B), "Move the chair." You should fill in (B) on your answer sheet.

1. (A) It's brand new.
   (B) She just repaired it.
   (C) Someone painted it.
   (D) It's just been sold.

2. (A) Give the woman cash.
   (B) Go to his car.
   (C) Return some merchandise.
   (D) Look for his credit card.

3. (A) He shouldn't have thrown away the list.
   (B) He doesn't have to read all the books.
   (C) All of the books on the list are required.
   (D) Some of the books are available now.

4. (A) She enjoyed it very much.
   (B) She thought it was too long.
   (C) She thought it was boring.
   (D) She only liked the ending.

5. (A) Either a pen or pencil can be used.
   (B) It's not necessary to fill out the form.
   (C) He should fill out a different form.
   (D) A pen is better than a pencil.

6. (A) The software isn't convenient to use.
   (B) He's not familiar with the software.
   (C) Using the software is simple.
   (D) He wishes he'd bought that software.

7. (A) The man ordered it, but it hasn't arrived yet.
   (B) It isn't working.
   (C) Someone else is using it.
   (D) The man doesn't know how to operate it.

8. (A) What time his brother called.
   (B) Where to meet his brother.
   (C) Why his brother called.
   (D) When to meet his brother.

9. (A) He left on a long trip yesterday.
   (B) His letter arrived unexpectedly.
   (C) He seemed to be sad yesterday.
   (D) The letter he sent was very funny.

10. (A) It's on the wrong floor.
    (B) There are too many bedrooms.
    (C) It's too small.
    (D) The rent is too high.

Go on to the next page

11. (A) He'll probably give the man another grade.
    (B) He doesn't teach chemistry anymore.
    (C) He rarely changes his grades.
    (D) He'll probably retire soon.

12. (A) She mailed the grades to her students.
    (B) She left the students' tests in her office.
    (C) She can't get into her office.
    (D) She put a list of grades on the door.

13. (A) He should get something for his friends to eat.
    (B) There isn't time for him to go out now.
    (C) The game won't be played today.
    (D) He should have invited his friends to the game.

14. (A) His class has been canceled.
    (B) He shouldn't drop the class.
    (C) An earlier class would be better for him.
    (D) He doesn't need to study political science.

15. (A) Sitting in other seats.
    (B) Going home.
    (C) Turning up the music.
    (D) Asking the usher for a refund.

16. (A) He has a good excuse for being late.
    (B) He's been feeling very weak recently.
    (C) He's still waiting to be contacted.
    (D) He doesn't take responsibility for errors.

17. (A) She doesn't have her camera.
    (B) The sun hasn't set yet.
    (C) There isn't any film in the camera.
    (D) Her camera is broken.

18. (A) He got on the wrong bus.
    (B) He's afraid he'll be late for his flight.
    (C) He's sorry he took a bus instead of flying.
    (D) He had to wait for the bus.

19. (A) The meeting will have to be rescheduled.
    (B) She doesn't care whom the board picks as dean.
    (C) She's not sure where the meeting will be.
    (D) The board will not choose a dean this month.

20. (A) He's upset about the card game.
    (B) He's getting ready for the game.
    (C) He knocked over the card table.
    (D) He sat down to have dinner.

Go on to the next page ➤

1 1 1 1 1 1 1 1 1 1 1

21. (A) They wish they hadn't paid attention to Harvey.
    (B) They asked for some information about Harvey.
    (C) Harvey told them not to ignore him.
    (D) Only Harvey could give them any assistance.

22. (A) Most of the audience joined in the performance.
    (B) Some people don't enjoy performing.
    (C) Not many people were in the audience.
    (D) A few people didn't like the performance.

23. (A) A hotel room.
    (B) The man's family.
    (C) A reasonable offer.
    (D) The man's schedule.

24. (A) He must change his syllabus.
    (B) The woman cannot take his class.
    (C) He has extra copies of the syllabus.
    (D) Some students are not on his list.

25. (A) It's inconvenient for him to go to Mount Pleasant Street.
    (B) Those antique stores aren't very nice.
    (C) There are many inexpensive shops on Mount Pleasant Street.
    (D) The antiques in those stores are a little expensive.

26. (A) He's gone to San Diego many times.
    (B) He's attended a lot of conferences.
    (C) He has already gotten enough information.
    (D) He's living in San Diego now.

27. (A) He once drove in a race.
    (B) He's going to the races soon.
    (C) He drives quite fast.
    (D) He's thinking about a new car.

28. (A) The bowls are stacked on the shelves.
    (B) This soup is no worse than the other brands.
    (C) The new bowls are very attractive.
    (D) He plans to stock up on this soup.

29. (A) Peter wouldn't be favored in the match.
    (B) The match had already been played.
    (C) The match wouldn't be played.
    (D) Peter would win the match.

30. (A) He hasn't finished working on the bookshelves.
    (B) The tools have been misplaced.
    (C) He's not very good with tools.
    (D) The tools have already been returned.

Go on to the next page ➡

Part B

Directions: This part of the test consists of extended conversations between two speakers. After each of these conversations, there are a number of questions. You will hear each conversation and question only once, and the questions are *not* written out.

When you have heard the questions, read the four answer choices and select the *one*—(A), (B), (C), or (D)—that best answers the question based on what is directly stated or on what can be inferred. Then fill in the space on your answer sheet that matches the letter of the answer that you have selected.

Don't forget: during actual exams, taking notes or writing in your test book is *not* permitted.

| 1 | 1 | 1 | 1 | 1 | 1 | 1 | 1 | 1 | 1 | 1 | 1 |

31. (A) Student and advisor.
    (B) Museum curator and visitor.
    (C) Manager and job applicant.
    (D) Professor and teaching assistant.

32. (A) In a few weeks.
    (B) Next year.
    (C) In three years.
    (D) In four years.

33. (A) Change her major.
    (B) Make a quick decision.
    (C) Take elective courses in art history.
    (D) Work full time at a museum.

34. (A) She couldn't get an airline reservation.
    (B) She can't find an important book.
    (C) She's been studying too much.
    (D) She doesn't have a car.

35. (A) Amounts of money.
    (B) Distances.
    (C) Types of cars.
    (D) Regions of the United States.

36. (A) Information about places to visit.
    (B) Help with expenses and driving.
    (C) An airline reservation.
    (D) A used car.

37. (A) In the campus cinema.
    (B) Next door to the Student Union building.
    (C) In a travel agent's office.
    (D) On the second floor of the Student Union building.

Go on to the next page ➤

Part C

Directions: This part of the test consists of several talks, each given by a single speaker. After each of these talks, there are a number of questions. You will hear each talk and question only once, and the questions are *not* written out.

When you have heard each question, read the four answer choices and select the *one*—(A), (B), (C), or (D)—that best answers the question based on what is directly stated or on what can be inferred. Then fill in the space on your answer sheet that matches the letter of the answer that you have selected.

Here is an example.

You will hear:

Now here is a sample question.

You will hear:

Sample Answer

You will read: (A) Philosophy.
(B) Meteorology.
(C) Astronomy.
(D) Photography.

The lecture concerns a lunar eclipse, a topic that would typically be discussed in an astronomy class. The choice that best answers the question "In what course is this lecture probably being given?" is (C), "Astronomy." You should fill in (C) on your answer sheet.

Here is another sample question.

You will hear:

Sample Answer

You will read: (A) The Earth's shadow moves across the Moon.
(B) Clouds block the view of the Moon.
(C) The Moon moves between the Earth and the Sun.
(D) The Sun can be observed without special equipment.

From the lecture you learn that a lunar eclipse occurs when the Earth moves between the Sun and the Moon and the shadow of the Earth passes across the Moon. The choice that best answers the question "According to the speaker, which of the following occurs during a lunar eclipse?" is (A), "The Earth's shadow moves across the Moon."

Don't forget: during actual exams, taking notes or writing in your test book is *not* permitted.

1 **1** **1** **1** **1** **1** **1** **1** **1** **1** **1** **1**

38. (A) An airplane.
    (B) A satellite.
    (C) A fireworks display.
    (D) A flying saucer.

39. (A) To change tires.
    (B) To avoid danger.
    (C) To get a hotel room.
    (D) To change drivers.

40. (A) From the news on the radio.
    (B) From a magazine.
    (C) From his mother.
    (D) From the news on television

41. (A) It burned up in the upper atmosphere.
    (B) It injured a woman as she was sleeping.
    (C) It caused damage to a parked car.
    (D) It broke into pieces before striking the ground.

42. (A) Frightened.
    (B) Upset.
    (C) Fortunate.
    (D) Relieved.

43. (A) On board a bus.
    (B) At the top of the Washington Monument.
    (C) On an elevator.
    (D) At the Lincoln Memorial.

44. (A) Four years.
    (B) Thirty-six years.
    (C) Forty years.
    (D) Forty-eight years.

45. (A) Walk up 898 steps.
    (B) Take the elevator to the top.
    (C) Come down on the elevator.
    (D) Walk down the stairs.

46. (A) They jumped over it.
    (B) They took pictures of it.
    (C) They wrote their names on it.
    (D) They touched it.

47. (A) Music appreciation.
    (B) American history.
    (C) Dance.
    (D) Geography.

48. (A) They were an important part of the daily lives of the people.
    (B) They were all extremely old.
    (C) They were all written as theme songs for political campaigns.
    (D) They were primarily written as dance music.

49. (A) They weren't as enduring.
    (B) They were harder to sing and play.
    (C) They were livelier.
    (D) They weren't concerned with politics.

50. (A) Sing songs.
    (B) Look at some sheet music.
    (C) Go to a dance.
    (D) Listen to a recording.

THIS IS THE END OF THE SAMPLE LISTENING COMPREHENSION TEST.

STOP WORK ON THIS TEST.

STOP   STOP   STOP   STOP   STOP   STOP

Dialogs

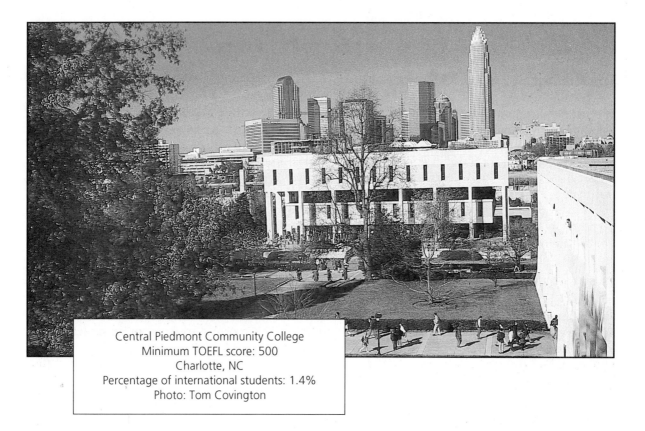

Central Piedmont Community College
Minimum TOEFL score: 500
Charlotte, NC
Percentage of international students: 1.4%
Photo: Tom Covington

About Dialogs

The first part of the Listening Comprehension section consists of spoken dialogs (conversations) between two speakers. A third speaker asks a question about what was said or implied in the conversation. You must decide which of the four answer choices printed in your test book is the best answer for the question you hear and then mark that choice on your answer sheet. Between each of the dialogs is a twelve-second pause. There are thirty dialogs on the standard form, forty-five on the long form.

Sample Item

You will hear:

> M1: Do you think I should leave this chair against the wall or put it somewhere else?
>
> F1: Over by the window, I'd say.
>
> M2: What does the woman think the man should do?

You will read:

> (A) Open the window.
> (B) Move the chair.
> (C) Leave the room.
> (D) Take a seat.

The woman indicates that she thinks the man should put the chair over by the window rather than leave it where it is. In other words, he should move it. The best answer is therefore (B).

Note: M1 = first male voice
M2 = second male voice
F1 = first female voice
F2 = second male voice

The Dialogs

Most of the dialogs in Part A involve a man and a woman. A few involve two men or two women. Each speaker usually speaks one or two sentences. Many dialogs (about 25%) are about facets of life at American universities: attending classes, talking to professors, writing research papers, taking tests. Other dialogs are about more general activities: shopping in grocery stores, looking for housing, taking vacations, going to meetings and parties. The tone of the dialogs is informal. Idioms, first names, contractions (*I'm, doesn't, can't*) are often heard. Some of the items test your ability to understand various language functions. For example, you must be able to determine if a speaker is agreeing or disagreeing with the other speaker, or if one speaker is accepting or rejecting the other speaker's offer.

The Questions

Most of the questions about the dialogs focus on what the second speaker says. However, it is usually necessary to understand the entire dialog in order to choose the correct answer. For example, in the Sample Item, it is not clear what the woman means when she says "Over by the window" unless you understand what the man says first. One or two questions in each test may focus instead on what the first speaker says.

Common Part A Question Types	Examples
1. *Meaning questions* These are the most common questions (about 50%). They ask for a restatement of what the second speaker or both speakers say. They may be general questions or ask what the speakers say about some specific topic. They often follow dialogs that contain idioms.	"What does the man/woman mean?" "What do the speakers say about ———?"
2. *Inference questions* These are the second most common Part A questions (about 20%). The answers for these questions are not directly stated in the dialog, but they can be inferred (concluded) from what the speakers say.	"What does the man/woman imply?" "What can be inferred from the conversation about ———?" "What can be concluded from the conversation about———?"
3. *Questions about suggestions* Generally, the first speaker talks about a problem or asks for advice. The second speaker makes a suggestion for solving the problem.	"What does the woman suggest the man do?" "What does the man suggest they do?" "What does the woman suggest?" "What does the woman think the man should do?"
4. *Questions about future actions* These ask what one or both of the speakers will do next or in the near future, or what one or both are planning to do.	"What will the man do?" "What will they probably do next?" "What are the speakers planning to do?"

Common Part A Question Types	Examples
5. *Topic questions* These ask about the subject of the dialog.	"What are they talking about?" "What are they discussing?"
6. *Questions about opinions* These ask how one or both of the speakers feel about some topic.	"How does the man/woman feel about ———?" "What is their opinion of ———?"
7. *Questions about assumptions* These ask what the second speaker thought (assumed) before he or she spoke to the first speaker.	"What had the man assumed about ———?" "What had the woman previously assumed?"
8. *Questions about questions* The first speaker makes a statement; the second speaker asks a question to get more information.	"What does the man want to know?"
9. *Questions about time* These ask when a conversation is taking place or when an event the speakers mention in the conversation will take place.	"When is this conversation taking place?" "When will the ——— take place?"
10. *Questions about reasons* These ask why one or both of the speakers did something.	"Why did the man/woman ———?"
11. *Questions about problems* These ask about some trouble one or both of the speakers are having.	"What problem is the man having?" "What is the problem?"
12. *Questions about activities* These ask what one or both of the speakers are doing.	"What are the speakers probably doing?"

Note: Two types of questions that were commonly asked about dialogs in the past are seldom or never asked about in the new-format test. These are location questions ("Where does this conversation probably take place?") and occupation questions ("What is the man's occupation?" or "Who is the man?").

The Answer Choices

All four of the answer choices are logical answers for the question, but only one—the key—is correct according to the dialog. However, as in all parts of TOEFL, not all of the answer choices are equally attractive. You can often eliminate one or two choices easily even if you are not sure which answer is correct and so make a better guess.

Correct answers are seldom stated word for word by either of the speakers. Correct answers often contain synonyms (words with the same meaning) for words in the dialogs and use different sentence structures.

Grammatically, there are three types of answer choices:
1. Complete sentences (about 75%)
2. Incomplete sentences, usually beginning with verb forms—most often the simple form of the verb (about 20%)
3. Short noun or prepositional phrases

The form of the answer choice can sometimes help you guess what the question will be, and you can therefore focus your listening.

Question Types and Examples	Usual Form of Answer Choice and Examples
Meaning questions: "What does the man mean?"	Complete sentences: (A) He prefers coffee to tea. (B) He'd like some lemon in his tea.
Questions about inferences: "What does the woman imply about the article?"	Complete sentences: (A) She will probably read it today. (B) She wasn't able to find it in the library.
Questions about suggestions: "What does the woman suggest John do?" "What does the man suggest?"	Incomplete sentences beginning with simple forms of verbs or -ing forms: (A) Call his cousin. (B) Take his cousin home. (A) Taking a bus to campus. (B) Walking to class.
Questions about future actions: "What will the speakers probably do next?"	Incomplete sentences beginning with simple forms of verbs: (A) Park their car. (B) Get some gasoline.
Topic questions: "What are the speakers discussing?"	Noun phrases: (A) The man's new schedule. (B) A homework assignment.
Questions about opinions: "What was their opinion of the play?" "How does the man feel about the announcement he heard?"	Complete sentences or adjective phrases: (A) They didn't enjoy it very much. (B) They liked it more than they thought they would. (A) Angry. (B) Enthusiastic.
Questions about assumptions: "What had the man assumed about Kathy?"	Complete sentences often containing the auxiliary verb *would* or *had*: (A) She had already finished the paper. (B) She wouldn't finish the research on time.
Questions about questions: "What does the woman ask about Professor Tolbert?" "What does the man ask about the department store?"	Incomplete sentences beginning with the word *if* or one of the *wh-* words or noun phrases: (A) If she is still in her office. (B) Where her office is. (A) Its location. (B) Its hours of operation.
Questions about time: "When will the man play the piano?"	Prepositional phrases of time: (A) At noon. (B) Before the ceremony.
Questions about reasons: "Why did Jerry miss the party?" "Why did Linda talk to Professor Delgado?"	Complete sentences or incomplete sentences beginning with infinitives (*to* + simple form): (A) He didn't receive an invitation. (B) He had other plans for the evening. (A) To ask him about a grade. (B) To explain why she missed class.

Question Types and Examples	Usual Form of Answer Choice and Examples

Questions about problems:
   "What problem did the man have?"
	Complete sentences:
	   (A) He didn't bring enough money for the tickets.
	   (B) There were no tickets available.

Questions about activities:
   "What are they probably doing?"
	Incomplete sentences beginning with *-ing* verbs:
	   (A) Buying groceries.
	   (B) Cooking breakfast.

The test writers sometimes make it more difficult to pick the correct answer by using sound-alike words, homonyms, words with multiple meaning, and other techniques. You'll practice avoiding these traps in this part of the *Guide.*

Tactics for Dialogs

- Be familiar with the directions for Part A.

- Remember that the answer for the question is generally contained in what the second speaker says.

- If you are not sure of the answer, eliminate as many answer choices as you can.

- After you have chosen an answer, use the remaining time to preview the choices for the next item. If the answer choices are long, just skim over them quickly. Try to anticipate what the question will be by the form of the answer choices.

- If you don't understand all or part of a conversation, guess and go on.

LESSON 1

ANTICIPATING QUESTIONS ABOUT DIALOGS

Between each dialog in Part A, there is a twelve-second pause. During the pause, here's what you should do:

- Answer the question you have just heard as quickly as you can.
- Preview the choices for the next item.

A look at the answer choices may tell you the topic of the upcoming dialog and what question will be asked about it. Consider the answer choices below:

       (A) Before she leaves her dormitory.
       (B) During chemistry class.
       (C) After the lab period.
       (D) While she's eating lunch.

Even a quick glance will tell you that the dialog must be about a student's schedule and that the question will begin, "When. . . ."

If you have an idea of the topic of the dialog and if you know what the question about the dialog will be, you will know what to listen for, and your listening task will be easier.

Exercise 1

Focus: Guessing which type of question will be asked about dialogs by looking at the four answer choices.

Directions: Quickly look over the five Part A items in each set. Try to guess the topic of the dialog and the type of question that would be asked about it. Then look at the list of questions following each set of items. Put the letter of the appropriate question in the blank provided. One question in each set will *not* be used. The first one is done as an example.

Note: There is no taped material for this exercise.

Set A

1. (A) Pleased.
   (B) Cold.
   (C) Disappointed.
   (D) Hungry.
Question: __**b**__

2. (A) Go to her office.
   (B) Call a taxi.
   (C) Show the man where to find a taxi.
   (D) Get directions.
Question: _____

3. (A) Cloudy but much warmer.
   (B) Rainy.
   (C) Clear but cold.
   (D) The same as today's.
Question: _____

4. (A) He left it in the lock.
   (B) It's still in his dorm room.
   (C) He put it in his pocket.
   (D) It doesn't work in this lock.
Question: _____

5. (A) Playing a game.
   (B) Attending a play.
   (C) Learning some lines.
   (D) Trying to find tickets.
Question: _____

   a) What will tomorrow's weather probably be like?
   b) How does the man feel?
   c) What are these people doing?
   d) Where will the man go tomorrow?
   e) What does John say about the key?
   f) What will the woman do next?

Set B

6. (A) He had given his textbooks to a friend.
   (B) He would receive more money.
   (C) He wouldn't get to the bookstore on time.
   (D) He hadn't sold his textbooks.

Question: _____

7. (A) She enjoyed it very much.
   (B) She thought it was too long.
   (C) She liked it more than the movie reviewer did.
   (D) She found it confusing.

Question: _____

8. (A) A tuition increase.
   (B) A policy change.
   (C) A new class.
   (D) A recent proposal.

Question: _____

9. (A) Buy some new software.
   (B) Get her computer fixed.
   (C) Use the computers at the library.
   (D) Borrow his computer.

Question: _____

10. (A) He doesn't have the right notebook.
    (B) He forgot to bring a pen.
    (C) He went to the wrong lecture hall.
    (D) He was late for the lecture.

Question: _____

    a) What did the woman think about the movie?
    b) What is the man's problem?
    c) What does the man suggest Ann do?
    d) What had the woman assumed about the man?
    e) What information does the man want?
    f) What are they discussing?

Set C

11. (A) His brother helped him move the piano.
    (B) He moved the piano to his brother's house.
    (C) His brother taught him to play the piano.
    (D) He and his brother hired professional movers.

Question: _____

12. (A) To ask her a question.
    (B) To get her advice.
    (C) To give her a suggestion.
    (D) To disagree with her idea.

Question: _____

13. (A) Who Katie is.
    (B) What was said.
    (C) When Katie called.
    (D) What the problem was.

Question: _____

14. (A) She's probably an expert on modern art.
    (B) She didn't paint the picture herself.
    (C) She's just begun to study painting.
    (D) She probably doesn't like modern art.

Question: _____

15. (A) At the beginning of the spring semester.
    (B) During spring break.
    (C) During final exams.
    (D) Right after final exams.

Question: _____

    a) How does the man feel about the woman's remark?
    b) Why did the man call Professor Wilkey?
    c) What does the woman want to know?
    d) When does this conversation take place?
    e) What does the man mean?
    f) What can be inferred about the woman?

LESSON 2

DIALOGS WITH SOUND CONFUSION

Some of the items in Part A involve a confusion between words that have similar sounds. Here's how they work: one of the speakers uses a word or phrase that sounds like a word or phrase in one or more of the answer choices. If you don't hear the word clearly, you might incorrectly choose an option with a sound-alike word or phrase.

Sample Item

You will hear:

      M1: I've never had this type of fruit before. I don't even know what to do with it.
      F1: You just have to peel it and eat it.
      M2: What does the woman mean?

You will read:

      (A) She doesn't feel like eating fruit.
      (B) The man should take the pill before eating.
      (C) The fruit shouldn't be eaten until it's been peeled.
      (D) She isn't familiar with this type of fruit either.

The word *feel* in choice (A) sounds like the word *peel* in the dialog. In a different way, the word *pill* in choice (B) also sounds like the word *peel*. Notice that choice (C)—the correct answer—and choice (D) do not contain sound-alike words.

Many sound-alike expressions in Part A are **minimal pairs.** Minimal pairs are two words that are pronounced alike except for one vowel sound (*peel* and *pill, lack* and *lake, point* and *paint*) or one consonant sound (*peel* and *feel, vine* and *wine, mop* and *mob*).

Another sound problem involves two words that sound like one word, such as *mark it* and *market, sent her* and *center, in tents* and *intense.*

A third type of sound problem involves one word that sounds like part of a longer word, such as *nation* and *imagination, mind* and *remind, give* and *forgive.*

> **Hint:** If an answer choice contains a word that sounds like a word in the spoken dialog, that choice is probably wrong. For example, if you hear the word *spell* and you read the word *spill* in an answer choice, you can eliminate that choice.

When you're taking Part A during an actual exam, you can use the **context** of the dialogs to help you solve problems with sound confusion. If you hear and understand all of the dialog, you won't have much trouble eliminating choices involving sound-alike words. However, if you only understand part of a dialog or if you "mis-hear" one or two words, you may easily choose an incorrect answer.

Exercise 2.1

Focus: Discriminating between sound-alike words in dialogs and answer choices.

Directions: Listen to the dialogs. Decide which of the two choices, (A) or (B), best answers the question, and mark the appropriate blank. The first one is done as an example.

Now start the tape.

1. (A) _____ Get in a different lane.
   (B) __✔__ Stand in another line.

2. (A) _____ Went down the slide.
   (B) _____ Played on the sled.

3. (A) _____ Put them in a file.
   (B) _____ Throw them in a pile.

4. (A) _____ He can't shut his suitcase.
   (B) _____ His suitcase doesn't fit in the closet.

5. (A) _____ She made bread from whole wheat.
   (B) _____ She baked some white bread.

6. (A) _____ Brenda is typing it.
   (B) _____ It's being taped.

7. (A) _____ Emily recently moved.
   (B) _____ Emily bought new clothes.

8. (A) _____ Its taste has improved.
   (B) _____ It tastes slightly bitter.

9. (A) _____ How much the ticket cost.
   (B) _____ What she might win.

10. (A) _____ It's been chipped.
    (B) _____ There's a ship inside it.

11. (A) _____ He tripped in the aisle.
    (B) _____ He slipped in some oil.

12. (A) _____ For its fast horses.
    (B) _____ For its natural resources.

13. (A) _____ Thinking about the decision.
    (B) _____ Arguing about the issue.

14. (A) _____ The color is too bright.
    (B) _____ It doesn't fit around the neck.

15. (A) _____ Wrote his name on the paper.
    (B) _____ Told his students to write a paper.

Exercise 2.2

Focus: Identifying sound-alike expressions in answer choices and choosing correct answers.

Directions: Listen to the dialogs. Each dialog contains a word or phrase that sounds like a word or phrase in two of the answer choices. Underline these words. Underline only those words with similar sounds, not words that are exactly the same. Then mark the answer choice that has the same meaning as the spoken sentence. (The correct answer will not contain any sound-alike words.) The first one is done as an example.

Now start the tape. If necessary, repeat this exercise to make sure that you have underlined all the sound-alike words.   [🔲]

1. (A) _____ She went to the <u>center</u> with her friend.
   (B) __✔__ She wrote her friend a letter.
   (C) _____ She told her friend to call her <u>later</u>.

2. (A) _____ He has an appointment with the president.
   (B) _____ He was just appointed vice-president.
   (C) _____ He's unhappy because he lost the election.

3. (A) _____ It is a study of the life of plants.
   (B) _____ It concerns the breeding of cattle.
   (C) _____ It deals with life on Earth.

4. (A) _____ They can't leave until the rain is over.
   (B) _____ Their drain has stopped up.
   (C) _____ He shouldn't board the train until it completely stops.

5. (A) _____ He offered his help to Darlene.
   (B) _____ He made an offer to Darlene's sister.
   (C) _____ When Darlene was gone, he missed her.

6. (A) _____ Get a copy made.
   (B) _____ Buy some cough drops.
   (C) _____ Eat in the coffee shop.

7. (A) _____ He didn't hear what was said.
   (B) _____ He can lend the man a pen.
   (C) _____ He had a pain behind his ear.

8. (A) _____ The food in this town isn't very good.
   (B) _____ She needed boots when she left home.
   (C) _____ The flooding in her neighborhood was severe.

9. (A) _____ She's been weakened by the sickness.
   (B) _____ She was awakened by the coughing.
   (C) _____ She missed class because of her cough.

10. (A) _____ Evaluate the texts.
    (B) _____ Correct the exams.
    (C) _____ Collect the tests.

11. (A) _____ His apartment is more comfortable now.
    (B) _____ He recently bought a new van.
    (C) _____ He's been feeling fine lately.

12. (A) _____ Her name is not on the list.
    (B) _____ The lease is difficult to read.
    (C) _____ The lawyer told her to call the police.

LESSON 3

DIALOGS WITH HOMONYMS AND WORDS WITH MULTIPLE MEANINGS

Two words are **homonyms** if they have the same pronunciation but are spelled differently and have different meanings. The words *flour* and *flower, bare* and *bear* are homonyms. In some items in Part A, one or more incorrect answer choices refer to a homonym of a word that is used on the tape, as in the example below.

Sample Item

You will hear:

      M1: Eugene missed a lot of classes last week.

      F1: That's because he was sick. I think he had the flu.

      M2: What is learned about Eugene?

You will read:

      (A) He has been feeling weak for a long time.

      (B) Because of sickness, Eugene was absent.

      (C) Eugene's eyesight isn't very strong, so he needs glasses.

      (D) Eugene flew to another city this week.

The dialog contains the word *week,* meaning a seven-day period. Choices (A) and (C) refer to a homonym of that word, *weak,* which means "not strong." The dialog also contains the word *flu,* an illness similar to a bad cold. Choice (D) refers to a homonym of that word, *flew* (took a trip by plane).

The dialogs may also contain **words with multiple meanings.** In these items, one or two of the answer choices refer to another definition of a word as it is used in the dialog.

Sample Item

You will hear:

      F1: Are you sure this is how Lois spells her last name?

      M1: It doesn't look right, does it? In fact, I'm not even sure it starts with that letter.

      M2: What does the man mean?

You will read: (A) The letter to Lois was incorrectly addressed.

      (B) Lois' last name may be incorrectly spelled.

      (C) Lois' name appeared on the right side of the page.

      (D) Lois hasn't begun writing the letter yet.

The dialog contains the words *right,* meaning "correct," and the word *letter,* meaning a character in the alphabet. Choices (A) and (D) also contain the word *letter,* but in those choices the word has another definition—a message sent through the mail. Choice (C) also contains the word *right,* but in that choice, it refers to a direction—the opposite of left.

You won't be confused by these items if you understand the entire dialog. Again, the **context** of the dialog can help you choose the correct answer. But if you focus only on single words, like *week* and *flu* or *letter* and *right* in the two samples, you can easily make mistakes.

Exercise 3.1

Focus: Using the context of dialogs to identify homonyms.

Directions: Listen to the dialogs. Decide which of the pair of homonyms appears in the dialogs and mark the appropriate answer, (A) or (B). The first one is done as an example.

Now start the tape.

1. __✔__ (A) presents
   _____ (B) presence

2. _____ (A) overdue
   _____ (B) overdo

3. _____ (A) pain
   _____ (B) pane

4. _____ (A) where
   _____ (B) wear

5. _____ (A) fined
   _____ (B) find

6. _____ (A) right
   _____ (B) write

7. _____ (A) board
   _____ (B) bored

8. _____ (A) brakes
   _____ (B) breaks

9. _____ (A) sail
   _____ (B) sale

10. _____ (A) site
    _____ (B) sight

11. _____ (A) rose
    _____ (B) rows

12. _____ (A) aloud
    _____ (B) allowed

Exercise 3.2

Focus: Using the context of dialogs to identify the definitions of words with multiple meanings.

Directions: Listen to the dialogs. One word from the dialog is given, along with two possible definitions of the word. Choose the definition of the word as it is used in the dialog and mark the appropriate answer, (A) or (B). The first one is done as an example.

Now start the tape.

1. cold
   __✔__ (A) minor illness
   _____ (B) chilly weather

2. kind
   _____ (A) type
   _____ (B) considerate

3. light
   _____ (A) not heavy
   _____ (B) not dark

4. wing
   _____ (A) part of an airplane
   _____ (B) part of a building

5. tables
   _____ (A) charts
   _____ (B) furniture

6. coat
   _____ (A) layer
   _____ (B) warm clothing

7. field
   _____ (A) outside the classroom
   _____ (B) area of study

8. playing
   _____ (A) taking part in a game
   _____ (B) appearing

9. party
   _____ (A) celebration
   _____ (B) group

10. period
    _____ (A) punctuation mark
    _____ (B) class time

Exercise 3.3

Focus: Using the context of dialogs to answer questions involving both homonyms and words with multiple definitions.

Directions: Listen to the statements. Decide which of the two choices best answers the question and mark the appropriate answer, (A) or (B). The first one is done as an example.

Now start the tape.　🖭

1. __✔__ (A) Look for mistakes.
   _____ (B) Write a check.

2. _____ (A) Events in the past.
   _____ (B) The man's performance in class.

3. _____ (A) He'd never heard buffaloes before.
   _____ (B) This was the first herd he'd ever seen.

4. _____ (A) Follow the directions on the sign.
   _____ (B) Sign up for another class.

5. _____ (A) Buy a second suit.
   _____ (B) Consider it for a little while.

6. _____ (A) He can't carry them by himself.
   _____ (B) The handle on one of them is broken.

7. _____ (A) He was surprised by the rain.
   _____ (B) He just got out of the shower.

8. _____ (A) The class has a better opinion of him.
   _____ (B) He had to stand in front of the class.

9. _____ (A) She works in an office by herself.
   _____ (B) She's in charge of making loans.

10. _____ (A) She's sorry the seminar is over.
    _____ (B) She was often absent from the seminar.

11. _____ (A) They can park their car at the zoo.
    _____ (B) The park is located near the zoo.

12. _____ (A) If she has some money for a phone call.
    _____ (B) If the phone number has changed recently.

LESSON 4

DIALOGS WITH IDIOMATIC EXPRESSIONS

On many TOEFL exams, up to half the dialogs in Part A contain idiomatic expressions. Many of the idiomatic expressions are two- or three-word verbs, such as *call off* and *look out for.*

Sample Item

You will hear:

F1: I wonder where Mike is.
M1: He'll show up as soon as the work is done, I bet.
M2: What does the man say about Mike?

You will read:

(A) He probably won't arrive until the work is finished.
(B) He went to a show instead of going to work.
(C) He can show them how to do the work.
(D) He'll probably work late today.

The idiom *show up* means "arrive." Choices (B) and (C) contain the word *show,* but it is not used in the idiomatic sense.

In most dialogs, the second speaker uses the idiomatic expression. Most questions about this type of dialog are questions about meaning ("What does the man mean?" for example), but some are inference questions or other types of questions. The correct answer often contains a synonym for the idiom (*arrive* for *show up* in choice (A) of the Sample Item). Incorrect choices often contain references to the literal meaning of idioms, as in choices (B) and (C).

The Mini-Lessons for Section 1, at the end of the Listening Comprehension section (pages 81–100), are intended to familiarize you with a large number of idioms. You should work on these lessons and study these expressions as often as possible.

However, memorizing these phrases does not guarantee that you will recognize all the idiomatic expressions that you will hear in the Listening Comprehension section. There are, after all, thousands of these expressions in English. You must develop "a good ear" for guessing the meaning of idioms. The context of the sentence will help you understand the expression, even if you're unfamiliar with it.

Exercise 4.1

Focus: Recognizing synonyms for idiomatic expressions.

Directions: Listen to the spoken statements. Each contains an idiomatic or figurative expression which is written out. First decide which of the two choices best answers the question and mark the appropriate answer, (A) or (B). Then underline the phrase in the correct answer that has the same meaning as the idiom. If necessary, rewind the tape and listen to the exercise again. The first one has been done as an example.

Now start the tape.

1. get into hot water
  ___✔___ (A) She <u>was in trouble</u>.
  _____ (B) She took a warm bath.

2. run into
  _____ (A) He met Caroline unexpectedly at the coffee shop.
  _____ (B) Caroline and he jogged to the coffee shop.

3. hit it off
  _____ (A) He and Chuck argued as soon as they met.
  _____ (B) He and Chuck quickly became friends.

4. piece of cake
  _____ (A) The exam was simple.
  _____ (B) She had a snack after the test.

5. at the drop of a hat
  _____ (A) He can't leave until he finds his hat.
  _____ (B) He's ready to leave immediately.

6. on edge
  _____ (A) He walks back and forth when he's nervous.
  _____ (B) He likes to walk along the edge.

7. under the weather
  _____ (A) She didn't want to practice because of the bad weather.
  _____ (B) She wasn't there because she felt a little sick.

8. take after
  _____ (A) He looks like his grandfather.
  _____ (B) He takes care of his grandfather.

9. for good
  _____ (A) He doesn't want the professor to quit teaching permanently.
  _____ (B) He hopes Professor Holmes has a good reason for quitting.

10. give a hand with
  _____ (A) Hand her the box.
  _____ (B) Help her carry the box.

11. a stone's throw away
  _____ (A) He likes to throw rocks in the park.
  _____ (B) He lives close to the park.

12. not think much of
  _____ (A) She didn't consider it.
  _____ (B) She didn't like it.

Exercise 4.2

Focus: Understanding dialogs involving idiomatic and figurative expressions.

Directions: Look over the idiomatic expressions listed before each set of items. If you are unfamiliar with any of the idioms, you may want to look them up in the Mini-Lessons for Section 1 that follow the Listening Comprehension section of this book (pages 81–100). The dialogs each contain one of the listed expressions. Listen to the dialogs and mark the one answer choice, (A) or (B), that best answers the question. The first one has been done as an example.

Now start the tape.

Set A

clear up	get off the ground	hours on end	over one's head
push one's luck	run of the mill	short for	turn in

1. __✔__ (A) He's not sure Max's business will succeed.
   _____ (B) He doesn't know where Max has gone.

2. _____ (A) Gary is lucky to have such a good car.
   _____ (B) It's time for Gary to get some new tires.

3. _____ (A) Go to bed.
   _____ (B) Watch a different program.

4. _____ (A) She didn't understand all the jokes.
   _____ (B) She left before the performance was over.

5. _____ (A) If the weather gets better.
   _____ (B) If he doesn't have any other plans.

6. _____ (A) Elizabeth is taller than Liz.
   _____ (B) People call Elizabeth "Liz."

7. _____ (A) She's stopped listening to it.
   _____ (B) She listens to it constantly.

8. _____ (A) The service is very fast there.
   _____ (B) It's just an average restaurant.

Set B

believe one's eyes	a breeze	chip in	get in one's blood
lend a hand	look who's talking	music to one's ears	what the doctor ordered

9. _____ (A) Ice water sounds perfect.
   _____ (B) The doctor told her to drink a lot of water.

10. _____ (A) Skiing can be a dangerous sport.
    _____ (B) It's easy to get into the habit of skiing.

11. _____ (A) She enjoys the sounds of nature.
    _____ (B) She wishes she'd brought a radio.

12. _____ (A) She wants to talk to Norman.
    _____ (B) Norman doesn't study much himself.

13. _____ (A) There's not enough wind to go sailing today.
    _____ (B) It won't be too hard to learn to sail.

14. _____ (A) Lend him some money.
    _____ (B) Give him some help.

15. _____ (A) They'll all pay for the gasoline.
    _____ (B) Gasoline is very inexpensive.

16. _____ (A) She doesn't think the man is telling the truth.
    _____ (B) She was surprised to see the snow.

Set C

| by heart | call it a day | come around | go without saying |
| ring a bell | slowly but surely | take a lot of nerve | take into account |

17. _____ (A) She seems too nervous.
    _____ (B) She took a bold approach.

18. _____ (A) He doesn't want to do any more painting today.
    _____ (B) He'll phone the woman later today.

19. _____ (A) He spoke the lines in an emotional way.
    _____ (B) He's memorized all the lines.

20. _____ (A) At some point, they'll agree to let her go.
    _____ (B) They'll come with her to Hawaii.

21. _____ (A) Rob Martin hasn't called him yet.
    _____ (B) He doesn't think Rob Martin was on the team.

22. _____ (A) He didn't count his money carefully.
    _____ (B) He didn't remember the tax.

23. _____ (A) She's making steady progress.
    _____ (B) She thinks the work is going too slowly.

24. _____ (A) Of course she was sorry that Molly left.
    _____ (B) Molly left without saying goodbye.

Exercise 4.3

Focus: Using the context of dialogs to understand the meaning of idioms.

Directions: Listen to the following dialog. Decide which of the choices—(A), (B), or (C)—best answers the question about the dialog and mark the appropriate answer. The first one is done as an example.

Now start the tape. [cassette]

1. _____ (A) Go to work with Jim.
   _____ (B) Go out for coffee.
   ___✔___ (C) Get some exercise.

2. _____ (A) If the woman will go to the party with him.
   _____ (B) If the red tie looks good with his shirt.
   _____ (C) If he should wear a tie to the party.

3. _____ (A) She missed Friday's class, too.
   _____ (B) They both missed class because they went sailing.
   _____ (C) He should take better notes during Professor Morrison's class.

4. _____ (A) He's never cut himself while preparing food.
   _____ (B) He doesn't want to work in a restaurant.
   _____ (C) He's planning to open up his own restaurant.

5. _____ (A) He wants to know if the woman is joking.
   _____ (B) He wants the woman to leave him alone.
   _____ (C) He'd like to know what the quiz will be about.

6. _____ (A) The program was canceled.
   _____ (B) The shuttle was launched yesterday.
   _____ (C) The launch was delayed.

7. _____ (A)   She stood up and left the lecture.
   _____ (B)   She was waiting outside the lecture hall.
   _____ (C)   Her sweater made her easy to spot.

8. _____ (A)   He deserved to get a ticket.
   _____ (B)   He was going to a good restaurant.
   _____ (C)   He probably wasn't speeding.

9. _____ (A)   He'll be glad to help.
   _____ (B)   If he helps, it will save the man some money.
   _____ (C)   He won't be very cooperative.

10. _____ (A)   It's about buying large real estate properties.
    _____ (B)   There are too many students in it.
    _____ (C)   In general, he likes it.

11. _____ (A)   The man didn't get Jill a watch.
    _____ (B)   The weather will be cool on graduation day.
    _____ (C)   Jill won't be graduating.

12. _____ (A)   She ordinarily works in a florist shop.
    _____ (B)   In the end, she won't have a problem.
    _____ (C)   She wears too much perfume to work.

13. _____ (A)   She doesn't want any fruit.
    _____ (B)   She doesn't want to celebrate her birthday.
    _____ (C)   She doesn't like candy.

14. _____ (A)   He doesn't have any questions for her.
    _____ (B)   He won't be able to take a trip.
    _____ (C)   He can't study during spring break.

15. _____ (A)   Mick's father told him to go to medical school.
    _____ (B)   Mick's father studied medicine.
    _____ (C)   Mick and his father walked to the school.

16. _____ (A)   Fred would be upset if he'd lost money.
    _____ (B)   Fred shouldn't be paid for singing.
    _____ (C)   Fred is generally very sympathetic.

17. _____ (A)   If Wally has been injured.
    _____ (B)   If Wally has been informed.
    _____ (C)   If Wally's trip has been canceled.

18. _____ (A)   He can't find some of his pictures.
    _____ (B)   He didn't go to the Grand Canyon.
    _____ (C)   Not all of his photos were good.

19. _____ (A)   She thinks they're certain to do well.
    _____ (B)   She thinks they're talented but lack experience.
    _____ (C)   She doesn't like their style of photography.

20. _____ (A)   The lake is not very scenic.
    _____ (B)   Her parents won't let them use the cabin.
    _____ (C)   The cabin is not luxurious.

LESSON 5

ANSWERING INFERENCE QUESTIONS ABOUT DIALOGS

Sometimes the answer to a question about a dialog is not directly stated in the dialog. How can you answer this type of question? You must be able to make an **inference** about the dialog. In other words, information in the dialog will indirectly provide you with the answer to the question.

This type of question can be phrased in two ways:

- What does the man/woman imply?
- What can be inferred from the conversation?

Some inference questions involve **overstatement,** or exaggeration.

> F: Are you interested in selling your car?
> M: Sure—if someone has a million dollars!

Because of the exaggeration, we can infer that the man doesn't want to sell his car at all.

Sample Item

You will hear:

> M1:   Can I take this bus to the art museum?
> F1:   No, this bus goes north to Bank Street. You want a bus that goes the opposite way.
> M2:   What can be inferred from this conversation?

You will read:

> (A) The man needs to take a southbound bus.
> (B) There is no bus to the museum.
> (C) It takes a long time to get to the museum by bus.
> (D) The art museum is on Bank Street.

From the information in the dialog it can be inferred that (A) is correct because the first bus is going north, but the man must take a bus going in the opposite direction to get to the art museum. Choice (B) is incorrect; it *is* possible to get to the museum by bus. There is no information about (C). Choice (D) can't be true because Bank Street is where the first bus is going.

Exercise 5

Focus: Listening to dialogs that are followed by inference questions and identifying the best answers.

Directions: Listen to the following dialogs. Decide which of the three choices—(A), (B), or (C)— best answers the question and mark the appropriate answer. The first one has been done as an example.

Now start the tape.

1. _____ (A)   He's not related to Larry.
   _____ (B)   He doesn't believe Larry won the contest.
   ___✔___ (C)   He's not a very good dancer.

2. _____ (A) The suit costs a lot of money.
   _____ (B) The man dresses as if he were very wealthy.
   _____ (C) The man already has an expensive suit.

3. _____ (A) There is just enough food.
   _____ (B) Many uninvited guests will come.
   _____ (C) The woman has prepared too much food.

4. _____ (A) Dave is a painter.
   _____ (B) Dave's apartment has been recently painted.
   _____ (C) Dave's brother doesn't like the smell of paint.

5. _____ (A) He's changed his major often.
   _____ (B) He hasn't really changed his major.
   _____ (C) He won't do well in his new major.

6. _____ (A) His lectures put his students to sleep.
   _____ (B) He's a middle-aged man.
   _____ (C) He lectures about history.

7. _____ (A) He hasn't been to the dentist for years.
   _____ (B) He wasn't able to see the dentist yesterday.
   _____ (C) Before he saw the dentist, he had a long wait.

8. _____ (A) They have agreed on it.
   _____ (B) They have different opinions about it.
   _____ (C) It depends on their co-operation.

9. _____ (A) Louis's new boss shouldn't have been promoted.
   _____ (B) Louis and his old boss argued.
   _____ (C) Louis should get a better job.

10. _____ (A) There's not enough snow to cause a cancellation yet.
    _____ (B) It will probably snow all night.
    _____ (C) The university has already decided to cancel classes.

11. _____ (A) He's been interested in folk dancing for a long time.
    _____ (B) He's interested in making new friends.
    _____ (C) He wants to form a new folk-dancing club.

12. _____ (A) She didn't enjoy the music.
    _____ (B) She couldn't see the concert very well.
    _____ (C) She had a good seat near the stage.

13. _____ (A) Last summer was even hotter.
    _____ (B) This is the hottest summer he can remember.
    _____ (C) He didn't live here last year.

14. _____ (A) Students must pay to swim in the pool.
    _____ (B) The public cannot use the pool on campus.
    _____ (C) The pool can be used by students for free.

15. _____ (A) They can't see the stars clearly.
    _____ (B) They're not in the city tonight.
    _____ (C) They are looking at the lights of the city.

16. _____ (A) He doesn't know many people at work.
    _____ (B) He wasn't expecting a phone call.
    _____ (C) He's not allowed to get phone calls at work.

17. _____ (A) Those aren't Shelly's photographs.
     _____ (B) Shelly has begun to take color photographs.
     _____ (C) Shelly took the photographs hanging in the hall.

18. _____ (A) That scarf looks great on Fran.
     _____ (B) Fran wears that scarf too often.
     _____ (C) In this weather, Fran needs a scarf.

19. _____ (A) She doesn't have an accent.
     _____ (B) Her parents have very strong accents.
     _____ (C) Her accent is stronger than her parents'.

20. _____ (A) Robert usually has trouble skiing.
     _____ (B) That's not a difficult slope.
     _____ (C) Robert is an excellent skier.

LESSON 6

DIALOGS INVOLVING AGREEMENT AND DISAGREEMENT

To answer questions about some of the dialogs in Part A, it is necessary to understand if the second speaker agrees or disagrees with the first speaker's ideas or proposals.

There are many ways to express agreement and disagreement:

Agreement	
So do I.	I'll say!
Me too.	You can say that again.
Neither do I.*	Is/Has/Was it ever!
I don't either.*	You bet!
Who wouldn't?	I couldn't agree with you more.
Isn't he/she/it though! (Didn't he/wasn't she/hasn't it though!)	I feel the same way you do about it.
I'll second that.	

*These two expressions show agreement with a negative statement:
    I don't really like my schedule this term.
    I don't either. *OR* Neither do I.

Disagreement	
I don't think so.	I'm afraid I don't agree.
That's not what I think.	Probably not.
That's not the way I see it.	Not necessarily.
Not really.	I'm afraid not.
I can't say I agree.	I'm not so sure.
I couldn't agree with you less.	

There are, of course, other expressions that show agreement and disagreement. Some are practiced in the exercises.

Sample Items

You will hear:

        M1: Howard certainly is a talented journalist.
        F1: Isn't he though!
        M2: What does the woman mean?

You will read:

        (A) She doesn't know if Howard is a journalist.
        (B) She agrees that Howard is talented.
        (C) She read Howard's journal.
        (D) She doesn't think Howard is talented.

Although the woman's reply seems negative in form, it actually signals agreement. Therefore, the best answer is (B).

You will hear:

> F1:   I thought Cheryl's photographs were the best at the exhibit.
> M1:   I didn't really see it that way.
> M2:   What does the man mean?

You will hear:

> (A) He thought Cheryl's photos were the best.
> (B) He didn't look at Cheryl's photos.
> (C) He thought other photos were better than Cheryl's.
> (D) He didn't go to the exhibit.

The man's response, "I didn't really see it that way," means that he disagreed with the woman's opinion that Cheryl's photographs were the best. The best answer is therefore (C).

Exercise 6.1

Focus: Determining if one speaker agrees or disagrees with the other speaker.

Directions: Listen to the following dialogues. Decide if the second speaker agrees or disagrees with the first speaker, and mark the appropriate blank. The first one is done as an example.

Now start the tape.

1. __✔__ (A) Agrees
   _____ (B) Disagrees

2. _____ (A) Agrees
   _____ (B) Disagrees

3. _____ (A) Agrees
   _____ (B) Disagrees

4. _____ (A) Agrees
   _____ (B) Disagrees

5. _____ (A) Agrees
   _____ (B) Disagrees

6. _____ (A) Agrees
   _____ (B) Disagrees

7. _____ (A) Agrees
   _____ (B) Disagrees

8. _____ (A) Agrees
   _____ (B) Disagrees

9. _____ (A) Agrees
   _____ (B) Disagrees

10. _____ (A) Agrees
    _____ (B) Disagrees

11. _____ (A) Agrees
    _____ (B) Disagrees

12. _____ (A) Agrees
    _____ (B) Disagrees

Exercise 6.2

Focus: Listening to dialogs that involve agreement and disagreement, and answering questions about them.

Directions: Listen to the following dialogs. Decide which choice—(A), (B), or (C)—best answers the question and mark the appropriate answer. The first one is done as an example.

Now start the tape.

1. _✔_ (A) He prefers taking a final exam.
   _____ (B) He's thinks an exam takes too much time.
   _____ (C) He'd rather write a research paper.

2. _____ (A) It was difficult, but she understood it.
   _____ (B) It wasn't very useful.
   _____ (C) It's probably easier than the other chapters.

3. _____ (A) He completely disagrees with it.
   _____ (B) He doesn't believe the university will accept it.
   _____ (C) He thinks it's a good one.

4. _____ (A) She doesn't think that Jack wrote it.
   _____ (B) She thinks it had too many details.
   _____ (C) She found it well-written.

5. _____ (A) He thinks it's a good day for bike riding, too.
   _____ (B) He doesn't agree with the woman's opinion of the weather.
   _____ (C) He didn't hear what the woman said.

6. _____ (A) Arthur wasn't doing well in the class.
   _____ (B) She's not sure why Arthur dropped the class.
   _____ (C) She believes Arthur dropped the class for no reason.

7. _____ (A) It might work.
   _____ (B) It's very impractical.
   _____ (C) It's unnecessary.

8. _____ (A) He didn't understand it.
   _____ (B) It made him angry.
   _____ (C) He agreed with it.

9. _____ (A) She's never been there during final exam week.
   _____ (B) It's crowded because students will be taking exams soon.
   _____ (C) It's not crowded now, but it soon will be.

10. _____ (A) He likes the costumes Madelyn made.
    _____ (B) He wouldn't recommend the play.
    _____ (C) He doesn't think the costumes are attractive.

11. _____ (A) It was very happy.
    _____ (B) It was exciting.
    _____ (C) It was unhappy.

12. _____ (A) She thinks Pamela is right.
    _____ (B) She thinks the regulations are fair.
    _____ (C) She disagrees with the man's opinion.

LESSON 7

DIALOGS INVOLVING SUGGESTIONS, INVITATIONS, OFFERS, AND REQUESTS

A number of dialogs in Part A involve a speaker making and/or responding to **suggestions, invitations, offers,** and **requests.** There are many ways to express these language functions. Some are listed in the charts in this lesson, while others are practiced in the exercises.

A) Suggestions

These are pieces of advice that one speaker gives another. In most dialogs, the first speaker poses a problem and the second speaker suggests a possible solution to that problem. In some dialogs, the first speaker makes a suggestion, and the second speaker responds to that suggestion positively or negatively.

Making Suggestions	
Why don't you/we . . .	If I were you . . .
Why not . . .	If I were in your shoes . . .
Have you ever thought of . . .	You/We should . . .
You/We might want to . . .	Shouldn't you/we . . .
You/We could always . . .	What about . . .
Maybe you/we could . . .	What if you/we . . .
Try . . .	How about . . .
You'd better . . .	

Positive Responses	Negative Responses
Why not!	I don't think so
Good idea!	I don't believe so.
That's an idea.	I already thought of that.
Sounds good to me.	I don't think that will work.
By all means!	Don't look at me!
Why didn't I think of that?	
That's worth a try.	
Thanks, I'll give that a try.	

▼ **Sample Item**

You will hear:

> M1: I'm doing so poorly in math class, I think I'm going to have to drop it.
>
> F1: You know, Frank, you should talk to Professor de Marco before you do anything. He's given special help to lots of students who were having trouble.
>
> M2: What does the woman suggest Frank do?

You will read:

> (A) Study with a group of students.
> (B) Drop his mathematics course.
> (C) Discuss the problem with the professor.
> (D) Take no action at this time.

The woman suggests that the man talk to Professor de Marco because the professor has helped many students in the past. ▲

B) Invitations

These are requests for someone to come somewhere or to take part in some activity. The first speaker may invite the second speaker to do something and the second speaker responds, or the second speaker may invite the first speaker to do something.

Making Invitations	
Shall we . . .	Let's . . .
Would you like to . . .	Do you want to . . .
Would you care to . . .	Could you . . .
Would you be able to . . .	Can you . . .
Want to . . .	

Positive Responses	Negative Responses
Yes, let's.	I'm sorry, but . . .
Sure, thanks.	I'd like to, but . . .
Sounds good.	I'd love to, but . . .
All right, I'd love to.	Thanks a lot, but . . .
I'd like that.	That sounds nice, but . . .
What a great idea!	I'll pass.
Sure. Thanks for inviting me.	Thanks for the invitation, but . . .
If you want me to.	I don't think I'll be able to make it this time.
Don't mind if I do.	Can I take a rain check?*

*This means, "Could we do this some other time?"

▼   **Sample Item**

You will hear:

M1: Would you like to join us on Sunday?
We're going to go on a picnic at the lake.
F1:   I'd love to, but I have a test Monday, and I have
to get ready for it.
M2: What will the woman probably do on Sunday?

You will read:

(A) Study for a test.
(B) Go on a picnic.
(C) Take an exam.
(D) Join a club.

The man invites the woman to come to a picnic. The woman says that she'd love to
go, but that she must study for a test she is taking Monday. (If the woman had
accepted the man's invitation, Choice (B) would have been correct.)   ▲

C) Offers

These are proposals to help someone or allow someone to do something. Either speaker in the dialog
may make an offer.

Making Offers	
Let me . . .	Can I . . .
Shall I . . .	May I . . .
Would you like me to . . .	Should I . . .
Do you want me to . . .	I could . . .
How does . . . sound?	

Positive Responses	Negative Responses
That would be nice.	I don't think so.
Yes, please	I'm afraid not.
Please do.	That won't be necessary.
Sure, thanks.	Thanks anyway.
If you wouldn't mind.	Please don't.
	Don't bother.
	Not on my account.

▼   **Sample Item**

You will hear:

F1:   Should I make reservations for dinner Friday night?
M1:   Thanks anyway, but I've already made them.
M2:   What does the man mean?

You will read:

(A) He can't go to dinner Friday night.
(B) Reservations won't be required.
(C) He made reservations earlier.
(D) He'd like the woman to make reservations.

The woman offers to make reservations, but the man replies that he's already made them.   ▲

D) Requests

To make a request is to ask someone to do something, or to ask for help or information.

Making Requests	
Would you . . .	Will you . . .
Could you/I . . .	May I . . .
Do you mind if . . .	Can you/I . . .
Would you mind if . . .	

Positive Responses	Negative Responses
I'd be glad to.	Sorry, but . . .
I'd be delighted.	I'm afraid not.
Sure thing.	I'd like to, but . . .
Certainly.	I wish I could, but . . .
Why not?	Actually, I do/would.*
If you want to.	I'm afraid I do/would.*
If you'd like.	As a matter of fact, I do/would.*
You bet.	
Be my guest.	
Not at all.*	
Of course not.*	

*Responses for "Do you mind if . . .?" or "Would you mind if . . .?"

▼ **Sample Item**

You will hear: M1: I have to make one more phone call before I go.
F2: Take your time. Would you just lock the office door when you finish?
M2: What does the woman want the man to do?

You will read:

(A) Lock the office.
(B) Finish his phone call quickly.
(C) Tell her what time it is.
(D) Look up a phone number.

● (B) (C) (D)

The woman requests that the man lock up the office. ▲

Exercise 7.1

Focus: Identifying suggestions, invitations, offers, and requests and responses to them.

Directions: Listen to the following dialogs. Decide which of the two choices best completes the sentence, and mark the appropriate space. The first one is done as an example.

Now start the tape.

1. The man is . . .
   ✔ (A) declining an offer
   ____ (B) making a suggestion

2. The woman is . . .
   ____ (A) accepting an invitation
   ____ (B) making an offer

3. The woman is . . .
   ____ (A) declining an offer
   ____ (B) making a suggestion

4. Mark is . . .
   ____ (A) rejecting a request
   ____ (B) agreeing to a request

5. The woman is . . .
   ____ (A) giving an invitation
   ____ (B) making a suggestion

6. The man is . . .
   ____ (A) agreeing to a request
   ____ (B) turning down an offer

7. Ed is probably going to . . .
   ____ (A) receive a suggestion
   ____ (B) make an offer

8. The woman is . . .
   ____ (A) suggesting a solution
   ____ (B) offering help

9. Cynthia is . . .
   ____ (A) giving an invitation
   ____ (B) accepting an offer

10. The woman is . . .
    ____ (A) declining an offer
    ____ (B) making a request

11. The man will probably . . .
    ____ (A) do what the woman suggests
    ____ (B) turn down the woman's invitation

12. Bob is . . .
    ____ (A) agreeing to an offer
    ____ (B) refusing a request

13. The man is . . .
    ____ (A) making a suggestion
    ____ (B) accepting an invitation

14. The man is . . .
    ____ (A) requesting that the man do something
    ____ (B) giving the woman a suggestion

15. Paul is . . .
    ____ (A) rejecting a suggestion
    ____ (B) agreeing with a suggestion

16. James tells the woman that . . .
    ____ (A) he can't accept her invitation
    ____ (B) he'd enjoy another sandwich

Exercise 7.2

Focus: Listening to dialogs involving suggestions, invitations, offers, and requests, and answering questions about them.

Directions: Listen to the following dialogs. Decide which choice—(A), (B), or (C)—best answers the question about the dialogs, and mark the appropriate answer. The first one is done as an example.

1. _____ (A) He would like a cigarette.
   _____ (B) The woman can smoke if she likes.
   _✔_ (C) He doesn't want the woman to smoke.

2. _____ (A) The man wears it quite often.
   _____ (B) It needs to be cleaned.
   _____ (C) The man should wear it.

3. _____ (A) Make more popcorn.
   _____ (B) Go to another theater.
   _____ (C) Buy some popcorn.

4. _____ (A) She could plan the trip.
   _____ (B) She may not feel well.
   _____ (C) She can go on the class trip.

5. _____ (A) He doesn't want more coffee.
   _____ (B) He doesn't want to use his credit card.
   _____ (C) He'd like to make coffee.

6. _____ (A) She doesn't think it's warm.
   _____ (B) She'll open the window herself.
   _____ (C) She wants the window closed.

7. _____ (A) The soup is more expensive than sandwiches.
   _____ (B) She doesn't know what kind of soup there is.
   _____ (C) The man might enjoy some soup.

8. _____ (A) The kitchen also needs cleaning.
   _____ (B) The living room doesn't have to be cleaned.
   _____ (C) The man shouldn't do the cleaning.

9. _____ (A) Go with her to the registrar's office.
   _____ (B) Help her find her way to the registrar's office.
   _____ (C) Tell her where to get her own map.

10. _____ (A) Work on their chemistry homework.
    _____ (B) Have breakfast.
    _____ (C) Stop studying for a little while.

11. _____ (A) Buy a new toaster.
    _____ (B) Replace her old shoes.
    _____ (C) Have repairs done.

12. _____ (A) He'd like her to go away.
    _____ (B) She can read his magazine.
    _____ (C) He hasn't finished reading.

13. _____ (A) Get an antique desk.
 _____ (B) Buy a new computer.
 _____ (C) Sit down and get to work.

14. _____ (A) He's already passed the test.
 _____ (B) He doesn't like to study at the library.
 _____ (C) He doesn't plan to study tonight.

15. _____ (A) He hasn't seen the letters.
 _____ (B) He doesn't know the right answers.
 _____ (C) He doesn't want to respond to the letters.

16. _____ (A) She wants to come even though it's raining.
 _____ (B) She can't come to lunch today.
 _____ (C) She'll pay for their lunch.

LESSON 8

DIALOGS INVOLVING CONTRADICTIONS, ASSUMPTIONS, AND QUESTIONS

A) Contradictions

These involve the second speaker correcting what the first speaker says, as in the samples below:

▼ **Sample Items**

You will hear:

> F1: Amy didn't work overtime last week.
> M1: As a matter of fact, she *did*.
> M2: What does the man say about Amy?

You will read:

> (A) She is always late for work.
> (B) She never works overtime.
> (C) She worked extra hours last week.
> (D) She hasn't had her job very long.

The man's emphatic use of the auxiliary verb *did* shows that he is contradicting what the woman said.

You will hear:

> M1: Martin always talks about how he loves to dance.
> F1: Yes, but you don't see him out on the dance floor very often, do you?
> M2: What does the woman say about Martin?

You will read:

> (A) He is an excellent dancer.
> (B) He doesn't like dancing very much.
> (C) He doesn't talk about dancing very often.
> (D) He goes dancing four times a week.

The woman's use of the word *but* and the tag question (". . . do you?") suggests that she doesn't believe that Martin really loves to dance.

You will hear:

> F1: All of the students voted for the proposal to expand the Student Council.
> M1: Well, most of them did, anyway.
> M2: What does the man mean?

You will read:

> (A) All of the students voted.
> (B) Some of the students opposed the proposal.
> (C) The proposal was defeated.
> (D) The Student Council voted.

The man says that most of the students voted for the proposal, contradicting the idea that all of them did. Therefore, some of the students must have opposed the proposal.

In some dialogs, such as the third Sample Item, the second speaker does not completely contradict what the first speaker says but rather limits the first speaker's idea. ▲

B) Assumptions

These are the beliefs that one speaker has until he or she receives information from a second speaker. You will generally hear dialogs involving assumptions near the end of Part A. These questions are considered difficult, but once you understand how they work and practice answering them, you should find them no more difficult than any other type of question. In this type of dialog, the first speaker makes a statement. The second speaker is surprised because the first statement contradicts what he or she believes to be true. The second speaker's response often begins with the word "Oh" and ends with the phrase ". . . after all." The answer to assumption questions is the reverse of what the second speaker initially thinks, and so what is "true" according to the first speaker is not the correct choice.

▼ **Sample Item**

You will hear:

    F1:   No, Judy's not here right now. She's at her economics class.
    M1:   Oh, so she decided to take that course after all.
    M2:   What had the man assumed about Judy?

You will read:

    (A) She wouldn't take the course.
    (B) She had already completed that course.
    (C) She was busy studying economics.
    (D) She wouldn't find economics difficult.

The man is surprised that Judy is in economics class because he thought that she had decided not to take the course. Therefore, he had obviously assumed that Judy was not going to take the course before he spoke to the woman. ▲

C) Questions

The second speaker in a dialog sometimes asks about what the first speaker says. The third speaker then asks what the second speaker wants to know.

▼ **Sample Item**

You will hear:

    F1:   Professor Petrakis said that Mark Twain was his favorite writer.
    M1:   When did he say that?
    M2:   What does the man want to know?

You will read:

> (A) When Mark Twain lived.
> (B) What the professor said about Mark Twain.
> (C) When the professor made his remark.
> (D) What books Mark Twain wrote.

The man asks when Professor Petrakis called Mark Twain his favorite author.   ▲

Two question phrases that may give you trouble are *What . . . for?* and *How come . . . ?* Both mean *Why . . . ?*

Exercise 8

Focus: Answering questions about dialogs involving contradictions, assumptions, and questions.

Directions: Listen to the following dialogs. Decide which one of the answer choices—(A), (B), or (C)—is correct, and mark the appropriate answer. The first one is done as an example.

Now start the tape.   🖭

1. _____ (A) She is definitely coming to dinner.
   _____ (B) She likes fish better than chicken.
   __✔__ (C) She likes chicken.

2. _____ (A) She had already moved.
   _____ (B) She hadn't found a new apartment yet.
   _____ (C) She'd already made an appointment.

3. _____ (A) What the man's name is.
   _____ (B) Who told the man to see the dean.
   _____ (C) Who the dean is.

4. _____ (A) He wants to take part in the election.
   _____ (B) He's not interested in running for office.
   _____ (C) He wants to get more facts from the president.

5. _____ (A) She couldn't type very fast.
   _____ (B) She had already finished the final draft.
   _____ (C) She hadn't completed the research.

6. _____ (A) He doesn't really like horseback riding.
   _____ (B) He rides horses whenever possible.
   _____ (C) He doesn't talk about riding very much.

7. _____ (A) When his insurance agent called.
   _____ (B) What his insurance agent wanted.
   _____ (C) What time he should return the call.

8. _____ (A) He was working full time.
   _____ (B) He was eating in the cafeteria.
   _____ (C) He didn't want a job.

9. _____ (A) When they returned.
   _____ (B) How long their hike was.
   _____ (C) Where they hiked.

10. _____ (A) He thinks the clothes are expensive.
    _____ (B) He doesn't think the clothes are very nice.
    _____ (C) He thinks the woman is being unreasonable.

11. _____ (A) Where the meeting will be held.
    _____ (B) When the meeting will start.
    _____ (C) Where the recreation center will be built.

12. _____ (A) Joy did not want to study abroad.
    _____ (B) The overseas program had been canceled.
    _____ (C) Joy would study overseas sooner than next year.

13. _____ (A) If the party was at Ben's house.
    _____ (B) What time the party ended.
    _____ (C) If he enjoyed the party.

14. _____ (A) All of Ted's answers were incorrect.
    _____ (B) Most of the problems were done correctly.
    _____ (C) Ted doesn't have to solve the problems.

15. _____ (A) How she got to the grocery store.
    _____ (B) Why she went to the grocery store.
    _____ (C) How much she paid for groceries.

16. _____ (A) Robin's brother didn't help her get a job.
    _____ (B) Robin didn't get a job.
    _____ (C) Robin was able to help her brother.

17. _____ (A) The flashlight had needed batteries.
    _____ (B) There had been some other problem with the flashlight.
    _____ (C) The man hadn't changed the batteries.

18. _____ (A) Professor Brennon surely won't lead the seminar.
    _____ (B) Professor Brennon's permission is not required.
    _____ (C) The woman doesn't need to take the seminar.

19. _____ (A) Why Steve is in the Pacific Northwest.
    _____ (B) How long Steve has been traveling.
    _____ (C) When Steve will return from his trip.

20. _____ (A) It hadn't been released yet.
    _____ (B) It wouldn't be very good.
    _____ (C) It can no longer be considered new.

LESSON 9

ANSWERING QUESTIONS ABOUT ACTIVITIES, PLANS, TOPICS, AND PROBLEMS

A) Questions About Activities

These questions follow dialogs that involve people talking about what they are doing. They are a kind of inference question because the activity itself is not mentioned in the dialog. Instead, you must determine the activity from the special vocabulary used by the speakers.

▼   **Sample Item**

You will hear:

> F1:   Is there room for that box up there?
> M1:   I can fit it in the trunk. And this suitcase should fit in the back seat.
> M2:   What are the speakers probably doing?

You will read:

> (A) Boarding an airplane.
> (B) Unpacking a box.
> (C) Loading a car.
> (D) Buying a suitcase.

The words *box*, *trunk*, *suitcase*, and *back seat* all indicate that the speakers are putting things into a car.   ▲

B) Questions About Plans

These questions follow dialogs in which two speakers discuss what one or both of them are going to do in the future.

▼   **Sample Item**

You will hear:

> F1:   Are you going to go to Boston with Michael this summer?
> M1:   Wish I could, but if I want to graduate next year, I've got to stay here and take a couple classes.
> M2:   What does the man plan to do this summer?

You will read:

> (A) Graduate.
> (B) Attend classes.
> (C) Visit Michael.
> (D) Go to Boston.

The man indicates that he must stay where he is and take classes in order to graduate next year.   ▲

C) Questions About Topics

The third speaker asks what the other two speakers are talking about. The topic is not usually mentioned directly in the dialog; it must be inferred from a general understanding of the dialog. The topic can be a person, a thing, or an activity.

▼ **Sample Item**

You will hear:

    F1:   Have you seen this letter from the bursar's office?

    F2:   Oh, no, not another increase! If you ask me, we're already spending too much to go to school here.

    M2: What are these speakers talking about?

You will read:

    (A) Higher tuition costs.

    (B) A poor grade.

    (C) Higher postage rates.

    (D) A letter from a relative.

From the fact that the letter comes from the bursar's office (the financial office of a university) and that the second woman is upset about an increase and feels they are spending too much to go to school, it is clear that they are talking about an increase in tuition. ▲

D) Questions About Problems

These questions follow dialogs in which the speakers are discussing some trouble one or both of them are having. The third speaker asks what the problem is.

▼ **Sample Item**

You will hear:

    M2: Gordon, what happened to your window?

    M1: When I was painting the house last week, I hit it with the ladder.

    M2: What problem does Gordon probably have?

You will read:

    (A) His house needs painting.

    (B) He broke his ladder.

    (C) He spilled some paint.

    (D) His window is broken.

Gordon, the second speaker, says that he hit the window with the ladder when he was painting the house. The logical result—a broken window. ▲

Exercise 9

Focus: Answering questions about activities, plans, topics, and problems.

Directions: Listen to the dialogs and the questions about them. Decide which of the answer choices—(A), (B), or (C)—best answers the question, and mark the appropriate blank.

Now start the tape. 〔▭〕

1. __✔__ (A) Road conditions.
   _____ (B) A weather report.
   _____ (C) Motel reservations.

2. _____ (A) Go to the concert.
   _____ (B) Listen to jazz on the radio.
   _____ (C) Buy more tickets.

3. _____ (A) The man's car is not running.
   _____ (B) The man isn't going to the party.
   _____ (C) The car isn't big enough for four people.

4. _____ (A) Stay inside.
   _____ (B) Find his umbrella.
   _____ (C) Look outside.

5. _____ (A) A store.
   _____ (B) A bridge.
   _____ (C) A street.

6. _____ (A) Shop for groceries.
   _____ (B) Leave for a camping trip.
   _____ (C) Go to a circus.

7. _____ (A) Ask the doctor for medicine for his headaches.
   _____ (B) Buy some new frames for his eyeglasses.
   _____ (C) get different lenses for his glasses.

8. _____ (A) Clothing.
   _____ (B) Hair styling.
   _____ (C) Painting.

9. _____ (A) Take a trip.
   _____ (B) Watch television.
   _____ (C) Examine some documents.

10. _____ (A) He lent it to someone else.
    _____ (B) It was ruined in the rain.
    _____ (C) He forgot where he left it.

11. _____ (A) A car.
    _____ (B) A magazine.
    _____ (C) A computer.

12. _____ (A) Go directly to business school.
    _____ (B) Look for a job with a big company.
    _____ (C) Start her own business.

13. _____ (A) Playing cards.
    _____ (B) Making dinner.
    _____ (C) Repairing a boat.

14. _____ (A) He doesn't have Phyllis's address.
    _____ (B) He's upset with Phyllis.
    _____ (C) He doesn't have a stamp.

15. _____ (A) Order a salad.
    _____ (B) Go to another restaurant.
    _____ (C) Put some salt in her soup.

LESSON 10

DIALOGS WITH SPECIAL VERBS

A) Causative Verbs

These verbs indicate that someone causes someone else to do something. When a dialog contains a causative verb, you must understand who performs the action. The verbs *have, get, make,* and *let* are the most common causative verbs. They are used in the following patterns:

<u>Have</u>

have someone do something   Dave had the mechanic fix his car.
have something done   Dave had his car fixed.

The causative verb *have* indicates that one person asks or pays another to do something. The subject of this sentence, *Dave,* does not perform the action. In the first sentence, the mechanic does. In the second sentence, an unnamed person does.

<u>Get</u>

get someone to do something   Jerry got his cousin to cut his hair.
get something done   Jerry got his hair cut.

The causative verb *get* usually means to persuade someone to do something. Again note that the subject, *Jerry,* does not perform the action. In the first sentence, Jerry's cousin does. In the second sentence, an unnamed person does.

<u>Make</u>

make someone do something   Cathy made her son do his homework.

The causative verb *make* means to force someone or compel someone to do something. Cathy's son is compelled to do his homework.

<u>Let</u>

let someone do something   The boss let us go home.

The verb *let* means *permit* or *allow.* The boss gives permission; we go home.

▼ Sample Item

You will hear:
    M1: Did you speak to the head of the department?
    F1: No, she had her assistant meet with me.
    M2: What does the woman mean?

You will read:

    (A) She spoke to the head of the department.
    (B) The head of the department had a meeting with her assistant.
    (C) She met with the assistant to the head of the department.
    (D) The assistant will soon become head of the department.

According to the dialog, the head of the department directed her assistant to meet with the woman. ▲

B) *Used to*

The expression *used to* has two functions:

used to + simple form

I used to live in New York. ——— means ———▶ I once lived in New York (but now I don't).

be/get + used to $\Bigg\langle$ + gerund (*-ing* verb)
+ noun phrase

I'm not used to driving on the left side of road. ——— means ———▶ I'm not accustomed to driving on the left side.

I've finally gotten used to my new job. ——— means ———▶ I've finally become accustomed to my new job.

The dialogs in Part A sometimes take advantage of these two functions of *used to*.

▼   **Sample Items**

You will hear:

> F1:   What does Hank's father do for a living?
> M1:   He's a salesman now, but he used to be a truck driver.
> M2:   What does the man say about Hank's father?

You will read:

> (A) He once drove trucks.
> (B) He sells used trucks.
> (C) His truck is still useful.
> (D) He's accustomed to his job.

The man says that Hank's father used to be a truck driver. In other words, Hank's father once drove trucks, but he no longer does so.

You will hear:

> F1:   Nancy is working late again today?
> M1:   Yeah, she must be getting used to it by now.
> M2:   What does the man say about Nancy?

You will read:

> (A) She probably has a more difficult job now.
> (B) She once worked later than she does now.
> (C) She seldom comes to work late.
> (D) She is becoming accustomed to late hours at work.

The second speaker indicates that Nancy has probably adjusted to working late.

Exercise 10

Focus: Listening to dialogs that contain causative verbs or expressions with *used to*.

Directions: Listen to the dialogs and the questions about them. Then decide which of the two answer choices—(A) or (B)—best answers the question, and mark the appropriate blank. The first one is done as an example.

Now start the tape.

1. _____ (A) Doug is happy to be Rose's friend.
   __✓__ (B) Doug and Rose are no longer good friends.

2. _____ (A) He can do the job as well as a professional.
   _____ (B) He should hire an electrician to do the job.

3. _____ (A) This station now plays classical music.
   _____ (B) The station doesn't broadcast anything but news.

4. _____ (A) Changing the oil was easy for her.
   _____ (B) The oil didn't need to be changed.

5. _____ (A) He's not accustomed to the early class either.
   _____ (B) His classes are difficult, too.

6. _____ (A) She's finally accustomed to roller-skating.
   _____ (B) She doesn't go skating as often as she once did.

7. _____ (A) He's going to clean his tie.
   _____ (B) He's going to take his tie to the laundry.

8. _____ (A) He moved the poster.
   _____ (B) He still likes the poster.

9. _____ (A) She may not be able to take a vacation in August.
   _____ (B) She's not sure when the busiest time will be.

10. _____ (A) She asked Greg to explain the point.
    _____ (B) She explained the point to Greg.

11. _____ (A) He isn't accustomed to his glasses.
    _____ (B) He looks quite different without glasses.

12. _____ (A) This type of weather is not new to him.
    _____ (B) He once lived in a very different climate.

13. _____ (A) She's going to take a picture of the members of her club.
    _____ (B) Someone is going to photograph her club.

14. _____ (A) She's never cooked with it.
    _____ (B) She doesn't feel comfortable using it.

15. _____ (A) If the deer will come near them.
    _____ (B) If they can approach the deer.

ANSWER SHEET
MINI-TEST 1: DIALOGS

1. (A) (B) (C) (D)   11. (A) (B) (C) (D)   21. (A) (B) (C) (D)
2. (A) (B) (C) (D)   12. (A) (B) (C) (D)   22. (A) (B) (C) (D)
3. (A) (B) (C) (D)   13. (A) (B) (C) (D)   23. (A) (B) (C) (D)
4. (A) (B) (C) (D)   14. (A) (B) (C) (D)   24. (A) (B) (C) (D)
5. (A) (B) (C) (D)   15. (A) (B) (C) (D)   25. (A) (B) (C) (D)
6. (A) (B) (C) (D)   16. (A) (B) (C) (D)   26. (A) (B) (C) (D)
7. (A) (B) (C) (D)   17. (A) (B) (C) (D)   27. (A) (B) (C) (D)
8. (A) (B) (C) (D)   18. (A) (B) (C) (D)   28. (A) (B) (C) (D)
9. (A) (B) (C) (D)   19. (A) (B) (C) (D)   29. (A) (B) (C) (D)
10. (A) (B) (C) (D)   20. (A) (B) (C) (D)   30. (A) (B) (C) (D)

MINI-TEST 1: DIALOGS

Directions: Listen to the conversations and the questions about them. Decide which of the four answer choices—(A), (B), (C), or (D)—is the best answer to the questions. Then mark the appropriate answer either in the blanks next to the answer choices or on the answer sheet above.

Now start the tape.

1. _____ (A) He met her during the summer.
   _____ (B) He's never liked her very much.
   _____ (C) He warned her of a problem.
   _____ (D) His impression of her has changed.

2. _____ (A) Review the last point.
   _____ (B) Go on to the next chapter.
   _____ (C) Leave the classroom.
   _____ (D) Point out the teacher's mistake.

3. _____ (A) The weather will not be as nice tomorrow.
   _____ (B) She no longer reads the weather report.
   _____ (C) She went to the store for a newspaper.
   _____ (D) The weather reports will change soon.

4. _____ (A) Watching television.
   _____ (B) Playing a game.
   _____ (C) Looking at a newspaper.
   _____ (D) Discussing a book.

5. _____ (A) Grace may want to live with the man's sister.
   _____ (B) The woman thinks Grace already has a roommate.
   _____ (C) The woman doesn't know where Grace has moved.
   _____ (D) Grace doesn't know the man's sister.

6. _____ (A) Go to a meeting.
   _____ (B) Keep a budget.
   _____ (C) Reduce his expenses.
   _____ (D) Get some exercise.

7. _____ (A) The man should clean out his closet.

_____ (B) The lamp will look better in a small space.

_____ (C) She doesn't like the lamp very much.

_____ (D) The living room is the best place for the lamp.

8. _____ (A) What Mark is writing.

_____ (B) Where Mark is living now.

_____ (C) Why Mark doesn't want to go.

_____ (D) Why Mark is in a hurry.

9. _____ (A) He certainly likes Ernie's red car.

_____ (B) The man in the red car resembles Ernie.

_____ (C) Ernie has a car just like that red one.

_____ (D) He can't see the man in the red car.

10. _____ (A) The man doesn't need his hat.

_____ (B) It's not very cold today.

_____ (C) She likes the way the hat looks.

_____ (D) The man ought to wear his hat.

11. _____ (A) She's never seen it.

_____ (B) It was made a long time ago.

_____ (C) She likes it a lot.

_____ (D) It's a very unusual movie.

12. _____ (A) He doesn't believe what the woman told him.

_____ (B) He thinks the team was unprepared too.

_____ (C) He disagrees with the woman's idea.

_____ (D) He isn't ready to go to the game either.

13. _____ (A) The man would like to use that computer.

_____ (B) Becky will need the computer for a long time.

_____ (C) There are no longer any computers in the library.

_____ (D) Becky would like the man to go to the library.

14. _____ (A) He hurt his hand when he was scuba diving.

_____ (B) He hasn't gone scuba diving for a long time.

_____ (C) He's not too old to go scuba diving.

_____ (D) He's an experienced scuba diver.

15. _____ (A) His shoes hurt his feet.

_____ (B) He was injured in a skiing accident.

_____ (C) His shoes are old and in bad shape.

_____ (D) He walked so far that his legs hurt.

16. _____ (A) She doesn't have time to listen now.

_____ (B) She is not sure what song she wants to hear.

_____ (C) She wants to hear his song right away.

_____ (D) She prefers old songs to new ones.

17. _____ (A) A television commercial.

_____ (B) A history class.

_____ (C) The woman's field of study.

_____ (D) Some famous artists.

18. _____ (A) She was about to suggest the same thing.

_____ (B) She doesn't feel like giving a party.

_____ (C) She's completely surprised by the man's remark.

_____ (D) She isn't hungry right now.

19. _____ (A) Sophie won't be at her apartment.
    _____ (B) The man can inform Sophie at the meeting.
    _____ (C) The man shouldn't bother Sophie.
    _____ (D) Sophie will think this is bad news.

20. _____ (A) He doesn't go out as often as he once did.
    _____ (B) He doesn't always tell the truth.
    _____ (C) He isn't as friendly as he once was.
    _____ (D) He hasn't always been so sociable.

21. _____ (A) The ring is quite attractive.
    _____ (B) Laura got a bargain on the ring.
    _____ (C) The ring was probably expensive.
    _____ (D) Laura had to sell her ring.

22. _____ (A) The woman didn't realize Bill had to work.
    _____ (B) Bill has not finished his work.
    _____ (C) The break has not lasted long enough.
    _____ (D) The work didn't take long to complete.

23. _____ (A) The woman has just begun to collect rocks.
    _____ (B) The man is unwilling to help.
    _____ (C) The box is very heavy.
    _____ (D) There's nothing in the box.

24. _____ (A) She doesn't like the length of her hair.
    _____ (B) She thinks the haircut took too long.
    _____ (C) She doesn't know where to get a haircut.
    _____ (D) She thinks haircuts are too expensive.

25. _____ (A) Professor Clayburn is going to speak some other night.
    _____ (B) He's never heard of Professor Clayburn.
    _____ (C) He didn't realize Professor Clayburn was speaking tonight.
    _____ (D) Professor Clayburn is giving his speech in this room.

26. _____ (A) The man may see the drawing.
    _____ (B) She'd like the man to visit.
    _____ (C) The man should draw a second picture.
    _____ (D) She's going to take a guess.

27. _____ (A) The weather has been very hot.
    _____ (B) Her car doesn't need a tune-up.
    _____ (C) She's starting to feel ill.
    _____ (D) She's already too warm.

28. _____ (A) Joe has been making too much noise.
    _____ (B) Dogs are not allowed in the dorm.
    _____ (C) No one understands the parking regulations.
    _____ (D) Joe is not allowed to leave his room.

29. _____ (A) Where the Medical Center is located.
    _____ (B) Which office Dr. Norton is in.
    _____ (C) What Dr. Norton told the man.
    _____ (D) Why the man went to see Doctor Norton.

30. _____ (A) She liked chemistry.
    _____ (B) She would graduate in May.
    _____ (C) She didn't have to repeat a course.
    _____ (D) She hadn't completed the required courses.

Extended Conversations

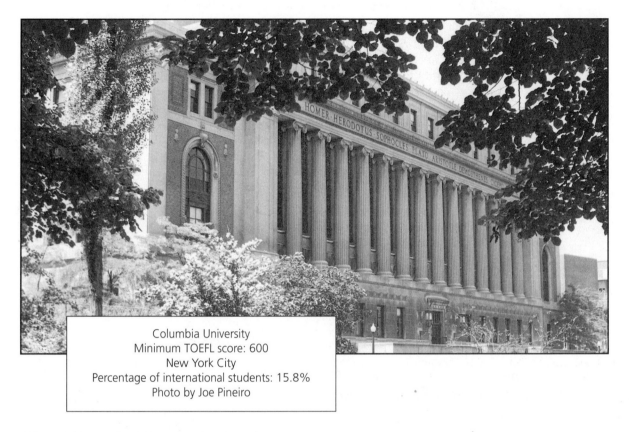

Columbia University
Minimum TOEFL score: 600
New York City
Percentage of international students: 15.8%
Photo by Joe Pineiro

About Extended Conversations

The second part of the Listening Comprehension section consists of longer conversations between a man and a woman or (sometimes) between two men or two women. Each conversation lasts from thirty to ninety seconds. It is preceded by brief introductory comments. After each of the conversations, there are from three to five questions. The questions are separated by a twelve-second pause. You must decide which one of the four answer choices in your test book is the best answer for the question, then mark that answer on your answer sheet. You're not permitted to take notes. There are two longer conversations on the standard form, three or four on the long form.

The Introductory Comments

These comments tell you which questions the conversation refers to and provide some brief information about the conversation:

> "Questions 31 to 34: Listen to two students talk about their psychology class."
> "Questions 31 to 35: Listen to a conversation about plans for a class trip."
> "Questions 35 to 38: Listen to two friends discussing a performance that they attended."
> "Questions 36 to 39: Listen to a conversation in a student housing office."
> "Questions 35 to 39: Listen to a conversation between two teaching assistants."

Not only do these introductory comments tell you to get ready to listen; they also tell you how many questions in your test book to preview at one time. Moreover, they give you a general idea of what to expect as you listen.

▼ **Sample Item**

You will hear:

M2: Listen to a conversation between two students.

F1: Bill, you're a physics major, aren't you?
M1: That's right.
F1: I need some advice. I want to take an introductory physics class, and I have to choose between two teachers, Professor Hunter and Professor McVey. Do you know much about them?
M1: I've taken classes from both of them. To tell you the truth, I don't really like Hunter's style of teaching. He doesn't seem to care if his students understand or not, and his lectures are pretty dry.
F1: Well, then, what about McVey? I've heard his course is difficult.
M1: It's not easy, but you'll learn a lot, and he always encourages his students to ask questions and join in discussions.

You will then hear:

M2: What does the woman ask Bill to do?

You will read:

(A) Give her information about two teachers.
(B) Help her with a physics assignment.
(C) Speak to a professor for her.
(D) Lead a discussion.

The woman asks Bill for some advice about the two professors who are teaching basic physics courses. Therefore, the best answer is (A).

You will then hear:

M2: What does Bill imply that the woman should do?

You will read:

(A) Change her major to physics.
(B) Discuss her problem with Professor Hunter.
(C) Sign up for an easy class.
(D) Take Professor McVey's class.

Bill speaks critically of Professor Hunter's teaching methods, but favorably of Professor McVey's, so he would probably advise her to take McVey's course. The best answer is (D). ▲

The Conversations

The extended conversations are similar to the Part A dialogs in style, but are longer. They frequently take place in a campus setting between two students or between a professor and a student.

The Questions

The questions may be overview questions or detail questions. The first question after the conversation is often an overview question. Overview questions require a broad understanding of the entire conversation. To answer them correctly, you must understand what *both* speakers say. There are several types of overview questions:

Type of Overview Question	Sample Question
Topic question	"What are the speakers discussing?"
Questions about setting (time and location)	"Where did this conversation take place?" "When did this conversation take place?"
Questions about the speakers	"Who are the speakers?" "What is the probable relationship between the speakers?"

It's important to listen carefully to the first few lines of an extended conversation to answer overview questions because this part of the talk often sets the scene. It often establishes the time and location of the conversation, the identity of the speakers, and the main idea of the rest of the conversation.

Detail questions ask about specific points in the conversation. The answer will usually be contained in what *one* speaker says. Detail questions follow the order of information in the conversation. In other words, the first of these questions refers to a point made early in the conversation, and the last asks about a point made near the end of the conversation. Most detail questions are factual questions; the answers are directly stated in the conversation. Many factual questions begin with these phrases:

According to the conversation, . . .
According to the man, . . .
According to the woman, . . .

A few of the detail questions are inference questions. In other words, the information is not directly given by the speakers; it can be concluded from the information that *is* stated, however.

What can be inferred from the man's comment about . . . ?
What does the man imply about . . . ?
What will the speakers probably try to do?

The Answer Choices

The four choices are all plausible answers for the question. Usually the answer choices are mentioned in some way in the conversation, but only one, the key, answers that particular question correctly.

Some people prefer to close their eyes or look away while listening to the extended conversations in order to concentrate on the voices on the tape. However, it is better if you read over the answer choices in the test book while listening. This technique is difficult, but it has several advantages:

- It allows you to get an overall sense of what the topic of the conversation will be.
- It enables you to anticipate what the questions will be, then concentrate on listening for those points.
- It permits you to confirm some of the details that you hear by comparing them with the answer choices in the test book.

In the next section of this *Guide*, you will practice previewing answer choices, listening to Part B conversations, and answering both overview and detail questions about the conversations.

TACTICS FOR EXTENDED CONVERSATIONS

- Be familiar with the directions, but remember that you cannot turn the page to look over answer choices while the directions are being read.

- Pay attention to the introductory comment for each conversation. These comments will tell you which items each conversation refers to and may give you an idea of what the conversation will be about.

- Preview the answer choices during the conversations and the pauses between questions. Try to guess what the questions will be.

- Listen for overall concepts:

  - Who is taking part in the conversation?

  - Where and when does the conversation take place?

  - What is the main topic of the conversation?

  The answers to these questions are often suggested in the first few lines of the conversations.

- You are not permitted to take written notes, but try to take "mental notes" on specific details: facts, figures, dates, places, and so on. You can sometimes check the information you think you hear against information you read in the answer choices while you are previewing.

- Answer items right away.

- Never leave any blanks on your answer sheet. Always guess.

LESSON 11

ANTICIPATING QUESTIONS ABOUT EXTENDED CONVERSATIONS

When you are previewing the items in Part B, you should try to anticipate what the questions will be by the form of the answer choices. You usually won't be able to guess exactly what the question will be, but you can guess what type of question will be asked. For example, if the four answer choices are the names of places, a "Where . . ." question will be asked; if the answer choices are times of day or dates, you will hear a "When . . ." question. If you have some idea of what the question will be, you can focus your listening during the talks.

You can also get a good idea of the situation in which the conversation is taking place by previewing the items.

Remember: The introductory comments at the beginning of the conversation tell you which items to preview.

Exercise 11

Focus: Guessing the questions that will be asked about an extended conversation and the situation in which the conversation takes place by previewing answer choices.

Directions: Look over the answer choices below. First try to guess the general type of question that will be asked about each item. Then look at the list of questions after each group of items and match the letter of the appropriate question with the item. Then answer the question about the overall topic of the conversation. The first one is done as an example.

There is no taped material for this exercise.

Conversation 1

1. (A) A grade the student received.
   (B) A story about a dance recital.
   (C) The need for correct spelling.
   (D) The role of a reporter.

   Question: ___b___

2. (A) Business.
   (B) Architecture.
   (C) Journalism.
   (D) Dance.

   Question: _____

3. (A) She submitted it too late.
   (B) It was too long.
   (C) Some important details were omitted.
   (D) Almost every word was misspelled.

   Question: _____

4. (A) Rewrite the story.
   (B) Buy a better dictionary.
   (C) Go to more dance recitals.
   (D) Get a job as a reporter.

   Question: _____

Questions for Conversation 1

   a) For what class did the man do the assignment?
   b) What is the main topic of this conversation?
   c) What does the man advise the woman to do?
   d) What problem does the man mention in connection with the story?

Situation Question: Conversation 1

Which of the following best describes the situation in which the first conversation probably takes place?

   _____ (A) One student is telling another a story about a dance.
   _____ (B) A professor is criticizing a student's story about a dance performance.
   _____ (C) An instructor is teaching a student a new dance.
   _____ (D) One student is suggesting ways in which the other student can improve her spelling.

Conversation 2

5. (A) He doesn't get enough exercise.
   (B) He's nervous about an important test.
   (C) He's spending too much time at the Recreation Center.
   (D) He doesn't know how to swim.

Question: _____

6. (A) Across campus from the Student Center building.
   (B) South of the stadium.
   (C) On the north side of campus.
   (D) Between the Student Center and the stadium.

Question: _____

7. (A) Sign up for some classes at the Recreation Center.
   (B) Spend more time studying for exams.
   (C) Take a break from his studies.
   (D) Take a bus to the Recreation Center.

Question: _____

8. (A) Just before the beginning of the semester.
   (B) During mid-term exams.
   (C) Near the end of the semester.
   (D) Just after the end of the semester.

Question: _____

Questions for Conversation 2
  a) Where is the Recreation Center?
  b) What does the woman suggest the man do?
  c) What problem does the man complain about?
  d) At what point in the semester does this conversation take place?

Situation Question: Conversation 2
Which of the following best describes the situation in which the conversation probably takes place?

_____ (A) One student recommends that another get some exercise in order to relax during exams.
_____ (B) Two students discuss their plans for a vacation.
_____ (C) A physical education instructor suggests that a student register for classes in her department.
_____ (D) A student explains to a visitor to campus how to get to the stadium.

Conversation 3

9. (A) At an art gallery.
   (B) At an art museum.
   (C) In an artist's studio.
   (D) In a special room in the library.

Question: _____

10. (A) Paintings.
    (B) Sculptures.
    (C) Book covers.
    (D) Photographs.

Question: _____

11. (A) A story in a newspaper.
    (B) An article in an art magazine.
    (C) A class she attended.
    (D) A show she saw on television.

Question: _____

12. (A) An art historian and a student.
    (B) Two students.
    (C) Two visitors to a museum.
    (D) A tour guide and a tourist.

Question: _____

13. (A) Primitive.
    (B) Life-sized.
    (C) Realistic.
    (D) Stylized.

Question: _____

Questions for Conversation 3

    a) Who is taking part in this conversation?
    b) How would the woman probably describe the works of art that she saw?
    c) What was the source of the woman's information?
    d) Where did the exhibit take place?
    e) What kind of art are the speakers discussing?

Situation Question: Conversation 3

Which of the following best describes the situation in which the conversation probably takes place?

_____ (A) One speaker describes to the other her techniques for painting pictures.
_____ (B) The woman tells the man about a recent book she read.
_____ (C) An art expert gives some advice to the other speaker about becoming an artist.
_____ (D) One speaker tells the other about some art she saw at an exhibit.

LESSON 12

ANSWERING OVERVIEW QUESTIONS ABOUT EXTENDED CONVERSATIONS

After each extended conversation in Part B, there are three to five questions. Usually the first and sometimes the last question are **overview questions**. To answer these questions, you need an understanding of the whole conversation rather than of any specific point.

Overview Questions for the Extended Conversations

- What is the main topic of this conversation?
- What are these people primarily discussing?
- Where does this conversation take place?
- When does this conversation take place?
- What is the relationship between the speakers?
- What is the man's/woman's occupation?
- What is one speaker's attitude toward the other speaker?

Main topic questions must correctly summarize the conversation. Incorrect answers for these questions are too general, too specific, or incorrect according to the conversation.

Although these questions require an overall understanding of the conversations, the first few sentences often "set the scene." In other words, the opening lines of the talk establish the time, place, and main topic. Read the opening lines of the extended conversation given below:

M1: (Answering phone) Hello?

F1: Hi, Rod, this is Rita—I'm in your nine o'clock class. I missed class because of a cold, and I was wondering if I could borrow your notes.

M1: I don't know if you could read my notes—I have terrible handwriting. But I can tell you what happened. Professor Phillips went over the material in Chapter 4, about different types of stars in our galaxy. And she talked about what the mid-term exam is going to be like.

F1: Uh-oh, you better tell me all about the mid-term—I really need to do well on it.

From this portion of a conversation, we learn that

. . . both of the speakers are students
. . . they are probably taking a course in astronomy
. . . the class is about halfway over (because they are taking mid-term exams)
. . . the rest of the talk will probably deal with the material that will be on the examination

Not all conversations begin with so much detail. However, it is important to concentrate on the opening lines to learn this kind of information.

Exercise 12

Focus: Listening to the opening lines of extended conversations, and answering overview questions about the topics, settings, and speakers.

Directions: Listen to the conversations and the questions about them. Then mark the answer choice—(A), (B), or (C)—that correctly completes the sentence. The first one is done as an example.

Now start the tape.

1. _____ (A) Methods of predicting earthquakes.
   __✔__ (B) Ways to improve the man's presentation.
   _____ (C) The many new uses of computer graphics.

2. _____ (A) Statistics.
   _____ (B) Computer science.
   _____ (C) Geology.

3. _____ (A) A language teacher and a student.
   _____ (B) A dean and a teacher.
   _____ (C) A teacher and an assistant.

4. _____ (A) The language of the deaf.
   _____ (B) Methods of teaching German.
   _____ (C) Communication networks.

5. _____ (A) Professor Quinn's approach to teaching.
   _____ (B) The process of getting a student identification card.
   _____ (C) Procedures for checking out reserve material.

6. _____ (A) At a university library.
   _____ (B) In a psychology class.
   _____ (C) In a laboratory.

7. _____ (A) To ask for a job.
   _____ (B) To get some advice.
   _____ (C) To discuss medical research.

8. _____ (A) Academic advisor.
   _____ (B) Physician.
   _____ (C) Administrator.

9. _____ (A) Helpful.
   _____ (B) Discouraging.
   _____ (C) Inconsiderate.

10. _____ (A) The art of raising dogs.
    _____ (B) A softball game.
    _____ (C) A dogsled race.

11. _____ (A) An archaeologist.
    _____ (B) An anthropologist.
    _____ (C) A university student.

12. _____ (A) Their plans for the coming school year.
    _____ (B) Tina's volunteer position.
    _____ (C) Tina's trip to Europe.

13. _____ (A) A clerk at a bookstore.
    _____ (B) A librarian.
    _____ (C) A publisher's sales officer.

14. _____ (A) Before the spring term begins.
    _____ (B) In the middle of the spring term.
    _____ (C) After the spring term ends.

15. _____ (A) In Nicholson Hall.
    _____ (B) In the Graduate Admissions Office.
    _____ (C) In the Financial Aid Office.

16. _____ (A) Requirements for graduate admission.
    _____ (B) Directions to another office.
    _____ (C) The woman's need for a scholarship.

LESSON 13

ANSWERING DETAIL QUESTIONS ABOUT
EXTENDED CONVERSATIONS

Most of the questions in Part B are **detail questions** that require an understanding of specific points in the conversation. A majority of these questions are **factual questions,** asking what, where, when, why, and how much. To answer the question, you need to listen carefully.

Other questions are **inference questions.** As previously explained, the answers to inference questions are not directly stated, but are suggested by information in the lecture. Many of these questions begin, "What do the speakers imply about . . ." or "What can be inferred from the conversation about . . ."

Remember that the order of detail questions follows the order of the conversation. In other words, the first detail question will be about something mentioned early in the conversation while the last one is about something mentioned near the end of the conversation.

If anything in the conversation is emphasized, it will probably be asked about. In other words, if something one speaker says is repeated by the second speaker, or if one speaker talks about something in an emphatic tone of voice, there will probably be a question about that information, as in this section of a conversation:

> M1: My project for my film-making class took me six weeks to finish.
> F1: Six weeks! I can hardly believe it. Doesn't the teacher realize you have other classes too?

You can be fairly sure that there will be a question such as this: "How long did the man's project take to complete?"

Exercise 13.1

Focus: Answering detail and inference questions based on specific points in short portions of extended conversations.

Directions: You will hear three extended conversations, each one divided into several short portions. After each portion, there will be a number of questions based on that part of the talk. Mark the best answer choice—(A), (B), or (C)—for each question. The first one is done as an example.

Now start the tape.

1. _____ (A) A doctor.
   _____ (B) A newspaper.
   ✔ (C) A magazine.

2. _____ (A) It's too tiring.
   _____ (B) It can cause injuries.
   _____ (C) It's not demanding enough.

3. _____ (A) Downhill skiing.
   _____ (B) Jogging.
   _____ (C) Cross-country skiing.

4. _____ (A) It doesn't require much snow.
   _____ (B) It is a recently developed sport.
   _____ (C) It can be done in flat areas.

5. _____ (A) Use a cross-country ski machine.
   _____ (B) Travel to ski resorts.
   _____ (C) Take up jogging.

6. _____ (A) The expense.
   _____ (B) The weather conditions.
   _____ (C) The danger.

7. _____ (A) He stayed up most of the night.
   _____ (B) He's been studying all morning.
   _____ (C) He took an exam last night.

8. _____ (A) It was an improvement.
   _____ (B) It was disappointing.
   _____ (C) It was unfair.

9. _____ (A) Undergraduate students.
   _____ (B) Teachers.
   _____ (C) Graduate students.

10. _____ (A) She learned how to do research.
    _____ (B) She was prepared for her sociology test.
    _____ (C) She learned teaching techniques.

11. _____ (A) Basic scientific research.
    _____ (B) Business management.
    _____ (C) Test-taking skills.

12. _____ (A) In Staunton Hall.
    _____ (B) In the Physics Tower.
    _____ (C) In the library.

13. _____ (A) Study for his next exam.
    _____ (B) Go to the Study Skills Center.
    _____ (C) Get some sleep.

14. _____ (A) To buy something at an auction.
    _____ (B) To pay for employees' salaries.
    _____ (C) To improve their broadcasts.

15. _____ (A) Apply for a job at the station.
    _____ (B) Donate his services for the station's auction.
    _____ (C) Direct the construction of a new tower.

16. _____ (A) She must work on her own research project.
    _____ (B) She has to help her parents.
    _____ (C) She must study for exams.

17. _____ (A) They seldom attend auctions.
    _____ (B) They might bid on the man's services.
    _____ (C) They often watch that station.

Exercise 13.2

Focus: Answering detail and inference questions based on specific points in complete extended conversations.

Directions: You will hear three extended conversations. After each conversation, there will be a number of questions based on it. Mark the best answer choice—(A), (B), or (C)—for each question. The first one is done as an example.

Now start the tape.

1. _____ (A) North of Los Angeles.
   ___✔___ (B) Between Los Angeles and San Diego.
   _____ (C) East of San Diego.

2. _____ (A) They are a type of insect.
   _____ (B) They are a kind of fish.
   _____ (C) They are a type of bird.

3. _____ (A) In March.
   _____ (B) In early summer.
   _____ (C) In October.

4. _____ (A) About 700 miles.
   _____ (B) About 1,000 miles.
   _____ (C) About 7,000 miles.

5. _____ (A) The swallows' arrival.
   _____ (B) The parade.
   _____ (C) The swallows' departure.

6. _____ (A) Only during the first week of classes.
   _____ (B) Whenever students ask for it.
   _____ (C) Only in the afternoon.

7. _____ (A) A tour guide.
   _____ (B) A classroom.
   _____ (C) A map.

8. _____ (A) In the Science Building.
   _____ (B) In the Student Center Building.
   _____ (C) In the University Recreation Center.

9. _____ (A) A test in a composition class.
   _____ (B) A road test.
   _____ (C) The written test for her driver's license.

10. _____ (A) He drove too fast.
    _____ (B) He couldn't park well.
    _____ (C) He made an improper turn.

11. _____ (A) Drive her to the test site.
    _____ (B) Help her get ready for the road test.
    _____ (C) Sell her a car.

12. _____ (A) It doesn't belong to her.
    _____ (B) She's not a licensed driver.
    _____ (C) It isn't running right.

**ANSWER SHEET
MINI-TEST 2**

1. (A) (B) (C) (D)   5. (A) (B) (C) (D)
2. (A) (B) (C) (D)   6. (A) (B) (C) (D)
3. (A) (B) (C) (D)   7. (A) (B) (C) (D)
4. (A) (B) (C) (D)   8. (A) (B) (C) (D)

MINI-TEST 2: EXTENDED CONVERSATIONS

Directions: Listen to the conversations and the questions about them. Decide which one of the four answer choices—(A), (B), (C), or (D)—is the best answer to the question. Then mark the appropriate answer either in the blanks next to the answer choices or on the answer sheet above.

Now start the tape.

1. _____ (A) To look up some terms.
   _____ (B) To meet Stanley.
   _____ (C) To get a snack.
   _____ (D) To prepare for an exam.

2. _____ (A) His library card.
   _____ (B) A statistics book.
   _____ (C) Some index cards.
   _____ (D) A notebook.

3. _____ (A) Piles of note cards.
   _____ (B) The part of the library where journals are stored.
   _____ (C) The part of the library where books are shelved.
   _____ (D) A place to get something to eat.

4. _____ (A) Behind the main desk.
   _____ (B) The periodicals room.
   _____ (C) A lost and found office.
   _____ (D) The reference room.

5. _____ (A) The sport of mountain climbing.
   _____ (B) Classes the man is taking.
   _____ (C) An exhibit the man saw in a museum.
   _____ (D) A new activity the man is involved in.

6. _____ (A) A means of descending slopes.
   _____ (B) A method of climbing cliffs.
   _____ (C) A way to clean walls.
   _____ (D) A type of graffiti.

7. _____ (A) Educating people about geology.
   _____ (B) Cleaning up after careless people.
   _____ (C) Photographing mountain peaks.
   _____ (D) Rescuing people who are in danger.

8. _____ (A) Explore a cave with him.
   _____ (B) Take some photographs.
   _____ (C) Attend a meeting.
   _____ (D) Examine a crystal.

Mini-Talks

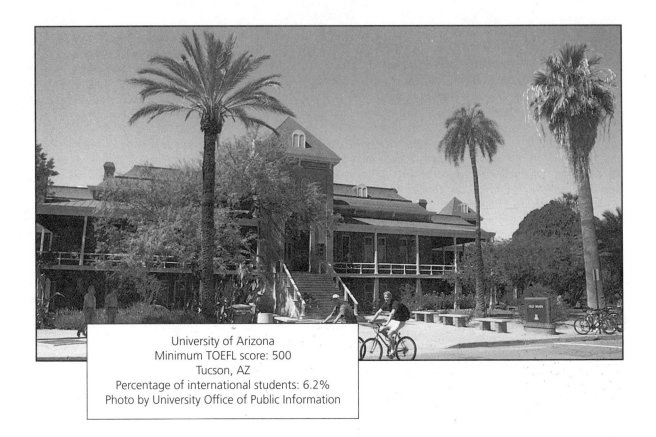

University of Arizona
Minimum TOEFL score: 500
Tucson, AZ
Percentage of international students: 6.2%
Photo by University Office of Public Information

About Mini-Talks

The third part of Section 1 consists of Mini-Talks. These are monologues (talks involving only one speaker). Each Mini-Talk lasts from thirty to ninety seconds. Like the Extended Conversations, they are preceded by introductory comments. After each talk, there are from three to five questions. The questions are separated by a twelve-second pause. You have to decide which of the four answer choices in the test book best answers the question, then mark that answer on your answer sheet. You are not allowed to take notes. There are three Mini-Talks on the standard form, four on the long form.

The Introductory Comments

These comments tell you which questions the Mini-Talks refer to and provide some brief information about the conversation:

"Questions 35 to 40: Listen to a lecture given at a botanical garden."
"Questions 31 to 35: Listen to a talk about the university's housing policy."
"Questions 35 to 38: Listen to a lecture given in a history class."

The introductory comments tell you how many questions in your test book to preview at one time and give you a general idea of the topic of the talk.

▼ **Sample Items**

You will hear:

M2: Listen to this lecture given in a university classroom.

M1: Students, this evening we'll have a chance to observe a phenomenon that we've discussed several times in class. Tonight there will be a lunar eclipse. As we've said, when an eclipse of the Moon occurs, the Earth passes between the Sun and the Moon. Therefore, the shadow of the Earth moves across the surface of the Moon and obscures it. Because you won't be looking at the Sun, it is not necessary to use the special lenses and filters that you need when observing a solar eclipse. You can observe a lunar eclipse with your unaided eye or with a telescope, and photograph it with an ordinary camera. So if the weather's not cloudy tonight, go out and take a look at this eclipse of the Moon. I'm sure you'll find it interesting.

You will hear:

M2: In what course is this lecture probably being given?

You will read:

(A) Philosophy.
(B) Meteorology.
(C) Astronomy.
(D) Photography.

The lecture concerns a lunar eclipse, a topic that would typically be discussed in an astronomy class.

You will hear:

M2: According to the speaker, which of the following occurs during a lunar eclipse?

You will read:

(A) The Earth's shadow moves across the Moon.
(B) Clouds block the view of the Moon.
(C) The Moon moves between the Earth and the Sun.
(D) The Sun is too bright to be observed without special equipment.

The speaker says "the shadow of the Earth moves across the Moon and obscures it." The best answer is therefore (A). ▲

The Talks

The Mini-Talks are usually somewhat more formal in style than the Extended Conversations. Some of the talks resemble lectures given as part of a university course in history, literature, or biology, for example. Other Mini-Talks resemble talks you would hear at a university, but not in a classroom. For example, you might hear talks about campus organizations, registration procedures, or the services at a campus medical center. Still others have nothing to do with university life; you may hear a tour guide speaking to a group of tourists or a curator speaking to visitors at a museum.

The Questions

As with the Extended Conversations, the questions about Mini-Talks may be overview questions or detail questions. The first question after the talk is usually an overview question. Overview questions require an understanding of the entire conversation. There are several types of overview questions:

Type of Overview Question	Sample Question
Topic/main idea/ purpose questions	"What is the lecture mainly about?" "What is the speaker mainly talking about?" "What is the main idea of this lecture?" "Why is the speaker giving this talk?" "What is the main point of this lecture?"
Questions about setting (course, time, and location)	"In what course was this lecture probably given?" "Where was this talk probably given?" "When was this talk probably given?"
Questions about the speaker	"Who is the speaker?" "What is the speaker's occupation?"

You should listen carefully to the first few lines of the mini-talk to answer overview questions because this part of the talk often sets the scene. It often establishes the time and location of the conversation, the identity of the speaker, and the main idea of the rest of the conversation.

Detail questions ask about specific points in the talk. Detail questions follow the order of information in the lecture. In other words, the first of these questions refers to a point made early in the lecture; the last asks about a point made near the end of the lecture. Most detail questions are factual questions; the answers are directly stated in the talk. Some factual questions begin with these phrases:

According to the speaker, . . .
According to the lecture, . . .

A few are inference questions. The answers to these are not directly stated in the talk; they are only suggested. These questions usually contain some form of the words *infer* or *imply* or the word *probably*.

What can be inferred about . . . ?
What does the speaker imply about . . . ?
What is probably true about . . . ?

The Answer Choices

The four choices are all plausible answers for the question. Usually the answer choices are mentioned in some way in the talk. As with the conversations, it is better to read over the answer choices in the test book while listening so that you can preview the answer choices than to look away or close your eyes.

In the next section of this *Guide*, you will practice previewing answer choices, listening to Part C Mini-Talks, and answering both overview and detail questions about the talks.

Tactics for Mini-Talks

- Be familiar with the directions, but remember that you cannot turn the page to look over answer choices while the directions are being read.

- Pay attention to the introductory comment for each talk. These comments will tell you which items each talk refers to and may give you an idea of what the talk will be about.

- Preview the answer choices while the talks are being read and during the pauses between questions. Try to guess what the questions and the topic will be.

- Listen for overall concepts:

  - Who is giving the talk?

  - Where and when is the talk being given?

  - What is the main topic or purpose of the talk?

  The answers to these questions are often suggested in the first few lines of the talks.

- You are not permitted to take written notes, but try to take "mental notes" on specific details: facts, figures, dates, places, and so on. You can sometimes check the information you think you hear against information you read in the answer choices while you are previewing.

- Answer items right away.

- Never leave any blanks on your answer sheet. Always guess.

LESSON 14

ANTICIPATING QUESTIONS ABOUT MINI-TALKS

As in the other two parts of the Listening Comprehension section, you should preview the items in Part C and try to anticipate what the questions will be by the form of the answer choices. You may not be able to guess exactly what the questions will be, but you can guess what type of question will be asked. For example, if the four answer choices are the names of places, a "Where . . ." question will be asked; if the answer choices are times of day or dates, you will hear a "When . . ." question.

   If you have some idea of what the question will be, you can focus your listening during the talks.

Exercise 14

Focus: Guessing what Part C questions will be asked by looking at the answer choices.

Directions: Look over the answer choices below. First try to guess the general type of question that will be asked about each item. Then look at the list of questions after each group of items and match the letter of the appropriate question with the item. One question in each set will *not* be used. The first one is done as an example.

There is no taped material for this exercise.

1. (A) The life of Clara Barton.
   (B) A short history of the American Red Cross.
   (C) The role of nurses in the Civil War.
   (D) The writings of Clara Barton.

   Question: ___*b*___

2. (A) In Virginia.
   (B) In Switzerland.
   (C) In Massachusetts.
   (D) In Texas.

   Question: _____

3. (A) Teacher.
   (B) Superintendent of a hospital.
   (C) Clerk in a government office.
   (D) Diplomatic official.

   Question: _____

4. (A) In 1845.
   (B) During the American Civil War.
   (C) During a trip to Europe.
   (D) In 1881.

   Question: _____

5. (A) To help wounded soldiers.
   (B) To provide relief for hurricane victims.
   (C) To prevent famines.
   (D) To publish books about nursing.

   Question: _____

Questions for items 1–5

   a) What was Clara Barton's first occupation?
   b) What is this talk mainly about?
   c) Where was Clara Barton born?
   d) When did Clara Burton found the American Red Cross?
   e) What was the original purpose of the American Red Cross?
   f) When was this lecture probably given?

6. (A) To honor a student.
   (B) To introduce a speaker.
   (C) To discuss the creative writing program.
   (D) To criticize a new book.

   Question: _____

7. (A) A science fiction novel.
   (B) Poetry.
   (C) Criticism.
   (D) A collection of short stories.

   Question: _____

8. (A) A cash prize.
   (B) Publication of his works.
   (C) A free trip.
   (D) A scholarship.

   Question: _____

Questions for items 6-8

a) How does the speaker feel about Jim McKee?
b) What award did Jim McKee receive?
c) What kind of writing has Jim McKee done?
d) What is the main purpose of this talk?

9. (A) A radio announcer.
   (B) A waitress.
   (C) A television announcer.
   (D) A chef.

Question: _____

10. (A) Vegetarian food.
    (B) Food from New Mexico.
    (C) Food from Louisiana.
    (D) Fresh seafood.

Question: _____

11. (A) On Atlantic Avenue.
    (B) On a boat.
    (C) On a dock.
    (D) On First Street.

Question: _____

12. (A) Most of the dishes are reasonably priced.
    (B) All but a few of the dishes are delicious.
    (C) The service has improved lately.
    (D) It's not too crowded on weekday nights.

Question: _____

Questions for Items 9-12

a) What does the speaker say about the Tangerine Café?
b) What kind of food does the Tangerine Café mainly serve?
c) What problem did the speaker have when she went to the Tangerine Café?
d) Who is the speaker?
e) Where is the Tangerine Café located?

LESSON 15

ANSWERING OVERVIEW QUESTIONS ABOUT MINI-TALKS

After each talk in Part C, there are three or four questions. Usually the first question is an **overview question**. To answer this type of question, you need an understanding of the whole talk rather than of any specific point.

Overview Questions for the Mini-Talks

- What is the main idea/main point/main topic of the lecture?
- What is the purpose of this talk?
- Where was this lecture given?
- When was this talk given?
- In what course was this lecture given?
- What is the speaker's occupation?
- Who is the audience for this talk?

Main idea, main topic, and main point questions must correctly summarize the talk. Incorrect answers for these questions are usually too general, too specific, or incorrect according to the lecture.

Although these questions require an overall understanding of the talks, the first few sentences often "set the scene." In other words, the opening lines of the talk frequently establish the time, place, and main topic. Read the opening lines of the Mini-Talk given below:

Good morning, everyone. As you probably know, this class is a continuation of a course that began last term. Last term we focused on American writers of the nineteenth century. Today we'll begin our study of twentieth-century novelists with a look at Ernest Hemingway.

From this introduction, we know that

. . . the speaker is a teacher
. . . the audience is a group of students
. . . the course is in American literature
. . . the talk will concern Ernest Hemingway

Not all talks will begin with so much detail. However, it is important to concentrate on the opening lines to learn this kind of information.

Exercise 15

Focus: Listening to the opening lines of Mini-Talks and answering overview questions about the main ideas, speakers and audiences, settings, and so on.

Directions: Listen to the introductions and the questions about them. Then mark the answer choice—(A), (B), or (C)—that correctly completes the sentence. The first one is done as an example.

Now start the tape.

1. _____ (A) A teacher.
   __✔__ (B) A tour guide.
   _____ (C) A photographer.

2. _____ (A) A description of the wildlife preserve.
   _____ (B) Advice about outdoor photography.
   _____ (C) The scientific classification of buffaloes.

3. _____ (A) To explain the traditions of handball.
   _____ (B) To give information about the rules of tennis.
   _____ (C) To discuss the rules of handball.

4. _____ (A) At the end of a tournament.
   _____ (B) Before an exhibition game.
   _____ (C) During a game.

5. _____ (A) Factory workers.
   _____ (B) Visitors to a factory.
   _____ (C) Management trainees.

6. _____ (A) The process of canning soft
   drinks.
   _____ (B) Management-labor teamwork.
   _____ (C) The life cycle of plants.

7. _____ (A) The physical rewards of
   dancing.
   _____ (B) The importance of the program
   to the university.
   _____ (C) The disadvantages of being in
   the program.

8. _____ (A) Director of a dance program.
   _____ (B) Professor of psychology.
   _____ (C) Athletics coach.

9. _____ (A) The host at a party.
   _____ (B) The president of a society.
   _____ (C) The captain of a ship.

10. _____ (A) The role of the State Historical
    Society.
    _____ (B) The history of New England.
    _____ (C) The story of some shipwrecks.

11. _____ (A) Composition.
    _____ (B) Fine arts.
    _____ (C) Architecture.

12. _____ (A) The use of blueprints.
    _____ (B) Methods of organization.
    _____ (C) Editing papers.

13. _____ (A) Experienced skiers.
    _____ (B) Ski instructors.
    _____ (C) Beginning skiers.

14. _____ (A) The fundamentals of skiing.
    _____ (B) Championship skiing.
    _____ (C) The development of ski resorts.

15. _____ (A) Law.
    _____ (B) Economics.
    _____ (C) Classical languages.

16. _____ (A) A few weeks after the beginning
    of class.
    _____ (B) In the first class meeting.
    _____ (C) During the final exam.

17. _____ (A) On a boat.
    _____ (B) At an aquarium.
    _____ (C) On an island.

18. _____ (A) The habits of whales.
    _____ (B) Types of whales.
    _____ (C) Efforts to protect whales.

19. _____ (A) Students who own bicycles.
    _____ (B) New members of the campus
    police force.
    _____ (C) Pedestrians concerned about
    safety.

20. _____ (A) To describe some recent
    accidents.
    _____ (B) To introduce a new program.
    _____ (C) To provide safety and security
    hints.

LESSON 16

ANSWERING DETAIL QUESTIONS ABOUT MINI-TALKS

Most of the questions about Part C talks are **detail questions** that ask about specific points in the talk. The majority of these questions are **factual questions,** asking about facts, reasons, places, or dates mentioned by the speaker. This type of question often begins, "According to the speaker, . . ." Incorrect answers are often mentioned at some point in the talk but are not appropriate answers to the questions as asked.

You are not permitted to take written notes while listening to the lecture.

A few questions about the Part C talks are **inference questions.** Many of these questions begin, "What does the speaker imply about . . ." or "What can be inferred from the lecture about . . ."

As in Part B, if a speaker emphasizes a point in the lecture by going back to it or repeating it, there will probably be a question about it.

> M: . . . Now, in the days of the California Gold Rush, the journey by ship from the East Coast to San Francisco took about six months. Can you imagine that—gold-seekers spent six months at sea just getting to California!

There will almost certainly be a question about how long it took to get from the East Coast to San Francisco during the Gold Rush.

Exercise 16.1

Focus: Answering detail and inference questions based on specific points in Part C talks.

Directions: You will hear three talks, each one divided into several short portions. After each portion, there will be a number of questions based on that part of the talk. Mark the best answer choice—(A), (B), or (C)—for each question. The first one is done as an example.

Now start the tape. 🎧

Talk A

1. _____ (A) It covers some difficult topics.
   __✔__ (B) It's unlike other biology courses.
   _____ (C) It has never been offered by this department.

2. _____ (A) By visiting a coral reef.
   _____ (B) By going to the library.
   _____ (C) By going to a farm.

3. _____ (A) Diving.
   _____ (B) Photography.
   _____ (C) Biology.

4. _____ (A) As harmful.
   _____ (B) As easily damaged.
   _____ (C) As frightening.

5. _____ (A) Transportation.
   _____ (B) Housing.
   _____ (C) Basic equipment.

6. _____ (A) Traveling by ship.
   _____ (B) Trying to get financial aid.
   _____ (C) Applying to another university.

Talk B

7. _____ (A) They have such impressive appetites.
   _____ (B) They sometimes walk on two legs.
   _____ (C) They frequently attack people.

8. _____ (A) They will eat anything except plants.
   _____ (B) They eat only honey.
   _____ (C) They aren't limited to a few types of food.

9. _____ (A) Five feet.
   _____ (B) Ten feet.
   _____ (C) Fifteen feet.

10. _____ (A) In Alaska.
    _____ (B) In Yellowstone National Park.
    _____ (C) All over the United States.

11. _____ (A) The kodiak bear.
    _____ (B) The grizzly bear.
    _____ (C) The black bear.

12. _____ (A) They are sometimes not as friendly as they seem.
    _____ (B) They are much more dangerous than grizzly bears.
    _____ (C) They look dangerous but are usually friendly.

Talk C

13. _____ (A) In the 1950's.
    _____ (B) In the 1970's.
    _____ (C) In the 1990's.

14. _____ (A) They fly off into deep space.
    _____ (B) They remain in orbit forever.
    _____ (C) They burn up in the atmosphere.

15. _____ (A) Three to four hundred.
    _____ (B) Eight thousand.
    _____ (C) Half a million.

16. _____ (A) They are too small.
    _____ (B) They are too far away.
    _____ (C) They are moving too fast.

17. _____ (A) A large booster rocket.
    _____ (B) A piece of metal the size of an aspirin.
    _____ (C) A tiny fleck of paint.

18. _____ (A) Their high speed.
    _____ (B) Their jagged shape.
    _____ (C) Their tremendous size.

19. _____ (A) An aspirin.
    _____ (B) A piece of debris.
    _____ (C) A model of the debris collector.

20. _____ (A) They detect the debris.
    _____ (B) They store the debris.
    _____ (C) They collect the debris.

21. _____ (A) It has already been tested on Earth.
    _____ (B) It has not been built yet.
    _____ (C) It has already been used on a spacecraft.

Exercise 16.2

Focus: Answering detail questions about complete Part C talks.

Directions: You will hear a number of Part C Mini-Talks. After each talk, there will be a number of questions based on that part of the talk. Mark the best answer choice—(A), (B), or (C)—for each question. The first one is done as an example.

Now start the tape.   🔲

1. _____ (A) Two years.
   ___✔___ (B) Three years.
   _____ (C) Five years.

2. _____ (A) Student fees.
   _____ (B) Room-and-board charges at the dormitory.
   _____ (C) Student insurance rates.

3. _____ (A) Its tuition rates are going up faster than the ones at Hambleton University.
   _____ (B) It has the highest tuition rates in the state.
   _____ (C) Its tuition rates are still lower than those at Hambleton University.

4. _____ (A) An executive on the Student Council.
   _____ (B) A member of the Board of Regents.
   _____ (C) A spokesperson for the administration.

5. _____ (A) A new dormitory will not be built.
   _____ (B) The proposal to increase student services will not be adopted.
   _____ (C) The tuition will not be raised.

6. _____ (A) A starfish.
   _____ (B) A salamander.
   _____ (C) A mammal.

7. _____ (A) A snake sheds its skin and grows a new one.
   _____ (B) An insect grows a new limb.
   _____ (C) A baby gets its first set of teeth.

8. _____ (A) Embryonic cells.
   _____ (B) Specialized cells.
   _____ (C) Nerve cells.

9. _____ (A) To treat diseases among animals.
   _____ (B) To learn to speed up the process among lower animals.
   _____ (C) To apply what they learn to human medicine.

10. _____ (A) Before the Revolutionary War.
    _____ (B) During the Revolutionary War.
    _____ (C) After American independence.

11. _____ (A) A history book.
    _____ (B) A dictionary.
    _____ (C) A spelling book.

12. _____ (A) His military service.
    _____ (B) His political philosophy.
    _____ (C) His dictionary.

13. _____ (A) T-H-E-A-T-R-E instead of T-H-E-A-T-E-R.
    _____ (B) L-A-B-O-U-R instead of L-A-B-O-R.
    _____ (C) N-I-F instead of K-N-I-F-E.

ANSWER SHEET
MINI-TEST 3: MINI-TALKS

1. (A) (B) (C) (D)   5. (A) (B) (C) (D)   9. (A) (B) (C) (D)
2. (A) (B) (C) (D)   6. (A) (B) (C) (D)   10. (A) (B) (C) (D)
3. (A) (B) (C) (D)   7. (A) (B) (C) (D)   11. (A) (B) (C) (D)
4. (A) (B) (C) (D)   8. (A) (B) (C) (D)   12. (A) (B) (C) (D)

MINI-TEST 3: MINI-TALKS

Directions: Listen to the talks and the questions about them. Decide which one of the four answer choices—(A), (B), (C), or (D)—is the best answer to the question. Then mark the appropriate answer either in the blanks next to the answer choices or on the answer sheet above.

Now start the tape.

1. _____ (A) An improved toothbrush.
   _____ (B) Recent developments in genetics.
   _____ (C) New uses for bacteria.
   _____ (D) A means of fighting tooth decay.

2. _____ (A) They have many side effects.
   _____ (B) They occur naturally in people's mouths.
   _____ (C) They attack one type of bacteria.
   _____ (D) They cause tooth decay.

3. _____ (A) Microbiology.
   _____ (B) Genetic engineering.
   _____ (C) Dentistry.
   _____ (D) Civil engineering.

4. _____ (A) Plan A includes dinner, but Plan B does not.
   _____ (B) Plan B is more expensive than Plan A.
   _____ (C) Plan B includes Sunday dinner, but Plan A does not.
   _____ (D) Plan A provides for three meals on most days while Plan B provides for only two.

5. _____ (A) The Bengal Grill.
   _____ (B) Restaurants near campus.
   _____ (C) The Tigers Lair
   _____ (D) The dormitory cafeterias.

6. _____ (A) A receipt.
   _____ (B) A check.
   _____ (C) A student ID card.
   _____ (D) A friend.

7. _____ (A) Selling one's meal tickets to anyone else.
   _____ (B) Eating at a dormitory where one does not live.
   _____ (C) Eating at a cafeteria if one lives off campus.
   _____ (D) Going back for more than one serving of food.

8. _____ (A) They are open longer hours.
   _____ (B) They serve many more students.
   _____ (C) They offer a wider variety of foods.
   _____ (D) They charge lower prices.

9. _____ (A) Visitors to the Bronx Zoo.
   _____ (B) Zoology students.
   _____ (C) Visitors to the City Zoological Gardens.
   _____ (D) New employees at the zoo.

10. _____ (A) They were usually sleeping when visitors were present.
    _____ (B) They were uncomfortable because they were exposed to direct sunlight.
    _____ (C) They couldn't be observed because they were always in darkness.
    _____ (D) They couldn't sleep well and therefore became ill.

11. _____ (A) To make them visible to observers.
    _____ (B) To put them to sleep.
    _____ (C) To simulate natural daylight.
    _____ (D) To allow them to see clearly.

12. _____ (A) Study marsupial mammals.
    _____ (B) Leave the zoo.
    _____ (C) Look at the nocturnal animals.
    _____ (D) Go to the World Down Under exhibit.

Mini-Lessons for Section 1
Idiomatic Expressions

A knowledge of idioms is important for the Listening Comprehension section, especially Part A. These Mini-Lessons contain lists of some 300 expressions and their definitions as well as exercises to familiarize you with most of these expressions. Many of the expressions listed here have appeared on the Listening Comprehension sections of TOEFL exams in the past, some of them several times.

Notes:

1. If a phrase contains a word in parentheses, that word is used only if the verb is followed by an noun or pronoun.

   Example:
   catch up (with)

   You go ahead. I'll catch up later. (no noun or pronoun)
   I'll catch up with you later. (pronoun)

2. The words *one* and *someone* are used to indicate that any pronoun (or sometimes a noun) can be used in this expression.

   Example:
   on one's own

   How long have you been on *your* own?
   Tom's been on *his* own for several years.

Mini-Lesson 1.1

about to   almost ready to
above all   most importantly
add up   make sense; be logical
all at once   suddenly; without warning
all of a sudden   all at once; suddenly
as a matter of fact   in reality; actually
as a rule   generally; customarily
at ease   not nervous; calm
at the drop of a hat   quickly; without any preparation time

back out (of)   withdraw an offer
bank on   depend on; count on
be my guest   do what you want; feel free; help yourself
be rusty   need practice or review
beats me   I don't know; I have no idea (often used in response to a question)
better off   in an improved condition.
bite off more than one can chew   take on more responsibility than one can handle
bound to   certain to; sure to
break down   stop functioning (a machine, for example)
break in (on)   interrupt
break the ice   break through social barriers (as at a party)
break the news (to)   inform; give bad news
break up   end (a meeting, for example)
break up (with)   stop being a couple (a boyfriend and girlfriend, for example)
a breeze   something very simple and easy to do

bring about   cause to happen
bring up   (1) raise (a child)
             (2) introduce (a topic, for example)
brush up on   review; study; practice
bump into   meet unexpectedly; run into
by and large   mostly; generally; on the whole
by heart   by memory; learned word for word
by no means   in no way; not at all

Exercise: Fill in the blanks in the sentences or dialogs with idioms from the list above. There will be one word per blank. It may be necessary to change the verb forms in order for the sentence to be grammatically correct. The first one is done as an example.

1. "Can you talk now?"
   "No, I'm __about__ ___to___ go to the grocery store, but I'll call you as soon as I get back."

2. "You're probably too tired to play another game of racquetball, right?"
   "I'm not that tired, really. _____ _____ _____ _____ _____, I'd enjoy another game."

3. "Will you support my proposal at the meeting?"
   "Certainly. You can _____ _____ my support."

4. I was talking to my aunt when suddenly my cousin George Ann _____ _____ _____ our conversation.

5. "I understand Diane lost her job."
   "Yes, but she's actually _____ _____. She found a more interesting job with a higher salary."

6. _____ _____ _____, Carlos is very punctual, but he sure was late tonight.

7. My car _____ _____ last week, and I had to take the bus to work until it was repaired.

8. I was taking a quiet walk last night when, _____ _____ _____ _____, there was a loud explosion.

9. Kent is _____ _____ fail that class if he doesn't start studying.

10. They _____ _____ their children to be honest.

11. There were a few things I didn't like about Professor Wong's class, but _____ _____ _____ I enjoyed it.

12. "I think Matthew was cheating on that quiz."
    "That doesn't _____ _____. Why should the best student in the class cheat?"

13. "Can I have another sandwich?"
    "Sure, _____ _____ _____. I made plenty."

14. Actors and actresses must know their lines _____ _____.

15. If you don't want to talk about this problem, why did you _____ it _____?

16. Many accidents are _____ _____ by carelessness.

17. Their team won the game, but they _____ _____ _____ dominated it. It was a very close game.

18. "What a boring party. No one is talking to one another."
    "Maybe we should put on some music and start dancing. That might _____ _____ _____."

19. "Have you studied Spanish before?"
    "Yes, but it's been years since I took a Spanish class, so I'll need to _____ _____ _____ it before I go to Venezuela."

20. "You're taking five classes this term?"
    "Yes, and I'm having trouble getting caught up. I'm afraid I _____ _____ _____ _____ I _____ _____ this time."

21. "You're all packed and ready to go, I see."
    "I could leave _____ _____ _____ _____ _____ _____."

22. "Do you know what the name of this street is?"
    "_____ _____. This is the first time I've ever been in this town."

23. "How's that biology class you're taking?"
    "So far, it's been _____ _____. We've just been going over things I studied last semester."

24. "What time did the party _____ _____ last night?"
    "I don't know. It was still going on when I went home."

25. "I was awfully nervous when I gave that speech."
    "Really? You hid it well. I thought you were completely _____ _____."

Mini-Lesson 1.2

call it a day   stop working for the day; go home
call off   cancel
call on   visit
calm down   relax
care for   (1) take care of
           (2) like; feel affection for
catch on   become popular
catch on (to)   understand; learn
catch up (with)   go as fast as; catch
check in (or **into**)   register (at a hotel)
check out (of)   (1) leave (a hotel)
           (2) take material (from a library, for example)
cheer up   become cheerful; be happy
chip in (on/for)   contribute
clear up   (1) clarify; make understandable
           (2) become nice and sunny (used to talk about the weather)
come across   find; meet; encounter
come around (to)   begin to change one's opinion; begin to agree with
come down with   become sick with (an illness)
come up with   think of (an idea)
cost an arm and a leg   be very expensive
count on   depend on; rely on; bank on
count out   eliminate; no longer consider as a factor
cut off   stop; discontinue (a service, for example)
cut out for   have an aptitude for; be qualified for

Exercise: Fill in the blanks in the sentences or dialogs with idioms from the list above. There will be one word per blank. It may be necessary to change the verb forms in order for the sentence to be grammatically correct.

1. The reception in the garden was _____ _____ because of a thunderstorm.

2. Don't get so excited. Just _____ _____ and tell us what happened.

3. I was looking up some information in the almanac when I _____ _____ an interesting fact.

4. I can _____ _____ my car. It's very dependable and never breaks down.

5. How did you _____ _____ _____ such a strange idea?

6. I arrived in town last night at seven-thirty and _____ _____ my hotel at around eight. This morning I plan to _____ _____ at about nine.

7. "Did you rent this videotape?"
   "No, I _____ it _____ _____ the library."

8. You look tired. Why don't we _____ _____ _____ _____ and finish up tomorrow?

9. It won't be too expensive to buy Professor McMillen a present if we all _____ _____.

10. If Arthur doesn't pay his electric bill soon, the utilities company might _____ _____ his electricity.

11. "I don't understand this theorem at all."
    "Talk to Professor Adler. I'll bet she can _____ _____ your confusion."

12. Who _____ _____ your cat while you were out of town?

13. A good stereo system doesn't have to _____ _____ _____ _____ _____ _____. You can find one for a reasonable price.

14. Cauliflower isn't my favorite vegetable. In fact, I don't _____ _____ it at all.

15. "I'm depressed. I didn't do very well on the first quiz."
    "_____ _____! That quiz only counted for 10% of the total grade, and I'm sure you'll do better on the other tests."

16. "How did Eric do in the cross-country ski race?"
    "He got off to a bad start, so he never _____ _____ _____ the leading skiers."

17. "Why did Brenda drop out of business school?"
    "She decided she wasn't _____ _____ _____ a career in business. She's going to study art instead."

18. This song wasn't very popular when it was first recorded, but now it's starting to _____ _____.

19. "Your roommate is still planning to vote for Smithson for president of the Student Council?"
    "Yes, but I'm going to keep talking to him. I think eventually he'll _____ _____ _____ our point of view and vote for Brannigan."

20. That saleswoman _____ _____ her clients at least once a month because she thinks personal contact is important.

21. "Is it still raining?"
    "No, the rain has stopped and it's starting to _____ _____."

Mini-Lesson 1.3

day in and day out   constantly; for a long time
die down   become less severe; quiet down
do over   do again; repeat
do without   not have
down the drain   wasted; done for no reason (work, for example)
dream up   invent; think of; come up with
drop (someone) a line   send someone a letter
drop in (on)   visit informally
drop off   (1) leave something (a package, for example)
               (2) take (someone) home; let someone out of a car
drop out (of)   stop attending (classes, for example)

easy as pie   very simple; a piece of cake
eyes bigger than one's stomach   said of someone who takes more food than he or she can eat

fall behind   not move as quickly as; lag behind
fall through   fail to happen

a far cry from   not similar to; not as good as
fed up (with)   not able to tolerate; disgusted with; annoyed by
feel free   do something if one wants
feel like   be inclined to; want to
feel like a million dollars   feel very good
feel up to   feel able to do something; ready to
few and far between   uncommon and infrequent
figure out   understand; solve

Exercise: Fill in the blanks in the sentences or dialogs with idioms from the list above. There will be one word per blank. It may be necessary to change the verb forms in order for the sentence to be grammatically correct.

1. It took me hours to _____ _____ how to record programs on my VCR.

2. If you could _____ _____ the laundry on the way to work, I'll pick it up on Monday.

3. "What a wonderful masquerade party!"
   "People certainly _____ _____ some interesting costumes, didn't they?"

4. "Do you _____ _____ going out tonight?"
   "No, I'd rather stay home and read."

5. "Why have you _____ _____ in your French class?"
   "I was sick and I missed a few classes. But I'm studying hard to catch up."

6. "Why do we need to get gas now? We have quite a bit left."
   "This highway goes through some very empty country, and gas stations are _____ _____ _____ _____."

7. Howard's teacher wasn't satisfied with the work he had done, so she asked him to _____ it _____.

8. I'm _____ _____ _____ my roommate's lack of responsibility. He never pays his bills or his share of the rent on time.

9. "Isn't your class picnic today?"
   "No, our plans for the picnic _____ _____."

10. "The food at that new restaurant isn't bad."
    "It's all right, but it's _____ _____ _____ _____ the food at Mario's. Now *that* is a great restaurant!"

11. Ben had to _____ _____ _____ the university because of financial problems.

12. After blowing furiously all day, the wind finally _____ _____.

13. "Do you telephone friends before you visit, or just _____ _____ _____ them?"
    "It depends. If they're close friends, I just visit them. If they're acquaintances, I generally call first."

14. "I'm tired of the same old routine."
    "I know how you feel. I get tired of doing the same things _____ _____ _____ _____ _____ too."

15. "Ralph really loaded up his tray with food."
    "He'll never eat it all. Ralph's _____ are _____ _____ his _____."

16. "I need to use a computer for a few hours."
    "_____ _____ to use my laptop computer. I don't need it this morning."

17. "I've missed James since he moved to Seattle."
    "You should _____ him _____ _____ and let him know how you're doing. I'm sure he'd love to get a letter from you."

Mini-Lesson 1.4

fill in   write in a blank (on an application form, for example)
fill in (for)   substitute for
fill one in   provide missing information
fill out   complete (an application form, for example)
find out   learn; discover
a fish out of water   someone not in his or her normal surroundings
fix up   repair; renovate
follow in one's footsteps   do what someone else did (especially a parent)
for good   permanently; forever
for the time being   temporarily; for now
from out of the blue   unexpectedly; without warning

get a kick out of (doing something)   enjoy; have fun (doing something)
get along with   have good relations with
get carried away   go too far; do too much; buy too much
get in one's blood   become a habit; become customary
get in over one's head   take on too much responsibility; bite off more than one can chew
get in the way   block; obstruct
get in touch with   contact
get off   leave (a vehicle)
get off the ground   start to be successful
get on   board (a vehicle)
get over   recover from (a disease)
get rid of   discard; no longer have
get under way   begin; start
give (someone) a cold shoulder   act unfriendly toward someone; ignore
give away   distribute (for free)

Exercise: Fill in the blanks in the sentences or dialogs with idioms from the list above. There will be one word per blank. It may be necessary to change the verb forms in order for the sentence to be grammatically correct.

1. "How did you _____ _____ where Warren lives?"
   "I just looked it up in my address book."

2. "I'm interested in the job that was advertised in the newspaper."
   "Fine. Just _____ _____ this application form."

3. Don't forget to _____ _____ the date on your check.

4. "Is Agnes still mad at you?"
   "I suppose so. I saw her at a party last weekend, and she just _____ me _____ _____ _____."

5. "Are you moving to Baltimore _____ _____?"
   "No, just _____ _____ _____ _____. I'll be back here in a month or two."

6. "That old paint that you have stored in your garage is a fire hazard."
   "You're right. I should _____ _____ _____ it."

7. Some companies _____ _____ free samples of new products in order to familiarize consumers with them.

8. "How's that advanced computer class you're taking, Polly?"
   "Not so good. I can't understand a word that the teacher or any of the other students are saying. I really feel like _____ _____ _____ _____ _____."

9. "Don't you just hate all this graffiti?"
   "It *is* ugly, isn't it? I've never understood why people _____ _____ _____ _____ _____ writing on walls. It doesn't seem like much fun to me."

10. When the train stopped, a mysterious looking woman in a black raincoat _____ _____ the train and found her seat.

11. "Maxwell's project will be very successful, I think."
"Oh, I don't know. I'm not sure it will ever _____ _____ _____ _____."

12. Do you _____ _____ _____ your new roommate, or do you two argue?

13. "That run-down old house that David bought looks terrific."
"Yes, he's _____ it _____ beautifully, hasn't he?"

14. "Has Edward _____ _____ _____ _____ you lately?"
"No, he hasn't. I don't think he has my new telephone number."

15. "Will the concert start soon?"
"It should _____ _____ _____ any minute now."

16. Living by the ocean really _____ _____ your _____. Once you've lived here, you never want to leave.

17. This is the last stop. Everyone has to _____ _____ the bus here.

18. Professor Dunbar came down with the flu, so her teaching assistant _____ _____ _____ her for a few days.

Mini-Lesson 1.5

get the hang of something   learn how to do something
give a hand   applaud; clap
give a hand (with)   assist
go easy on   not punish severely
go on (with)   continue
go overboard   do too much; buy too much
go with   (1) accompany
           (2) look good together; complement (for example, two articles of clothing)
go without saying   be clear; be obvious
grow up   mature; become an adult

hand in   give back to; return
hand out   distribute
hang on   wait
hard to come by   difficult to find
have a heart   be compassionate; show mercy
have a hunch   have an intuitive feeling
have a word with (someone)   talk to someone briefly
have on   wear
have one's hands full   be very busy; have a challenging job
have the time of one's life   have fun; have a great time
hear firsthand (from)   get information directly from someone
hear from   be contacted by; be in touch with
hear of   know about; be familiar with
hit it off   become friendly (especially at a first meeting)
hit the road   leave; go away
hold on   wait
hold on (to)   grasp
hold still   not move
hold up   delay

Exercise: Fill in the blanks in the sentences or dialogs with idioms from the list above. There will be one word per blank. It may be necessary to change the verb forms in order for the sentence to be grammatically correct.

1. Everett was born in the South, but he _____ _____ in Michigan.

2. At the beginning of the class, the instructor _____ _____ the quizzes and told the students they had ten minutes in which to finish.

3. After ten minutes, the students _____ _____ their quizzes to the instructor.

4. "Have you ever _____ _____ William Carlos Williams?"
   "I believe so. He was a poet, wasn't he?"

5. "Hello, is Gina there?"
   "Yes, _____ _____ a minute and I'll get her."

6. "You're graduating next month, right?"
   "Yes, but I'm going to _____ _____ _____ my studies in graduate school."

7. _____ _____ while I take your photograph. I don't want the picture to be blurry.

8. "I got stopped by the police for speeding. I have to pay a big fine."
   "Well, you could talk to the judge and ask him to reduce it. Since you've never been stopped for speeding before, maybe he'll _____ _____ _____ you."

9. "Do you like this blouse?"
   "Yes, but I think the grey silk one would _____ better _____ your jacket."

10. "So, Dave is teaching you how to wind surf?"
    "Yes, and he's such a good teacher that I'm already _____ _____ _____ _____ it."

11. The audience _____ the cast a big _____ after their wonderful performance.

12. "Do you think Iris will pass the history test?"
    "That _____ _____ _____. In fact, she'll probably have the best grade in the class."

13. "What _____ _____ your flight?"
    "There was a big snowstorm in Denver that delayed a lot of flights."

14. "Have you _____ _____ Maureen since she went to Hawaii?"
    "Yeah, I got a postcard from her yesterday. She said she's _____ _____ _____ _____ her _____ and never wants to come home."

15. Can you _____ me _____ _____ _____ this luggage? It's too heavy for me to carry myself.

16. The wind is starting to blow. You'd better _____ _____ _____ your hat.

17. "Oh, you bought that new book by Richard Stone."
    "Yes, but that book is _____ _____ _____ _____. I looked for it in three or four bookstores before I finally found it."

18. It's getting late. I'd better _____ _____ _____ if I want to get home by midnight.

19. "Can I _____ _____ _____ _____ you now, Professor Rivera?"
    "I've got to go to class right now. Drop by my office later, and we'll talk then."

20. "You sure bought a lot of groceries."
    "Yeah, I guess I _____ _____. I should never go grocery shopping when I'm hungry."

Mini-Lesson 1.6

in a nutshell   in summary; in brief
in favor of   in agreement with; supporting
in hot water   in trouble
in no time   very soon; very quickly
in person   face to face (not by telephone, letter, etc.)
in store   in the future; coming up
in the dark   not knowing; confused
in the long run   over a long period of time
in the same boat   in the same situation; having the same problem
iron out   solve (a problem)

join the club   have the same problem as other people
jump to conclusions   form opinions without sufficient evidence

keep an eye on   watch; take care of; look after
keep an eye out (for)   look for
keep on (with)   continue
keep track of   know where something or someone is
keep up (with)   maintain the same speed as
kill time   spend time doing unimportant things (before an appointment, for example)
know like the back of one's hand   be very familiar with

lay off   put out of work
learn the ropes   become familiar with; get used to; get the hang of
leave out   not include; omit
leave someone/something alone   not disturb
let someone down   disappoint
let up   decline in intensity (rain, for example)
look after   take care of; mind
look for   try to locate
look forward to   anticipate (with pleasure)
look into   investigate

Exercise: Fill in the blanks in the sentences or dialogs with idioms from the list above. There will be one word per blank. It may be necessary to change the verb forms in order for the sentence to be grammatically correct.

1. Will you _____ _____ _____ _____ my dog while I go in the drugstore?

2. Kathy's daughter has such short legs that she has a hard time _____ _____ _____ the other children.

3. The store had to _____ _____ a number of clerks because sales were down.

4. "You must be anxious to go on your vacation."
   "I certainly am. I'm really _____ _____ _____ this trip."

5. Don't _____ _____ _____ . Maybe your jewelry wasn't stolen after all.

6. "I need to find a new apartment."
   "There might be some vacancies in the building where I live. I'll _____ _____ _____ _____ _____ one."

7. The company may lose some money now, but _____ _____ _____ _____ , this is a good investment.

8. Alex complained that no one invited him to any social events and that he felt _____ _____ .

9. "Can you hurry over here? I need to see you right away."
   "Sure. I'll be there _____ _____ _____ ."

10. "May I help you, sir?"
    "No, I'm just looking around and trying to _____ some _____ until my wife finishes shopping."

11. "Has it stopped raining yet?"
    "No, but it's beginning to _____ _____ a little."

12. "I can't go to Daryl's party this weekend. I have to study."
    "Guess we're _____ _____ _____ _____. I've got to study too."

13. "Should we stop and spend the night at this motel?"
    "No, let's _____ _____ driving for a few more miles."

14. If you find a baby animal in the woods, don't touch it. Just _____ it _____.

15. I _____ all over town _____ a good used car, but I couldn't find one.

16. Stella's sister _____ _____ her baby while Stella is at work.

17. "If you don't know how to use this software, why don't you ask Joanne to help?"
    "I *did* ask her, but I'm still _____ _____ _____. I didn't understand a word she said."

18. The police are _____ _____ the crime.

19. "Did Amanda ever complete her project?"
    "She's almost finished. She just has a few minor problems left to _____ _____."

20. Alfred is _____ _____ _____ with his boss because he didn't finish an important project by the deadline.

21. "Has Marilyn gotten used to her new job at the bank yet?"
    "It took her awhile, but I think she's finally _____ _____ _____ there."

22. Are you _____ _____ _____ this proposal or against it?

23. "Are you familiar with this neighborhood?"
    "I grew up here, so I _____ it _____ _____ _____ _____ my _____."

24. "Is your roommate at home now?"
    "I have no idea. I can never _____ _____ _____ his comings and goings."

25. "I understand that you have a new dean over at the Business School."
    "Yes, his name is Dean Nishimura. He has a completely different philosophy of business education from the one Dean Woodford had, so I'm sure that some big changes are _____ _____ for us."

Mini-Lesson 1.7

look like   resemble
look out (for)   be careful
look over   examine; read
look up   (1) find information (especially in a reference book)
          (2) try to locate someone
look up to   respect; admire

make a fool of oneself   act embarrassingly
make a point of   make a special effort
make ends meet   balance a budget
make sense (of)   be logical and clear; understand
make up   invent; create
make up one's mind   decide
make way for   allow space for; provide a path for
mean to   intend to

mixed up   confused
music to one's ears   something that sounds pleasant

a nervous wreck   someone who is very nervous
next to nothing   very little (money, for example); cheap
no doubt about it   certainly; definitely
no harm done   there was no damage done
not at all   not in any way; not to any degree
not believe one's ears (or **eyes**)   be unable to believe what one hears (or sees)
not think much of   not like; not have a good opinion of

odds and ends   small, miscellaneous items
an old hand (**at**)   an experienced person
on edge   nervous
on end   consecutively, without a break (*days on end*, for example)
on hand   easily available
on needles and pins   nervous; anxious
on one's own   independent
on second thought   after reconsidering
on the go   always busy; always moving
on the tip of one's tongue   almost able to remember
on the whole   in general
out of (something)   not having something
out of one's mind   insane; illogical; irrational
out of order   broken; not functioning properly
out of the question   definitely not; impossible
over and over   again and again; repeatedly
over one's head   not understandable (a joke, for example); obscure

Exercise: Fill in the blanks in the sentences or dialogs with idioms from the list above. There will be one word per blank. It may be necessary to change the verb forms in order for the sentence to be grammatically correct.

1. "Have you _____ _____ this contract yet?"
   "Not yet. I'll try to read it this weekend."

2. "I think I'll have the prime rib, waiter."
   "All right, sir."
   "Wait, no— _____ _____ _____, I think I'll have the chicken."

3. Is this story true, or did you just _____ it _____?

4. You can't get a soda from that machine. There's a sign on it that says " _____ _____
   _____."

5. Sherry _____ _____ _____ her father because of all the help and good advice he's
   given her.

6. I don't have much cash _____ _____, but I can get some from an automatic teller
   machine.

7. What a confusing movie! I couldn't _____ _____ _____ it.

8. "You did a fine job on this research paper, especially on the bibliography."
   "Thanks. I _____ _____ _____ getting the bibliography exactly right. I did
   it _____ _____ _____ until it was perfect."

9. "What's Fritz's cousin's name?"
   "It's _____ _____ _____ _____ my _____, but I can't quite remember."

10. "Hello. I'd like to reserve a room for this weekend."
    "I'm afraid that's _____ _____ _____ _____. The hotel is fully booked this
    weekend."

11. "Do you have any fresh peaches?"
    "Sorry, I'm _____ _____ them. I just sold the last crate of peaches."

12. "Listen to the roar of the engines."
    "Yeah, it's _____ _____ my _____. I just love going to these car races."

13. The plane was delayed for hours _____ _____. I thought we'd never get off the ground.

14. "Have you finished moving into your new apartment?"
    "Almost. There are still a few _____ _____ _____ in my old apartment that I need to move today."

15. "Brad sure is busy, isn't he?"
    "Yeah, he's involved in so many activities that he's always _____ _____ _____."

16. There are so many interesting dishes on the menu that it's hard for me to _____ _____ my _____ which one to order.

17. If you go into the swamp, _____ _____ _____ alligators.

18. "When will you be informed of the test results?"
    "Not until Monday, so I'll be _____ _____ _____ _____ all weekend."

19. "Do you know what the capital of South Dakota is?"
    "I'm not sure. Let's _____ it _____ in this atlas."

20. They're going to tear down those old warehouses to _____ _____ _____ a big new hotel.

21. "I like that painting you bought. Did it cost much?"
    "No, the artist sold it to me for _____ _____ _____."

22. "How was your final exam, Laurie?"
    "A couple of questions were tricky, but _____ _____ _____ it was pretty easy."

23. "I'm sorry I knocked that vase over. I didn't mean to."
    "_____ _____ _____. It wasn't damaged."

24. I must have been _____ _____ my _____ when I signed the lease on this apartment. I can't afford this much rent.

25. He didn't _____ _____ break the plate; it was an accident.

26. "I didn't know you could play horseshoes so well."
    "Oh, I'm _____ _____ _____ _____ horseshoes. I've been playing since I was a kid."

27. You must be _____ _____. This isn't River Street; it's Laurel Avenue.

28. "How long have you been living alone?"
    "I've been _____ my _____ since I graduated from high school."

29. "Did you find that lecture boring?"
    "_____ _____ _____. In fact, I thought it was fascinating."

30. "Christine is so funny, she should be a stand-up comic."
    "I suppose, but a lot of her jokes go right _____ my _____. I just don't get them."

Mini-Lesson 1.8

part with   no longer have; get rid of; not be in the company of
pass up   not accept; not choose
pass with flying colors   do very well (on a test)
pat oneself on the back   congratulate oneself
pay attention (to)   concentrate on; focus on
pick out   choose; select

pick up   (1) take something from a surface (for example, a floor)
(2) go to a location and get someone or something
(3) learn (especially without formal training)
pick up the tab (for)   pay for
the picture of   a perfect example of something
play it by ear   do something without a definite plan
play it safe   choose a cautious plan
point out   indicate
a pretty penny   a lot of money
pull one's leg   joke with someone; make up a story
push one's luck   to continue doing something too long; to keep taking chances
put aside   save for later; set aside
put away   return something to its proper place
put off   delay; postpone
put on   begin to wear
put together   assemble
put up with   tolerate

Exercise: Fill in the blanks in the sentences or dialogs with idioms from the list above. There will be one word per blank. It may be necessary to change the verb forms in order for the sentence to be grammatically correct.

1. Vanessa is allergic to tobacco smoke, so she can't _____ _____ _____ smoking.

2. "That conference you attended in San Diego must have been very expensive."
"Yes, but fortunately, the company I work for _____ _____ _____ _____ _____ it."

3. I asked my teacher to _____ _____ the mistakes that I made in my essay so that I could correct them.

4. "What do you want to do tomorrow?"
"I don't know. Let's just _____ _____ _____ _____."

5. "You should get rid of that old leather jacket."
"I know, but I hate to _____ _____ it. I've had it for years."

6. "How did you learn how to make such beautiful pottery? Did you take a class in ceramics?"
"No, I just _____ it _____ on my own."

7. "Can you read that sign?"
"Just a minute. Let me _____ my glasses _____."

8. It took Linda weeks to _____ _____ that thousand-piece jigsaw puzzle.

9. This bike cost _____ _____ _____, but I think it was worth it.

10. "I passed the first two quizzes in this class, and I scarcely studied for them at all."
"Well, if I were you, I wouldn't _____ my _____ any further. You should study for the next quiz because it's going to be a lot harder."

11. I'll _____ _____ the laundry that you dropped off at the cleaners on Friday.

12. The child _____ _____ her toys from the floor and then _____ them _____ in her toy box.

13. Bert and Mary had to _____ _____ their dinner party until next weekend because Bert wasn't feeling well.

14. "Who _____ _____ that tie for you?"
"No one. I chose it myself."

15. "Are you going to take that job?"
"No, I decided to _____ it _____ because I don't want to relocate."

16. _____ _____ as I read the directions or you won't understand what to do.

17. "I finally finished collecting all the materials I need to write my report."
    "Great, but don't be too quick to _____ yourself _____ _____ _____. You still have to write the report and then word-process it."

18. "How did you do on your final exams?"
    "Great! I _____ them all _____ _____ _____."

19. I'm going to _____ this magazine _____ for now and read it later.

20. I wouldn't believe a word Lynn told you. She's just _____ your _____.

Mini-Lesson 1.9

right away   immediately
ring a bell (with)   sound familiar to
rough it   experience somewhat difficult or primitive conditions
rule out   say something is impossible; eliminate
run a temperature   have a fever
run for office   try to get elected
run into   (1) meet unexpectedly; bump into
          (2) collide with
run late   be late; be in a hurry
run of the mill   ordinary
run out of   exhaust the supply of

save one's breath   don't bother asking someone
search me   I don't know; I have no idea; beats me
see eye to eye (with someone) (on something)   have the same opinion; be in agreement
see (someone) off   accompany (to an airport or train station, for example)
see to   take care of; check on; fix
serve one right   receive the proper punishment; get the penalty one deserves
short for   a nickname for
show around   orient; give a tour
show off   try to attract attention by unusual behavior
show up   arrive
shut down   close
sign up (for)   enroll (for a class, for example)
sing another tune   change one's opinion; feel differently
size up   measure; estimate
sleep on it   postpone a decision until the next day
slowly but surely   gradually; steadily but not quickly
snowed under   very busy
so far, so good   up until now, there are no problems
sooner or later   at some indefinite future time
speak one's mind   say what one is thinking
speak up   speak more loudly
speak up for   support verbally
spell out (for)   make something very clear; explain in detail

Exercise: Fill in the blanks in the sentences or dialogs with idioms from the list above. There will be one word per blank. It may be necessary to change the verb forms in order for the sentence to be grammatically correct.

1. "Has John gone back to Minneapolis yet?"
   "Yes, I just _____ him _____ at the airport."

2. "This pipe is leaking again."
   "We'd better have a plumber _____ _____ it."

3. I was late because I _____ _____ _____ gasoline.

4. Write down your ideas _____ _____. If you wait to write them down, you may forget them.

5. When the factory _____ _____, hundreds of workers were laid off.

6. "Did you _____ _____ _____ Professor Carmichael's class?"
   "No, I decided to take Professor Knudson's class instead."

7. "Vicki, how's that project you're working on coming along?"
   "_____ _____, _____ _____, but the tricky part will be next week."

8. "Have you ever heard of an actor named Anthony Reed?"
   "Hmmm. I don't think so. The name doesn't _____ _____ _____ _____ me at all."

9. "Frank doesn't take a hint very well, does he?"
   "No, you have to _____ things _____ _____ Frank. He likes everything crystal clear."

10. I'd heard that the clothes in this store were very nice, but I found them _____ _____ _____ _____.

11. "Bennet thought those stories Tina told about you were pretty funny."
    "They weren't funny; they were embarrassing. Bennet would be _____ _____ _____ if Tina had told that kind of story about him."

12. Norman doesn't like to _____ _____ when he goes on vacation. He prefers to stay at luxury hotels.

13. I don't like to go to parties too early. I'd rather _____ _____ a little bit late.

14. It's expensive to _____ _____ _____ these days. Political campaigns cost a lot of money.

15. "So, do you plan to buy this motorcycle or not?"
    "I'm still not sure. Can I _____ _____ it and let you know tomorrow morning?"

16. "Have you seen the campus yet?"
    "Yes, my cousin Melissa is a student there, and she _____ me _____."

17. "I'm collecting money for the Red Cross. I think I'll ask Pat to contribute."
    "_____ your _____. Pat never contributes to anything."

18. "Are you going to medical school?"
    "Not this year, but I wouldn't _____ it _____ in the future."

19. I _____ _____ my old friend Leslie downtown yesterday. I hadn't seen her for months.

20. "I understand you're learning how to speak Russian."
    "Yes, and it was really hard for me, especially at first. Now, though, I'm _____ _____ _____ getting the hang of it."

21. "Your sister's name is Jessie?"
    "That's what everyone calls her—it's _____ _____ Jessica."

22. "Have a busy night at the restaurant?"
    "We weren't just busy—we were _____ _____! I've never seen so many customers!"

23. "I feel terrible. I have a terrible cold or maybe even the flu."
    "Are you _____ _____ _____? If you have a fever, then you probably have the flu."

24. My brother and I agree on most issues, but I sure don't _____ _____ _____ _____ _____ him _____ this proposal to build a new stadium.

Mini-Lesson 1.10

spick and span   extremely clean; spotless
stack up against   compare with
stamp out   eliminate; wipe out
stand for   (1) tolerate; put up with
                (2) symbolize; represent
stand out   be noticeable
stay out   not come home
stay out (or up) to all hours   come home (or go to bed) very late
stay up   not go to bed
stick with   not change; stay with
stock up (on)   get a large supply of something
a stone's throw from   not far away from; close to
stop by   visit informally; go to see
straighten up   clean up; make tidy
stuck with   have something one cannot get rid of

take a break   stop working for a short time
take a lot of nerve   require a lot of courage
take a lot out of (someone)   be hard on someone; drain energy from someone
take advantage of   utilize; make use of; exploit
take after   resemble; look like (especially an older relative)
take apart   disassemble
take it easy   relax; calm down

Exercise: Fill in the blanks in the sentences or dialogs with idioms from the list above. There will be one word per blank. It may be necessary to change the verb forms in order for the sentence to be grammatically correct.

1. Vaccines have permitted doctors to virtually _____ _____ a number of diseases, including smallpox and polio.

2. "How late do you usually _____ _____?"
   "I'm normally in bed by eleven on weekdays."

3. "How late do you usually _____ _____ on weekends?"
   "I sometimes don't come home until two or three in the morning."

4. "Do you _____ _____ your mother or father?"
   "I don't think I look much like either one of them."

5. Earl had no trouble _____ _____ the engine on the lawn mower, but then he couldn't put it back together.

6. You look a little tired. Why don't you _____ _____ _____ and finish your homework later?

7. The teacher won't __ _____ _____ cheating. When she caught one student cheating on the mid-term exam, she gave him a zero on that test.

8. "I tried and tried to find a buyer for this old car."
   "Looks like you're _____ _____ it for now."

9. "My brother is going to invest all his savings in a new business venture."
   "That _____ _____ _____ _____ _____. I'd be afraid to take a risk like that."

10. "I give up. I can't solve this chemistry problem."
    "_____ _____ it. Eventually, you'll figure it out."

11. We have to leave the apartment _____ _____ _____. The landlord said that if it wasn't clean when we moved out, we'd lose part of our security deposit.

12. Don was wearing jeans and a T-shirt while all the other guests had on formal dinner wear. He really _____ _____.

13. "I'm nervous about my interview."
"_____ _____ _____. You'll make a better impression if you're relaxed."

14. The fifty stars on the American flag _____ _____ the fifty states.

15. "Do you _____ _____ your apartment before guests _____ _____?"
"A little bit. I don't mind if it's a little messy, but I don't want it to look like a disaster area."

16. "My new roommate is from Italy."
"You should _____ _____ _____ this opportunity to learn some Italian."

17. "I just heard on the news that the Florida orange crop was damaged by the hurricane last week, and that orange juice prices are going to go way up."
"If we had a big freezer, we could _____ _____ _____ frozen orange juice now and we wouldn't have to pay those prices."

18. "Do you live near Cecilia?"
"Oh, sure. My apartment building is just _____ _____ _____ _____ hers."

19. "So you ran in that ten-kilometer race?"
"Yes, but it _____ _____ _____ _____ _____ me. I can hardly move."

20. "Tim, you've eaten at both these restaurants—how does Chez Michelle _____ _____ _____ the Oak Room?"
"Oh, they're both good. I think the Oak Room has slightly better food, but the service is better at Chez Michelle."

Mini-Lesson 1.11

take a short cut   take a more direct or faster route than usual
take off   (1) remove (clothing, for example)
                    (2) ascend (a plane, for example)
                    (3) become popular quickly
take over   assume control or responsibility
take part (in)   participate in
take the plunge   finally take action; do something different
take time off (from)   take a vacation or a break from work or school
take up   begin to study some topic or engage in some activity
talk down to   speak to someone as if he or she were a child; patronize
talk into   persuade; convince
talk out of   dissuade; convince not to do something
talk over   discuss
tear oneself away from something   stop doing something interesting
tear up   rip into small pieces
tell apart   distinguish
things are looking up   the situation is improving
think over   consider
throw away   discard; get rid of
throw cold water on   discourage; force to cancel (a plan, for example)
throw the book at someone   give someone the maximum punishment
try on   test clothing before buying (for size, style, and so on)
try out   test a product before buying
try out (for)   audition for (a role in a play, for example); attempt to join (a team, for example)

Exercise: Fill in the blanks in the sentences or dialogs with idioms from the list above. There will be one word per blank. It may be necessary to change the verb forms in order for the sentence to be grammatically correct.

1. You'd better _____ _____ these gloves before you buy them; they may not fit.

2. At first, I didn't want to go to the party, but I'm glad Annette _____ me _____ it. It was fun.

3. The spy _____ _____ the document so that no one else could read it.

4. The twins look so much alike that almost no one can _____ them _____.

5. "I need more excitement in my life."
   "Why don't you give up stamp collecting and _____ _____ sky-diving instead?"

6. "Who made the final decision?"
   "All of the people who were at the meeting _____ _____ _____ the decision-making process."

7. Most air accidents take place when a plane is _____ _____ or landing.

8. You've got to _____ yourself _____ _____ those computer games and do your homework.

9. Dan was afraid the judge would _____ _____ _____ _____ him because he had been charged with the same offense several times.

10. _____ _____ your boots before you go into the house.

11. I wish I'd _____ _____ this calculator before I bought it. It doesn't seem to be working right.

12. Marvin was going to drop out of school, but his grandfather _____ him _____ _____ it.

13. I'm not sure if this is a suitable topic for a research paper. I need to _____ it _____ with my teacher before I start writing.

14. "I'm going to _____ _____ those old newspapers."
    "Don't just put them in the trash—recycle them instead."

15. "Are you going on the class trip?"
    "I need to _____ it _____ before I decide."

16. "How did you get home so quickly?"
    "I _____ _____ _____ _____ through the fields."

17. "So, Louisa, you decided to _____ _____ _____ a part in the play?"
    "Yes, I've been interested in acting for quite a while, so I finally decided to _____ _____ _____."

18. Akiko is going to _____ some _____ _____ _____ teaching to finish writing her dissertation.

Mini-Lesson 1.12

turn around   face in a different direction
turn down   (1) reject an offer
                        (2) decrease the intensity of
turn in   (1) return; give back; hand in
                    (2) go to bed
turn into   change to; transform into
turn off   stop the operation (of an appliance, for example); shut off

turn on   start the operation (of an appliance, for example)
turn out   (1) result; end up; be the final product
                       (2) produce
                       (3) arrive; gather (for a meeting, for example)
turn up   (1) increase the intensity of
                     (2) arrive

under the weather   slightly ill
use up   use completely

wait on   serve
walk on air   be very happy
warm up   (1) heat
                     (2) practice; prepare for
warm up (to)   become friendly with; start to enjoy
watch out (for)   be alert; look out for
wear out   become no longer useful because of wear
what the doctor ordered   exactly what was needed; the perfect thing
wipe out   eliminate; stamp out
without a hitch   without a problem
work out   (1) exercise
                     (2) bring to a successful conclusion; solve

Exercise: Fill in the blanks in the sentences or dialogs with idioms from the list above. There will be one word per blank. It may be necessary to change the verb forms in order for the sentence to be grammatically correct.

1. The story of Dr. Jekyll and Mr. Hyde is about a scientist who _____ _____ a monster after drinking a chemical potion.

2. _____ _____ the water or the tub will overflow.

3. It's warm in here. Could you _____ _____ the heater a little?

4. I love that song. Could you _____ _____ the radio a little?

5. I can't see a thing. Please _____ _____ the light.

6. This sweater looked nice when it was new, but now it's _____ _____.

7. "I'm hungry!"
   "Why don't you _____ _____ some of the leftovers from lunch? You can use the microwave oven."

8. Not many people _____ _____ for the meeting last night.

9. It's been a rough day. I'm going to _____ _____ early and get a good night's sleep.

10. "How about a nice cup of hot tea?"
    "That's exactly what I'm in the mood for. It's just _____ _____ _____ _____."

11. "How was your presentation?"
    "Great. It went off _____ _____ _____."

12. I'm going to the gym to _____ _____ on the exercise machines.

13. If you're on a crowded bus or subway car, you must _____ _____ _____ pickpockets.

14. "A bear! I don't see a bear! Where is it?"
    "_____ _____ slowly. It's right behind you."

15. Maria had quite a few problems last year, but she _____ them all _____.

16. Don't ask me to _____ _____ you! I'm not your servant.

17. Brian was offered the manager's job, but he _____ it _____. He said he didn't want the responsibility.

18. Before the game starts, the players need to _____ _____.

19. "This cake Holly baked for the wedding _____ _____ very well, don't you think?"
    "Yes, indeed. It was delicious."

20. "Mitchell looked pale and tired."
    "He told me he was feeling a little _____ _____ _____."

21. "You must be happy about getting that scholarship."
    "Are you kidding? I'm still _____ _____ _____."

Guide to Structure and Written Expression

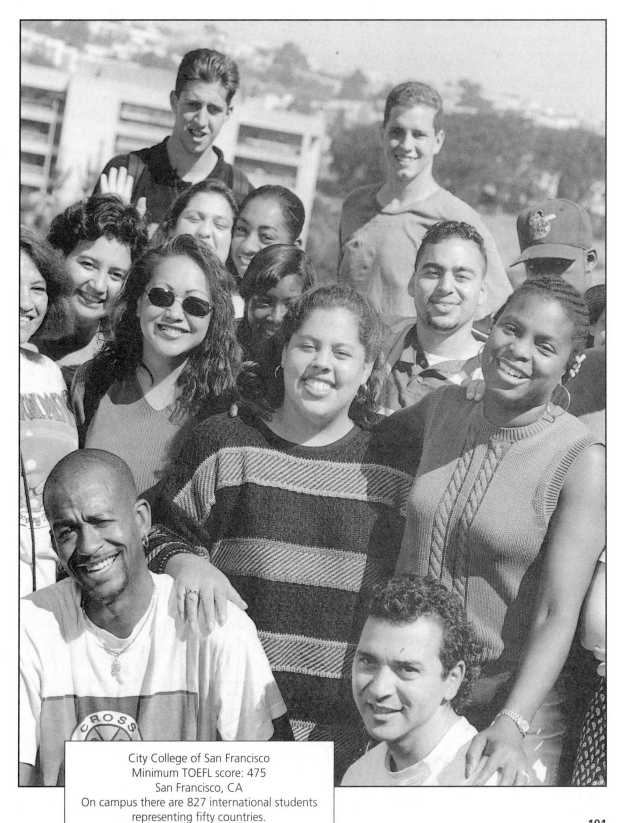

City College of San Francisco
Minimum TOEFL score: 475
San Francisco, CA
On campus there are 827 international students
representing fifty countries.
Photo courtesy of City College of San Francisco

About Structure and Written Expression

The second section of TOEFL tests your understanding of English grammar and usage. This section is divided into two parts: Structure (sentence completion) and Written Expression (error identification). The length of these parts varies depending on the form of the test.

	Standard Form	Long Form
Structure (Sentence Completion)	15 items	23 items
Written Expression (Error Identification)	25 items	37 items
Totals	40 items	60 items
Time	25 minutes	35 minutes

Section 2 is important! Your best chance for improving your score on TOEFL in a short time is to improve your score on this section, and therefore pull up your total score. Although a wide range of grammar points are tested, there are certain points that appear again and again, and you can master these points with the information and practice this *Guide* provides. Also, there are fewer items in this part than in the other two, so each item that you answer correctly adds more to your total score.

Section 2 may seem less stressful for you than Section 1 because you don't have to divide your attention between the tape and the test book. It may seem less stressful than Section 3 because it is easier to finish all the items before time is called.

Section 2 sentences are generally about academic subjects: the physical sciences (such as astronomy or geology), the social sciences (such as psychology or economics), or the humanities (such as music or literature). You will *not* see sentences that deal with "controversial" subjects such as abortion, illegal drugs, or sensitive political issues.

Any cultural references in the sentences are to the culture of the United States or Canada. Many of the sentences contain references to people, places, and institutions that you will not be familiar with. (In fact, many North Americans are not familiar with these either!) It's not necessary to know these references; you should simply concentrate on the structure of the sentences. It's also not necessary to understand all the vocabulary in a sentence; you can often answer a question correctly without a complete understanding of that sentence.

There are two possible approaches to Section 2 problems: an analytical approach and an intuitive approach. A test-taker who uses the analytical approach quickly analyzes the grammar of a sentence to see what element is missing (in Structure) or which element is incorrect (in Written Expression). Someone who uses the second approach simply chooses the answer that "sounds right" (in Structure) or the one that "sounds wrong" (in Written Expression). Although this *Guide* emphasizes the first approach, the second can be useful too, especially for people who learned English primarily by speaking it and listening to it rather than by studying grammar and writing. If you aren't sure which approach works best for you, take Section 2 of one of the Practice Tests using the first method, and Section 2 of another test using the second approach. Did one approach give you a significantly better score? You can also combine the two approaches: if you get "stuck" (unable to choose an answer) using one method, you can switch to another.

> **Hint:** An excellent way to prepare for Section 2 is to write your own Structure and Written Expression items. Write several items for each of the lessons in this part of the *Guide*. There's no better way to start thinking like a test-writer.

Strategies for Section 2

- Be familiar with the directions for both parts. Don't waste time reading the directions or examples. Begin immediately with question 1.

- You can spend an average of about thirty seconds on each item. If an item seems difficult, make a guess and lightly mark the item on your answer sheet so that you can come back to it later. Erase all such marks before time is up. Don't spend too much time working on difficult items; it's better to work on items that you will probably get correct.

- Never answer any item too quickly, even if it seems easy. Always consider all four answer choices. On both parts of this section, it's easy to make mistakes because of carelessness.

- Never leave any answers blank. Always guess even if you have no idea what the answer is.

- If you finish before time is called, go back and work on items that you found difficult. You are not permitted go ahead to Section 3.

Now begin your preparation for Section 2 by taking the Sample Structure and Written Expression Test. Be sure to observe the twenty-five-minute time limit.

2 Sample Structure and Written Expression Test

Time: 25 minutes

This section tests your ability to recognize grammar and usage suitable for standard written English. This section is divided into two parts, each with its own directions.

Structure

Directions: Items in this part are incomplete sentences. Following each of these sentences, there are four words or phrases. You should select the one word or phrase—(A), (B), (C), or (D)—that best completes the sentence. Then fill in the space on your answer sheet that matches the letter of the answer that you have selected.

Example I

Pepsin _____ an enzyme used
in digestion.

(A) that
(B) is
(C) of
(D) being

Sample Answer

ⒶⒷ ⒸⒹ

This sentence should properly read "Pepsin is an enzyme used in digestion." You should fill in (B) on your answer sheet.

Example II

_____ large natural lakes are found
in the state of South Carolina.

(A) There are no
(B) Not the
(C) It is not
(D) No

Sample Answer

ⒶⒷⒸ ●

This sentence should properly read "No large natural lakes are found in the state of South Carolina." You should fill in (D) on your answer sheet.

As soon as you understand the directions, begin work on this part.

Go on to the next page ➤

2 2 2 2 2 2 2 2 2 2 2 2

1. Martha Graham, _____ of the pioneers of modern dance, didn't begin dancing until she was twenty-one.

   (A) who, as one
   (B) she was one
   (C) one
   (D) was one

2. Tiger moths _____ wings marked with stripes or spots.

   (A) have
   (B) with
   (C) their
   (D) whose

3. Platinum is harder than copper and is almost as pliable _____ .

   (A) gold
   (B) than gold
   (C) as gold
   (D) gold is

4. Most of Annie Jump Cannon's career as an astronomer involved the observation, classification, and _____ .

   (A) she analyzed stars
   (B) the stars' analysis
   (C) stars were analyzed
   (D) analysis of stars

5. Many communities are dependent on groundwater _____ from wells for their water supply.

   (A) that obtained
   (B) obtained
   (C) is obtained
   (D) obtain it

6. _____ experimental studies of the aging process, psychologist Ross McFarland determined that people could work productively much longer than had previously been thought.

   (A) In that
   (B) Through
   (C) Since
   (D) Into

7. _____ often raise funds from the sale of stock.

   (A) For corporations to operate
   (B) The operations of corporations, which
   (C) Corporations operate by
   (D) To operate, corporations

8. While all birds are alike in that they have feathers and lay eggs, _____ great differences among them in terms of size, structure, and color.

   (A) there are
   (B) but are
   (C) if there are
   (D) their

Go on to the next page ➡

②②②②②②②②②②②②

9. There were _____ federal laws regulating mining practices until 1872.

(A) none
(B) not
(C) no
(D) nor

10. The Masters, one of the most important of all golf tournaments, _____ every year in Augusta, Georgia.

(A) has held
(B) being held
(C) is held
(D) holding

11. Not only _____ places of beauty; they serve scientific and educational purposes as well.

(A) are botanical gardens
(B) botanical gardens to be
(C) botanical gardens are
(D) to be botanical gardens

12. _____ quicksand can be found all over the world, little was known about its composition until recently.

(A) Except
(B) Although
(C) Even
(D) Despite

13. In 1791 Quebec was divided into two sections, Upper Canada and Lower Canada, _____ were ruled by elected assemblies.

(A) they both
(B) both of them
(C) in which both
(D) both of which

14. _____ are a form of carbon has been known since the late eighteenth century.

(A) Diamonds
(B) Because diamonds
(C) That diamonds
(D) Diamonds, which

15. Designed by Frédéric Auguste Bartholdi, _____ .

(A) the United States was given the Statue of Liberty by the people of France
(B) the people of France gave the Statue of Liberty to the United States
(C) the Statue of Liberty was given to the United States by the people of France
(D) the French people presented the United States with a gift, the Statue of Liberty

Go on to the next page ➤

Written Expression

Directions: The items in this part have four underlined words or phrases, (A), (B), (C) and (D). You must identify the one underlined expression that must be changed for the sentence to be correct. Then find the number of the question on your answer sheet and fill in the space corresponding to
the letter.

Example I   Sample Answer

Lenses may <u>to have</u> either <u>concave</u> <u>or</u> convex <u>shapes</u>.
                 A   B   C   D

This sentence should read "Lenses may have either concave or convex shapes." You should therefore select answer (A).

Example II   Sample Answer

<u>When</u> painting a fresco, an artist <u>is applied</u> paint <u>directly</u> to the damp plaster <u>of a wall</u>.
  A   B   C   D

This sentence should read "When painting a fresco, an artist applies paint directly to the damp plaster of a wall." You should therefore select answer (B).

As soon as you understand the directions, begin work on this section.

Go on to the next page

16. There are thousand of different types of roses.
        A   B   C   D

17. Since 1908 breeders set out to produce chickens that could survive Canada's cold climate.
       A   B   C   D

18. From 1865 to 1875, a remarkable various of inventions was produced.
       A   B   C   D

19. The simplest kind of plant, alike the simplest kind of animal, consists of only one cell.
      A   B   C   D

20. The first recorded use of natural gas to light streetlamps it was in the town of Frederick,
                 A   B   C   D

     New York, in 1825.

21. A museum in Denver, Colorado, chronicles black cowboys and his role in the history of the
                                       A   B   C   D

     American West.

22. Bluegrass music is a kind of country music who was pioneered by Bill Monroe of Rosine,
                          A   B   C   D

     Kentucky.

23. A number of the materials used in manufacturing paint are potential dangerous if mishandled.
            A   B   C   D

24. There are several races of giraffes, but there are only one species.
       A   B   C   D

25. Chestnuts were once the most common tree in the eastern United States, but almost of them
                A   B   C

     were destroyed by a disease called chestnut blight.
                                  D

Go on to the next page ➤

26. Despite they are small, ponies are strong and have great stamina.
    ‾‾A‾‾   ‾B‾   ‾C‾   ‾D‾

27. Physical therapists help patients relearn how to use their bodies after disease or injure.
                                 ‾‾A‾‾   ‾B‾ ‾‾   ‾C‾   ‾D‾

28. Liquids take the shape of any container which in they are placed.
                 ‾‾A‾‾   ‾B‾   ‾‾C‾‾   ‾‾D‾‾

29. The Sun supplies the light and the warmth that permit life on Earth existing.
    ‾A‾   ‾‾‾B‾‾‾   ‾C‾   ‾‾D‾‾

30. For seventeen years, between 1932 to 1949, Fred Allen was one of the most popular
                                  ‾A‾   ‾B‾ ‾‾C‾‾

    comedians on radio.
              ‾‾D‾‾

31. Boolean algebra is most often used to solve problems in logic, probability, and engineer.
                     ‾‾‾A‾‾‾   ‾‾B‾‾   ‾C‾   ‾‾D‾‾

32. Attorney Clarence Darrow is knowing for his defense of unpopular persons and causes.
                            ‾‾‾A‾‾‾   ‾B‾ ‾‾C‾‾   ‾‾D‾‾

33. Phi Beta Kappa is a honor society that encourages scholarship in science and art.
                   ‾A‾   ‾B‾   ‾‾‾C‾‾‾   ‾D‾

34. The French Quarter is the most famous and the most old section of New Orleans.
                      ‾A‾ ‾‾B‾‾   ‾‾C‾‾   ‾D‾

35. There was once a widespread believe that all lizards were poisonous.
    ‾‾A‾‾   ‾‾B‾‾   ‾‾C‾‾   ‾‾D‾‾

36. In the late nineteenth century, many public buildings, especially that on college campuses,
    ‾‾A‾‾   ‾B‾

    were built in the in the Romanesque Revival style of architecture.
    ‾‾C‾‾   ‾‾D‾‾

Go on to the next page ➡

37. Sponges <u>have</u> neither <u>heads</u> <u>or</u> separate body <u>organs</u>.
       A   B   C   D

38. A <u>wooden</u> barrel is made from <u>strips</u> of wood called staves <u>holding</u> together with <u>metal</u> hoops.
       A   B   C   D

39. Salt was once <u>too</u> scarce <u>and</u> precious that it <u>was used</u> <u>as</u> money.
                     A   B   C   D

40. Sharks acquire <u>many</u> sets of <u>tooth</u> <u>during</u> <u>their</u> lifetimes.
                      A   B   C   D

THIS IS THE END OF SECTION 2.

IF YOU FINISH BEFORE THE TIME LIMIT, CHECK YOUR WORK ON SECTION 2 ONLY.
DO NOT READ OR WORK ON ANY OTHER SECTION OF THE TEST.

Structure

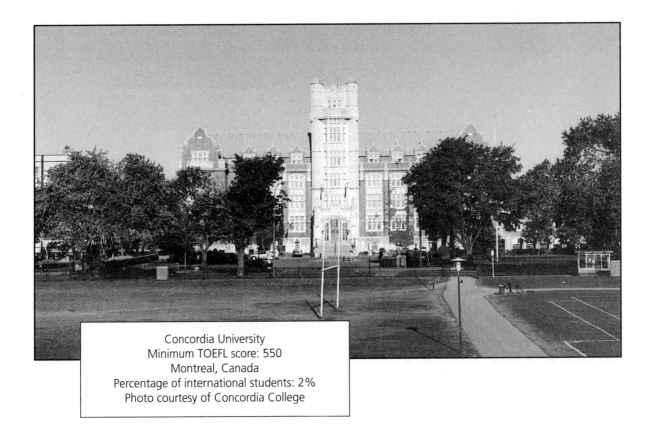

Concordia University
Minimum TOEFL score: 550
Montreal, Canada
Percentage of international students: 2%
Photo courtesy of Concordia College

About Structure

This part of the test consists of fifteen incomplete sentences (twenty-three on the long form). Some portion of each sentence has been replaced by a blank. Under each sentence, four words or phrases are listed. One of these completes the sentence grammatically and logically.

▼ Sample Item

Pepsin _____ an enzyme used in digestion.

(A) that
(B) is
(C) of
(D) being

The sentence consists of a single clause (*Pepsin is an enzyme*) and a reduced (shortened) adjective clause (*used in digestion*). Each clause must contain a subject and a verb. There is a subject but no main verb. (The verbal form *used* is NOT the main verb in this sentence; it is a past participle.) Therefore, a main verb is needed. Only choices (B) and (D) are verb forms. However, an *-ing* verb can never be used alone as a main verb. The only possible choice is (B), the main verb *is*. ▲

What Is Tested in This Section?

In general, there are five main points tested. The chart below shows how these are presented in the next section of the *Guide*.

Main Testing Points	Lesson
Sentence Structure	Lesson 17: Incomplete Independent Clauses
	Lesson 18: Incomplete Adjective Clauses
	Lesson 19: Incomplete/Missing Participial Phrases
	Lesson 20: Incomplete/Missing Appositives
	Lesson 21: Incomplete Adverb Clauses
	Lesson 22: Incomplete Noun Clauses
	Lesson 23: Incomplete/Missing Prepositional Phrases
Word Order	Lesson 24: Word Order Items
Verbs and Verbals	Lesson 25: Items Involving Verb Problems
	Lesson 26: Incomplete/Missing Infinitive and Gerund Phrases
Proper Style	Lesson 27: Items Involving Parallel Structures
	Lesson 28: Items Involving Misplaced Modifiers
Word Choice	Lesson 29: Incomplete/Missing Comparisons
	Lesson 30. Missing Conjunctions
	Lesson 31: Missing Negative Words

The points practiced in the first group of lessons (Lessons 17 to 23) are tested on almost every TOEFL exam. The points in the second group (Lessons 24 to 31) are tested on many TOEFL exams.

What Is the Best Way to Answer Structure Items?

If the answer choices are fairly short, you should begin by taking a quick look at the answer choices to get an idea of what to look for when you read the sentence. A look at the answer choices can often tell you that you are looking at a problem involving verb forms, word order, parallel structure, misplaced modifiers, or others.

If the answer choices are long or complicated, begin by reading the stem. Don't analyze it word for word, but as you are reading, try to form a picture of the sentence's overall structure. How many clauses will there be in the complete sentence? Does each clause have a complete subject and verb? Is there a connecting word to join clauses? Are any other elements obviously missing?

Then look at the answer choices. If you're not sure of the answer, try to eliminate as many distractors as possible. Distractors in Structure are generally incorrect for one of the following reasons:

- A necessary word or phrase is missing, so the sentence is still incomplete.
- An unnecessary word or phrase is included.
- Part of the answer choice is ungrammatical when put into the stem.

Never choose an answer until you've read the sentence completely; sometimes an option seems to fit in the sentence unless you read every word.

After you have eliminated as many answer choices as possible, read the sentence quickly to yourself with the remaining choice or choices in place of the blank. If an answer doesn't "sound right," it probably isn't. If you still can't decide, guess and go on. If you have time, come back to these more difficult items later.

Punctuation clues can sometimes help you solve Structure problems. For example, if there are a series of items in a sentence separated by commas (A, B, and C), you will probably see a problem involving parallel structures.

Tactics for Structure

- If the answer choices are short, look them over before you read the sentence. Try to get an idea of what type of problem you are working with.

- Read the sentence, trying to determine which elements are missing. Never choose an answer until you have read the entire sentence; sometimes an answer will seem to fit until you have read the last few words of the sentence.

- Mark your choice immediately if the answer is obvious. If you're not sure, try to eliminate incorrect answers.

- Read the sentence with the remaining answer choices in place of the blank. Choose the option that sounds best.

- If you are still unable to decide on an answer, guess and and go on. Lightly mark these items on your answer sheet and come back to them if time permits.

- Go on to the second part of this section (Written Expression) as soon as you've finished Structure. Don't spend so much time working on Structure that you don't have enough time to finish Written Expression.

LESSON 17

INCOMPLETE INDEPENDENT CLAUSES

The structures practiced in this lesson are the ones that are most often tested in the Structure section. About 20% of all problems in the section (usually three or four per test) involve incomplete independent clauses.

A) Clauses

All sentences consist of one or more clauses. A **simple sentence** consists of one clause.

> People need vitamins.
> The man took a vitamin pill.
> Judy lives in northern California.
> In the summer, Tom walks to his office.

A **compound sentence** consists of two independent clauses joined by a coordinating conjunction (such as *and* and *but*).

> The man took a vitamin pill, and he drank a glass of orange juice.
> Judy lives in northern California now, but she was raised in Ohio.

A **complex sentence** consists of an independent clause (called the main clause) and a dependent (subordinate) clause. Subordinate clauses may be adverb clauses, noun clauses, or adjective clauses. In the sentences below, the independent clauses are italicized.

> *The man took a vitamin pill* because he had a cold.
>   (independent clause + adverb clause)
> *I didn't realize* that Nancy was here.
>   (independent clause + noun clause)
> *Tom walks to his office*, which is located on Broadway, *every day during the summer*.
>   (independent clause + adjective clause)

All three types of subordinate clauses are commonly seen in the Structure part of the test, and each is considered in separate lessons (Lessons 18, 21, and 22). The emphasis in this chapter, however, is on the basic components of independent clauses.

B) Missing Subjects, Verbs, Objects, and Complements

All clauses have a **subject** and a **verb.** Clauses with an action verb often take a **direct object** as well.

Subject	Verb	Object
People	need	vitamins.

The verb missing from an independent clause may be a single-word verb (*need, was, took, had, walked*) or a verb phrase consisting of one or more auxiliary verbs and a main verb (*will need, has been, should take, would have had, had walked*). The verbs may be active (*need, take*) or passive (*was needed, is taken*).

The missing subject and direct object may be a noun (*people, vitamins, Tom*) a noun phrase (*some famous people, a vitamin pill, my friend Tom*) or a pronoun. (*He, she, it,* and *they* are subject pronouns; *him, her, it* and *them* are object pronouns.)

After the verb *to be* and certain other non-action verbs, a **subject complement** is used rather than a direct object. (Subject complements are also known as predicate nominatives and predicate adjectives.)

Subject	Verb	Complement
She	is	an architect.
The teacher	seemed	upset.

In the Structure section of TOEFL, it is common for any of these elements or a combination of two or more of these elements to be missing from the stem. The most common problem in Structure involves a missing verb. A missing subject and a missing subject-verb combination are common as well. The missing element may also be part of rather than all of the verb or noun phrase.

▼ Sample Items

The art of storytelling _____ almost as old as humanity.

(A) that is
(B) is
(C) it is
(D) being

The correct answer supplies the missing verb. Choice (A) is incorrect because the word *that* is used to connect a relative clause to a main clause; in this sentence, there is only one verb, so there can only be one clause. Choice (C) is incorrect because there is an unnecessary repetition of the subject (*The art of storytelling it . . .*). Choice (D) is not correct because an *-ing* form (*being*) cannot be the main verb of a clause.

_____ a few of the sounds produced by insects can be heard by humans.

(A) Only
(B) There are only
(C) That only
(D) With only

The correct answer completes the noun phrase that is the subject of the sentence. The expletive *There* in choice (B) is incorrectly used. In (C), the word *That* creates a noun clause, but each clause must have its own verb. (*Produced* is used as a participle, not a main verb, in this sentence.) Choice (D) is incorrect because a preposition may not be used directly before the subject.

_____ when lava cools very rapidly.

(A) Because pumice is formed
(B) To form pumice
(C) Pumice is formed
(D) Forming pumice

The best answer supplies an independent clause to join to the adverb clause *when lava cools very rapidly*. Choice (A) consists of an adverb clause; two adverb clauses cannot be joined to form a complete sentence. Choices (B) and (D) are incorrect because they do not contain main verbs, and an independent clause must contain a main verb. (*To form* and *forming* are not main verbs.) Only choice (C) could serve as an independent clause because it contains a subject (*Pumice*) and a full verb, the passive verb *is formed*.

Duke Ellington wrote _____ during his career.

(A) that over a thousand songs
(B) over a thousand songs
(C) over a thousand songs were
(D) there were over a thousand songs

The direct object is missing from this sentence. In choice (A), the connecting word *that* is used unnecessarily. In (C), the verb *were* is used unnecessarily because there is only one clause and it has a verb (*wrote*). In choice (D) the phrase *there were* is not needed between a verb and its direct object. Choice (B) correctly supplies a noun phrase that serves as the direct object.

Before the invention of the printing press, books _____.

(A) that were very rare
(B) were very rarely
(C) were very rare
(D) as very rare

Choice (A) incorrectly forms an adjective clause; an adjective must be joined to a main clause. Choice (B) contains an adverb; after the verb *to be*, an adjective is required. Choice (D) lacks a verb. Choice (C) correctly supplies a verb (*were*). ▲

C) Clauses with *There* and *It*

Some clauses begin with the introductory words *there* or *it* rather than with the subject of the sentence. These introductory words are sometimes called **expletives.**

The expletive *there* shows that someone or something exists, usually at a particular time or place. These sentences generally follow the pattern *there* + verb *to be* + subject:

There are many skyscrapers in New York City.
There was a good movie on television last night.

The expletive *it* is used in a number of different situations and patterns:

It is important to be punctual for appointments.
      (with the verb *to be* + adjective + infinitive)
It was in 1959 that Alaska became a state.
      (with the verb *to be* + adverbial + noun clause)
It takes a long time to learn a language.
      (with the verb *to take* + time phrase + infinitive)
It was David who did most of the work.
      (with the verb *to be* + noun + relative clause)

It and *there*, along with the verb and other sentence elements, may be missing from the stem.

▼ **Sample Items**

In Michigan, _____ over six hundred feet deep.

(A) salt deposits
(B) where salt deposits are
(C) having salt deposits
(D) there are salt deposits

Ⓐ Ⓑ Ⓒ ⬤

Choice (D) correctly supplies an introductory word (*there*), a verb, and a subject. Choice (A) lacks a verb. Choice (B) contains a subordinator, used to introduce a clause; there is only one verb, however, so there can only be one clause. Choice (C) also lacks a main verb.

_____ a tomato plant from 75 to 85 days to develop into a mature plant with ripe fruit.

(A) It takes
(B) To take
(C) That takes
(D) By taking

⬤ Ⓑ Ⓒ Ⓓ

Choice (A) correctly completes the sentence with the introductory word *It* and a verb. Choices (B) and (D) do not supply main verbs. Choice (C) incorrectly creates a noun clause. ▲

Exercise 17

Focus: Completing structure problems involving incomplete independent clauses. (Note: Three or four items in this exercise do *not* focus on missing subjects, verbs, complements, or introductory words; these items are marked in the answer key with asterisks.)

Directions: Choose the one option—(A), (B), (C), or (D)—that correctly completes the sentences, and then mark the appropriate blank. The first one is done as an example.

1. In the United States, _____ is generally the responsibility of municipal governments.
   _____ (A) for water treatment
   __✔__ (B) water treatment
   _____ (C) where water treatment
   _____ (D) in which water treatment

2. Crop rotation _____ of preserving soil fertility.
   _____ (A) it is one method
   _____ (B) one method
   _____ (C) a method is one
   _____ (D) is one method

3. _____ the dollar as its monetary unit in 1878.
   _____ (A) Canada adopted
   _____ (B) Adopted by Canada,
   _____ (C) It was adopted by Canada
   _____ (D) The Canadian adoption of

4. _____ almost impossible to capture the beauty of the aurora borealis in photographs.
   _____ (A) Being
   _____ (B) It is
   _____ (C) There is
   _____ (D) Is

5. Usually, political cartoons _____ on the editorial page of a newspaper.
   _____ (A) appear
   _____ (B) whose appearance
   _____ (C) by appearing
   _____ (D) when they appear

6. _____ two major art museums, the Fogg and the Sadler.
   _____ (A) Harvard University has
   _____ (B) At Harvard University
   _____ (C) Harvard University, with its
   _____ (D) There at Harvard University

7. American actress and director Margaret Webster _____ for her production of Shakespearean plays.
   _____ (A) who became famous
   _____ (B) famous as she became
   _____ (C) becoming famous
   _____ (D) became famous

8. _____ gas tanks connected to welding equipment, one full of oxygen and the other full of acetylene.
   _____ (A) It is two
   _____ (B) Of the two
   _____ (C) There are two
   _____ (D) Two

9. _____ is more interested in rhythm than in melody is apparent from his compositions.
   _____ (A) That Philip Glass
   _____ (B) Philip Glass, who
   _____ (C) Philip Glass
   _____ (D) Because Philip Glass

10. Compressed air _____ the power to drive pneumatic tools.
    _____ (A) by providing
    _____ (B) provides
    _____ (C) that provides
    _____ (D) the provision of

11. _____ by cosmic rays.
    _____ (A) The earth is constantly bombarded
    _____ (B) Bombarded constantly, the earth
    _____ (C) Bombarding the earth constantly
    _____ (D) The earth's constant bombardment

12. _____ primary colors are red, blue, and yellow.
    _____ (A) There are three
    _____ (B) The three
    _____ (C) Three of them
    _____ (D) That the three

13. _____ who was elected the first woman mayor of Chicago in 1979.
_____ (A) It was Jane Byrne
_____ (B) Jane Byrne
_____ (C) That Jane Byrne
_____ (D) When Jane Byrne

14. Every computer consists of a number of systems _____ together.
_____ (A) by working
_____ (B) work
_____ (C) they work
_____ (D) that work

15. On the Moon, _____ air because the Moon's gravitational field is too weak to retain an atmosphere.
_____ (A) there is no
_____ (B) where no
_____ (C) no
_____ (D) is no

16. The Glass Mountains of northwestern Oklahoma _____ with flecks of gypsum, which shine in the sunlight.
_____ (A) they are covered
_____ (B) covered them
_____ (C) that are covered
_____ (D) are covered

17. In some cases, _____ to decide if an organism is a plant or an animal.
_____ (A) difficult if
_____ (B) it is difficult
_____ (C) the difficulty
_____ (D) is difficult

18. The first American novelist to have a major impact on world literature _____.
_____ (A) who was James Fenimore Cooper
_____ (B) James Fenimore Cooper was
_____ (C) it was James Fenimore Cooper
_____ (D) was James Fenimore Cooper

19. _____ important railroad tunnel in the United States was cut through the Hoosac Mountains in Massachusetts.
_____ (A) At first
_____ (B) It was the first
_____ (C) The first
_____ (D) As the first of

20. Generally, _____ in the valleys and foothills of the Pacific Coast ranges.
_____ (A) the California poppy grown
_____ (B) the growth of the California poppy
_____ (C) the California poppy grows
_____ (D) growing the California poppy

21. When bats are at rest, _____ hang upside-down.
_____ (A) they
_____ (B) and
_____ (C) to
_____ (D) as

22. _____ that the capital of South Carolina was moved from Charleston to Columbia.
    _____ (A) In 1790 was
    _____ (B) There was in 1790
    _____ (C) In 1790
    _____ (D) It was in 1790

23. Although not as important as they once were, _____ a major form of transportation in North America.
    _____ (A) there are still railroads
    _____ (B) railroads, which are still
    _____ (C) railroads are still
    _____ (D) railroads still being

24. The Loop, which is the commercial heart of Chicago, _____ within a rectangular loop of elevated train tracks.
    _____ (A) that is enclosed
    _____ (B) enclosing it
    _____ (C) is enclosed
    _____ (D) enclosed

25. _____ amino acids that serve as the basic building blocks of all proteins.
    _____ (A) About twenty
    _____ (B) For about twenty of
    _____ (C) About twenty are
    _____ (D) There are about twenty

LESSON 18

INCOMPLETE ADJECTIVE CLAUSES

As mentioned in the previous lesson, there are three types of dependent clauses, all of which are tested in Structure. **Adjective clauses**—also called **relative clauses**—are the most commonly tested of the three. You will see one or two items involving adjective clauses on most tests.

Adjective clauses are a way of joining two sentences. In the joined sentence, the adjective clause modifies (describes) a noun (called the **head noun**) in another clause of the sentence. It usually begins with an **adjective clause marker.**

> I wanted the book. The book had already been checked out.
> The book *which I wanted* had already been checked out.

The adjective clause in this example begins with the marker *which* and modifies the head noun *book*.

Adjective clause markers are relative pronouns such as *who, that,* or *which* or the relative adverbs *when* or *where.*

Adjective Clause Marker	Use	Example
who	Subject (people)	A neurologist is a doctor *who* specializes in the nervous system.
whom	Object (people)	This is the patient *whom* the doctor treated.
whose	Possessive (usually people)	Mr. Collins is the man *whose* house I rented.
which	Subject/Object (things)	That is a topic *which* interests me. (*which* as subject)
		That is the topic *on which* I will write. (*which* as object of preposition)
that	Subject/Object (people/things)	Art *that* is in public places can be enjoyed by everyone. (*that* as subject)
		The painting *that* Ms. Wallace bought was very expensive. (*that* as object)
where	Adverb (place)	Here is the site *where* the bank plans to build its new headquarters.
when	Adverb (time)	This is the hour *when* the children usually go to bed.

Like all clauses, adjective clauses must have a subject and a verb. In some cases the adjective-clause marker itself is the subject; in some cases, there is another subject.

> The painting was very expensive. Ms. Wallace bought it.
> The painting *which Ms. Wallace bought* was very expensive.

The adjective-clause marker in the joined sentence replaces *it*, the object of the verb *bought*. In the joined sentence, the adjective clause keeps the subject—*Ms. Wallace*—that it had in the original sentence.

This is a topic. It interests me.
This is a topic *that interests me*.

The adjective-clause marker in the joined sentence replaces *it*, the subject of the second original sentence. In the joined sentence, the marker itself is the subject of the adjective clause. Notice that the inclusion of the pronoun *it* in the joined sentences above would be an error.

> **Incorrect:** *The painting which Ms. Wallace bought *it* was very expensive.
> *This is a topic which *it* interests me.

This type of mistake is sometimes seen in distractors.

When the markers *which*, *that*, and *whom* are used as objects in relative clauses, they can correctly be omitted.

> The painting Ms. Wallace bought is very expensive. (*which* omitted)

The adjective-clause markers *which* and *whom* can also be used as objects of prepositions:

> That is the topic. I will write on it.
> That is the topic *on which I will write*.

You may also see sentences with quantifiers (*many, both, most, none, a few*, and so on) and adjective clauses used in this pattern:

> quantifier + *of* + relative clause

> He met with two advisors. He had known both of them for years.
> He met with two advisors, *both of whom he had known for years*.

> I read a number of articles. Most of them were very useful.
> I read a number of articles, *most of which were very useful*.

Any part of a relative clause can be missing from the stem of Structure items, but most often, the marker and the subject (if there is one) and the verb are missing. Any word or phrase from another clause—usually the head noun—may also be missing from the stem.

▼ **Sample Items**

Cable cars are moved by cables _____ underground and are powered by a stationary engine.

(A) they run
(B) that they run
(C) run
(D) that run

Choice (A) is incorrect because the pronoun *they* cannot be used to join two clauses. Choice (B) is not appropriate because the subject *they* is not needed in the adjective clause; the marker *that* serves as the subject of the clause. Choice (C) is incorrect because there is no marker to join the adjective clause to the main clause.

The melting point is the temperature _____ a solid changes to a liquid.

(A) which
(B) at which
(C) which at
(D) at

Choice (A) is incorrect because a preposition is needed before the adjective clause.
Choice (C) is incorrect because the relative pronoun comes before the preposition.
Choice (D) is incorrect because the relative pronoun has been omitted.

> There are six types of flamingos, all _____ have long legs, long necks, and beaks that curve sharply downward.
>
> (A) of them
> (B) that
> (C) of which
> (D) they

Ⓐ Ⓑ ⬤ Ⓓ

Choices (A) and (D) do not contain connecting words needed to join clauses. Choice (B) does not follow the correct pattern of relative clauses after a quantifier (*all*). The correct pattern needed to complete this sentence is quantifier + *of* + marker. Only (C) follows this pattern. ▲

Exercise 18

Focus: Answering structure problems involving incomplete adjective clauses. (Note: One or two items in this exercise do *not* focus on adjective clauses; these items are marked in the answer key with asterisks.)

Directions: Choose the one option—(A), (B), (C), or (D)—that correctly completes the sentence, and then mark the appropriate blank. The first one is done as an example.

1. Most folk songs are ballads _____ have simple words and tell simple stories.
   _____ (A) what
   _____ (B) although
   _____ (C) when
   ✔ (D) that

2. After its introduction in 1969, the float process _____ the world's principal method of manufacturing flat sheets of glass.
   _____ (A) by which it became
   _____ (B) it became
   _____ (C) became
   _____ (D) which became

3. In 1850 Yale University established Sheffield Scientific School, _____.
   _____ (A) engineers were educated there
   _____ (B) where engineers were educated
   _____ (C) in which were engineers educated
   _____ (D) where were engineers educated

4. Many of Louise Nevelson's sculptures consisted of a number of large wooden structures _____ in complex patterns.
   _____ (A) which she arranged
   _____ (B) she arranged them
   _____ (C) which arranged
   _____ (D) arranged them

5. In addition to being a naturalist, Stewart E. White was a writer _____ the struggle for survival on the American frontier.

    _____ (A) whose novels describe

    _____ (B) he describes in his novels

    _____ (C) his novels describe

    _____ (D) who, describing in his novels

6. Diamonds are often found in rock formations called pipes, _____ the throats of extinct volcanoes.

    _____ (A) in which they resemble

    _____ (B) which resemble

    _____ (C) there is a resemblance to

    _____ (D) they resemble

7. William Samuel Johnson, _____ helped write the Constitution, became the first president of Columbia College in 1787.

    _____ (A) whom he had

    _____ (B) and he had

    _____ (C) who had

    _____ (D) had

8. Seals appear clumsy on the land, _____ are able to move short distances faster than most people can run.

    _____ (A) but they

    _____ (B) which they

    _____ (C) they

    _____ (D) which

9. The instrument panel of a light airplane has at least a dozen instruments _____.

    _____ (A) the pilot must watch

    _____ (B) what the pilot must watch

    _____ (C) which the pilot must watch them

    _____ (D) such that the pilot must watch them

10. A keystone species is a species of plants or animals _____ absence has a major effect on an ecological system.

    _____ (A) that its

    _____ (B) its

    _____ (C) whose

    _____ (D) with its

11. The size and shape of a nail depend primarily on the function _____ intended.

    _____ (A) which it is

    _____ (B) for which it is

    _____ (C) which it is for

    _____ (D) for which is

12. In geometry, a tangent is a straight line _____ a curve at only one point.

    _____ (A) it touches

    _____ (B) whose touching

    _____ (C) its touching

    _____ (D) that touches

13. It was the ragtime pianist Scott Joplin _____ the "Maple Leaf Rag," perhaps the best known of all ragtime tunes.
    _____ (A) wrote
    _____ (B) the writer of
    _____ (C) who wrote
    _____ (D) writing

14. There are over 2,000 varieties of snakes, _____ are harmless to humans.
    _____ (A) mostly they
    _____ (B) most of them
    _____ (C) most of which
    _____ (D) which most

15. Smokejumpers are _____ descend into remote areas by parachute to fight forest fires.
    _____ (A) firefighters
    _____ (B) when firefighters
    _____ (C) who, as firefighters
    _____ (D) firefighters who

16. Charlotte Gilman's best known book _____ she urges women to become financially independent.
    _____ (A) is *Women and Economics,* in which
    _____ (B) *Women and Economics,* in which
    _____ (C) is *Women and Economics,* which
    _____ (D) *Women and Economics,* in that

LESSON 19

INCOMPLETE OR MISSING PARTICIPIAL PHRASES

Participial phrases generally occur after nouns. They are actually **reduced** (shortened) **relative clauses. Present participles** (which always end in *-ing*) are used to reduce adjective clauses that contain active verbs.

> Minnesota, *which joined the Union in 1858*, became the thirty-second state.
> (adjective clause with active verb)
> Minnesota, *joining the Union in 1858*, became the thirty-second state.
> (participial phrase with a present participle)

Most **past participles** end in *-ed*, but there are also many irregular forms. Past participles are used to reduce adjective clauses with passive verbs.

> William and Mary College, *which was founded in 1693*, is the second oldest university in
> the United States.
> (adjective clause with a passive verb)
> William and Mary College, *founded in 1693*, is the second oldest university in the United States.
> (participial phrase with a past participle)

Participial phrases can also come before the subject of a sentence.

> *Joining the Union in 1858*, Minnesota became the thirty-second state.
> *Founded in 1693*, William and Mary College is the second oldest university in the United States.

Usually, the participle itself is missing from this type of Structure item, but any part of a participial phrase as well as parts of a main clause may be missing.

▼ Sample Item

Natural resources provide the raw materials _____ to produce finished goods.

(A) needed
(B) are needed
(C) which need
(D) needing

Option (B) is a passive verb; the sentence cannot contain two main verbs (*are needed* and *provide*) in the same clause. Choice (C) creates an adjective clause, but the verb in the clause is active and a passive verb is required. (However, a relative clause with a passive verb (*which are needed*) would be a correct answer.) Choice (D) is a present participle and has an active meaning; a past participle is needed. ▲

Exercise 19

Focus: Completing structure problems involving incomplete or missing participial phrases. (Note: One or two items in this exercises do *not* focus on participial phrases; these items are marked on the answer key with asterisks.)

Directions: Choose the one option—(A), (B), (C), or (D)—that correctly completes the sentence, and then mark the appropriate blank. The first one is done as an example.

1. Aerodynamics is the study of the forces _____ on an object as it moves through the
    atmosphere.
    __✔__ (A) acting
    _____ (B) act
    _____ (C) are acting
    _____ (D) acted

2. _____ for their strong fiber include flax and hemp.
    _____ (A) Plants are grown
    _____ (B) Plants grown
    _____ (C) Plants that grow
    _____ (D) To grow plants

3. _____, José Limon's dance troupe often toured abroad.
    _____ (A) The U.S. State Department sponsored it
    _____ (B) Sponsored by the U.S. State Department
    _____ (C) The U.S. State Department, which sponsored it
    _____ (D) The sponsorship of the U.S. State Department

4. Elfreth's Alley in Philadelphia is the oldest residential street in the United States, with
    _____ from 1728.
    _____ (A) houses are dated
    _____ (B) the dates of the houses
    _____ (C) the dating of houses
    _____ (D) houses dating

5. In 1821 the city of Indianapolis, Indiana, was laid out in a design _____ after that of
    Washington, D.C.
    _____ (A) patterned
    _____ (B) was patterned
    _____ (C) a pattern
    _____ (D) that patterned

6. _____ in front of a camera lens changes the color of the light that reaches the film.
    _____ (A) Placed a filter
    _____ (B) A filter is placed
    _____ (C) A filter placed
    _____ (D) When a filter placed

7. The Massachusetts State House, _____ in 1798, was the most distinguished building in
    the United States at that time.
    _____ (A) completing
    _____ (B) which was completed
    _____ (C) was completed
    _____ (D) to be completed

8. Barbara McClintock _____ for her discovery of the mobility of genetic elements.
    _____ (A) known
    _____ (B) who knows
    _____ (C) knowing
    _____ (D) is known

9. The solitary scientist _____ by himself or herself has in many instances been replaced by
    a cooperative scientific team.
    _____ (A) to make important discoveries
    _____ (B) important discoveries were made
    _____ (C) has made important discoveries
    _____ (D) making important discoveries

10. Geometry is the branch of mathematics _____ the properties of lines, curves, shapes, and surfaces.
    _____ (A) that concerned with
    _____ (B) it is concerned with
    _____ (C) concerned with
    _____ (D) its concerns are

11. _____ an average of 471 inches of rain a year, Mount Waialeale in Hawaii is the wettest spot in the world.
    _____ (A) It receives
    _____ (B) Receiving
    _____ (C) To receive
    _____ (D) Received

12. Amber is a hard, yellowish-brown _____ from the resin of pine trees that lived millions of years ago.
    _____ (A) substance formed
    _____ (B) to form a substance
    _____ (C) substance has formed
    _____ (D) forming a substance

LESSON 20

INCOMPLETE OR MISSING APPOSITIVES

An **appositive** is a noun phrase that explains or rephrases another noun phrase. It usually comes after the noun which it rephrases. It may also come before the subject of a sentence.

> Buffalo Bill, *a famous frontiersman*, operated his own Wild West Show.
>   (appositive following a noun)
> *A famous frontiersman*, Buffalo Bill operated his own Wild West Show.
>   (appositive before the subject)

Appositives are actually reduced adjective clauses. However, unlike adjective clauses, they do not contain a marker or a verb.

> Oak, *which is one of the most durable hardwoods*, is often used to make furniture.
>   (adjective clause)
> Oak, *one of the most durable hardwoods*, is often used to make furniture.
>   (appositive)

Appositives are usually separated from the rest of the sentence by commas, but some short appositives (usually names) are not.

> Economist *Paul Samuelson* won a Nobel Prize in 1970.

In Structure items, all or part of an appositive phrase may be missing. In addition, the noun that the appositive refers to or other parts of the main clause may be missing.

▼ **Sample Item**

> The National Road, _____ of the first highways in North America, connected the East Coast to the Ohio Valley.
>
> (A) which one
> (B) it was one
> (C) one
> (D) was one

Choice (A) is incorrect; there is no verb in the relative clause. Choice (B) has no connecting word to join the clause to the rest of the sentence. Choice (D) is incorrect because a verb cannot be used in an appositive phrase. Note: *which was one* would also be a correct answer. ▲

Exercise 20

Focus: Completing structure problems involving appositives. (Note: The focus for one or two items in this exercises is *not* appositives; these sentences are marked in the answer key with asterisks.)

Directions: Choose the one option—(A), (B), (C), or (D)—that correctly completes the sentences, and then mark the appropriate blank. The first one is done as an example.

1. The Democratic Party is older than the other major American political party, _____.
   _____ (A) which the Republican party
   __✔__ (B) the Republican party
   _____ (C) it is the Republican party
   _____ (D) the Republican party is

2. _____ relations with friends and acquaintances, play a major role in the social development of adolescents.

_____ (A) What are called peer group relations are

_____ (B) Peer group relations are

_____ (C) Peer group relations, the

_____ (D) By peer group relations, we mean

3. Joseph Henry, _____ first director of the Smithsonian Institute, was President Lincoln's advisor on scientific matters.

_____ (A) the

_____ (B) to be the

_____ (C) was the

_____ (D) as the

4. The Wassatch Range, _____ extends from southeastern Idaho into northern Utah.

_____ (A) which is a part of the Rocky Mountains,

_____ (B) a part of the Rocky Mountains that

_____ (C) is a part of the Rocky Mountains

_____ (D) a part of the Rocky Mountains, it

5. _____ Ruth St. Dennis turned to Asian dances to find inspiration for her choreography.

_____ (A) It was the dancer

_____ (B) The dancer

_____ (C) That the dancer

_____ (D) The dancer was

6. The organs of taste are the _____ which are mainly located on the tongue.

_____ (A) groups of cells, are taste buds

_____ (B) taste buds, are groups of cells

_____ (C) taste buds, these are groups of cells

_____ (D) taste buds, groups of cells

7. In 1878 Frederick W. Taylor invented a concept called scientific management, _____ of obtaining as much efficiency from workers and machines as possible.

_____ (A) it is a method

_____ (B) a method which

_____ (C) a method

_____ (D) called a method

8. A group of Shakers, _____ settled around Pleasant Hill, Kentucky, in 1805.

_____ (A) members of a strict religious sect which

_____ (B) whose members of a strict religious sect

_____ (C) members of a strict religious sect,

_____ (D) were members of a strict religious sect

9. In physics, _____ "plasma" refers to a gas which has a nearly equal number of positively and negatively charged particles.

_____ (A) the term

_____ (B) by the term

_____ (C) is termed

_____ (D) terming

10. Norman Weiner, _____ mathematician and logician, had an important role in the development of the computer.

_____ (A) who, as a

_____ (B) was a

_____ (C) whom a

_____ (D) a

11. Jerome Kern's most famous work is *Showboat*, _____ most enduring musical comedies.

_____ (A) it is one of the finest,

_____ (B) one of the finest,

_____ (C) the finest one

_____ (D) as the finest of the

12. _____ a marshland that covers over 750 square miles in North Carolina and Virginia.

_____ (A) In the Great Dismal Swamp,

_____ (B) The Great Dismal Swamp, which

_____ (C) The Great Dismal Swamp,

_____ (D) The Great Dismal Swamp is

LESSON 21

INCOMPLETE ADVERB CLAUSES

A) Full Adverb Clauses

An **adverb clause** consists of a connecting word, called an **adverb clause marker** (or subordinate conjunction), and at least a subject and a verb.

> The demand for economical cars increases *when gasoline becomes more expensive*.

In this example, the adverb clause marker *when* joins the adverb clause to the main clause. The adverb clause contains a subject (*gasoline*) and a verb (*becomes*).

An adverb clause can precede the main clause or follow it. When the adverb clause comes first, it is separated from the main clause by a comma.

> *When gasoline becomes more expensive*, the demand for economical cars increases.

The following markers are commonly seen in the Structure section:

Adverb Clause Marker	Use	Example
because	cause	*Because* the speaker was sick, the program was canceled.
since	cause	*Since* credit cards are so convenient, many people use them.
although	opposition (contrary cause)	*Although* he earns a good salary, he never saves any money.
even though	opposition (contrary cause)	*Even though* she was tired, she she stayed up late.
while	contrast	Some people arrived in taxis *while* others took the subway.
if	condition	*If* the automobile had not been invented, what would people use for basic transportation?
unless	condition	I won't go *unless* you do.
when	time	Your heart rate increases *when* you exercise
while	time	Some people like to listen to music *while* they are studying.
as	time	One train was arriving *as* another was departing.
since	time	We haven't seen Professor Hill *since* she returned from her trip.
until	time	Don't put off going to the dentist *until* you have a problem.
once	time	*Once* the dean arrives, the meeting can begin.
before	time	*Before* he left the country, he bought some traveler's checks.
after	time	She will give a short speech *after* she is presented with the award.

In Structure items, any part of a full adverb clause—the marker, the subject, the verb, and so on—can be missing from the stem.

B) Clause Markers with *-ever*

Words that end with *-ever* are sometimes used as adverb clause markers. (In some sentences, these words are actually noun-clause markers, but they are seldom used that way in Structure items.)

The three *-ever* words that you are likely to see in the Structure Section are given in the chart below:

Adverb Clause Marker with *-ever*	Meaning	Example
wherever	any place that . . .	Put that box *wherever* you can find room for it.
whenever	any time that . . .	They stay at that hotel *whenever* they're in Boston.
however	any way that . . .	*However* you solve the problem, you'll get the same answer.

C) Reduced Adverb Clauses

When the subject of the main clause and the subject of the adverb clause are the same person or thing, the adverb clause can be reduced (shortened). Reduced adverb clauses do not contain a main verb or a subject. They consist of a marker and a participle (either a present or a past participle) or a marker and an adjective.

> *When astronauts are orbiting the earth*, they don't feel the force of gravity.
> (full adverb clause)
> *When orbiting the earth*, astronauts don't feel the force of gravity.
> (reduced clause with present participle)

> *Although it had been damaged*, the machine was still operational.
> (full adverb clause)
> *Although damaged*, the machine was still operational.
> (reduced clause with a past participle)

> *Although he was nervous*, he gave a wonderful speech.
> (full adverb clause)
> *Although nervous*, he gave a wonderful speech.
> (reduced clause with an adjective)

You will most often see reduced adverb clauses with the markers *although, while, if, when, before, after*, and *until*. Reduced adverb clauses are NEVER used after *because*.

D) Prepositional Phrases with the Same Meaning as Adverb Clauses

There are also certain prepositions that have essentially the same meaning as adverb-clause markers but are used before noun phrases or pronouns, not with clauses.

Preposition	Related Marker	Example
because of	because/since	He chose that university *because of* its fine reputation.
due to	because/since	The accident was *due to* mechanical failure.
on account of	because/since	Visibility is poor today *on account of* air pollution.
in spite of	although/even though	He enjoys motorcycle riding *in spite of* the danger.
despite	although/even though	*Despite* its loss, the team is still in first place.
during	when/while	Her father lived in England *during* the war.

In structure items where the correct answer is an adverb-clause marker, one of these words often appears as a distractor.

▼ **Sample Items**

No one knows what color dinosaurs were _____ no sample of their skin has survived.

(A) because of
(B) because that
(C) it is because
(D) because

Choice (A) is incorrect; *because of* can be used only before nouns or pronouns. In choice (B), *that* is unnecessary. In (C), the phrase *it is* is used unnecessarily.

_____ rises to the surface of the earth, a volcano is formed.

(A) Liquid magma
(B) Whenever liquid magma
(C) Liquid magma, which
(D) That liquid magma

Choice (A) creates two clauses, but there is no connecting word to join them. (C) creates a sentence with a main clause and an adjective clause, but the main clause has two subjects (*liquid magma* and *a volcano*). (D) creates a noun clause. In a correct sentence, when a noun clause begins a sentence, the clause itself is the subject of the verb in the main clause, but this sentence already has a subject (*volcano*).

_____ invisible to the unaided eye, ultraviolet light can be detected in a number of ways.

(A) Although is
(B) Despite
(C) Even though it
(D) Although

Ⓐ Ⓑ Ⓒ ⬤

The best answer completes a reduced adverb clause. In choice (A), the adverb clause lacks a subject and is not a correct reduction because it contains a verb. In choice (B), *despite* cannot be used with an adjective (only with a noun phrase or pronoun). (C) does not supply a verb for the adverb clause and is not a correct reduction because it contains a subject.

Because _____, the mineral alabaster can be easily carved.

(A) is soft
(B) softness
(C) of its softness
(D) of soft

Ⓐ Ⓑ ⬤ Ⓓ

Choice (A) lacks a subject in the adverb clause. Choice (B), a noun, could only be used with *because of*. In (D), *because of* is followed by an adjective; to be correct, it must be followed by a noun phrase or pronoun.   ▲

Exercise 21

Focus: Completing structure problems involving adverb clauses, reduced adverb clauses, and related prepositional expressions. (Note: Two or three items do *not* focus on one of these structures. These items are marked in the answer key with an asterisk.)

Directions: Choose the one option—(A), (B), (C), or (D)—that correctly completes the sentences, and then mark the appropriate blank. The first one is done as an example.

1. Small sailboats can easily capsize _____ they are not handled carefully.
   _____ (A) but
   _____ (B) which
   ___✔___ (C) if
   _____ (D) so

2. _____ they are tropical birds, parrots can live in temperate or even cold climates.
   _____ (A) Despite
   _____ (B) Even though
   _____ (C) Nevertheless
   _____ (D) But

3. _____ added to a liquid, antifreeze lowers the freezing temperature of that liquid.
   _____ (A) That
   _____ (B) As is
   _____ (C) It is
   _____ (D) When

4. _____ advertising is so widespread in the United States, it has had an enormous effect on American life.
_____ (A) Why
_____ (B) The reason
_____ (C) On account of
_____ (D) Since

5. _____ towards shore, its shape is changed by its collision with the shallow sea bottom.
_____ (A) During a wave rolls
_____ (B) As a wave rolls
_____ (C) A wave rolls
_____ (D) A wave's rolling

6. _____ people are increasingly linked over long distances by electronic communications, but many of them still prefer face-to-face encounters.
_____ (A) Although
_____ (B) Despite
_____ (C) Today
_____ (D) The fact that

7. _____ together in one place, they form a community.
_____ (A) When people who live
_____ (B) When people living
_____ (C) Whenever people live
_____ (D) Whenever living people

8. _____ managed by an independent governor and board of directors, the Bank of Canada is owned by the Canadian government.
_____ (A) And yet
_____ (B) In spite of it
_____ (C) Although
_____ (D) It is

9. _____ pieces of rope are of different thickness, the weaver's knot can be used to join them.
_____ (A) Two of
_____ (B) What two
_____ (C) Two such
_____ (D) If two

10. _____, the seeds of the Kentucky coffee plant are poisonous.
_____ (A) Until they have been cooked
_____ (B) Cooking them
_____ (C) They have been cooked
_____ (D) Cooked until

11. Natural silk is still highly prized _____ similar artificial fabrics.
_____ (A) although is available
_____ (B) despite there are available
_____ (C) in spite of the availability of
_____ (D) even though an availability of

12. Cattle ranches are found almost _____ in Utah.
_____ (A) wherever
_____ (B) everywhere
_____ (C) overall
_____ (D) somewhere

13. _____ through a prism, a beam of white light breaks into all the colors of the rainbow.
_____ (A) When shines
_____ (B) It shines
_____ (C) It is shone
_____ (D) When shone

14. _____ most people think of freezing as a relatively modern method of food preservation, it is actually one of the oldest.
_____ (A) Even
_____ (B) As though
_____ (C) However
_____ (D) Even though

15. _____ large bodies of water never freeze solid is that the sheet of ice on the surface protects the water below it from the cold air.
_____ (A) Because
_____ (B) Why do
_____ (C) The reason that
_____ (D) For the reason

16. _____ granted by the Patent Office, it becomes the inventor's property and he or she can keep it, sell it, or license it to someone else.
_____ (A) Once a patent is
_____ (B) When a patent
_____ (C) A patent, once
_____ (D) A patent, whenever it

17. Owls can hunt in total darkness _____ their remarkably keen sense of smell.
_____ (A) since
_____ (B) because of
_____ (C) the result
_____ (D) that

18. _____ most bamboo blooms every year, there are some species that flower only two or three times a century.
_____ (A) Whenever
_____ (B) That
_____ (C) While
_____ (D) However

LESSON 22

INCOMPLETE NOUN CLAUSES

Noun clauses are the third type of subordinate clause. They begin with **noun-clause markers.** Noun clauses that are formed from statements begin with the noun-clause marker *that*. Noun clauses formed from *yes/no* questions begin with the noun-clause markers *whether* or *if*. Those formed from information questions begin with *wh-* words: *what, where, when,* and so on.

> Dr. Hopkins' office is in this building.   (statement)
> I'm sure that Dr. Hopkins' office is in this building.

> Is Dr. Hopkins' office on this floor?   (yes/no question)
> I don't know *if (whether)* Dr. Hopkins' office is on this floor.

> Where is Dr. Hopkins' office?   (information question)
> Please tell me *where* Dr. Hopkins' office is.

Notice that the word order in direct questions is not the same as it is in noun clauses. The noun clause follows statement word order (subject + verb), not question word order (auxiliary + subject + main verb). Often one of the distractors for noun-clause items will incorrectly follow question word order.

> *I don't know what *is her name*.
> (Incorrect use of question word order)

> I don't know what *her name is*.
> (Correct word order)

> *She called him to ask what time *did his party start*.
> (Incorrect use of question word order)

> She called him to ask what time *his party started*.
> (Correct word order)

Noun clauses function exactly as nouns do: as subjects, as direct objects, or as complements after the verb *to be*.

> *When the meeting will be held* has not been decided.
> (noun clause as subject)

> The weather announcer said *that there will be thunderstorms*.
> (noun clause as direct object)

> This is *what you need*.
> (noun clause after *to be*)

Notice that when the noun clause is the subject of a sentence, the verb in the main clause does not have a noun or pronoun subject.

In Structure items, the noun-clause marker, along with any other part of the noun clause—subject, verb, and so on—may be missing from the stem, or the whole noun clause may be missing.

▼ **Sample Items**

_____ was caused by breathing impure air was once a common belief.

(A) Malaria
(B) That malaria
(C) Why malaria
(D) Because malaria

$\text{(A)} \ \bullet \ \text{(C)} \ \text{(D)}$

Choice (A) is incorrect because there are two verbs (*was caused* and *was*) but only one subject. Choice (C) is incorrect because *Why* is not the appropriate noun-clause marker in this sentence; the noun clause is based on a statement, not on an information question. Choice (D) is incorrect because it forms an adverb clause, but the main clause lacks a subject. In the correct answer the noun clause itself (*That malaria was caused by breathing impure air*) is the subject of the verb *was* in the main clause.

One basic question psychologists have tried to answer is _____.

(A) people learn
(B) how do people learn
(C) people learn how
(D) how people learn

$\text{(A)} \ \text{(B)} \ \text{(C)} \ \bullet$

Choice (A) is incorrect; there is no connector between the first clause and the second. Choice (B) incorrectly follows question word order. (C) is incorrect because *how* is in the wrong position. ▲

Exercise 22

Focus: Completing structure problems involving incomplete noun clauses. (Note: Two or three items in this exercise do *not* focus on noun clauses. These items are marked in the answer key with asterisks.)

Directions: Choose the one option—(A), (B), (C), or (D)—that correctly completes the sentences, and then mark the appropriate blank. The first one is done as an example.

1. _____ begin their existence as ice crystals over most of the earth seems likely.
   _____ (A) Raindrops
   _____ (B) If raindrops
   _____ (C) What if raindrops
   __✔__ (D) That raindrops

2. Scientists cannot agree on _____ related to other orders of insects.
   _____ (A) that fleas are
   _____ (B) how fleas are
   _____ (C) how are fleas
   _____ (D) fleas that are

3. It was in 1875 _____ joined the staff of the astronomical observatory at Harvard University.
   _____ (A) that Anna Winlock
   _____ (B) Anna Winlock, who
   _____ (C) as Anna Winlock
   _____ (D) Anna Winlock then

4. _____ is a narrow strip of woods along a stream in an open grassland.
   _____ (A) Ecologists use the term "gallery forest"
   _____ (B) What do ecologists call a "gallery forest"
   _____ (C) "Gallery forest" is the term ecologists use
   _____ (D) What ecologists call a "gallery forest"

5. _____ developed very rapidly in Alabama primarily because of its rich natural resources.
   _____ (A) That heavy industry
   _____ (B) Heavy industry
   _____ (C) Heavy industry that was
   _____ (D) When heavy industry

6. _____ so incredible is that these insects successfully migrate to places that they have never even seen.
   _____ (A) That makes the monarch butterflies' migration
   _____ (B) The migration of the monach butterflies is
   _____ (C) What makes the monarch butterflies' migration
   _____ (D) The migration of the monarch butterflies, which is

7. Art critics do not all agree on what _____ a painting great.
   _____ (A) qualities make
   _____ (B) are the qualities for making
   _____ (C) qualities to make
   _____ (D) do the qualities that make

8. In order to grow vegetables properly, gardeners must know _____.
   _____ (A) what the requirements for each vegetable are
   _____ (B) that the requirements for each vegetable
   _____ (C) what are each vegetable's requirements
   _____ (D) that is required by each vegetable

9. When _____ is not known.
   _____ (A) was the wheel invented
   _____ (B) the invention of the wheel
   _____ (C) inventing the wheel
   _____ (D) the wheel was invented

10. For many years people have wondered _____ exists elsewhere in the universe.
    _____ (A) that life
    _____ (B) life which
    _____ (C) whether life
    _____ (D) life as it

11. _____ of all modern domestic poultry is the red jungle fowl is widely believed.
    _____ (A) The ancestor
    _____ (B) The ancestor is
    _____ (C) How the ancestor
    _____ (D) That the ancestor

12. _____ the right side of a person's brain is dominant, that person is left-handed.
    _____ (A) That
    _____ (B) If
    _____ (C) Which
    _____ (D) For

LESSON 23

INCOMPLETE OR MISSING PREPOSITIONAL PHRASES

A **prepositional phrase** consists of a **preposition** (*in, at, with, for, until,* and so on) followed by a noun phrase or pronoun, which is called the **prepositional object.** Prepositional phrases often describe relationships of time and location, among others.

> *In the autumn,* maple leaves turn red.
> Beacon Hill is one of the most famous neighborhoods *in Boston.*
> *With luck,* there won't be any more problems.
> This house was built *by John's grandfather.*

Often, prepositional phrases come at the beginning or end of sentences, but they may appear in other parts of the sentence as well.

The correct answer for this type of item may be a preposition, its object, or both, as well as other parts of the sentence.

You may see prepositions in distractors, especially before the subject of a sentence. Remember, the object of a preposition cannot correctly be the subject of a sentence, as in these examples:

> **In the autumn* is my favorite season.
> **Without a pencil* is no way to come to a test.

▼ Sample Items

_____ the unaided eye can see about 6,000 stars.

(A) A clear night
(B) It's a clear night
(C) On a clear night
(D) A clear night, when

Choice (A) is incorrect because there is no connector to join the noun phrase *a clear night* to the rest of the sentence. Choice (B) consists of an independent clause, but there is no connector to join it to the other clause. (D) seems to form a subordinate clause, but the clause lacks a verb.

_____ all the field crops grown in the United States are harvested with machines called combines.

(A) Of nearly
(B) Nearly
(C) That nearly
(D) Nearly of

Choices (A) and (D) are incorrect because the subject of a sentence (*all the field crops*) cannot be the object of a preposition (*of*). Choice (C) creates a noun clause, but the noun clause lacks a verb. ▲

Exercise 23

Focus: Completing structure problems involving prepositional phrases. (Note: One or two items in this exercises do *not* focus on prepositional phrases. These items are marked in the answer key with asterisks.)

Directions: Choose the one option—(A), (B), (C), or (D)— that correctly completes the sentence, and then mark the appropriate blank. The first one is done as an example.

1. Dynamite is ordinarily detonated _____ called a blasting cap.
   - _____ (A) a device is used
   - _____ (B) that a device
   - __✔__ (C) with a device
   - _____ (D) the use of a device

2. _____ seed of a flowering plant is covered by a dense protective coat.
   - _____ (A) On each
   - _____ (B) Each
   - _____ (C) Each of
   - _____ (D) That each

3. _____ 1900 there were some 300 bicycle factories in the United States, and they produced over a million bicycles.
   - _____ (A) In
   - _____ (B) Because in
   - _____ (C) It was in
   - _____ (D) That in

4. A thick layer of fat called blubber keeps whales warm even _____ coldest water.
   - _____ (A) although the
   - _____ (B) in the
   - _____ (C) the
   - _____ (D) of the

5. _____ the United States, the general movement of air masses is from west to east.
   - _____ (A) Across
   - _____ (B) To cross
   - _____ (C) They cross
   - _____ (D) It is across

6. The bark of a tree thickens _____.
   - _____ (A) with age
   - _____ (B) it gets older
   - _____ (C) as older
   - _____ (D) by age

7. A substance that is harmless to a person who has no allergies can cause mild to serious reactions in a person _____ allergies.
   - _____ (A) has
   - _____ (B) which having
   - _____ (C) whose
   - _____ (D) with

8. In 1886 a number of national unions formed the American Federation of Labor _____.
   - _____ (A) Samuel Gompers was its leader
   - _____ (B) under the leadership of Samuel Gompers
   - _____ (C) which, under Samuel Gompers' leadership
   - _____ (D) Samuel Gompers led it

9. Harmonicas, autoharps, and kazoos _____ folk instruments.
   _____ (A) are examples
   _____ (B) for example
   _____ (C) are examples of
   _____ (D) as examples of

10. _____ charming shops and restaurants, Old Town is the most picturesque section of Albuquerque.
    _____ (A) With its
    _____ (B) Its
    _____ (C) Because its
    _____ (D) For its

11. _____, such as banking and travel, in which computers are not a convenience but a necessity.
    _____ (A) Where some industries
    _____ (B) In some industries
    _____ (C) Some industries
    _____ (D) There are some industries

12. One of the oldest large suspension bridges still _____ today is the George Washington Bridge between New York City and Fort Lee, New Jersey.
    _____ (A) uses
    _____ (B) is used
    _____ (C) the use of
    _____ (D) in use

ANSWER SHEET
MINI-TEST 4: STRUCTURE

1. Ⓐ Ⓑ Ⓒ Ⓓ   6. Ⓐ Ⓑ Ⓒ Ⓓ   11. Ⓐ Ⓑ Ⓒ Ⓓ

2. Ⓐ Ⓑ Ⓒ Ⓓ   7. Ⓐ Ⓑ Ⓒ Ⓓ   12. Ⓐ Ⓑ Ⓒ Ⓓ

3. Ⓐ Ⓑ Ⓒ Ⓓ   8. Ⓐ Ⓑ Ⓒ Ⓓ   13. Ⓐ Ⓑ Ⓒ Ⓓ

4. Ⓐ Ⓑ Ⓒ Ⓓ   9. Ⓐ Ⓑ Ⓒ Ⓓ   14. Ⓐ Ⓑ Ⓒ Ⓓ

5. Ⓐ Ⓑ Ⓒ Ⓓ   10. Ⓐ Ⓑ Ⓒ Ⓓ   15. Ⓐ Ⓑ Ⓒ Ⓓ

MINI-TEST 4: STRUCTURE

Directions: The following sentences are incomplete. Beneath each of these sentences, there are four words or phrases, marked (A), (B), (C), and (D). Choose the one word or phrase that best completes the sentence. Then mark the appropriate answer either in the blanks next to the answer choices or on the answer sheet above.

1. _____ by Anna Baldwin in 1878.

_____ (A) The invention of the vacuum milking machine
_____ (B) That the vacuum milking machine was invented
_____ (C) The vacuum milking machine, which was invented
_____ (D) The vacuum milking machine was invented

2. Dry cleaning is the process _____ clothes are cleaned in liquids other than water.

_____ (A) by
_____ (B) which through
_____ (C) by which
_____ (D) through

3. Sand dunes are made of loose sand _____ up by the action of the wind.

_____ (A) it builds
_____ (B) builds
_____ (C) is building
_____ (D) built

4. _____ book *Jubilee*, which was based on the life of her great-grandmother, Margaret Walker was awarded the Pulitzer Prize.

_____ (A) For her
_____ (B) Her
_____ (C) It was her
_____ (D) That her

5. Job specialization takes place _____ of production is separated into occupations.

_____ (A) whenever the work is
_____ (B) when the work
_____ (C) is when the work
_____ (D) whenever working

6. _____ are hot is a common misconception.

    _____ (A) All deserts
    _____ (B) All deserts which
    _____ (C) Of all deserts
    _____ (D) That all deserts

7. _____ imaginative stories about the origin of the game of chess.

    _____ (A) Many of the
    _____ (B) Many
    _____ (C) There are many
    _____ (D) Of the many

8. _____ one of Canada's greatest engineering projects, is a twenty-seven mile long waterway between Lake Erie and Lake Ontario.

    _____ (A) Because the Welland Ship Canal is
    _____ (B) The Welland Ship Canal is
    _____ (C) That the Welland Ship Canal is
    _____ (D) The Welland Ship Canal,

9. A deep-tissue massage is a type of massage therapy _____ on one part of the body, such as the lower back.

    _____ (A) its concentration is
    _____ (B) concentrating
    _____ (C) why it concentrates
    _____ (D) to be concentrated

10. One of the most powerful optical telescopes, the "Big Eye" at Mt. Palomar _____ a two-hundred-inch mirror.

    _____ (A) has
    _____ (B) that has
    _____ (C) with
    _____ (D) it has

11. Elfego Baca, _____ legendary Mexican-American folk hero, was a lawman in New Mexico in the late 1880's.

    _____ (A) a
    _____ (B) who, as a
    _____ (C) was a
    _____ (D) and he was a

12. _____ relatively inexpensive, the metal pewter can be fashioned into beautiful and useful objects.

    _____ (A) Even it is
    _____ (B) Despite
    _____ (C) Nevertheless, it is
    _____ (D) Although

13. _____ is a general category that includes all mental states and activities.

    _____ (A) What do psychologists call cognition
    _____ (B) Psychologists call it cognition
    _____ (C) What psychologists call cognition
    _____ (D) Cognition, as it is called by psychologists, which

14. Nathaniel Hawthorne wrote four novels, _____ *The Scarlet Letter*, became an American literary classic.

    _____ (A) of which one,

    _____ (B) which one

    _____ (C) one of which,

    _____ (D) one was

15. _____ about four years for a new aircraft model to move from the preliminary design stage to the full-production stage.

    _____ (A) It takes

    _____ (B) Taking

    _____ (C) That takes

    _____ (D) To take

LESSON 24

WORD ORDER ITEMS

All of the answer choices for a Structure item involving **word order** contain more or less the same words, but they are arranged in four different orders. The word order is "scrambled" in three choices; one is correct. Most items consist of three or four words.

(A) X Y Z
(B) Y X Z
(C) Z Y X
(D) X Z Y

Word order problems are easy to identify because the answer choices are exactly—or almost exactly—the same length, so the answer choices form a rectangle.

(A) so far away from
(B) away so far from
(C) from so far away
(D) away from so far

Many different types of structures are used in word order problems. One of the most common is a phrase with a superlative adjective or adverb.

Word order items are the only Structure items in which the distractors can be ungrammatical. In other Structure problems, distractors are always correct in some context. However, at least two of the choices may be grammatical. The correct choice depends on the context of the sentence.

It sometimes is easy to eliminate distractors in word order items by making sure they "fit" the rest of the sentence. If you are not sure which remaining answer is correct, use your "ear." Say the sentence to yourself (silently) to see which sounds best. Sometimes in word order problems, the answer that looks best doesn't always sound best. Don't, however, go just by the sound of the answer choices; you must consider them as part of the whole sentence.

A special type of word order problem involves **inversions.** This type of sentence uses question word order even though the sentence is not a question. When are inversions used?

- **When the negative words listed below are placed at the beginning of a clause for emphasis**

not only	never
not until	seldom
not once	rarely
at no time	scarcely
by no means	no sooner
nowhere	

Not once *was he* on time.
Seldom *have I heard* such beautiful music.
Not only *did the company* lose profits, but it also had to lay off workers.

- **When the following expressions beginning with *only* occur at the beginning of a sentence (with these expressions, the subject and verb in that clause are inverted)**

only in (on, at, by, etc.)   only recently
only once

Only in an emergency *should you use* this exit.
Only recently *did she return* from abroad.
Only by asking questions *can you learn*.

- **When the following expressions beginning with *only* occur at the beginning of a sentence (with these expressions the subject and verb of the second clause are inverted)**

  only if   only when
  only because   only after
  only until

  Only if you have a serious problem *should you* call Mr. Franklin at home.
  Only when you are satisfied *is the sale* considered final.

- **When clauses beginning with the word *so* + an adjective or participle occur at the beginning of a sentence**

  So rare *is this coin* that it belongs in a museum.
  So confusing *was the map* that we had to ask a police officer for directions.

- **When clauses beginning with expressions of place or order occur at the start of a sentence (in these cases, the subject and main verb are inverted since auxiliary verbs are not used as they would be in most questions)**

  In front of the museum *is a statue*.
  Off the coast of California *lie the Channel Islands*.
  First *came a police car;* then *came an ambulance*.

▼ **Sample Items**

Andromeda is a galaxy containing millions of individual stars, but it is
_____ Earth that it looks like a blurry patch of light.

(A) so far away from
(B) away so far from
(C) from so far away
(D) away from so far

Only choice (A) involves the correct word order for this sentence. Choices (B) and (D) are incorrect word orders in any sentence. Choice (C) could be correct in certain sentences, but is not correct in the context of this sentence.

Not only _____ shade and beauty, but they also reduce carbon dioxide.

(A) do trees provide
(B) trees provide
(C) provide trees
(D) trees do provide

Only choice (A) correctly uses question word order after *not only*. Choices (B) and (C) do not use an auxiliary verb, which is required after *not only*. Choice (D) does not follow the correct word order: auxiliary + adjective + main verb. ▲

Exercise 24

Focus: Completing structure problems involving word order. (Note: *All* the items in this exercise focus on word order problems.)

Directions: Choose the one option—(A), (B), (C), or (D)—that correctly completes the sentence, and then mark the appropriate blank. The first one is done as an example.

1. Hills known as land islands, or salt domes, are _____ Louisiana's marshlands.
   - ___✔___ (A) extremely interesting features of
   - _____ (B) of extremely interesting features
   - _____ (C) interesting extremely features of
   - _____ (D) extremely interesting of features

2. _____ of chamber music is the string quartet.
   - _____ (A) The famous most form
   - _____ (B) The most famous form
   - _____ (C) The form most famous
   - _____ (D) Most the form famous

3. Not until the seventeenth century _____ to measure the speed of light.
   - _____ (A) did anyone even attempt
   - _____ (B) anyone did even attempt
   - _____ (C) did anyone attempt even
   - _____ (D) did even attempt anyone

4. Alfalfa is _____ for livestock.
   - _____ (A) a primarily grown crop
   - _____ (B) grown primarily a crop
   - _____ (C) a crop grown primarily
   - _____ (D) a grown crop primarily

5. The Franklin stove, which became common in the 1790's, burned wood _____ an open fireplace.
   - _____ (A) efficiently more than much
   - _____ (B) much more efficiently than
   - _____ (C) much more than efficiently
   - _____ (D) more efficiently much than

6. Reinforced concrete is concrete that is strengthened by metal bars _____.
   - _____ (A) in it that are embedded
   - _____ (B) embedded that are in it
   - _____ (C) are that it embedded in
   - _____ (D) that are embedded in it

7. The type of clothing people wear tells others a lot about _____.
   - _____ (A) who they are
   - _____ (B) are they who
   - _____ (C) they are who
   - _____ (D) who are they

8. Most Southern states had set up primary school systems by the late eighteenth century, but only in New England _____ and open to all students.
   - _____ (A) primary schools were free
   - _____ (B) were primary schools free
   - _____ (C) free were primary schools
   - _____ (D) were free primary schools

9. Fungi,_____, do not produce chlorophyll.
   _____ (A) as such mushrooms
   _____ (B) mushrooms as such
   _____ (C) such as mushrooms
   _____ (D) mushrooms such as

10. Seldom _____ more than twenty minutes a night.
    _____ (A) sleep giraffes
    _____ (B) do giraffes sleep
    _____ (C) giraffes do sleep
    _____ (D) giraffes sleep

11. _____ of the early years of space exploration was the discovery of the Van Allen radiation belt in 1958.
    _____ (A) Perhaps the greatest triumph
    _____ (B) The triumph perhaps greatest
    _____ (C) The greatest perhaps triumph
    _____ (D) The triumph greatest perhaps

12. Today _____ major new products without conducting elaborate market research.
    _____ (A) corporations hardly introduce ever
    _____ (B) hardly ever corporations introduce
    _____ (C) hardly ever introduce corporations
    _____ (D) corporations hardly ever introduce

13. Across the Chesapeake Bay from the rest of the state _____, whose farms produce beans, tomatoes, and other garden vegetables.
    _____ (A) there lies Maryland's Eastern Shore
    _____ (B) lies Maryland's Eastern Shore
    _____ (C) Maryland's Eastern Shore lies there
    _____ (D) Maryland's Eastern Shore lies

14. Acidophilus bacteria are _____ in an acid medium.
    _____ (A) those that grow best
    _____ (B) those grow best that
    _____ (C) that those grow best
    _____ (D) grow best those that

15. _____ of great apes, the gibbon is the smallest.
    _____ (A) Four of the types
    _____ (B) The four of types
    _____ (C) Four types of the
    _____ (D) Of the four types

16. It is difficult _____ through swamps because of tangled roots and shallow waterways.
    _____ (A) to navigate even for small boats
    _____ (B) for even small boats to navigate
    _____ (C) even small boats for to navigate
    _____ (D) even to navigate for small boats

17. A lodestone is _____.
    _____ (A) an occurring naturally magnet
    _____ (B) a magnet naturally occurring
    _____ (C) naturally a magnet occurring
    _____ (D) a naturally occurring magnet

18. So complicated _____ that consumers who use a product are seldom aware of where all its components come from.
    _____ (A) today trade is international
    _____ (B) today international trade is
    _____ (C) is international trade today
    _____ (D) international trade is today

19. The snow bunting is _____ winter birds in Canada.
    _____ (A) one most of the common
    _____ (B) the most common one of
    _____ (C) one of the most common
    _____ (D) the one of most common

20. Nashville has _____ the capital of country music.
    _____ (A) as long been known
    _____ (B) been known long as
    _____ (C) long been known as
    _____ (D) long as been known

LESSON 25

ITEMS INVOLVING VERB PROBLEMS

The answer choices for this type of problem are all or almost all different forms of the same verb. From the context of the sentence stem, you'll have to decide which form works best in the sentence. Distractors are generally incorrect for one of these reasons:

- **The "verb" is not really a verb.**

  Used alone, an infinitive, gerund, or participle cannot be a main verb.

- **The verb is active but should be passive, or it is passive but should be active.**
  If the subject of the sentence *performs* the action, the verb must be in the active voice. If the subject of the sentence *receives* the action, the verb must be in the passive.

  The architect *designed* the building.
      (active verb)
  The building *was designed* by the architect.
      (passive verb)

- **The verb does not agree with its subject.**
  Singular subjects require singular verbs; plural subjects require plural verbs.

- **The verb is not in the right tense.**
  According to the time words or ideas in the sentence, the appropriate tense must be used.

- **An unnecessary element comes before the verb.**
  Personal pronouns (*he, she, it*), relative pronouns (*who, which, that*, and so on), or conjunctions (*and, but*, and so on) may be used unnecessarily before verbs in some sentences.

▼ **Sample Item**

    Before the late eighteenth century, most textiles _____ at home.

    (A) produced
    (B) was produced
    (C) producing
    (D) were produced

Choice (D) is the best answer. (A) can be considered either an active verb in the past tense or a past participle; both are incorrect. An active verb is incorrect because a passive verb is needed; a past participle is incorrect because a past participle cannot serve as a main verb. (B) is incorrect because the plural subject *textiles* requires a plural verb, *were*. (C) is incorrect because, by itself, an *-ing* form can never be a main verb. ▲

Exercise 25

Focus: Completing structure problems involving verb forms. (Note: One or two items in this exercises do *not* focus on finite verb forms. These items are marked in the answer key with asterisks.)

Directions: Choose the one option—(A), (B), (C), or (D)—that correctly completes the sentence, and then mark the appropriate blank. The first one is done as an example.

1. R. M. Bartlett of Philadelphia _____ the first private business college in the United States in 1843.
   - _____ (A) founding
   - __✔__ (B) founded
   - _____ (C) was founded
   - _____ (D) founds

2. In 1989 the space probe *Voyager 2* _____ by the planet Neptune.
   - _____ (A) fly
   - _____ (B) flown
   - _____ (C) flying
   - _____ (D) flew

3. A cupful of stagnant water may _____ millions of microorganisms.
   - _____ (A) contains
   - _____ (B) to contain
   - _____ (C) contain
   - _____ (D) containing

4. Computers and new methods of communication _____ revolutionized the modern office.
   - _____ (A) have
   - _____ (B) have been
   - _____ (C) having
   - _____ (D) has

5. Sarah Knight _____ a fascinating account of a journey she made from Boston to New York in 1704.
   - _____ (A) written
   - _____ (B) write
   - _____ (C) wrote
   - _____ (D) writing

6. All animals _____ on other animals or plants.
   - _____ (A) feed
   - _____ (B) feeds
   - _____ (C) fed
   - _____ (D) feeding

7. Chromium _____ in the manufacture of stainless steel.
   - _____ (A) using
   - _____ (B) is used
   - _____ (C) uses
   - _____ (D) is using

8. The Baltimore and Ohio Railroad _____ the first air conditioning system for trains in 1931.
   _____ (A) has installed
   _____ (B) installed
   _____ (C) to have installed
   _____ (D) installing

9. Porous rocks such as chalk and sandstone allow water _____ through them.
   _____ (A) soaks
   _____ (B) is soaked
   _____ (C) to soak
   _____ (D) can soak

10. By 1790, rice _____ an important crop in the South.
    _____ (A) being
    _____ (B) has been
    _____ (C) was
    _____ (D) was being

11. Weavers are social birds that _____ complex nests housing hundreds of families.
    _____ (A) build
    _____ (B) are built
    _____ (C) are building
    _____ (D) built

12. The American dancer Maria Tallchief first _____ prominent in Europe.
    _____ (A) to become
    _____ (B) become
    _____ (C) has become
    _____ (D) became

LESSON 26

INCOMPLETE OR MISSING INFINITIVE AND GERUND PHRASES

An **infinitive** is a verbal form that consists of the word *to* and the simple form of the verb: *to be, to go, to give, to build*. Infinitives are often followed by an object: *to give directions, to build a house*. Together, an infinitive and its object form an **infinitive phrase.**

Infinitives can be used in a variety of ways. They may be the subjects or objects of verbs or used after *to be* + adjective.

> *To read* the directions is important.   (infinitive as subject of a verb)
> He forgot *to read* the directions.   (infinitive as object of a verb)
> It's important *to read* the directions.   (infinitive after *to be* + adjective)

Infinitives can be used as adjective phrases after noun phrases. You will often see this in Structure problems after noun phrases containing the word *first*.

> John Glenn was the first American astronaut *to orbit* the Earth.

Infinitives can also be used to show purpose. In other words, they explain why an action takes place. (The phrase *in order* + infinitive also shows purpose.) These infinitive phrases often come at the beginning of a sentence, and are set off by commas.

> *To learn how to dance*, he took lessons.
> *In order to learn how to dance*, he took lessons.

You may see Structure items that focus on **passive infinitives.** A passive infinitive consists of the word *to* + *be* + past participle.

> Roberta was the first person *to be asked* to speak at the meeting.

A **gerund** is a verbal form that ends in *-ing: being, going, giving, building*. Like infinitives, gerunds are often followed by objects: *giving directions, building a house*. Together, a gerund and its object form a **gerund phrase.**

Gerunds are verbal nouns, and are used as other nouns are used. You will generally see gerunds as subjects or objects of verbs or as objects of prepositions. (Note: Infinitives can also be subjects and objects but *never* objects of prepositions.)

> *Playing* cards is enjoyable.   (gerund as subject of a verb)
> He enjoys *playing* cards.   (gerund as object of a verb)
> He passes the time by *playing* cards.   (gerund as object of a preposition)

▼ **Sample Items**

_____ the eggs of most birds must be kept warm.

(A) Proper development
(B) By properly developing,
(C) They develop properly
(D) To develop properly,

The only one of these for phrases listed here that can show purpose is choice (D), an infinitive. This expression means *in order to develop properly.*

In 1959 the political philosopher Hannah Arendt became the first woman
_____ a full professor at Princeton University.

(A) to appoint
(B) was appointed
(C) to be appointed
(D) an appointment as

$$\text{(A)} \quad \text{(B)} \quad \bullet \quad \text{(D)}$$

After a noun phrase such as *the first woman* an infinitive is used as an adjective
phrase. Because a passive form is needed (Hannah Arendt receives the action; she
doesn't perform the action), choice (A) is not the correct infinitive form. Choice (C),
a passive infinitive, is best.

The ear is the organ of hearing, but it also plays a role in _____
balance.

(A) maintaining
(B) it maintains
(C) to maintain
(D) maintained

$$\bullet \quad \text{(B)} \quad \text{(C)} \quad \text{(D)}$$

A gerund is used correctly after a preposition. Choices (B), (C), and (D) would not
be appropriate after a preposition. ▲

Exercise 26

Focus: Completing structure problems involving infinitive and gerund phrases. (Note: One or two of
the items in this exercise do *not* focus on infinitives or gerunds. These items are marked in the
answer key with asterisks.)

Directions: Choose the one option—(A), (B), (C), or (D)—that correctly completes the sentence,
and then mark the appropriate blank. The first one is done as an example.

1. _____ for a career in dance generally begins at an early age.
   _____ (A) People train
   _____ (B) That people train
   _____ (C) If training
   ✔ (D) Training

2. A baby's first teeth _____ are generally the lower incisors.
   _____ (A) appearance
   _____ (B) appear
   _____ (C) to appear
   _____ (D) in appearing

3. A climbing helmet _____ protection for a rock-climber's head from falling rocks and
   other hazards.
   _____ (A) to provide
   _____ (B) provides
   _____ (C) providing
   _____ (D) that provides

4. Power tools require careful handling _____ injuries.
   _____ (A) by avoiding
   _____ (B) they avoid
   _____ (C) to avoid
   _____ (D) that avoid

5. An electromagnet is created _____ electrical current through a coil of wire.
   _____ (A) by passing
   _____ (B) passes by
   _____ (C) to be passed
   _____ (D) passed

6. _____ at home requires only three types of chemicals, several pieces of simple equipment, and running water.
   _____ (A) For the development of film
   _____ (B) To develop film
   _____ (C) When film is developed
   _____ (D) In developing film

7. The purpose of cost accounting is _____ involved in producing and selling a good or service.
   _____ (A) as a determination of its costs
   _____ (B) the costs determined
   _____ (C) that determines the costs
   _____ (D) to determine the costs

8. _____ was one of the most difficult tasks pioneers faced on their journeys west.
   _____ (A) Crossing rivers
   _____ (B) While crossing rivers
   _____ (C) Rivers being crossed
   _____ (D) By crossing rivers

9. Energy can be defined as the ability _____.
   _____ (A) do working
   _____ (B) to do work
   _____ (C) doing work
   _____ (D) work to be done

10. The process of _____ by hand has changed little since the fifteenth century.
    _____ (A) to bind books
    _____ (B) binding books
    _____ (C) books are bound
    _____ (D) bound books

11. A crescent wrench has adjustable jaws for _____ a nut, bolt, or pipe.
    _____ (A) to grip
    _____ (B) they grip
    _____ (C) gripping
    _____ (D) gripped

12. Compressed air is _____ air brakes, pneumatic tools, and other machinery.
    _____ (A) used to powering
    _____ (B) to use power
    _____ (C) used to power
    _____ (D) in use by powering

13. Some people believe that the crystals of certain minerals _____ curative powers.
    _____ (A) have
    _____ (B) having
    _____ (C) that have
    _____ (D) to have

14. The narrow blades of speed skates allow _____ speeds of up to 30 miles per hour.
    _____ (A) for skaters maintaining
    _____ (B) skaters to maintain
    _____ (C) skaters maintain
    _____ (D) maintenance by skaters

15. The first library _____ in the Nebraska Territory was built in Fort Atkinson in 1870.
    _____ (A) to be established
    _____ (B) was established
    _____ (C) could establish
    _____ (D) to establish

LESSON 27

ITEMS INVOLVING PARALLEL STRUCTURES

In certain Structure items, the correct use of **parallel structures** is tested. Parallel structures have the same grammatical form and function. Look at the following sentences:

> She spends her leisure time *hiking, camping,* and *fishing.*
> He *changed* the oil, *checked* the tire pressure, and *filled* the tank with gas.
> Nancy plans to either *study* medicine or *major* in biology.
> Nancy plans to study either *medicine* or *biology.*

All of the structures in italics are parallel. In the first, three gerunds are parallel; in the second, three main verbs; in the third, two simple forms; in the fourth, two nouns. Many other structures must be parallel in certain sentences: adjectives, adverbs, infinitives, prepositional phrases, noun clauses, and others.

The most common situation in which parallel structures are required is in a sequence (*A, B,* and *C*) as in the first two sentences above. Parallel structures are also required with correlative conjunctions such as *either . . . or* or *not only . . . but also.* (Correlative conjunctions are presented in Lesson 30.)

▼   **Sample Item**

San Francisco has a pleasant climate, _____ and many fascinating neighborhoods.

(A) exciting scenery,
(B) has exciting scenery
(C) that the scenery is exciting
(D) the scenery is exciting,

This sentence contains a series of three objects after the verb *has:* the first and third are noun phrases (*a pleasant climate* and *many fascinating neighborhoods*). To be parallel, the second object must also be a noun phrase. Therefore, choice (A) is the correct answer; (B), (C), and (D) are not parallel.   ▲

Exercise 27

Focus: Completing structure problems involving parallelism. (Note: One or two items in the exercise do *not* focus on items involving parallel structures. These items are marked in the answer key with asterisks.)

Directions: Choose the one option—(A), (B), (C), or (D)—that correctly completes the sentence, and then mark the appropriate blank. The first one is done as an example.

1. Insects provide many beneficial services, such as _____, breaking down deadwood, and pollinating plants.
   _____ (A) they condition soil
   _____ (B) to condition soil
   ✔ (C) conditioning the soil
   _____ (D) soil conditioned

2. Frozen orange juice must be packed, _____, and stored when the fruit is ripe.
   _____ (A) be frozen
   _____ (B) must be frozen
   _____ (C) frozen
   _____ (D) it must be frozen

3. Sioux is a North American Indian language that is spoken not only _____ Sioux but also by the Crow and Osage tribes.
   _____ (A) by the
   _____ (B) the
   _____ (C) do the
   _____ (D) and the

4. In 1900 electrically powered cars were more popular than gasoline powered cars because they were quiet, operated smoothly, and _____.
   _____ (A) handled easily
   _____ (B) ease of handling
   _____ (C) handling easily
   _____ (D) easy to handle

5. Roger Williams was a clergyman, _____ the colony of Rhode Island, and an outspoken advocate of religious and political freedom.
   _____ (A) founded
   _____ (B) the founder of
   _____ (C) was the founder of
   _____ (D) he founded

6. Paint can be applied to a surface with rollers, _____, or spray guns.
   _____ (A) brushes
   _____ (B) brushes can be used
   _____ (C) with brushes
   _____ (D) by brush

7. The use of labor-saving devices in homes, _____, and factories added to the amount of leisure time people had.
   _____ (A) at an office
   _____ (B) used in offices
   _____ (C) offices
   _____ (D) in offices

8. A dulcimer can be played by either striking its strings with a hammer or _____.
   _____ (A) to pluck them with the fingers
   _____ (B) fingers are used to pluck them
   _____ (C) they are plucked with the fingers
   _____ (D) plucking them with the fingers

9. Throughout history, trade routes have increased contact between people, _____, and greatly affected the growth of civilization.
   _____ (A) have resulted in an exchange of ideas
   _____ (B) an exchange of ideas has resulted
   _____ (C) resulted in an exchange of ideas
   _____ (D) resulting in an exchange of ideas

10. Walt Disney made many technical advances in the use of sound, color, and _____ in animated films.
    _____ (A) photographing
    _____ (B) using photography
    _____ (C) photography
    _____ (D) use of photographs

11. Artist Paul Kane traveled throughout Northwest Canada on foot, by canoe, and _____ to sketch Native Canadians going about their ordinary lives.
    _____ (A) on horseback
    _____ (B) riding a horse
    _____ (C) horseback
    _____ (D) by a horse

12. Barbara Jordan was the first woman in the South to win an election to the House of Representatives, _____ as Congresswoman from Texas from 1973 to 1979.
    _____ (A) to serve
    _____ (B) served
    _____ (C) serving
    _____ (D) has served

13. Photographers' choice of a camera depends on what kind of pictures they want to take, how much control they want over exposure, and _____ they want to spend.
    _____ (A) the amount of money
    _____ (B) what money
    _____ (C) how much money
    _____ (D) so much money that

14. Atlanta is the commercial, financial, and _____ of Georgia.
    _____ (A) center of administration
    _____ (B) administrative center
    _____ (C) center for administering
    _____ (D) administering center

15. Even after the Revolutionary War, American importers obtained merchandise from Britain because British merchants understood American tastes, offered attractive prices, and _____ .
    _____ (A) easy credit was provided
    _____ (B) because of easy credit
    _____ (C) easy credit
    _____ (D) provided easy credit

LESSON 28

ITEMS INVOLVING MISPLACED MODIFIERS

A **misplaced modifier** is a participial phrase or other modifier that comes before the subject, but does *not* refer to the subject.
Look at this sentence:

> *Driving down the road, a herd of sheep suddenly crossed the road in front of Liza's car.
> (INCORRECT)

This sentence is incorrect because it seems to say that a herd of sheep—rather than Liza—was driving down the road. The participial phrase is misplaced. The sentence could be corrected as shown:

> As Liza was driving down the road, a herd of sheep suddenly crossed the road in front of her. (CORRECT)

This sentence now correctly has Liza in the driver's seat instead of the sheep.
The following sentence structures are often misplaced:

Misplaced Structure	Example	Correction
present participle	Walking along the beach, the ship was spotted by the men.	Walking along the beach, the men spotted the ship.
past participle	Based on this study, the scientist could draw several conclusions.	Based on this study, several conclusions could be drawn by the scientist.
appositive	A resort city in Arkansas, the population of Hot Springs is about 35,000.	A resort city in Arkansas, Hot Springs has a population of about 35,000.
reduced adjective clause	While peeling onions, his eyes began to water.	While he was peeling onions, his eyes began to water.
adjective phrases	Warm and mild, everyone enjoys the climate of the Virgin Islands.	Everyone enjoys the warm, mild climate of the Virgin Islands.
expressions with *like* or *unlike*	Like most cities, parking is a problem in San Francisco.	Like most cities, San Francisco has a parking problem.

Structure items with misplaced modifiers are usually easy to spot. They generally consist of a modifying element at the beginning of the sentence followed by a comma, with the rest or most of the rest of the sentence missing. The answer choices tend to be long. To find the answer, you must decide what subject the modifier correctly refers to.

▼ Sample Item

Using a device called a cloud chamber, _____.

(A) experimental proof for the atomic theory was found by Robert Millikin
(B) Robert Millikin's experimental proof for the atomic theory was found
(C) Robert Millikin found experimental proof for the atomic theory
(D) there was experimental proof found for the atomic theory by Robert Millikin

Choice (A) and (B) are incorrect because the modifier (*Using a device called a cloud chamber . . .*) could not logically refer to the subjects (*experimental proof* and *Robert Millikin's experimental proof*). (D) is incorrect because a modifier can never properly refer to the introductory word *there* or *it*.   ▲

Exercise 28

Focus: Completing structure problems involving misplaced modifiers. (Note: *all* the items in this exercise focus on misplaced modifiers.)

Directions: Choose the one option—(A), (B), (C), or (D)—that correctly completes the sentences, and then mark the appropriate blank. The first one is done as an example.

1. Fearing economic hardship, _____.
    __✔__ (A) many New Englanders emigrated to the Midwest in the 1820's
    _____ (B) emigration from New England to the Midwest took place in the 1820's
    _____ (C) it was in the 1820's that many New Englanders emigrated to the Midwest
    _____ (D) an emigration took place in the 1820's from New England to the Midwest

2. Rich and distinctive in flavor, _____.
    _____ (A) there is in the United States a very important nut crop, the pecan
    _____ (B) the most important nut crop in the United States, the pecan
    _____ (C) farmers in the United States raise pecans, a very important nut crop
    _____ (D) pecans are the most important nut crop in the United States

3. Orbiting from 2.7 to 3.6 billion miles from the sun, _____.
    _____ (A) the astronomer Clyde Tombaugh discovered Pluto in 1930
    _____ (B) Pluto was discovered by the astronomer Clyde Tombaugh in 1930
    _____ (C) it was in 1930 that the astronomer Clyde Tombaugh discovered Pluto
    _____ (D) the discovery of Pluto was made by Clyde Tombaugh in 1930

4. A popular instrument, _____.
    _____ (A) only a limited role has been available to the accordion in classical music
    _____ (B) there is only a limited role for the accordion in classical music
    _____ (C) classical music provides only a limited role for the accordion
    _____ (D) the accordion has played only a limited role in classical music

5. Unlike most birds, _____.
    _____ (A) the heads and necks of vultures lack feathers
    _____ (B) feathers are not found on the heads and necks of vultures
    _____ (C) vultures do not have feathers on their heads and necks
    _____ (D) there are no feathers on vultures' heads and necks

6. Widely reproduced in magazines and books, _____.
    _____ (A) Ansel Adams depicted the Western wilderness in his photographs
    _____ (B) the Western wilderness was depicted in the photographs of Ansel Adams
    _____ (C) Ansel Adams's photographs depicted the Western wilderness
    _____ (D) it was through his photographs that Ansel Adams depicted the Western wilderness

7. Smaller and flatter than an orange, _____.
    _____ (A) a tangerine is easy to peel and its sections separate readily
    _____ (B) the peel of a tangerine is easily removed and its sections are readily separated
    _____ (C) it's easy to peel a tangerine and to separate its sections
    _____ (D) to peel a tangerine is easy, and its sections can be readily separated

8. Like the federal government, _____.

   _____ (A) taxation provides most of the funds for state and local governments as well

   _____ (B) state and local governments obtain most of their funds through taxation

   _____ (C) through taxation is how state and local governments obtain most of their funds

   _____ (D) funds are provided from taxation for state and local governments

9. Originally settled by Polynesians around 700 A.D., _____.

   _____ (A) Hawaii received its first European visitor in 1778, when Captain James Cook landed there

   _____ (B) Hawaii's first European visitor, Captain James Cook, landed there in 1778

   _____ (C) in 1778 the first European, Captain James Cook, visited Hawaii

   _____ (D) the first European to visit Hawaii was Captain James Cook, landing there in 1778

10. Unlike most modernist poets, _____ based on ordinary speech.

    _____ (A) Robert Frost's poems were

    _____ (B) the works of Robert Frost were

    _____ (C) Robert Frost wrote poems that were

    _____ (D) the poetry written by Robert Frost was

11. Named for its founder, _____ in Ithaca, New York.

    _____ (A) in 1865 Ezra Cornell established Cornell University

    _____ (B) Cornell University was established in 1865 by Ezra Cornell

    _____ (C) it was in 1865 that Cornell University was established by Ezra Cornell

    _____ (D) Ezra Cornell established Cornell University in 1865

12. While living in New Orleans, _____ the Creole people of Louisiana.

    _____ (A) a book of folklore, *Bayou Folk,* was written by Kate Chopin about

    _____ (B) *Bayou Folk,* a book of folklore, was written by Kate Chopin about

    _____ (C) the subject of Kate Chopin's book *Bayou Folk* was the folklore of

    _____ (D) Kate Chopin wrote *Bayou Folk,* a book about the folklore of

LESSON 29

INCOMPLETE OR MISSING COMPARISONS

You may see sentences in the Structure section that contain comparisons. Many of these involve the comparative forms of adjectives.

> On the average, the Pacific Ocean is *deeper than* the Atlantic.
> Rhonda is a *more experienced* performer *than* Theresa.
> This show is *less interesting than* the one we watched last night.

Be sure that the sentence compares similar things or concepts.

> **The ears of African elephants* are bigger than *Indian elephants*. (INCORRECT)
> *The ears of African elephants* are bigger than *those of of Indian elephants*. (CORRECT)

The first sentence above is incorrect because it compares two dissimilar things: African elephants' ears and Indian elephants. In the second, the word *those* refers to ears, so the comparison is between similar things.

Another type of comparison involves the phrase *as . . . as*.

> The lab session lasted *as long as* the class did.
> There weren't *as many people at the meeting as* I had thought there would be.

The words *like/alike* and *unlike/not alike* can also be used to express comparison:

Like A, B . . .	Unlike X, Y . . .
A, like B, . . .	X, unlike Y, . . .
A is like B.	X is unlike Y.
A and B are alike.	X and Y are not alike.

In these sentences, similar-looking words such as *likely, likewise, dislike,* and *unlikely* may appear as distractors.

Other phrases can be used in making comparisons:

A is the same as B	X is different from Y
A and B are the same	X and Y are different
A is similar to B	X differs from Y

A special kind of comparison is called a **proportional statement.** A proportional statement follows this pattern: *The more A . . . the more B.*

> *The higher* the humidity, *the more uncomfortable* people feel.

▼ Sample Items

Subtropical zones _____ temperate zones, but they still have distinct summer and winter seasons.

(A) that are warmer
(B) warmer
(C) are warmer as
(D) are warmer than

Choice (A) creates a relative clause, which is not appropriate in this sentence; also, the choice lacks the word *than.* Choice (B) lacks both a verb and the word *than.* (C) incorrectly uses *as* in place of *than.*

_____ other mammals, whales do not have a sense of smell.

(A) Not alike
(B) Unlike
(C) Unlikely
(D) Dislike

Ⓐ ⬤ Ⓒ Ⓓ

Choice (A) is used only in the pattern "A and B are not alike." (C) and (D) are not used in comparisons; *unlikely* is an adjective meaning "not probable"; *dislike* is a verb meaning "not enjoy, not admire."

_____ the diameter of a circle, the larger its circumference is.

(A) Greater than
(B) The greater
(C) Great as
(D) As great as

Ⓐ ⬤ Ⓒ Ⓓ

The correct pattern for a proportional statement is *the more A . . . the more B.* Only choice (B) follows this pattern. ▲

Exercise 29

Focus: Completing structure problems involving comparisons. (Note: *All* the items in this exercise focus on comparisons.)

Directions: Choose the option—(A), (B), (C), or (D)—that correctly completes the sentence, and then mark the appropriate blank. The first one is done as an example.

1. Sea bass _____ freshwater bass.
   __✔__ (A) are larger than
   _____ (B) the larger the
   _____ (C) are as large
   _____ (D) are larger

2. Wild strawberries are _____ as cultivated strawberries.
   _____ (A) not so sweet
   _____ (B) not as sweet
   _____ (C) less sweeter
   _____ (D) not as sweeter

3. Automobiles, airplanes, and buses use more energy per passenger _____.
   _____ (A) as do trains
   _____ (B) than trains do
   _____ (C) trains do
   _____ (D) like trains

4. The larger a drop of water, _____ freezing temperature.
   _____ (A) the higher its
   _____ (B) its higher
   _____ (C) higher than its
   _____ (D) higher of its

5. _____ San Diego and San Francisco, Los Angeles has no natural harbor.
   _____ (A) Dissimilar
   _____ (B) Unlike
   _____ (C) Dislike
   _____ (D) Different

6. The water of the Great Salt Lake is _____ seawater.
   _____ (A) saltier than that of
   _____ (B) as salty as that of
   _____ (C) saltier than
   _____ (D) so salty as

7. A psychosis is a severe mental disorder, _____ a neurosis.
   _____ (A) the most serious
   _____ (B) as serious
   _____ (C) more serious than
   _____ (D) as though serious

8. The social system of bumblebees is not as complex _____.
   _____ (A) than honeybees
   _____ (B) as honeybees
   _____ (C) that honeybees are
   _____ (D) as that of honeybees

9. The administration of private colleges is nearly _____ that of public colleges.
   _____ (A) same
   _____ (B) just as
   _____ (C) the same as
   _____ (D) similar

10. _____ a river on land, an ocean current does not flow in a straight line.
    _____ (A) Alike
    _____ (B) Like
    _____ (C) Likewise
    _____ (D) Likely

11. The skin temperature of humans is _____ their internal temperature.
    _____ (A) not high as
    _____ (B) not so high
    _____ (C) as low
    _____ (D) lower than

12. A butterfly _____ a moth in a number of ways.
    _____ (A) is different from
    _____ (B) is different
    _____ (C) the difference is
    _____ (D) differing from

LESSON 30

MISSING CONJUNCTIONS

Conjunctions are connecting words; they join parts of a sentence. In this lesson, we'll look at two types of conjunctions.

    Coordinate conjunctions are used to join equal sentence parts: single words, phrases, and independent clauses. When two full clauses are joined, they are usually separated by a comma. The coordinate conjunctions you will most often see in Structure problems are listed in the chart below:

Coordinate Conjunction	Use	Examples
and	addition	Hereford cows are brown *and* white. He washed his car *and* cleaned out the garage.
or	choice, possibility	This plant can be grown in a house *or* in a garden. Her action was very brave *or* very foolish.
but	contrast, opposition	He brought his wallet *but* forgot his checkbook. The book discussed some interesting ideas, *but* it wasn't very well written.
nor	negation	He's never taken a class in sociology, *nor* does he intend to.
so	effect	It was a bright day, *so* she put on her sunglasses.

(The conjunction *so* is used to join only clauses—not single words or phrases.)

Conjunctive adverbs (*moreover, therefore, however, nevertheless,* and so on) are also used to join clauses, but in Structure problems, these words are most often used as distractors—they seldom appear as correct answers.

    Correlative conjunctions are two-part conjunctions. Like coordinate conjunctions, they are used to join clauses, phrases, and words.

Correlative Conjunction	Use	Example
both . . . and	addition	*Both* wolves *and* coyotes are members of the dog family.
not only . . . but also	addition	Dominic studied *not only* mathematics *but also* computer science.
either . . . or	choice, possibility	We need *either* a nail *or* a screw to hang up this picture.
neither . . . nor	negation (not A and not B)	*Neither* the television *nor* the stereo had been turned off.

▼ **Sample Items**

The automobile began as a toy _____ developed into a powerful force for social change.

(A) it
(B) but
(C) when
(D) or

A ● C D

There is a contrast in this sentence; the role of the automobile as a toy in its early days is contrasted with its later role as a force for social change. The only word among the four choices that indicates contrast is choice (B), *but.*

Singer Marian Anderson trained _____ in the United States and abroad.

(A) not just
(B) and
(C) both
(D) not only

A B ● D

The correct structure for this sentence is *both . . . and.* Choices (A), (B), and (D) do not follow this pattern. (In choice (D), *not only* must be paired with *but also* to be correct.) ▲

Exercise 30

Focus: Completing structure problems involving conjunctions. (Note: One or two of the items in this exercise do *not* focus on conjunctions. These items are marked in the answer key with asterisks.)

Directions: Choose the one option—(A), (B), (C), or (D)—that correctly completes the sentence, and then mark the appropriate blank. The first one is done as an example.

1. Blindfish, which spend their whole lives in caves, have _____ eyes nor body pigments.
   _____ (A) not any
   ✔ (B) neither
   _____ (C) nor
   _____ (D) without

2. Specialty stores, unlike department stores, handle only one line of merchandise _____ a limited number of closely related lines.
   _____ (A) either
   _____ (B) but
   _____ (C) instead
   _____ (D) or

3. Thomas Eakins studied not only painting _____ anatomy when he was training to become an artist.
   _____ (A) moreover
   _____ (B) but also
   _____ (C) as well
   _____ (D) and

4. Although topology is the youngest branch of geometry, _____ is considered the most sophisticated.
   _____ (A) but it
   _____ (B) so it
   _____ (C) it
   _____ (D) however it

5. In 1923 Jean Toomer wrote a book titled *Cane*, which combined fiction _____ poetry to describe the experience of being black in the United States.
   _____ (A) and
   _____ (B) to
   _____ (C) also
   _____ (D) or

6. Endive can be used _____ as a salad green or as a cooking vegetable.
   _____ (A) such
   _____ (B) both
   _____ (C) either
   _____ (D) neither

7. Glucose does not have to be digested, _____ it can be put directly into the bloodstream.
   _____ (A) so
   _____ (B) while
   _____ (C) and since
   _____ (D) nor

8. Natural fiber comes from either animal _____ plant sources.
   _____ (A) or
   _____ (B) otherwise
   _____ (C) and
   _____ (D) nor

9. Paint is _____ used to protect wood.
   _____ (A) not only the substance
   _____ (B) the substance which is not only
   _____ (C) not only a substance which is
   _____ (D) not the only substance

10. An acoustic engineer's purpose in designing a factory is to suppress sound, _____ his or her purpose in designing a concert hall is to transmit sound faithfully.
    _____ (A) or
    _____ (B) so
    _____ (C) but
    _____ (D) which

11. Demographers believe most metropolitan areas will continue to grow in _____ population and area in the future.
    _____ (A) moreover
    _____ (B) both
    _____ (C) together
    _____ (D) besides

12. Most crustaceans live in the sea, _____ some live in fresh water and a few have ventured onto land.
    _____ (A) both
    _____ (B) also
    _____ (C) but
    _____ (D) and

LESSON 31

MISSING NEGATIVE WORDS

The answer choices for this type of item are four negative expressions, such as the ones listed below:

Negative Word	Use	Meaning	Example
no	adjective	not any	There was *no* milk in the refrigerator.
none	pronoun	not one	They took a lot of pictures, but almost *none* of them turned out.
nothing	pronoun	not anything	There was *nothing* in his briefcase.
no one	pronoun	not anyone	*No one* arrived at the meeting on time.
nor	conjunction	and . . . not	He's never been fishing, *nor* does he plan to go.
without	preposition	not having	She likes her coffee *without* milk or sugar.
never	adverb	at no time	I've *never* been to Alaska.

The negative word *not* is used to make almost any kind of word or phrase negative: verbs, prepositional phrases, infinitives, adjectives, and so on.

Both *no* and *not* can be used before nouns, depending on meaning.

There is *no* coffee in the pot.   (It's empty.)
This is *not* coffee.   (It's tea.)

The adjective *no* is also used before the word *longer* to mean "not anymore."

I *no longer* read the afternoon paper.

▼ Sample Item

There is almost _____ vegetation in the Badlands, a barren region of South Dakota.

(A) not
(B) nor
(C) none
(D) no

Choices (A), (B), and (C) cannot be used before nouns as adjectives. ▲

By the way, probably the most common correct answer for this type of problem is the adjective *no*.

Exercise 31

Focus: Completing structure problems involving negative words. (Note: *All* the items in this exercise focus on negative words.)

Directions: Choose the one option—(A), (B), (C), or (D)—that correctly completes the sentence, and then mark the appropriate blank. The first one is done as an example.

1. Old Faithful is the most famous but _____ the most powerful geyser in Yellowstone National Park.
   _____ (A) none of
   _____ (B) no
   _____ (C) nothing
   __✔__ (D) not

2. Early carpenters, having _____ nails, had to use wooden pegs to secure their constructions.
   _____ (A) no
   _____ (B) not
   _____ (C) without
   _____ (D) neither

3. Joseph Priestly, the discoverer of oxygen, had little _____ interest in science until he met Benjamin Franklin in Paris.
   _____ (A) and not
   _____ (B) or no
   _____ (C) but not
   _____ (D) nor any

4. Mobile homes were _____ counted as permanent houses until the 1960 census.
   _____ (A) not
   _____ (B) nor
   _____ (C) no
   _____ (D) none

5. Most solo musicians play _____ sheet music in front of them.
   _____ (A) without
   _____ (B) not having
   _____ (C) lacking
   _____ (D) and no

6. Desertification is the creation of deserts where _____ had existed before.
   _____ (A) never
   _____ (B) no one
   _____ (C) none
   _____ (D) not one

7. Glass snakes are actually legless lizards, _____ snakes.
   _____ (A) no
   _____ (B) not
   _____ (C) nor
   _____ (D) none

8. There is _____ truth to the old expression "Lightning never strikes the same place twice."
   _____ (A) without
   _____ (B) none
   _____ (C) no
   _____ (D) not

9. _____ single person can be said to have invented the automobile.
   _____ (A) There was not a
   _____ (B) Nor a
   _____ (C) Not one of
   _____ (D) No

10. A serious study of physics is impossible _____ some knowledge of mathematics.
   _____ (A) not with
   _____ (B) no
   _____ (C) not having
   _____ (D) without

11. _____ two fingerprints have ever been found to be exactly the same.
   _____ (A) No
   _____ (B) Never
   _____ (C) Not
   _____ (D) None

12. One of the few stands of forest on the East Coast of the United States that has _____ been harvested is Hutcheson Forest in New Jersey.
   _____ (A) no
   _____ (B) never
   _____ (C) none
   _____ (D) nothing

13. Until the 1960's, customers could open small savings accounts at U.S. Post Offices, but that service is _____ offered.
   _____ (A) no longer
   _____ (B) not longer
   _____ (C) no long
   _____ (D) not along

14. _____ the reptiles alive today is capable of flight.
   _____ (A) No
   _____ (B) None of
   _____ (C) Not one
   _____ (D) Not

**ANSWER SHEET
MINI-TEST 5: STRUCTURE**

1. A B C D	6. A B C D	11. A B C D
2. A B C D	7. A B C D	12. A B C D
3. A B C D	8. A B C D	13. A B C D
4. A B C D	9. A B C D	14. A B C D
5. A B C D	10. A B C D	15. A B C D

MINI-TEST 5: STRUCTURE

Directions: The following sentences are incomplete. Beneath each of these sentences, there are four words or phrases, marked (A), (B), (C), and (D). Choose the one word or phrase that best completes the sentence. Then mark the appropriate answer either in the blanks next to the answer choices or on the answer sheet above.

1. _____, an organism must be able to adapt to changing factors in its environment.

   _____ (A) If survival
   _____ (B) For surviving
   _____ (C) To survive
   _____ (D) It survives

2. The art of landscape architecture is _____ that of architecture itself.

   _____ (A) almost as old as
   _____ (B) as almost old
   _____ (C) almost as old than
   _____ (D) old as almost

3. The Mummers' Parade has _____ every year in Philadelphia on New Year's Day since 1901.

   _____ (A) holding
   _____ (B) been holding
   _____ (C) held
   _____ (D) been held

4. Rarely _____ more than fifty miles from the coast.

   _____ (A) redwood trees grow
   _____ (B) redwood trees do grow
   _____ (C) grow redwood trees
   _____ (D) do redwood trees grow

5. Microorganisms live in extreme conditions of heat and cold where _____ other organisms can survive.

   _____ (A) not
   _____ (B) never
   _____ (C) no
   _____ (D) none

6. The higher one rises in the atmosphere, _____ the temperature generally becomes.

   _____ (A) colder than
   _____ (B) the colder
   _____ (C) the colder as
   _____ (D) is colder

7. Medical researchers are constantly looking for ways to control, _____, and cure diseases.

_____ (A) prevention
_____ (B) preventing
_____ (C) prevent
_____ (D) to prevent

8. Nerve cells, or neurons, _____ in the human body.

_____ (A) the most complex cells are
_____ (B) are the most complex cells
_____ (C) most complex the cells are
_____ (D) most are the complex cells

9. Released in 1915, _____.

_____ (A) D. W. Griffith made an epic film about the Civil War, *Birth of a Nation*
_____ (B) the Civil War was the subject of D. W. Griffith's epic film, *Birth of a Nation*
_____ (C) D. W. Griffith's epic film *Birth of a Nation* was about the Civil War
_____ (D) the subject of D. W. Griffith's epic film *Birth of a Nation* was the Civil War

10. _____ on barren slopes can help prevent erosion.

_____ (A) Planting trees
_____ (B) For trees to be planted
_____ (C) In order to plant trees
_____ (D) Trees are planted

11. Vermont is the only state in New England _____ an Atlantic coastline.

_____ (A) without
_____ (B) not with
_____ (C) which not having
_____ (D) doesn't have

12. In 1867 Hiram R. Revels _____ the first black to be elected to the U.S. Senate.

_____ (A) becoming
_____ (B) became
_____ (C) to have become
_____ (D) has become

13. Jupiter's moons can be easily seen through _____ binoculars or a small telescope.

_____ (A) either
_____ (B) if
_____ (C) whether
_____ (D) or

14. The Colorado beetle is a beautiful insect, _____ it causes a great deal of damage to food crops.

_____ (A) but
_____ (B) what
_____ (C) so
_____ (D) that

15. Judge Francis Hopkins is probably best known as a signer of the Declaration of Independence, but he also excelled as a poet, _____, and an orator.

_____ (A) as a musician
_____ (B) by playing music
_____ (C) a musician
_____ (D) he played music

Written Expression

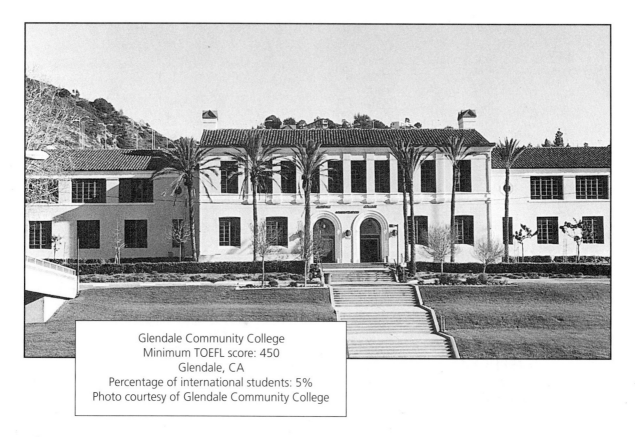

Glendale Community College
Minimum TOEFL score: 450
Glendale, CA
Percentage of international students: 5%
Photo courtesy of Glendale Community College

About Written Expression

In this part of the test, there are twenty-five sentences (thirty-seven on the long form). In each sentence, four expressions—single words or two- or three-word phrases—are underlined. Your job is to identify which of these phrases must be rewritten (it can't simply be omitted) in order for the sentence to be correct. All the errors involve grammar or usage—never punctuation or spelling.

▼ Sample Items

Music, <u>dramatic</u>, and <u>art</u> contribute to <u>the culture</u> of <u>any</u> community.
      A   B   C   D

This sentence should correctly read "Music, *drama*, and art contribute to the culture of any community." Choice (A) would have to be rewritten to correct the sentence, so (A) is the best answer.

Lenses may to have either concave or convex shapes.
         A   B   C   D

The correct verb form after a modal auxiliary is the simple form *have*. This sentence should read "Lenses may have either concave or convex shapes." The best answer is (A). ▲

What's the Best Way to Answer Written Expression Items?

You should begin with a quick reading of each sentence to find any obvious errors. **Don't** simply read the underlined portions, because in most items the underlined expression is incorrect only in the context of the sentence. **Don't** answer the question until you've read the entire sentence.

Easier questions can be answered after the first reading; mark your answer and go on. If you don't find the error immediately, re-read the sentence, now concentrating on the underlined expressions. You can't use the same techniques for reading these items as you would to read other materials, such as newspapers or magazine articles. Usually, a person's eyes move very quickly over "little words" like articles and prepositions because these words don't contain much information. However, in this part of the test, these expressions may be used incorrectly. It would be helpful, in fact, if you could read these sentences aloud, but of course that isn't permitted. You **can**, however, train your eyes to move slowly and to pronounce the sentences in your mind exactly as if you were speaking them.

If you haven't identified the error after a careful reading of the sentence, go through a mental checklist of the most common errors: word form, word choice, verb error, parallelism, pronoun errors, and singular/plural noun errors. Do the underlined expressions seem to fit into any of these categories?

If you still can't find an error, eliminate expressions that seem to be used correctly, and then make a guess from any choices that remain.

Type of Error	Frequency of Errors in Written Expression* Percentage
Word Form	21
Word Choice	15
Verbs	10
Parallel Structures	9
Pronouns	8
Singular/Plural Nouns	8
Verbals (Infinitives, Gerunds, and Participles)	6
Prepositions	6
Articles	5
Word Order	5
Comparatives and Superlatives	3
Conjunctions	2
Other Types of Errors	2

* Based on an analysis of 20 different exams that test-takers were allowed to keep after Disclosed Test Admissions.

In this section of the *Guide*, the lessons follow the same order as given in the chart above. The most common error, which involves incorrect word forms, is considered first, and so on. Each type of error is explained, and examples are provided. There are exercises to help you practice identifying all these types of errors.

When taking actual exams, once you've found an error, don't worry about how to correct it. However, while working the exercises in this *Guide*, it's important to understand **why** an item is incorrect, so most of the exercises ask you not just to identify errors but to supply corrections as well.

Tactics for Written Expression

- Skim each sentence, looking for obvious errors.

- If you haven't found the error, read the sentence again carefully, concentrating on the underlined parts. Go through a mental checklist of the most common types of errors (those involving word form, word choice, parallelism, verbs, pronouns, and singular/plural nouns) to see if any of the underlined expressions seem to fall into those categories.

- If you are still unable to find an error, try eliminating options that seem to be correct. If more than one option remains, put a mark by the number of that item on your answer sheet, and then take a guess and go on.

- If you finish before time is called, go back and work on Section 2 problems that you marked as difficult. Make sure you have an answer for every problem. Don't go on to Section 3.

LESSON 32

ERRORS WITH WORD FORMS

By far the most common type of Written Expression error involves word forms. As many as eight or nine items per test may be word-form problems. Most errors of this type involve using one part of speech in place of another. Both the incorrect word and the correction come from the same root (*rapid* and *rapidly*, for example, or *inform* and *information*). The four parts of speech generally involved are verbs, nouns, adjectives, and adverbs. The most common problems are adjectives in place of adverbs and adverbs in place of adjectives. Nouns in place of adjectives and adjectives in place of nouns are also commonly seen. In some word-form problems, different forms of the same part of speech may be involved. For example, a noun that refers to a person (*leader*) may be used in place of the field (*leadership*). A gerund (a verbal noun) may also be used in place of an ordinary noun (*judging* and *judgment*, for example).

Parts of speech can often be identified by their suffixes (word endings):

Common Noun Endings

-tion	information	-ery	recovery
-sion	provision	-ship	scholarship
-ence	existence	-tude	multitude
-ance	acceptance	-ism	capitalism
-ity	creativity	-cracy	democracy
-hood	childhood	-logy	biology
-dom	wisdom	-ness	happiness
-th	health	-ment	experiment

Endings for Nouns That Refer to Persons

-er	explorer	-ee	employee
-or	sailor	-ic	comic
-ist	psychologist	-ian	technician
-ent	student	-ant	attendant

Common Verb Endings

-ize	realize	-ify	satisfy
-en	shorten	-ate	incorporate
-er	recover		

Common Adjective Endings			
-ate	moderate	-y	sunny
-ous	dangerous	-ic	economic
-al	normal	-ical	logical
-ial	remedial	-ory	sensory
-able	comfortable	-less	hopeless
-ible	sensible	-ive	competitive
-ish	sluggish	-ly	friendly
-ant	resistant	-ful	colorful

Common Adverb Endings			
-ly	quickly	-ally	historically

A) Adjective/Adverb Errors

The most common type of word-form problem involves the use of an adverb in place of an adjective or an adjective in place of an adverb. A few points to keep in mind:

- Adjectives modify nouns, noun phrases, and pronouns.
  - Adjectives often come before nouns.
    an *important* test
    a *quiet* evening
    a *long* letter

  - They often answer the question *What kind?*

    She is a *brilliant* doctor. (What kind of a doctor is she? A *brilliant* one.)

  - Adjectives also follow the verb *to be* and other linking verbs.

    The glass was *empty*.
    That song sounds *nice*.
    They look *upset*.

  - Adverbs may modify verbs, participles, adjectives, prepositions, adverb clause markers, and other adverbs.

    Ann *eagerly* accepted the challenge.
        (adverb modifying the main verb *accepted*)
    It was a *rapidly* changing situation.
        (adverb modifying the present participle *changing*)
    She wore a *brightly* colored scarf.
        (adverb modifying the past participle *colored*)
    Ted seemed *extremely* curious about that topic.
        (adverb modifying the adjective *curious*)
    We arrived at the airport *shortly* before our flight left.
        (adverb modifying the adverb-clause marker *before*)
    We arrived at the airport shortly before noon.
        (adverb modifying the preposition *before*)
    The accident occurred *incredibly* quickly.
        (adverb modifying the adverb *quickly*)

- Sometimes adverbs are used at the beginning of sentences, often followed by a comma. These adverbs sometimes modify the entire sentence rather than one word in the sentence.

  Generally, I like my classes.
  Usually Professor Ingram's lectures are more interesting.

- Most adverbs tested in this section are adverbs of manner. They are formed by adding the suffix *-ly* or *-ally* to an adjective.

  | quick | quickly | comic | comically |
  | comfortable | comfortably | historic | historically |

- Adverbs of manner answer the question *How?*

  She treated her employees *honestly*. (How did she treat her employees? *Honestly*.)

- A few adverbs (*fast*, *hard*, *high*, for example) have the same form as adjectives.

  He bought a *fast* car. (adjective)
  He was driving so *fast* that he got a speeding ticket. (adverb)

- *Well* is the irregular adverb form of the adjective *good*.

  Juan is an exceptionally *good* student.
  He did very *well* on the last test.

- Some adjectives also end in *-ly*: *friendly*, *yearly*, *costly*, and *lively*, for example.

  That was a *costly* mistake.
  I found Houston a very *friendly* city.

▼ **Sample Items**

The Black Hills of South Dakota <u>are</u> covered <u>with</u> <u>densely</u> pine forests.
    A   B   C D

The best answer is (D). An adjective, *dense*, not an adverb, is required to modify the noun phrase *pine forests*.

During solar storms, the <u>amount</u> of radiation <u>reaching</u> the Earth is
   A   B   C

<u>abnormal</u> high.
  D

The adverb *abnormally* is needed to modify the adjective *high*. ▲

B) Incorrect Forms of Words Connected with Certain Fields

This error involves a confusion between the names of fields (*biology*, for example) and the name of a person who practices in that field (*biologist*), or between one of those terms and the adjective that describes the field (*biological*).

▼ **Sample Item**

First <u>specializing</u> in <u>industrial</u> photography, Margaret Bourke-White later
      A   B

became a famous news <u>photographer</u> and <u>editorial</u> .
                    C   D

The adjective *editorial* is used to describe the field of editing. However, a noun referring to a person (*editor*) is needed in this sentence. ▲

C) Other Word-Form Problems

There are many other word-form problems. Some examples are given here:

▼ **Sample Items**

Corn played <u>an</u> important <u>role in</u> the <u>cultural</u> of the <u>cliff-dwelling</u>
          A   B   C   D
Indians of the Southwest.

The noun *culture,* not the adjective *cultural,* is needed.

<u>The galaxy</u> Andromeda is the most <u>distance</u> object <u>visible</u> to <u>observers</u>
   A   B   C   D
in the Northern Hemisphere.

The adjective *distant* is needed in place of the noun *distance*.

Scientists <u>belief</u> that the continents once <u>formed</u> a single continent
           A   B
surrounded <u>by</u> an <u>enormous</u> sea.
           C   D

In this sentence, the verb *believe* is needed in place of the noun *belief.*

Bunsen burners <u>are used</u> to <u>hot</u> materials <u>in a</u> <u>chemistry</u> lab.
             A   B   C   D

The verb *heat* is needed in place of the adjective *hot.*

A <u>sudden</u> <u>freezing</u> can <u>destroy</u> citrus <u>crops</u>.
   A   B   C   D

Rather than the gerund (*-ing*) form, the noun *freeze* is required. ▲

Exercise 32.1

Focus: Correctly providing word forms for parts of speech commonly confused in Written Expression problems.

Directions: Fill in the lines in the blanks below with the appropriate word forms. In some cases, there may be more than one correct answer. The first one is done as an example.

	Verb	Noun	Adjective	Adverb
1.	differ	difference	different	differently
2.			inventive	
3.	compete			
4.		symbol		
5.				deeply
6.		decision		
7.	beautify			
8.	prohibit			
9.	originate			
10.			emphatic	
11.			inconvenient	
12.		glory		
13.	mystify			
14.				equally
15.			general	
16.				simply
17.			familiar	
18.			pure	
19.	free			
20.	restrict			

Exercise 32.2

Focus: Providing word forms related to the names of fields, to adjectives describing those fields, and to people involved in those fields.

Directions: Fill in the blanks in the chart below with the appropriate form. The first one is done as an example.

	Field	**Person**	**Adjective**
1.	music	*musician*	*musical*
2.		surgeon	
3.			poetic
4.		electrician	
5.	administration		
6.			financial
7.		photographer	
8.	theory		
9.			athletic
10.	editing		
11.		philosopher	
12.		criminal	
13.			political
14.		lawyer	
15.	humor		

Exercise 32.3

Focus: Identifying errors and recognizing correct use of adjectives and adverbs.

Directions: Underline the form that correctly completes the sentence. The first one is done as an example.

1. In any animal community, herbivores (great/<u>greatly</u>) outnumber carnivores.
2. Floods cause billions of dollars worth of property damage (annual/annually).
3. (Regular/Regularly) airmail service in the United States began in 1918.
4. Writer Ernest Hemingway was known for his (simple/simply) language and his lively dialogue.
5. The tiny coral snake is (beautiful/beautifully) but deadly.
6. Skyscrapers developed (simultaneous/simultaneously) in Chicago and New York City.
7. (General/Generally), bauxite is found near the surface, so it is relatively (simple/simply) to mine.
8. A good proofreader (painstaking/painstakingly) examines a manuscript for errors in spelling and grammar as well as for factual mistakes.
9. The colony of New Hampshire was (permanent/permanently) separated from the Massachusetts Bay Colony in 1692.
10. The most numerous and (wide/widely) distributed of all insectivorous animals are the shrews.
11. The endocrine system functions in (close/closely) relationship with the nervous system.
12. A gap in the Coast Range of California provides (easy/easily) access to the San Francisco Bay area.
13. Mushrooms are found in an (incredible/incredibly) range of sizes, colors, and shapes.
14. Some airplanes have an automatic pilot that is connected to the airplane's controls and (automatic/automatically) keeps the plane on course.
15. Winslow Homer, who had no (formal/formally) training in art, became famous for his paintings of the sea.

16. The potter's wheel was an invention of (profound/profoundly) importance.

17. The nuclear-powered cargo ship *Savannah* proved (commercial/commercially) impractical.

18. Sojourner Truth spoke (persuasively/persuasive) in opposition to slavery.

19. In 1948 Stan Getz made a (masterful/masterfully) solo recording of the song "Early Autumn" which (deep/deeply) influenced younger musicians.

20. The planet Venus was once believed to be two (distinct/distinctly) objects: the morning star Phosphorous and the evening star Hesperus.

Exercise 32.4

Focus: Identifying which parts of speech are appropriate in sentences.

Directions: Underline the form that correctly completes the sentence. Then identify the parts of speech of the words in parentheses. You can use these abbreviations for parts of speech:

N = noun	G = gerund (*-ing*) noun
V = verb	ADJ = adjective
PN = "person" noun	ADV = adverb

The first one is done as an example.

1. Sinclair Lewis' novel *Babbitt* is set in the (fiction/<u>fictional</u>) town of Zenith. (_____N_____/_____ADJ_____)

2. By-products from chicken eggs are used by (industry/industrial) in manufacturing such (produces/products) as soap and paint. (_____/_____) (_____/_____)

3. The daylily is an attractive, (fragrance/fragrant) flower. (_____/_____)

4. An equation is a (mathematics/mathematical) statement which says that two expressions are (equal/equality). (_____/_____) (_____/_____)

5. The Supreme Court has ruled that (evidence/evident) obtained from (illegal/illegally) searches cannot be used in court. (_____/_____) (_____/_____)

6. The Richter Scale measures the (severely/severity) of earthquakes. (_____/_____)

7. Justin Winsom promoted the (developing/development) of libraries throughout the United States in the nineteenth century. (_____/_____)

8. Pipelines (transportation/transport) huge quantities of natural gas and liquid petroleum products. (_____/_____)

9. Scientists (differ/different) in their opinions of how snow crystals (originate/origin). (_____/_____) (_____/_____)

10. Harry Blackstone was a famous (magic/magician). (_____/_____)

11. Glass sponges are found in oceans at a (deep/depth) of 300 feet or more. (_____/_____)

12. Colorado shares with Wyoming the (distinction/distinctly) of having four (perfect/perfectly) straight borders. (_____/_____) (_____/_____)

13. Yale's Peabody Museum has a world-famous (collection/collecting) of fossils. (_____/_____)

14. Pronghorns, which are American antelopes, are (present/presence) in large numbers on the (open/openly) plains of Wyoming. (_____/_____) (_____/_____)

15. The President's (chooses/choices) for the members of the Cabinet must be (approved/approval) by the Congress. (_____/_____) (_____/_____)

16. Rose Han Lee wrote a number of (scholar/scholarly) accounts about the effects of (immigrant/immigration) on mining towns in the western United States. (_____/_____) (_____/_____)

17. Most snails venture out to look for (feed/food) only after sunset or on (rain/rainy) days. (_____/_____) (_____/_____)

18. Hats may (symbolize/symbol) social status or (occupation/occupational) as well as being fashion items. (_____/_____) (_____/_____)

19. Analgesics are used to (relieve/relief) pain and reduce fever. (_____/_____)

20. The process of (respire/respiration) in plants involves a complex series of (chemistry/chemical) reactions. (_____/_____) (_____/_____)

21. A (member/membership) of the Paiute tribe of Nevada, Sarah Winnemuca worked as a guide and (interpret/interpreter). (_____/_____) (_____/_____)

22. The (strong/strength) of a rope is (direct/directly) proportional to its cross-sectional area. (_____/_____) (_____/_____)

23. The Nassau grouper is a (tropics/tropical) fish that is noted for its (able/ability) to change color. (_____/_____) (_____/_____)

24. Alpha rays (loss/lose) energy (rapidity/rapidly) as they pass through matter. (_____/_____) (_____/_____)

25. The cherry is one of the only fruits that will not (ripe/ripen) if it is removed from the tree. (_____/_____)

Exercise 32.5

Focus: Identifying errors involving word-form problems. (Note: One or two items in this exercise do not focus on word-form errors. These are marked in the answer key with an asterisk.)

Directions: Decide which of the four underlined words or phrases—(A), (B), (C), or (D)—would not be considered correct, and write the letter of the expression in the blank. Then, in the line at the end of the sentence, write the correction for the underlined phrase. The first one is done as an example.

_B_ 1. Liberal arts colleges <u>cultivate</u> general <u>intellectually</u> <u>abilities</u> rather than technical or
     A   B   C

  <u>professional</u> skills. _intellectual_
   D

_____ 2. Goats are extremely <u>destruction</u> to <u>natural</u> <u>vegetation</u>, and are often <u>responsible</u> for soil
         A   B   C   D

  erosion. _____

_____ 3. <u>Wild</u> plants were of <u>considerable</u> <u>important</u> to early settlers, and many are still used
   A   B   C

  <u>medicinally</u> and as foods. _____
   D

_____   4. One important <u>branch</u> of <u>linguistics</u> is semantics, which <u>analysis</u> the <u>meaning</u> of words.
A   B   C   D

_____

_____   5. Unlike folk <u>dancers</u>, which are the <u>product</u> of a single <u>culture</u>, ballet is an <u>international</u>
A   B   C   D

art form. _____

_____   6. The Earth's <u>out</u> shell is <u>divided</u> into sections called plates, which are <u>constantly</u> in
A   B   C

<u>motion</u>. _____
D

_____   7. Black bears can move <u>rapidly</u> when <u>necessary</u> and are <u>skillful</u> tree-climbers for their size
A   B   C

and <u>weigh</u>. _____
D

_____   8. In an arboretum, trees are <u>cultivated</u> for <u>scientific</u> and <u>educational</u> <u>purpose</u>.
A   B   C   D

_____

_____   9. In most Western states, the first major <u>industry</u> was <u>mines</u>, which was <u>gradually</u>
A   B   C

supplemented by ranching and <u>farming</u>. _____
D

_____   10. Peach trees <u>grow</u> <u>good</u> in a <u>variety of</u> soil types, but do best in <u>sandy</u> loam.
A B   C   D

_____

_____   11. The <u>unit</u> of <u>measuring</u> called the foot was <u>originally</u> based on the <u>length</u> of the human
A   B   C   D

foot. _____

_____   12. <u>Philosopher Theodore A.</u> Langerman was <u>interested</u> in the fields of <u>literary</u> and <u>music</u>.
A   B   C   D

_____

_____   13. <u>Pure</u> nitric acid is colorless, but it <u>acquires</u> a yellow <u>color</u> when it is <u>exposed</u> of air.
A   B   C   D

_____

_____   14. A chemical <u>react</u> that <u>absorbs</u> <u>heat</u> is called endothermic. _____
A   B   C D

_____ 15. One <u>characteristic</u> of the <u>poems</u> of Emily Dickinson is the <u>sharp</u> of her <u>images</u>.
   A B C D
_____

_____ 16. Luther Gulick was a <u>teacher</u> and <u>physician</u> who spent much of his <u>live</u> promoting
   A B C

<u>physical fitness</u>. _____
   D

_____ 17. A dog should be checked <u>regularly</u> by a veterinarian <u>to ensure</u> that it <u>remains</u> in good
   A B C

<u>healthy</u>. _____
   D

_____ 18. <u>Southwestern</u> Boston is made up of Hyde Park, West Roxbury, and other <u>pleasant</u>
   A B

<u>residential</u> <u>neighbors</u>. _____
   C D

_____ 19. Hunting and fishing techniques were <u>highly developed</u> among the North American
   A

Indians, <u>particularly</u> in regions where <u>agriculture</u> was less <u>success</u>. _____
   B C D

_____ 20. <u>Science</u> requires the <u>careful</u> <u>collect</u> and <u>organization</u> of data. _____
   A B C D

_____ 21. The Natchez Trace was <u>an important</u> <u>commercial</u> and <u>military route</u> between Nashville,
   A B C

Tennessee <u>to</u> Natchez, Mississippi. _____
   D

_____ 22. Some games rely <u>mainly</u> on <u>skill</u> and practice while others <u>primarily</u> involve <u>lucky</u>.
   A B C D
_____

_____ 23. In the <u>absent</u> of <u>natural</u> enemies, the gypsy moth has <u>become</u> a <u>serious</u> pest in North
   A B C D

America. _____

_____ 24. Huey Long and his <u>brother</u> Earl were the two most <u>powerful</u> <u>politics</u> in the <u>history of</u>
   A B C D

Louisiana. _____

_____ 25. To make candles, pioneers <u>twisted</u> string into wicks, dipped the wicks into <u>hot</u> fat, then
   A B

<u>hung</u> the candles to cool and <u>hard</u>. _____
   C D

LESSON 33

ERRORS IN WORD CHOICE

Word-choice errors involve the incorrect use of one word in place of another. These two words may be related forms (*other* and *another*, for example), or they may be completely different (*do* and *make*, for example).

Descriptions of some of the most common word choice errors are given below.

A) Wrong Choice of *Make* or *Do*

The verb *to do* is often used in place of *to make*, and *to make* in place of *to do*. In its basic sense, *to make* means to produce, to create, to construct, while *to do* means to perform, to act, to accomplish. These verbs are also used in a number of set expressions:

Common Expressions with *Make*	
make advances	make an offer
make an attempt	make a plan
make a comparison	make a point
make a contribution	make a prediction
make a decision	make a profit
make a distinction	make a promise
make a forecast	make a sound/noise
make an investment	make a suggestion
make a law	

be made of (= be composed of)

make up (= compose)

To make is also used in this pattern: *make* + someone + adjective (The gift *made* her happy).

Common Expressions with *Do*	
do an assignment	do a job (errand, chore)
do business with	do research
do one's duty	do one's work
do someone a favor	

The auxiliary verb *do* is used rather than repeat main verbs (My computer doesn't operate as fast as theirs *does*).

Anytime you see the verb *make* or *do* underlined in the Written Expression section, suspect a word-choice error.

▼ **Sample Items**

Cement is <u>done</u> from <u>varying</u> <u>amounts</u> of limestone, clay, <u>and</u> gypsum.
         A   B   C   D

The verb *done* is incorrect in this sentence. The correct word choice is *made*.

Small town <u>newspapers</u> often <u>urge</u> readers to <u>make business</u> with <u>local</u> merchants.
                 A   B   C   D

The phrase should read *do business*. ▲

B) Wrong Choice of *Like* or *Alike* and *Like* or *As*

The word *alike* is incorrectly used in place of *like*, or *like* is used in place of *alike*. These words are used correctly in the following patterns:

Like A, . . .	Like birds, mammals are warm-blooded.
A, like B, . . .	Birds, like mammals, are warm-blooded.
A is like B . . .	Birds are like mammals in that they are both warm-blooded.
A and B are alike . . .	Birds and mammals are alike in that they are both warm-blooded.

Whenever you see the words *alike* or *like* underlined, you should suspect a word-choice error.
   The word *like* is also sometimes confused with the word *as*. When *like* is used in a comparison, it is followed by a noun or pronoun. When *as* is used in a comparison, it is followed by a clause containing a subject and a verb.

I did my experiment just *as* Paul did.
My results were much *like* Paul's.

The word *as* is also used before nouns when it means *in place of* or *in the role of*. This is particularly common after certain verbs: *serve*, *function*, and *use*, among others.

The Vice-President served *as* President when the President was sick.

▼ **Sample Items**

<u>Alike</u> their <u>close</u> relatives the <u>frogs</u>, toads <u>are</u> amphibians.
  A   B   C   D

Choice (A) doesn't follow the pattern *Like A, B* . . .

Asters, <u>as</u> <u>most</u> perennial plants, <u>bloom</u> once <u>a year</u>.
      A B   C   D

The word *like* should be used in place of the word *as* before a noun phrase (*most perennial plants*). ▲

C) Wrong Choice of *So, Such, Too,* and *As*

The words *so, such,* and *too* are used in the following patterns:

> *so* + adjective + *that* clause
>> These boxes are *so* heavy that we can't lift them.

> (*So* is also used with *many . . . that* and *much . . . that*.)
>> There were *so* many people in the auditorium that we could barely get in the front door.

> *such* + adjective + noun phrase + *that* clause
>> It was *such* a pretty view that he took a photograph.

> *too* + adjective + infinitive
>> It's *too* cold to go swimming today.

Notice that *so* and *such* are both followed by *that* clauses, but *too* is followed by an infinitive. The words *as* and *so* are also sometimes confused:

> *Jane did *so* well as I did on the economics exam. (INCORRECT)
> *The coffee was *as* hot that I couldn't drink it. (INCORRECT)

In the first sentence, the word *as* should be used in place of *so;* in the second, *so* should be used in place of *as*.

Also look for *so much* or *too much* used in place of *so* or *too*.

▼ **Sample Items**

> The sun is <u>so</u> bright to <u>look at</u> <u>directly</u>.
>   <u> </u>
> A   B   C   D

The correct pattern is *too* + adjective + infinitive.

> <u>In much</u> of Alaska, the growing season is <u>as</u> short that <u>crops</u> can't be raised.
>   A   B   C   D

The correct pattern is *so* + adjective + *that* clause.

> The giant squid is <u>so</u> an elusive animal that <u>at one time</u> it was <u>believed</u> to be
>   A   B   C
>
> <u>purely</u> mythical.
>   D

Before an adjective + noun + *that* clause, the word *such* should be used.

> The <u>mineral</u> grains in basalt are <u>so much</u> small that <u>they</u> cannot <u>be seen</u>
>   A   B   C   D
>
> with the unaided eye.

The phrase should read *so small* rather than *so much small*.

D) Wrong Choice of *Another* or *Other*

Use of *Another* and *Other*

	Another	Other
Used as an adjective	*another* + singular noun (Have *another* sandwich.)	*other* + plural noun (I wonder if there is life on *other* planets.) determiner + *other* + noun (There may be life on some *other* planet.)
Used as a pronoun	*another* (Thanks. I'll have *another.*)	determiner + *other* ("I have one book." "I have the *other.*")

Another means "one more, an additional one." It can be used as an adjective before a singular nouns or alone as a pronoun.

> He needs *another* piece of paper.
> I have one class in that building, and *another* in the building across the quadrangle.

Other is used as an adjective before a plural noun. It is also used as an adjective before a singular noun when preceded by a determiner such as *the, some, many, any, one,* or *no.* It can also be used alone as a pronoun when preceded by a determiner.

> There are *other* matters I'd like to discuss with you.
> One of the books was a novel; the *other* was a collection of essays.
> There's no *other* place I'd rather visit.

▼ **Sample Items**

Willa Cather <u>is known</u> for *My Antonia* and <u>another</u> novels
        A   B

<u>of the</u> American <u>frontier</u>.
  C   D

Before a plural noun, *other* must be used.

<u>An</u> understudy is an actor <u>who can</u> substitute for <u>other</u> actor
 A   B   C

<u>in case of</u> an emergency.
  D

Other is used incorrectly in place of *another* before a singular noun. ▲

E) Wrong Choice of *Because* or *Because Of* and Similar Expressions

Certain expressions, such as *because,* are adverb clause markers and are used only before clauses. Other expressions, such as *because of,* are prepositions and are used before nouns, noun phrases, or pronouns.

Adverb Clause Markers (Used with Clauses)	Prepositions (Used with Noun Phrases)
because	because of
although	despite in spite of
When while	during

▼ **Sample Items**

Because <u>migration</u> to the suburbs, the <u>population</u> of <u>many</u> large
A B C
American cities <u>declined</u> between 1950 and 1960.
D

Before a noun (*migration*), the preposition *because of* must be used.

<u>Despite</u> most people <u>consider</u> the tomato a vegetable, botanists <u>classify</u>
A B C
it <u>as a fruit</u> .
D

Before a full clause (*most people consider the tomato a vegetable*), the adverb
marker *although* must be used. ▲

F) Wrong Choice of *Much* or *Many* and Similar Expressions

Certain expressions can be used only in phrases with plural nouns; others can be used in expressions only with non-count nouns.

Used with Plural Nouns	Used with Non-count Nouns
many	much
few, a few	little, a little
fewer, the fewest	less, the least
number	amount

▼ **Sample Items**

Pearls are <u>found</u> in <u>much</u> colors, <u>including</u> cream, <u>blue</u>, lavender, and black.
A B C D

Many must be used with a plural noun (*colors*).

Even <u>during</u> <u>economic</u> booms, there is a small <u>number</u> of <u>unemployment</u>.
　　　　A　　　　B　　　　　　　　　　　　　　C　　　　　D

The word *amount* must be used to refer to a non-count noun such as *unemployment*. ▲

G) Other Word-Form Problems

Other pairs of words are sometimes confused in Written Expression, including those listed below. ***All of the sentences with asterisks are examples of errors and are INCORRECT.***

no	Used as an adjective before nouns; means "not any." Also used in the expression *no longer*.
not	Used to make all other words negatives.

*_Not_ gasoline was left in the tank.
*This is *no* the station that I usually listen to.
*I *not longer* listen to that station.

most	Used in superlative adjective phrases; also used to mean "the majority."
almost	Used as an adverb to mean "nearly."

*This is the al*most* interesting chapter in the book.
*I've read *almost* of the chapters in the book.
*I've solved *most* all of the problems in the book.

twice	Used as an adjective to mean "two times."
double	Used as a verb to mean "make twice as large."

*Henry has *double* as much money as he did before he invested it.
*Henry *twice* his money.

earliest	Used as a superlative adjective to mean "most distant in time."
soonest	Used as a superlative adverb to mean "most promptly."

*These are the *soonest* examples of the artist's works.

(You will probably not see *earliest* used incorrectly in place of *soonest*.)

percent	Used after a number.
percentage	Not used after a number.

*Fifty *percentage* of the people voted in favor of the initiative.
*The *percent* of people who approve of the initiative has been steadily growing.

after	Used as a preposition before a noun or as an adverb clause marker before a clause.
afterwards	Used as an adverb, means "after that."

*We'll go to dinner *after*wards the play.
*We'll go to dinner *after*wards the play is over.
*First the performer played the guitar and *after* she played the flute.

ago	Used to talk about a time earlier than the present.
before	Used to talk about a time earlier than some other point in time.

*Harold won a gold medal in the Olympics last year, and four years ago that, he won a silver medal.

(You will probably not see *before* used incorrectly in place of *ago*.)

tell	Used with an object; also used in certain set expressions: *tell a story, tell the truth, tell a secret.*
say	Used without an object.

*Mr. Hunter *said* us that he'd had a good trip.
*Joe *said* a wonderful story.
*Mr. Hunter *told* that he'd had a good trip.

ever	Means "at any time." Used with *not* to mean "never." Also used in some set expressions such as *ever since* and *hardly ever.*
never	Means "at no time." Not used with a negative word.

*He hardly n*ever* goes to that club.

(You will probably not see *ever* used incorrectly in place of *never*.)

alive	Used after the verb *to be.*
live	Used before a noun to modify that noun.

*Sue likes to have *alive* plants in her apartment.
*Although she forgot to water it for a week, the plant was still *live*.

around	Used as a preposition to mean "in a circular path."
round	Used as an adjective to mean "circular in shape."

*The new office building will be *an around* glass tower.

(You will probably not see *round* used incorrectly in place of *around*.)

age	Used as a noun, often in these patterns: at the age of twenty-one twenty-one years of age
old	Used as an adjective, often in this pattern: twenty-one years old

*Harriet will be thirty years age next week.
*Operators of motor vehicles must be sixteen years of old in this state.

near	Used as an adjective; means "close to."
nearly	Used as an adverb; means "almost."

*Lynn is looking for an apartment *nearly* the Medical Center.
*The two-bedroom apartment she looked at cost *near* a thousand dollars a month.

some	Used as a determiner before a noun to mean "an indefinite amount."
somewhat	Used as an adverb to mean "slightly."

*This bicycle is *some* more expensive than the one I looked at yesterday.

(You will probably not see *somewhat* used incorrectly in place of *some*.)

You can practice the distinctions between many of these words in Exercise 44.7.

Note: The distinctions between words such as *desert* and *dessert*, *stationary* and *stationery*, *capital* and *capitol*, which are really spelling problems, are NOT tested on TOEFL.

Exercise 33.1

Focus: Choosing correctly between *do* and *make*.

Directions: Underline the word that correctly completes each sentence below. The first one is done as an example.

1. The tips of high-speed dental drills are (done/<u>made</u>) of tungsten steel and often contain diamonds.

2. A cottage industry is a form of manufacturing (done/made) at home.

3. Margaret Mead (did/made) fundamental contributions to both the theory and field work of anthropology.

4. Many universities receive grants to (do/make) research for the federal government.

5. Research in genetics in the early nineteenth century (did/made) much to improve agriculture.

6. Futurologists study current trends to (do/make) predictions about the future.

7. Filmmaker George Lucas has (done/made) many advances in the production of motion pictures, especially in the use of special effects.

8. The distinction between wildflowers and weeds is one that is often difficult to (do/make).

9. The helicopter can (do/make) jobs that no other aircraft can.

10. Yeast is added to dough to (do/make) bread light and porous.

Exercise 33.2

Focus: Choosing correctly between *like* and *alike* and *like* and *as*.

Directions: Underline the word that correctly completes each sentence below. The first one is done as an example.

1. The government of the United States and that of Canada are (<u>alike</u>/like) in that both conduct a complete census every ten years.

2. Fashion design, (as/like) all types of design, has been greatly aided by computers.

3. (Alike/Like) stars, galaxies tend to congregate in clusters.

4. Fungi are the most important decomposers of forest soil, just (as/like) bacteria are the most important decomposers of grassland soil.

5. The spinal column is (alike/like) the brain in that its main functions can be classified as either sensory or motor functions.

6. A peanut is not actually a nut but a legume (alike/like) peas and beans.

7. The stately Government House in Annapolis serves (as/like) the residence of the Governor of Maryland.

8. The cetosaur was a dinosaur that looked much (as/like) the whales of today.

9. Fats are made up of carbon, hydrogen, and oxygen atoms just (like/as) carbohydrates are.

10. One way pumpkins and watermelons are (like/alike) is that both grow on vines trailing along the surface of the ground.

Exercise 33.3

Focus: Choosing correctly between *so, such, too,* and *as.*

Directions: Underline the word that correctly completes each sentence below. The first one is done as an example.

1. The mineral talc is (<u>so</u>/such) soft that it can be scratched with a fingernail.

2. Oceanographers use robots and unmanned submarines to explore parts of the ocean that are (so/too) deep for people to explore safely.

3. (So/As) much paper money was printed during the Revolutionary War that it became almost worthless.

4. The walking stick is an insect with (so/such a) close resemblance to a twig that it escapes the notice of its enemies.

5. At present, solar cells are (so/too) expensive and inefficient to be used in the commercial generation of electricity.

6. Acrylic plastics are very hard and are (so/as) clear as glass.

7. Founded in 1682, Norfolk developed (so/such a) prosperous sea trade that it quickly became the largest town in the colony of Virginia.

8. Continental islands are (so/so much) close to continents that their plant and animal life are identical to life on the mainland.

9. Timberline is the elevation on a mountainside above which temperatures become (so/too) cold for most trees to grow.

10. A few people have (such/too) good eyesight that they can actually see the brightest stars during full daylight.

Exercise 33.4

Focus: Choosing correctly between *other* and *another.*

Directions: Underline the word that correctly completes each sentence below. The first one is done as an example.

1. Lightning is a rush of electrical current from a cloud to the ground or from one cloud to (<u>another</u>/other).

2. A ballet dancer's techniques and skills are very different from those of (another/other) dancers.

3. The commercial center of New York City, the island of Manhattan is joined to the (another/other) boroughs by bridges and tunnels.

4. The legal surrender of a criminal suspect from one state or country to (another/other) is called extradition.

5. Rocky Mountain spotted fever is one type of disease that is carried by ticks, and Colorado tick fever is (another/other).

6. The art of photography has often been influenced by—and has influenced—(another/other) fine arts.

7. William O. Douglas was a Supreme Court Justice for thirty-six years, longer than any (another/other) justice in the history of the Court.

8. In physics, diffusion is the spread of one substance's molecules or atoms through those of (another/other).

9. A basketball player may advance the ball by dribbling it or passing it to (another/other) player.

10. Limkins are water birds that eat snails and (another/other) mollusks.

Exercise 33.5

Focus: Choosing correctly between *because of* or *because* and similar expressions.

Directions: Underline the word that correctly completes the sentences below. The first one is done as an example.

1. (<u>Although</u>/Despite) cats cannot see in complete darkness, their eyes are much more sensitive to light than humans' eyes.

2. (Because/Because of) cheese is essentially a concentrated form of milk, it contains the same nutrients as milk.

3. (Although/In spite of) its frightening appearance, the octopus is shy and completely harmless.

4. (Because/Because of) its acute sense of smell, the bloodhound is often used in tracking.

5. (When/During) the female oriole is absent from the nest, the male oriole stands guard.

6. (Although/Despite) their light weight, aluminum alloys can be very strong.

7. (Although/In spite of) Adlai Stevenson was never elected president, he was one of the preeminent American politicians of the mid-twentieth century.

8. Snakebirds were not given their name because they eat snakes, but (because/because of) their long, slender necks resemble snakes.

9. In the sixteenth century, it was thought that a compass needle pointed north (because/because of) some mysterious influence of the stars.

10. (Although/Despite) it can occur in adults, chicken pox is classified as a disease of childhood.

11. Opinion polls are often used (while/during) political campaigns to find out how voters feel about candidates and issues.

12. Geneticists often experiment with bacteria and viruses (because/because of) those organisms reproduce so quickly.

Exercise 33.6

Focus: Choosing correctly between *much* or *many* and similar words.

Directions: Underline the word that correctly completes each sentence below. The first one is done as an example.

1. (<u>Many</u>/Much) industrial products can be made from soybeans.

2. Desert plants compete fiercely for the (few/little) water that is available.

3. The American designer Louis Comfort Tiffany took (many/much) of his inspiration from nature.

4. A (few/little) simple precautions can prevent accidents at home and on the job.

5. In a formal debate, the same (number/amount) of persons speak for each team, and both teams are granted an equal (number/ amount) of time in which to make their arguments.

6. Bats do (few/little) damage to people, livestock, or crops.

7. Even small (numbers/amounts) of zinc can have a significant effect on the growth of plants.

8. The adrenal glands, one on top of each kidney, secrete (many/much) important hormones.

9. (Many/Much) of the stories in John Weems' biography of George Washington are difficult to believe.

10. Folk artists have (few/little) or no formal art training.

Exercise 33.7

Focus: Choosing correctly between other commonly confused words.

Directions: Underline the word that correctly completes each sentence below. The first one is done as an example.

1. At eight weeks of (<u>age</u>/old), red foxes begin to get their adult markings.

2. The Missouri River is about (double/twice) as long as the Colorado River.

3. Catherine Esther Beacher established schools in Connecticut and Ohio, and (after/afterwards) founded the American Women's Educational Association.

4. (Most/Almost) antibiotics are antibacterial agents, but some are effective against fungal, protozoal, or yeast infections.

5. In 1941 nylon was first used to make stockings, and the year (ago/before), it was first used to make toothbrush bristles.

6. Chuck Berry was one of the (soonest/earliest) and most influential performers of rock music.

7. Long before Columbus, various thinkers believed that the Earth was (around/round).

8. Apricots, which are (some/somewhat) smaller than peaches, are known for their delicate taste.

9. Huge radio telescopes aimed into space may someday (say/tell) us whether intelligent life exists elsewhere in the universe.

10. One of Canada's most beautiful botanical gardens is Butchart Gardens (near/nearly) Victoria, British Columbia.

11. Since 1945, the average size of American farms has more than (doubled/twice).

12. When the Hopi Indians perform the Snake Dance, the dancers handle (alive/live) rattlesnakes.

13. Around eighty-five (percentage/percent) of the bauxite produced in the United States is mined in Arkansas.

14. Artist Clementine Hunter continued to paint until she was over 100 years (age/old).

15. The period immediately (after/afterwards) the Civil War is known as Reconstruction.

16. (No/Not) plant has a nervous system, and most respond very slowly to stimuli in their environment.

17. (Most/Almost) every county in the United States has agricultural extension agents who provide help to farmers.

18. Murals (say/tell) narrative stories through visual images.

19. Forests cover (near/nearly) half the land area of Tennessee.

20. Giraffes hardly (ever/never) sleep more than twenty minutes a night.

Exercise 33.8

Focus: Identifying a variety of word-choice errors. (Note: One or two items in this exercise do not focus on word-choice errors. These are marked in the answer key with an asterisk.)

Directions: Decide which of the four underlined words or phrases—(A), (B), (C), or (D)—would not be considered correct, and write the letter of the expression in the blank. Then, in the line at the end of the sentence, write the correction for the underlined phrase. The first one is done as an example.

___C___   1. When a spacecraft is operating beyond the atmosphere, its fins and wings not longer
       A   B   C

         serve to stabilize it. ___no longer___
                D

_____   2. The University of Chicago is unlike most other U.S. universities in that it has emphasized
                              A   B

         graduate student programs so much as undergraduate programs ever since it opened.
                        C   D

         _____

_____   3. The mass production of paper bags cut costs so much that a bag soon became a routine
              A   B   C

         part of near every purchase. _____
              D

_____   4. A person must be at least thirty years age in order to serve as a U.S. senator.
                A   B   C   D

         _____

_____   5. No other state receives as few rainfall as the state of Nevada. _____
         A   B   C   D

_____   6. Because of refraction, the water in a tank ever looks as deep as it actually is.
             A   B   C   D

         _____

_____   7. Molds grow on bread, fruit, paper, and much other substances. _____
             A   B   C   D

_____   8. The *lei*, which is made of flowers, shells, and other materials, is presented to visitors
                     A   B

         as a symbolize of Hawaiian hospitality. _____
         C   D

_____   9. The botanists Katherine Hunter and Emily Fose spent many difficult months making
              A   B   C

         research in the Rocky Mountains. _____
         D

_____ 10. Early explorers in Utah named the cliffs they encountered "reefs" because they thought
          A   B   C
these cliffs looked alike coral formations. _____
                     D

_____ 11. Today oysters are grown and harvested much like any another crop. _____
             A   B   C   D

_____ 12. Walter Hunt invented an enormous amount of devices, including the safety pin and a
                                            A   B
machine for making nails. _____
   C   D

_____ 13. Connecticut, like the other New England states, are dotted with many little lakes.
                         A   B   C   D
_____

_____ 14. The soonest parachutes were made of canvas, but later, silk and then nylon were used .
                 A   B   C   D
_____

_____ 15. When vigorous exercise, muscles require a much greater amount of oxygen than
             A   B   C
when they are at rest. _____
   D

_____ 16. One should never throw water on an alive electrical fire. _____
                    A   B   C   D

LESSON 34

ERRORS WITH VERBS

Whenever the verb is underlined in a Written Expression problem, you should check for the common verb errors outlined in this lesson.

A) Errors in Subject-Verb Agreement

If a subject is singular, the verb must be singular. If the subject is plural, the verb must be plural. Most problems involving subject-verb agreement on TOEFL are simple, but a few are tricky.

▼ **Sample Items**

> Minerals in seawater exists in the same proportions in
>   A   B   C
> all of the oceans of the world.
>   D

The plural subject *minerals* requires a plural verb, *exist*. You might have found this question tricky because the singular noun *seawater* comes between the subject and the verb, and you may have mistaken that word for the true subject.

> Bowling, one of the most popular indoor sports, are popular all over
>   A   B   C
> the United States and in other countries.
>   D

The subject of the sentence is *bowling*, not *sports*. The singular verb form *is* should therefore be used.

There are some special rules about subject-verb agreement that you should be familiar with:

- **A sentence with two subjects joined by *and* takes a plural verb.**

  The chemistry lab and the physics lab *are* . . .

- **Some words end in -*s* but are singular in form. Many of these words are the names of fields of study (*economics*, *physics*, and so on). *News* is another word of this kind.**

  Economics *is*. . .
  The news *was*. . .

- **Irregular plurals (*children, feet, mice,* and so on) do not end in -*s* but take plural verbs.**

  The women *were*. . .
  His feet *are*. . .

- **When a clause begins with the expletive *there*, the verb may be singular or plural, depending on the thematic subject.**

  There *was* a loud noise. . .
  There *were* a few problems. . .

- **Subjects with *each* and *every* take singular verbs. (This includes compound words like *everyone* and *everything*.)**

> Each state *has*. . .
> Each of the representatives *was* . . .
> Every person *was*. . .
> Everyone *wants*. . .

- **The verb in many relative clauses depends on the noun that the relative pronoun refers to.**

> The house that *was* built . . .
> The students who *were* selected . . .

> Other relative clauses contain noun or pronoun subjects that determine the verb.

> The houses that he *builds* . . .
> The students whom the teacher *selects* . . .

- **The phrase *the number of* + plural noun takes a singular verb. The phrase *a number of* + plural noun takes a plural verb.**

> The number of trees *is*. . .
> A number of important matters *have*. . .

- **Singular subjects used with phrases such as *along with*, *accompanied by*, *together with*, *as well as*, and *in addition to* take singular verbs.**

> The mayor, along with the city council, *is*. . .
> Together with his friends, Mark *has*. . .

- **Quantities of time, money, distance, and so on usually take a singular verb.**

> Five hundred dollars *was*. . .
> Two years *has*. . .
> Ten miles *is*. . .

B) Errors Involving Tense

Most tense errors involve the simple present tense, the simple past tense, and the present perfect tense.

- **The simple present tense is a general-time tense.**

It usually indicates that a condition is always true or that an action always occurs. It may also indicate that an action regularly occurs.

> The atmosphere *surrounds* the earth.
> Dana often *stays* at this hotel.
> Generally, the lectures in this class *are* very interesting.

- **The simple past tense indicates that an action took place at a specific time in the past.**

> They *moved* to Phoenix five years ago.
> This house *was built* in the 1920's.
> Dinosaurs *lived* millions of years ago.

- **The present perfect tense usually indicates that an action began at some time in the past and continues to the present. It may also indicate that an action took place at an unspecified time in the past.**

> Mr. Graham *has worked* for this company since 1990.
> She *hasn't been* to a doctor for a year.
> Jennifer *has* recently *returned* from Europe.

▼ Sample Items

The <u>most important</u> period of physical <u>growth</u> in humans <u>occurred</u>
         A   B   C

during <u>their</u> first two years.
       D

Choice (C) is best. The simple present tense, not the past tense, should be used because the situation described in this sentence always occurs.

<u>Personal</u> taxes <u>for</u> Americans <u>rose</u> <u>sharply</u> since 1945.
   A   B   C   D

Option (C) is again best. The time phrase *since 1945* means *from 1945 until now*. Therefore, the present perfect (*have risen*) is required in place of the past tense. ▲

C) Incorrect Verb Forms

Some of the verb errors are errors in form. An *-ing* form may be used in place of a part participle, a simple form in place of an *-ing* form, an infinitive in place of a simple form, and so on. Some involve irregular verbs that have different forms for the past tense and the past participle—*took* and *taken*, for example. The following information may help you choose the correct form of the main verb.

- **The simple form follows all modal auxiliaries.**

might be	can remember	should study
must know	could go	may follow

Certain similar auxiliary verbs require infinitives.

ought to attend	used to play	have to hurry

- **The past participle is used after a form of *have* in all perfect forms of the verb.**

has done	had called	should have said
have run	will have read	could have made

- **The *-ing* form is used after a form of *be* in all progressive forms of the verb.**

is sleeping	has been writing	should have been wearing
was working	had been painting	will be waiting

- **The past participle is used after a form of *be* in all passive forms of the verb.**

is worn	has been shown
is being considered	had been promised
were told	will have been missed
would have been lost	might have been canceled

Verb-form problems may also involve auxiliary verbs: *has* may be used in place of *did*, *is* in place of *does*, and so on.

▼ **Sample Items**

The first bicycle race on record in the United States
    A   B

taken place in 1883.
  C   D

The correct verb is the past tense form (*took*), not a past participle.

The Michigan Dunes, located on Lake Michigan's eastern
              A   B

shore, may to reach a height of 200 feet.
        C   D

After a modal auxiliary, the simple form of the verb (*reach*) should be used in place of the full infinitive (*to reach*).

Dextrose does not taste as sweet as table sugar is.
            A   B C   D

The correct auxiliary verb in this sentence is *does*, not *is*. The auxiliary *does* replaces the present tense verb *tastes*. ▲

Exercise 34.1

Focus: Choosing correct verb forms to achieve subject-verb agreement.

Directions: Underline the form that correctly completes each sentence. The first one is done as an example.

1. Ethics (is/are) the study of moral duties, principles, and values.

2. The first bridge to be built with electric lights (was/were) the Brooklyn Bridge.

3. There (is/are) two types of calculus, differential and integral.

4. George Gershwin, together with his brother Ira, (was/were) the creator of the first musical comedy to win a Pulitzer Prize.

5. In a chess game, the player with the white pieces always (moves/move) first.

6. The Earth and Pluto (is/are) the only two planets believed to have a single moon.

7. A number of special conditions (is/are) necessary for the formation of a geyser.

8. Each of the Ice Ages (was/were) more than a million years long.

9. The battery, along with the alternator and starter, (makes/make) up the electrical system of a car.

10. Teeth (is/are) covered with a hard substance called enamel.

11. The more-or-less rhythmic succession of economic booms and busts (is/are) referred to as the business cycle.

12. The number of protons in the nucleus of an atom (varies/vary) from element to element.

13. All trees, except for the tree fern, (is/are) seed-bearing plants.

14. Fifteen hundred dollars a year (was/were) the per capita income in the United States in 1950.

15. Everyone who (goes/go) into the woods should recognize common poisonous plants such as poison ivy and poison oak.

Exercise 34.2

Focus: Recognizing and correcting errors in verb tense and form.

Directions: If the underlined form is correct, mark the sentence *C*. If the underlined form is incorrect, mark the sentence *X* and write a correction for the underlined form in the blank at the end of the sentence. The first one is done as an example.

__X__ 1. Coal, grain, steel, and other products are often <u>shipping</u> by barge on inland waterways.
____shipped____

_____ 2. The first cotton mill in Massachusetts <u>has built</u> in the town of Beverly in 1787.
_____

_____ 3. Physician Alice Hamilton <u>is known</u> for her research on industrial diseases. _____

_____ 4. When scientists search a site for fossils, they begin by examining places where the soil has <u>wore</u> away from the rock. _____

_____ 5. The popularity of recreational vehicles <u>has been grown</u> over the last few decades. _____

_____ 6. Experts have estimated that termites cause as much property damage every year as fire <u>has</u>. _____

_____ 7. In music, a chord is the sound of two or more notes that <u>are playing</u> together. _____

_____ 8. The white pine <u>is</u> the most commercially important forest tree in North America until the beginning of the twentieth century. _____

_____ 9. In 1846 the Swiss naturalist Louis Agassiz <u>come</u> to the United States to give a series of lectures. _____

_____ 10. Parrots and crows <u>are considered</u> the most intelligent birds. _____

_____ 11. Portable fire extinguishers generally <u>containing</u> liquid carbon dioxide. _____

_____ 12. The first experimental telegraph line in the United States <u>run</u> from Baltimore to Washington, a distance of forty miles. _____

_____ 13. The first seven American astronauts <u>were chose</u> in 1959. _____

_____ 14. Since ancient times, farmers <u>used</u> scarecrows to protect their crops from hungry birds. _____

_____ 15. In the late nineteenth century, many important theories in both the biological and the physical sciences <u>have been produced</u>. _____

Exercise 34.3

Focus: Identifying and correcting errors involving verb forms. (Note: One or two items in this exercise do not focus on word-form errors. These are marked in the answer key with an asterisk.)

Directions: Decide which of the four underlined words or phrases—(A), (B), (C), or (D)—would not be considered correct, and write the letter of the expression in the blank. Then, in the line at the end of the sentence, write a correction for the underlined phrase. The first one is done as an example.

__A__ 1. Medical students must to study both the theory and practice of medicine.
         __study__   A   B   C   D

_____ 2. The seal, like the sea lion and the walrus, is a descendant of ancestors that once live
                 A   B   C   D
on the land. _____

_____ 3. The top layer of the ocean stores as much heat as does all the gases in the atmosphere.
         A   B   C   D
        _____

_____ 4. Every one of the body's billions of cells require a constant supply of food and oxygen.
                      A   B   C   D
        _____

_____ 5. In science, the results of an experiment are not generally accepted until they had been
         A   B   C
duplicated in other laboratories. _____
  D

_____ 6. In colonial times, flax and wool required months of preparation before they could be
        A   B   C
dyed and spin into cloth. _____
      D

_____ 7. Although some people find bats terrifying, they are actually beneficial because they
                    A   B   C
ate harmful insects. _____
 D

_____ 8. Each of the four types of human teeth are suited for a specific purpose. _____
        A   B   C   D

_____ 9. Mathematicians taken centuries to develop the methods that now arc used in
                   A   B   C
arithmetic . _____
  D

_____ 10. Electric milking machines have made dairy farming a much easier job than it once did .
          A   B   C   D
       _____

_____ 11. Playwright Frank Shin has often describes the lives of Chinese Americans in his dramas .
        A   B   C   D
       _____

_____ 12. Cans of paint must be <u>shaking</u> to <u>mix</u> the pigments with the medium <u>in which</u> they are
                                    A   B   C

in <u>suspended</u>. _____
   D

_____ 13. Beavers <u>continuously</u> <u>repair</u> the dams <u>they</u> have <u>build</u>. _____
                          A   B   C   D

_____ 14. The <u>emphasize</u> on team sports has <u>become</u> even <u>stronger</u> in this century than it <u>was</u>
                    A   B   C   D

in the past. _____

_____ 15. Sheep <u>are</u> often <u>dip</u> in liquid chemicals to <u>eliminate</u> ticks and <u>other</u> external parasites.
                      A   B   C   D

_____

LESSON 35

ERRORS WITH PARALLEL STRUCTURES

Written Expression items involving errors with parallel structures are similar to those in the Structure part of the test (Lesson 24). These sentences most often contain a series of three expressions: *X*, *Y*, and *Z*. One of these expressions is *not* grammatically parallel to the other two items in the series.

Structures that are often involved in parallelism are nouns, adjectives, verbs, prepositional phrases, gerunds, and infinitives.

Some problems with parallelism are actually word-form problems similar to those in Lesson 32.

▼ **Sample Item**

As a young <u>man</u>, George Washington liked <u>boating</u>, <u>to hunt</u>,
     A   B   C

and <u>fishing</u>.
    D

Option (C) is not parallel with the other items in the series: *to hunt* is an infinitive, while the other items are gerunds. You may have considered the other options that are part of the series, (B) and (D), but if you rewrote only one of these, the three expressions would still not be parallel.

In general, errors involving parallelism are easy to identify.

Exercise 35.1

Focus: Identifying and correcting errors involving parallelism.

Directions: If the underlined form is parallel to other forms in the sentence, mark the sentence *C*. If the underlined form is not parallel, mark the sentence *X* and write a correction for the underlined form in the blank at the end of the sentence. The first one is done as an example.

<u> X </u> 1. Because of their hardness, industrial diamonds can be used for cutting, <u>grind</u>, and drilling. <u> grinding </u>

_____ 2. Sacramento is the commercial, <u>industry</u>, and financial center of California's Central Valley, as well as being the state capital. _____

_____ 3. Philosophers are concerned with questions about nature, <u>human behavior</u>, society, and reality. _____

_____ 4. When taking part in winter sports, one should wear clothing that is lightweight, <u>warmth</u>, and suitable for the activity. _____

_____ 5. Folklore consists of the beliefs, customs, traditions, and <u>telling stories</u> that people pass from generation to generation. _____

_____ 6. Major sources of noise pollution include automobiles and other vehicles, industrial plants, and <u>heavy construction equipment</u>. _____

_____ 7. Steel is alloyed with manganese to increase its strength, hardness, and <u>resistance</u> to wear. _____

_____ 8. Scholar John Fiske wrote on history, <u>religious</u>, and social issues. _____

_____ 9. Electricity is used to light, <u>hot</u>, and cool buildings. _____

_____ 10. T. S. Eliott was equally distinguished as a poet, <u>he wrote criticism</u>, and a dramatist. _____

_____ 11. Jute is a glossy fiber that is strong, does not easily stretch, and <u>inexpensive</u>. _____

_____ 12. Wetlands were once considered useless areas, but they have been found to purify water, nurture wildlife, and <u>flood control</u>. _____

Exercise 35.2

Focus: Identifying and correcting errors with parallel structures. (Note: One or two items in this exercise do not focus on errors involving parallel structures. These are marked in the answer key with an asterisk.)

Directions: Decide which of the four underlined words or phrases—(A), (B), (C), or (D)—would not be considered correct, and write the letter of that expression in the blank. Then, in the line at the end of the sentence, write a correction for the underlined phrase. The first one is done as an example.

_B_ 1. Computers are <u>often used</u> to control, <u>adjustment</u>, and <u>correct</u> complex <u>industrial</u>
               A   B   C   D
operations. ___adjust___

_____ 2. The bellflower <u>is</u> a wildflower that <u>grows in</u> shady fields, in <u>marshes</u>, <u>and mountain</u>
                        A   B   C   D
slopes. _____

_____ 3. Eggs may be <u>boiled</u> in <u>the shell</u>, scrambled, <u>fried</u>, and cooked in countless <u>another</u>
                       A   B   C   D
ways. _____

_____ 4. Many places of <u>history</u>, scientific, <u>cultural</u>, or <u>scenic</u> importance have been designated
                         A   B   C
<u>national</u> monuments. _____
 D

_____ 5. R. Buckminster Fuller was <u>a design</u>, <u>an architect</u>, <u>an inventor</u>, and <u>an engineer</u>.
                                   A   B   C   D
_____

_____ 6. <u>Modern</u> motorcycles are <u>lighter</u>, faster, <u>and specialized</u> than <u>motorcycles</u> of 25 years
         A   B   C   D
ago. _____

_____ 7. Many people who live near the ocean <u>depend on</u> it as a source of <u>food</u>, <u>recreation</u>, and
                                                A   B   C
<u>to have economic</u> opportunities. _____
 D

_____ 8. Large commercial fishing vessels are <u>equipped</u> to clean, <u>packaging</u>, and <u>freeze</u> the fish
                                               A   B   C

                that they catch <u>at sea</u>. _____
                                            D

_____ 9. As <u>a breed</u>, golden retrievers are <u>intelligent</u>, <u>loyally</u>, and <u>friendly</u> dogs. _____
                  A   B   C   D

_____ 10. Mathematics can be considered a <u>language</u>, an art, <u>a science</u>, a <u>tool</u>, or <u>playing a game</u>.
                                                  A   B   C   D

       _____

_____ 11. <u>Paper</u> may contain <u>vegetable</u>, <u>minerals</u>, or <u>man-made</u> fibers. _____
              A   B   C   D

_____ 12. According to Susan Sontag, <u>our concepts</u> of <u>art</u>, beauty, and <u>nature</u> <u>has</u> been changed
                                            A   B   C   D

                by photography. _____

_____ 13. The economist Kenneth Boulding <u>proposed</u> a single social science that <u>would unify</u>
                                            A   B

                <u>economic</u>, sociology, and <u>political</u> science. _____
                  C   D

_____ 14. The <u>teeth front</u> are used to <u>bite</u> <u>food</u>, the canines to tear it, and the molars <u>to grind it</u>.
                             A   B   C   D

       _____

_____ 15. An ant's antennae provide <u>it</u> with the senses of <u>hear</u>, smell, <u>touch</u>, and <u>taste</u>.
                                           A   B   C   D

       _____

LESSON 36

ERRORS WITH PRONOUNS

Pronoun errors in Written Expression involve several types of pronouns:

- **Personal pronouns**
  (*he, she, it, they,* and so on)

- **Reflexive pronouns**
  (*himself, herself, itself, themselves,* and so on)

- **Relative pronouns** (adjective clause markers)
  (*who, whose, which, that,* and so on)

- **Demonstrative pronouns**
  (*this, that, these, those*)

For the purposes of this lesson, possessive adjectives (*his* house, *their* bicycles) are considered personal pronouns and demonstrative adjectives (*that* book, *those* horses) are considered demonstrative pronouns.

The greatest number of errors involve personal pronouns.

A) Errors in Pronoun/Noun Agreement

A pronoun must agree with the noun to which it refers (the pronoun's **referent**).

Most agreement errors with personal pronouns, reflexive pronouns, and demonstrative pronouns consist of a singular pronoun referring to a plural noun or a plural pronoun referring to a singular noun.

Agreement errors with relative pronouns usually involve the use of *who* to refer to things or *which* to refer to persons. (Note: The relative pronoun *that* can be used in certain sentences to refer to both persons and things.)

Another error involves the use of *this* or *these* in place of *that* and *those*. (*This* and *these* are used to refer to things that are perceived as close in time or space; *that* and *those* are used to refer to things that are perceived as distant in time or space.)

▼ **Sample Items**

Jackrabbits <u>have</u> powerful <u>rear legs</u> that enable <u>it</u> to leap long <u>distances</u>.
  A B C D

Ⓐ Ⓑ ⬤ Ⓓ

The pronoun referring to the plural noun *Jackrabbits* must be plural.

The <u>best way</u> for children to learn <u>science</u> is <u>to perform</u> experiments

<u>himself</u>.
  D

Ⓐ Ⓑ Ⓒ ⬤

The referent is plural (*children*), so the reflexive pronoun must also be plural (*themselves*) to agree with it. Therefore, the best answer is (D).

The Canadian Shield is a huge , rocky region who curves around Hudson
                       ─────   ───   ─────
                         A   B   C

Bay like a giant horseshoe.
    ────
      D

The referent for the pronoun *who* is *region*. To agree with the referent, the
relative pronoun *which* or *that* must be used. The pronoun *who* can refer
only to a person.

Trademarks enable a company to distinguish its products from these of
          ──────   ───   ─────
             A   B   C

another company.
───────
   D

The demonstrative *these* cannot be used to refer to the products of another
company. The demonstrative *those* should be used instead.   ▲

B) Errors in Pronoun Form

These errors usually involve personal pronouns. A subject form like *he* might be used in place of
an object form like *him*, or a possessive pronoun like *hers* might be used in place of a possessive
adjective like *her*. This type of pronoun error is usually easy to spot.

▼ **Sample Item**

Herman Melville gathered material for him novels, including *Moby Dick,*
                 ────────   ───
                    A   B

during his years at sea.
──────   ──────
   C   D

The possessive form *his,* not the object form *him,* is required.   ▲

C) Incorrect Type of Pronoun

In some sentences, the wrong type of pronoun is used. For example, a reflexive pronoun might be
used when a personal pronoun is needed, or a personal pronoun used when a relative pronoun is
required.

▼ **Sample Items**

As larvae, barnacles are free-swimming, but as adults they attach them
                     ───   ─────────   ─────
                      A   B   C

to stones, docks, and hulls of ships.
                            ────────
                               D

The reflexive pronoun is required because the subject and object are the
same entity: *they attach themselves.*

A barometer is <u>a</u> device <u>it is</u> used <u>to measure</u> atmospheric <u>pressure</u>.
         A   B   C   D

A personal pronoun (*it*) cannot be used to connect an adjective clause to the rest of the sentence. A relative pronoun (*which* or *that*) must be used instead.

D) Incorrect Inclusion of Pronouns

Some errors involve the unnecessary use of pronouns. Often, this type of error occurs when a personal pronoun is used as a subject in a sentence that already has a noun subject. It may also involve a personal pronoun used unnecessarily in a relative clause.

In a few items, a relative pronoun is used unnecessarily.

▼ **Sample Items**

Block Island <u>in</u> Long Island Sound <u>it is</u> <u>surrounded</u> by cold,
          A   B   C

<u>dangerous</u> waters.
  D

The subject of the sentence is *Block Island*; the personal pronoun *it* is an unnecessary repetition of the subject.

Dutch elm disease, <u>which</u> <u>it is</u> <u>caused</u> by a fungus, <u>can destroy</u> a
                            A   B   C

tree <u>within</u> four weeks.
    D

The relative pronoun *which* is the true subject of the relative clause; the personal pronoun *it* is not needed.

Certain <u>types</u> of turtles <u>that may</u> live <u>as long as</u> 100 <u>years</u>.
        A   B   C   D

The relative pronoun *that* is unnecessary in this sentence because there is only one verb (*may live*). A sentence that contains a relative clause must have a verb in each clause.

Exercise 36.1

Focus: Identifying and correcting errors of pronoun agreement.

Directions: If the underlined form is correct, mark the sentence *C*. If the underlined form is incorrect, mark the sentence *X* and write a correction for the underlined form in the blank at the end of the sentence. The first one is done as an example.

__X__ 1. One cannot see through translucent materials, but light can pass though <u>it</u>.
____them____

_____ 2. Unlike other cats, the cheetah cannot fully retract <u>their</u> claws. _____

_____ 3. Investment banking is concerned with the sale of government bonds, and <u>he</u> also deals with corporate stocks and bonds. _____

_____ 4. The oldest known forms of fossils are <u>those</u> of microscopic plants similar to algae. _____

_____ 5. Gene Krupa had one of the few big bands <u>who</u> was centered around a drummer. _____

_____ 6. Emeralds get <u>its</u> beautiful green color from titanium and chromium impurities in the stone. _____

_____ 7. The viola is larger and heavier than the violin, and <u>she</u> has a darker, somewhat nasal tone. _____

_____ 8. The Ringling Brothers were five brothers <u>which</u> built a small group of performers into the world's largest circus. _____

_____ 9. Storms on the planet Saturn may be larger than the planet Earth <u>itself</u>. _____

_____ 10. The molecules of a liquid are held together tighter than <u>that</u> of a gas. _____

_____ 11. Ducks make nests out of leaves and <u>its</u> own feathers. _____

_____ 12. The clipper ship *Flying Cloud* was one of the fastest ships of <u>their</u> kind. _____

_____ 13. There are thousands of kinds of bacteria, many of <u>whom</u> are beneficial. _____

_____ 14. When babies reach the age of one, <u>her</u> growth begins to slow down. _____

_____ 15. The arrangement of keys on the keyboard of a personal computer is almost the same as <u>those</u> on a standard typewriter. _____

Exercise 36.2

Focus: Identifying and correcting errors involving incorrect types and forms of pronouns.

Directions: If the underlined form is correct, mark the sentence *C*. If the underlined form is incorrect, mark the sentence *X* and write a correction for the underlined form in the blank at the end of the sentence. The first one is done as an example.

__X__ 1. Artist Margaret Leng Tan combined dance and piano playing in <u>hers</u> performances.
____her____

_____ 2. Over the years, the intensive breeding of domestic rabbits has given <u>their</u> softer, finer fur than wild rabbits. _____

_____ 3. New England poet Edwin A. Robinson moved to New York City in 1896 and devoted <u>himself</u> to his writing. _____

_____ 4. Yellow journalism was a form of news reporting <u>it</u> emphasized the spectacular aspects of the news. _____

_____ 5. There are between 100 and 400 billion stars in <u>ours</u> galaxy, the Milky Way. _____

_____ 6. The atoms of a crystal always arrange <u>them</u> into a specific array, called a lattice. _____

_____ 7. Fred Astaire and Gene Kelly were basically tap dancers, but <u>their</u> both added some ballet movements to their dance steps. _____

_____ 8. The Pritzken Prize is given every year to architects <u>their</u> work benefits humanity and the environment. _____

_____ 9. Charleston, South Carolina, has preserved to a remarkable degree <u>it</u> historic houses and famous gardens. _____

_____ 10. Ice fishermen sometimes build small, movable huts to protect <u>them</u> from the cold winds.
_____

Exercise 36.3

Focus: Identifying errors involving the incorrect inclusion of pronouns.

Directions: If the sentence contains a pronoun that is incorrectly included, mark that sentence *X* and underline the pronoun. If the sentence does not contain an incorrect pronoun inclusion, mark that sentence *C*. The first one is done as an example.

__X__ 1. The first great public library in the United States <u>it</u> was founded in Boston in the 1830's.

_____ 2. Floods which cause billions of dollars worth of property damage in the United States annually.

_____ 3. As a class, percussion instruments such as drums that are the simplest in construction of any musical instruments.

_____ 4. Richard G. Hatcher of Gary, Indiana, he was one of the first black mayors of a sizable American city.

_____ 5. Active stocks are stocks which are frequently bought and sold.

_____ 6. There are many species of plants and animals that they are peculiar to Hawaii.

_____ 7. Pipettes are glass tubes, open at both ends, which chemists use them to transfer small volumes of liquid.

_____ 8. When molten basalt cools, it forms six-sided columns.

_____ 9. Elizabeth Peabody, founder of the first American kindergarten, she helped gain acceptance of that institution as a regular part of public education.

_____ 10. Today meteorologists obtain the information which they use to make weather predictions chiefly from satellites.

_____ 11. Cells often obtain water through which the process of osmosis.

_____ 12. The lighting of large outdoor arenas it first became feasible in the 1930's.

Exercise 36.4

Focus: Identifying and correcting errors involving pronouns. (Note: One or two items in this exercise do not focus on pronoun errors. These are marked in the answer key with an asterisk.)

Directions: Decide which of the four underlined words or phrases—(A), (B), (C), or (D)—would not be considered correct, and write the letter of the expression in the blank. Then, in the line at the end of the sentence, write a correction for the underlined phrase. The first one is done as an example.

_C_   1. A caricature is a picture <u>in which</u> the subject's <u>distinctive</u> features <u>they are</u> deliberately
                              A   B   C

   <u>exaggerated</u> . _____*are*_____
        D

_____ 2. A beaver uses <u>its strong</u> front <u>teeth</u> to cut down trees and <u>peel off</u> <u>its</u> bark.
                            A   B   C   D

         _____

_____ 3. Ants are blind to red light, so <u>it is</u> possible to observe <u>themselves</u> in an artificial nest
                                         A   B

   <u>without</u> disturbing <u>their</u> activities. _____
        C   D

_____ 4. An auger is <u>a tool</u> which a carpenter <u>uses it</u> <u>to bore</u> holes <u>in wood</u> . _____
                        A   B   C   D

_____ 5. The glaciers in Olympia National Park are <u>unusually</u> because <u>they</u> are found at altitudes
                                                   A   B

   lower than <u>those</u> at <u>which</u> glaciers are usually found. _____
                 C   D

_____ 6. In <u>his</u> novels, Sinclair Lewis <u>drew</u> critical portraits of Americans <u>who</u> thought of <u>them</u>
                A   B   C   D

   as model citizens. _____

_____ 7. Jaguars <u>which resemble</u> leopards, but <u>they</u> are larger and are <u>marked</u> with rosettes
                      A   B   C

   <u>rather than</u> spots. _____
        D

_____ 8. Most bacteria <u>have</u> strong cell walls <u>much</u> <u>like</u> <u>that</u> of plants. _____
                          A   B   C   D

_____ 9. Bees <u>collect</u> pollen, <u>which</u> <u>furnishes</u> protein for <u>its</u> diet. _____
                  A   B   C   D

_____ 10. A small business <u>often</u> limits <u>their</u> operations to a single <u>neighborhood</u> or a group of
                              A   B   C

   neighboring <u>communities</u> . _____
                    D

_____ 11. Louisa May Alcott, <u>she</u> is best known for <u>her books</u> for children, <u>served as</u> a nurse
                                A   B   C

   <u>during</u> the Civil War. _____
        D

_____ 12. The <u>principles</u> used in air-conditioning are <u>basically</u> the same as <u>those</u> used by the
                  A   B   C

   human body to cool <u>himself</u> . _____
                          D

_____ 13. In that age of computers, it is difficult to imagine how tedious the work of accountants
               A   B   C

      and clerks must have been in the past. _____
                      D

_____ 14. In general, the only kind of cells that cannot replace itself are nerve cells.
           A   B   C   D

      _____

_____ 15. The naturalist Edwin Teal illustration his books with photographs he had taken himself.
                                   A   B   C   D

      _____

LESSON 37

ERRORS WITH SINGULAR AND PLURAL NOUNS

A) Plural Nouns in Place of Singular Nouns and Singular Nouns in Place of Plural Nouns

Underlined nouns in the Written Expression section may be incorrect because they are plural but should be singular, or because they are singular but should be plural.

Sometimes it is clear that a singular subject is incorrectly used because the verb is plural, or that a plural noun is used incorrectly because the verb is singular. In this type of item, the verb will *not* be underlined, because this is not a verb error.

Sometimes it is obvious that a plural or a singular noun is needed because of the determiners that precede the noun. Certain determiners are used only before singular nouns while other determiners are used only before plural nouns.

Determiners Used with Singular Nouns	Determiners Used with Plural Nouns
a/an	two, three, four, etc.
one	dozens of
a single	hundreds of
each	thousands of
every	a few (of)
this	many (of)
that	a number of
	the number of
	a couple (of)
	every one of
	each one of
	each of
	one of
	these
	those

Each *contestant* won a prize.
Each of the *contestants* won a prize.
This *flower* is a yellow rose.
These *flowers* are yellow roses.
I attended only one *game* this season.
It was one of the most exciting *games* that I had ever attended.

▼ **Sample Items**

Several of Washington Irving's story have become classics in
                  —————————— ———   ——————
                        A   B   C

American literature.
         —————————
              D

In this item, both the determiner before the noun (*Several of*) and the plural verb (*have*) indicate that a plural noun (*stories*) should be used.

Mauna Loa, an active volcano on the island of Hawaii, usually has
              ——————   —— ————————
                 A   B   C

one eruptions every three years.
     —————————
          D

A singular noun must be used after the determiner *one*.

One of the most beautiful state capitol is the Utah State Capitol,
    ——————   ——————————   ——————
        A   B   C

located in Salt Lake City.
————————
    D

The correct pattern is *one of the* + superlative adjective + plural noun. The plural noun *capitols* must therefore be used.   ▲

B) Errors Involving Irregular Plurals

Most plural nouns in English end in *-s*, but a few are irregular. Only the most common irregular plurals are tested on TOEFL. (Irregular plurals that come to English from Latin or Greek—*data*, *cacti*, *alumnae*, or *phenomena*, for example—will NOT be tested on TOEFL.)

Common Irregular Plural Nouns	
Singular Noun	*Plural Noun*
child	children
man	men
woman	women
foot	feet
tooth	teeth
mouse	mice
fish	fish

▼ **Sample Item**

As <u>childs</u> grow <u>older</u>, <u>their</u> bones become <u>thicker</u> and longer.
   _A   _B   _C   _D

The correct plural form of *child* is *children*.   ▲

C) Errors with Plural Forms of Non-Count Nouns

In some items a non-count noun (such as *furniture*, *research*, *sunshine*, *information*, or *bread*) is incorrectly given as a plural noun.

▼ **Sample Item**

Some encyclopedias <u>deal with</u> specific fields, such as <u>music</u> or
   _A   _B   _C

philosophy, and provide <u>informations</u> on only those subjects.
                          _D

Information is an uncountable noun and cannot be pluralized.   ▲

D) Errors with Plural Compound Nouns

Compound nouns consist of two nouns used together to express a single idea: *grocery store*, *travel agent*, *dinner party*, and *house cat*, for example. Only the second noun of compounds is pluralized: *grocery stores*, *travel agents*, *dinner parties*, and *house cats*.

   (There are rare exceptions to this rule—*sports cars* and *women doctors*, for example—but these won't be tested.)

▼ **Sample Item**

Raymond Chandler's <u>detectives stories</u> are <u>admired</u> by both critics
                      _A   _B

and general <u>readers</u>.
 _C   _D

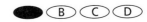

The correct plural form of this compound noun is *detective stories*.   ▲

E) Errors Involving Plural Forms of Numbers and Measurement

Some errors involve numbers + measurements:

   They went for a *six-mile* walk.
   They walked *six miles*.

In the first sentence, the number + measurement is used as an adjective, and the measurement is singular. In the second, the measurement is a noun and is therefore plural.

Numbers like *hundred*, *thousand*, and *million* may be pluralized when they are used indefinitely—in other words, when they do not follow other numbers.

seven thousand	thousands
five million dollars	millions of dollars

▼ Sample Items

The U.S. president serves a maximum of two four-years terms.
   A   B   C   D

When used before a noun, a number + measurement is singular.

Thousand of antibiotics have been developed, but only about
    A   B   C
thirty are in common use today.
    D

The plural form *Thousands* should be used.

Exercise 37

Focus: Identifying and correcting errors involving singular and plural nouns. (Note: One or two items in this exercise do not focus on singular-plural errors. These are marked in the answer key with an asterisk.)

Directions: Decide which of the four underlined words or phrases—(A), (B), (C), or (D)—would not be considered correct, and write the letter of the expression in the blank. Then, in the line at the end of the sentence, write a correction for the underlined phrase. The first one is done as an example.

__D__ 1. The male mandril baboon is one of the most colorful of all mammal. __mammals__
         A   B   C   D

_____ 2. Zoonoses are diseases that can be transmitted to humans beings by animals.
              A   B   C   D

         _____

_____ 3. Many championship automobiles and motorcycle races take place in Daytona Beach,
        A   B   C   D
Florida. _____

_____ 4. The Newberry Award is granted every years to the authors of outstanding books for
                      A   B   C
children. _____
   D

_____ 5. The major source of air pollution vary from city to city. _____
     A   B   C   D

_____   6. Around seventy-five percents of the Earth's surface is covered by water. _____
A   B   C   D

_____   7. All college and universities get their funds from a variety of sources. _____
A   B   C   D

_____   8. Russell Cave in northeastern Alabama was the home of cliff-dwelling Indians thousand of
A   B   C

years ago. _____
D

_____   9. In 1792 a corporation constructed a sixty-miles toll road from Philadelphia to Lancaster,
A   B   C   D

Pennsylvania. _____

_____   10. The mathematician and astronomer David Rittenhouse was one of the first man of
A   B   C

science in the American colonies. _____
D

_____   11. Publishers of modern encyclopedias employ hundreds of specialists and large editorials
A   B   C   D

staffs. _____

_____   12. The electric toaster was one of the earliest appliance to be developed for the kitchen.
A   B   C   D

_____

_____   13. Tornadoes can pick up objects as heavy as automobiles and carry them for hundreds of
A   B   C

foot. _____
D

_____   14. Many kinds of vegetables are growth in California's Imperial Valley. _____
A   B   C   D

_____   15. In typical pioneers settlements, men, women, and children worked from morning until
A   B   C

night at farm and household tasks. _____
D

_____   16. Some engineers have predicted that, within twenty years, automobiles will be make
A   B   C

almost completely of plastic. _____
D

_____   17. The pine tree is probably the more important lumber tree in the world. _____
A   B   C   D

_____ 18. Mary Lyon <u>founded</u> Mount Holyoke College, the first permanent <u>institution</u> of higher
                      A   B

learning for <u>woman</u> in the United States. _____
   C   D

_____ 19. <u>Adult</u> humans have more than a <u>trillions</u> <u>cells</u> in their <u>bodies</u> . _____
            A   B   C   D

_____ 20. Phytoplankton is <u>found</u> only in the upper <u>layers</u> of the <u>ocean</u>, where <u>sunlights</u> can
                             A   B   C   D

reach. _____

ANSWER SHEET
MINI-TEST 6: WRITTEN EXPRESSION

1. Ⓐ Ⓑ Ⓒ Ⓓ   10. Ⓐ Ⓑ Ⓒ Ⓓ   19. Ⓐ Ⓑ Ⓒ Ⓓ
2. Ⓐ Ⓑ Ⓒ Ⓓ   11. Ⓐ Ⓑ Ⓒ Ⓓ   20. Ⓐ Ⓑ Ⓒ Ⓓ
3. Ⓐ Ⓑ Ⓒ Ⓓ   12. Ⓐ Ⓑ Ⓒ Ⓓ   21. Ⓐ Ⓑ Ⓒ Ⓓ
4. Ⓐ Ⓑ Ⓒ Ⓓ   13. Ⓐ Ⓑ Ⓒ Ⓓ   22. Ⓐ Ⓑ Ⓒ Ⓓ
5. Ⓐ Ⓑ Ⓒ Ⓓ   14. Ⓐ Ⓑ Ⓒ Ⓓ   23. Ⓐ Ⓑ Ⓒ Ⓓ
6. Ⓐ Ⓑ Ⓒ Ⓓ   15. Ⓐ Ⓑ Ⓒ Ⓓ   24. Ⓐ Ⓑ Ⓒ Ⓓ
7. Ⓐ Ⓑ Ⓒ Ⓓ   16. Ⓐ Ⓑ Ⓒ Ⓓ   25. Ⓐ Ⓑ Ⓒ Ⓓ
8. Ⓐ Ⓑ Ⓒ Ⓓ   17. Ⓐ Ⓑ Ⓒ Ⓓ
9. Ⓐ Ⓑ Ⓒ Ⓓ   18. Ⓐ Ⓑ Ⓒ Ⓓ

MINI-TEST 6: WRITTEN EXPRESSION

Directions: The sentences below have four underlined words or phrases, (A), (B), (C), and (D). Identify the *one* underlined expression that must be changed for the sentence to be correct. Then find the number of the question on your answer sheet and fill in the space corresponding to the letter. Then mark the appropriate answer either in the blanks next to the items or on the answer sheet above.

Time: 12 minutes

_____ 1. Bricks <u>can be made</u> from <u>many</u> <u>difference</u> types of <u>clay</u> .
                 A   B   C   D

_____ 2. <u>Despite</u> most mushrooms are <u>edible</u> , some species <u>cause</u> serious <u>poisoning</u>.
          A   B   C   D

_____ 3. Judges in <u>dog shows</u> rate dogs on such points as <u>their</u> <u>colorful</u>, posture, shape, and <u>size</u>.
              A   B   C   D

_____ 4. The <u>medicine</u> of prehistoric people probably consisted of a <u>mixture of</u> scientific
              A   B

        practices, <u>superstitions</u> , and religious <u>believes</u>.
                    C   D

_____ 5. The game backgammon <u>has</u> been <u>playing</u> for <u>thousands</u> of years.
              A   B   C   D

_____ 6. <u>One of</u> the <u>greatest</u> of American automobile <u>designer</u> <u>was</u> Harley Earl.
           A   B   C   D

_____ 7. <u>Before</u> the late eighteenth century, most <u>textiles</u> were <u>done</u> <u>at home</u>.
          A   B   C   D

_____ 8. Political science, <u>alike</u> the <u>other</u> social <u>sciences</u>, is not <u>an exact</u> science.
                       A   B   C   D

_____ 9. About 8,000 <u>years</u> ago, people <u>began</u> using animals to carry <u>themselves</u> and their
               A   B   C   D
belongings.

_____ 10. Storks <u>constantly</u> rearrange their nests to keep <u>their</u> eggs <u>safety</u>, dry, and <u>warm</u>.
                   A   B   C   D

_____ 11. In its <u>purely</u> state, hydrochloric acid is <u>a gas</u>, but <u>it</u> is <u>almost always</u> used as a solution
              A   B   C   D
in water.

_____ 12. Animals <u>that</u> hibernate <u>usually</u> eat large <u>numbers</u> of food <u>in the</u> autumn.
                 A   B   C   D

_____ 13. <u>Many</u> folk <u>songs</u> have been <u>written</u> about railroads and <u>railroads</u> workers.
           A   B   C   D

_____ 14. Some plants and <u>insects</u> exhibit <u>so</u> high degree of interdependence that the elimination
                            A   B
of one <u>results</u> in the elimination of <u>the other</u>.
          C   D

_____ 15. <u>Lightly</u>, sandy soil <u>absorbs</u> water more <u>quickly</u> than clay <u>or</u> loam.
           A   B   C   D

_____ 16. Fannie Farmer, an <u>educator</u> and <u>cooking</u> expert, <u>she wrote</u> the first <u>distinctively</u>
                             A   B   C   D
American cookbook.

_____ 17. The rhesus monkey <u>has been</u> <u>widely</u> used in <u>biological</u>, psychological, and <u>medicine</u>
                         A   B   C   D
research.

_____ 18. <u>During</u> the Depression of the 1930's, <u>many</u> artists <u>were giving jobs</u> by the Federal Arts
           A   B   C   D
Project.

_____ 19. Crocodiles are sometimes <u>confused</u> with alligators, but are <u>different</u> from <u>they</u> in
                                A   B   C
<u>a number</u> of ways.
     D

_____ 20. As a concert <u>violinist</u>, conductor, and <u>he composed</u> both serious and popular <u>music</u>,
                   A   B   C
Leonard Bernstein achieved a series of <u>remarkable</u> successes.
                                            D

_____ 21. It is a <u>chemical</u> called capsaicin <u>that gives</u> hot peppers <u>their</u> <u>spice</u> flavor.
                  A   B   C   D

_____ 22. Flying snakes <u>can launch</u> <u>itself</u> from <u>the top of</u> one tree and glide to <u>another</u>.
                          A   B   C   D

_____ 23. A <u>basic</u> knowledge of social studies such as <u>history</u> and geography <u>are</u> considered an
              A   B   C
           important part of the education of every <u>child</u>.
                                                     D

_____ 24. The black walnut tree <u>is grown</u> principally for <u>its</u> lumber, <u>which is</u> used for cabinets and
                                 A   B   C
           <u>furnitures</u>.
            D

_____ 25. Plymouth was the <u>soonest</u> of the five <u>colonies</u> <u>established</u> by the Pilgrims <u>in</u>
                            A   B   C   D
           Massachusetts.

LESSON 38

ERRORS WITH VERBALS

Verbals are participles, gerunds, infinitives, and—for the purpose of this lesson—simple forms of the verb.

Participles are verbal adjectives. In this part of the test, participles are often seen before nouns as one-word adjectives. **Present participles** end with *-ing*. When used before a noun, present participles have an active meaning. **Past participles** of regular verbs end in *-ed*; the past participles of many common verbs are irregular. Before nouns, past participles have a passive meaning.

> It was an *exhausting* ten-kilometer race.   (present participle)
> The *exhausted* runners were too tired to move after the race.   (past participle)

In the first sentence, the race exhausts the runners. The race "performs" the action. In the second sentence, the runners are exhausted by the race. They receive the action.

Participles are also used in phrases after nouns as reduced (shortened) relative clauses. Again, present participles imply an active idea, past participles a passive one.

> The man *stealing* the money was arrested.
>   (present participle; means "who stole")
> The money *stolen* from the bank was recovered.
>   (past participle; means "which was stolen")

Gerunds are verbal nouns. Like present participles, gerunds end in *-ing*. They can be the subjects of verbs, the objects of prepositions, and the objects of certain verbs. (See the chart on the following page.)

> *Dancing* is good exercise.   (gerund as subject)
> You can solve this problem by *using* a calculator.   (gerund as object of a preposition)
> He enjoys *going* to good restaurants.   (gerund as object of a verb)

All two- and three-word verb phrases that can be followed by verbals are used with gerunds, not infinitives. This is true even when the verb phrase ends with the word *to*. (This can be tricky because infinitives always begin with the word *to*.)

> I'm looking forward to *going* to New Orleans.
> John is opposed to our *participating*.

Infinitives consist of the word *to* and the simple form of the verb. Like gerunds, infinitives can be the subjects of verbs and the objects of certain verbs (see chart). Unlike gerunds, infinitives can *never* be the objects of prepositions.

> *To help* others is rewarding.   (infinitive as subject)
> He attempted *to swim* across the river.   (infinitive as object of a verb)

Infinitives are used in several other ways:

> It's important *to change* the oil in your car frequently.
>   (infinitive after an adjective)
> The first man *to land* on the moon was Neil Armstrong.
>   (infinitive used as an adjective after a noun)
> She must take this class *to graduate*.
>   (infinitive used to show purpose)

Simple forms are the base forms of verbs; they consist of the infinitive without the word *to*.
Simple forms are used after the causative verbs *have, make,* and *let:*

He had the carpenter *repair* the door.
His father makes him *study* hard.
She let her son *go* on the trip.

Common Verbs That Take Verbal Objects		
Verbs Used with Gerunds	*Verbs Used with Infinitives*	*Verbs Used with Simple Forms*
admit	agree	have
avoid	allow	let
deny	arrange	make
enjoy	attempt	
finish	cause	
justify	choose	
quit	decide	
recommend	enable	
suggest	enjoy	
understand	hope	
	instruct	
	know (how)	
	learn (how)	
	permit	
	persuade	
	require	
	seem	
	teach (how)	
	tell	
	use	
	warn	

Watch for the following errors involving verbals:

A) Incorrect Choice of Verbal

Any of these verbals—participle, gerund, infinitive, or simple form—may be incorrectly used when another one of them is required.

▼ **Sample Items**

The writer Edgar Allan Poe is <u>usually</u> <u>credited</u> with <u>invent</u> the
         A   B   C

<u>short story</u>.
     D

After a preposition (*with*), a simple form cannot be used. The correct form is
a gerund (*inventing*).

A <u>single-lens</u> reflex <u>camera</u> allows a photographer <u>seeing</u> exactly what
       A   B   C

the camera <u>will photograph</u>.
                  D

After the verb *allow*, a gerund (*seeing*) cannot be used. An infinitive (*to see*)
is correct. ▲

B) Incorrect Choice of Participle

You may see past participles used incorrectly for present participles or present participles used
incorrectly for past participles.

You may also see a main verb used when a participle is required.

▼ **Sample Items**

There <u>are</u> probably <u>around</u> 3,000 languages <u>speaking</u> in <u>the world</u>.
       A   B   C   D

A past participle (*spoken*) is required because the idea is passive. The
sentence means, ". . . 3,000 languages *which are spoken* . . ."

<u>For decades</u>, journalist Theodore H. White <u>wrote</u> books <u>described</u>
       A   B   C

American <u>presidential</u> elections.
                D

The past participle *described* is used incorrectly because the idea is active:
the books described the elections. Therefore, a present participle,
describing, should be used. (The sentence could also be corrected by adding
a relative pronoun: *that described.*)

Nutmeg, widely <u>is used</u> as a <u>spice</u>, is <u>actually</u> the kernel of a
                   A   B   C

<u>tropical</u> nut.
    D

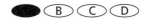

Rather than the main verb *is used*, a past participle (*used*) is required.

C) Incorrect Forms of Infinitives

Incorrect infinitive forms such as *for go* or *to going* may be used in place of the correct form, *to go*.

▼ **Sample Item**

Viral infections are generally more difficult to treating than bacterial
                 A   B   C

infections.
    D

The correct form of the infinitive is *to treat*. ▲

Exercise 38.1

Focus: Identifying incorrect and correct forms of gerunds, infinitives, and simple forms.

Directions: Underline the form that best completes each sentence. The first one is done as an example.

1. Sport parachutes are relatively easy (controlling/<u>to control</u>).

2. Sleeve bearings allow pistons (to move/move) back and forth.

3. One of the most important steps in (producing/to produce) a motion picture is film editing.

4. An opera singer is required (having/to have) a powerful and beautiful voice.

5. The Wampanoag Indians taught the Pilgrims how (growing/to grow) corn.

6. Frogs and certain kinds of birds use their tongues (to catch/catch) insects.

7. Isadora Martinez invented a knee implant that lets people with arthritis (to bend/bend) their knees easily.

8. Smells can be more effective than any other sensory stimuli in vividly (bringing/bring) back memories.

9. Modems permit computers (communicating/to communicate) with one another over telephone lines.

10. A sudden sound can make a golfer (to miss/miss) a shot.

11. Heavy spring snows may cause the branches of trees (snap/to snap).

12. Modern race cars store fuel in rubber bladders that are almost impossible (rupturing/to rupture).

13. New words are constantly being invented (describe/to describe) new objects and concepts.

14. Dr. Mary Walker, a surgeon in the Union Army during the Civil War, was the first and so far only woman (to be awarded/awarding) the Congressional Medal of Honor.

15. In 1957 Ralph Abernathy founded an organization devoted to (achieve/achieving) racial equality for black Americans.

Exercise 38.2

Focus: Identifying incorrect and correct forms of participles or verbs.

Directions: Underline the form that best completes each sentence. The first one is done as an example.

1. The largest (knowing/<u>known</u>) insects are found in tropical rain forests.

2. A bill of lading is a (writing/written) receipt for goods that are sent by public transportation.

3. A hummingbird's heart beats at the (astonishing/astonished) rate of 615 beats per minute.

4. At the peak of his jump, a pole vaulter performs a series of (twisting/twisted) body motions to clear the bar.

5. Anyone (working/worked) under conditions that cause a heavy loss of perspiration can suffer heat exhaustion.

6. A mosquito (filled/is filled) with blood is carrying twice its own body weight.

7. The state of Wisconsin has seventy-two counties, many (naming/named) after Indian tribes.

8. Sunspots occur in cycles, with the greatest number generally (appearing/are appearing) every eleven years.

9. A delta is a more-or-less triangular area of sediments (depositing/deposited) at the mouth of a river.

10. William H. Kilpatrick was a philosopher and scholar now generally (regarding/regarded) as the father of progressive education.

11. Checkerboard Mesa in Utah features a strangely (cracked/cracking) expanse of stone.

12. It has been known since the third century that coffee has a (stimulated/stimulating) effect.

Exercise 38.3

Focus: Identifying and correcting a variety of errors involving verbals. (Note: One or two items in this exercise do not focus on errors involving verbals. These are marked in the answer key with an asterisk.)

Directions: Decide which of the four underlined words or phrases—(A), (B), (C), or (D)—would not be considered correct, and write the letter of that expression in the blank. Then, in the line at the end of the sentence, write a correction for the underlined phrase. The first one is done as an example.

_C_ 1. The most <u>widely</u> used material for <u>package</u> consumer goods <u>is</u> cardboard.
        A   B   C   D

packaging

_____ 2. One of <u>the latest</u> methods <u>of quarrying</u> stone is <u>to cutting</u> the stone <u>with a</u> jet torch.
              A   B   C   D

_____ 3. In 1944 biologist Charles Michener <u>devised</u> a system for <u>to classify</u> the <u>approximately</u>
                                      A   B   C

    20,000 <u>species of</u> bees. _____
           D

_____   4. Most candles are made of paraffin wax <u>mix</u> with compounds <u>that have</u> higher melting

A   B

       points <u>to keep</u> them from <u>melting</u> in hot weather. _____

      C   D

_____   5. Machines <u>used</u> to <u>harvest</u> tree crops such as cherries or almonds can be <u>classified</u> either

A   B   C

       as shakers <u>and</u> as pick-up machines. _____

D

_____   6. Fishing cats, <u>found</u> in Southeast Asia, are <u>distinguished</u> by their <u>webbed</u> feet, which

        A   B   C

       enable them <u>catching</u> fish. _____

D

_____   7. Geothermal <u>energy</u> is energy <u>to obtain</u> by <u>using</u> heat from <u>the Earth's</u> interior.

      A   B   C   D

       _____

_____   8. <u>Bathe</u> in mineral water has <u>long been</u> believed <u>to have</u> beneficial <u>effects</u>. _____

A   B   C   D

_____   9. It is <u>the facets</u> <u>cut</u> into a diamond that <u>make</u> it <u>to sparkle</u>. _____

       A   B   C   D

_____ 10. Ralph Blakelock <u>specialized</u> in <u>paint</u> wild, lonely nighttime <u>landscapes</u>, usually with

              A   B   C

       black trees <u>silhouetted</u> against the moon. _____

D

_____ 11. The Farallon Islands are <u>a group of</u> <u>uninhabited</u> islands <u>lying</u> about <u>40 mile</u> west of San

                 A   B   C   D

       Francisco. _____

_____ 12. The <u>crushing</u> leaves of yarrow plants <u>can serve</u> as a <u>traditional</u> medicine for <u>cleansing</u>

     A   B   C   D

       wounds. _____

_____ 13. Robert A. Moog <u>developed</u> an electronic device that could <u>be</u> used <u>for play</u> <u>synthesized</u>

             A   B   C   D

       music. _____

_____ 14. Hypnosis <u>is sometimes</u> employed <u>as a</u> means of <u>helping</u> people to quit <u>to smoke</u>.

            A   B   C   D

       _____

_____ 15. Throughout his <u>long career</u>, Pete Seeger <u>has been</u> a <u>lead</u> figure in <u>reviving</u> folk music.

          A   B   C   D

       _____

LESSON 39

ERRORS WITH PREPOSITIONS

Errors with **prepositions** are among the most difficult errors to catch. Preposition use in English is very complex. For every rule, there seems to be an exception. Recently, there have been more errors involving prepositions in the Written Expression part of TOEFL, and the errors have been more difficult to spot.

Prepositions are used in the following ways:

- In adverbial phrases that show time, place, and other relationships

    in the morning   on Pennsylvania Avenue   to the park   by a student

- After certain nouns

    a cause of   a reason for   a solution to

- After certain adjectives and participles

    different from   aware of   disappointed in

- After certain verbs

    combine with   rely on   refer to

- In phrasal prepositions (two- and three-word prepositions)

    according to   together with   instead of   in spite of

- In certain set expressions

    by far   in general   on occasion   at last

Note: In Mini-Lessons for Section 2, found at the end of this section of the *Guide* (pages 260–267), all of these uses for prepositions are explained and practice exercises are provided.

There are two main types of preposition errors that you may see in the Written Expression part of the test:

A) Errors in Preposition Choice

The wrong preposition is used according to the context of the sentence.

Some of the rules for choosing the correct prepositions are given in the Mini-Lessons, but you will never be able to memorize all the rules for preposition use in English. The more you practice, though, the more you will develop a "feel" for determining which preposition is correct in any given situation.

There are two particular situations involving preposition choice that are often tested in Written Expression:

- **Errors with *from . . . to* and *between . . . and***

Both these expressions are used to give the starting time and ending time. They can also be used to show relationships of place and various other relationships.

> He lived in Seattle *from* 1992 *to* 1997.
> He lived in Seattle *between* 1992 *and* 1997.

> Route 66 ran *from* Chicago *to* Los Angeles.
> Route 66 ran *between* Chicago *and* Los Angeles.

Errors usually involve an incorrect pairing of those words, or the incorrect use of other prepositions:

between A *to* B   *from* X *and* Y
between A *with* B   *since* X *to* Y

■ Errors with *since, for,* and *in*

Since is used before a point in time with the present perfect tense—but never with the past tense. *For* is used before a period of time with the present perfect and other tenses. *In* is used before certain points in time (years, centuries, decades) with the past tense and other tenses—but never with the present perfect tense.

He's lived here *since* 1995.
He's lived here *for* two years.
He moved here *in* 1995.

Errors involve the use of one of these prepositions for another:

*He's lived here *in* 1995.
*He's lived here *since* two years.
*He lived here *since* 1995.

▼ Sample Items

The pitch of a <u>tuning fork</u> depends <u>of</u> the <u>size</u> and shape of <u>its</u> arms.
           A   B   C   D

The correct preposition after the verb *depend* is *on,* not *of.*

The Alaskan Pipeline <u>runs</u> <u>between</u> Prudhoe Bay on the Arctic
                      A   B

Coastal Plain to the <u>port</u> of Valdez, a <u>distance</u> of 789 miles.
                     C   D

The correct pattern is *from . . . to.*

Candles were <u>mankind's</u> chief <u>source of</u> illumination <u>since</u>
               A   B   C

at <u>least</u> 2,000 years.
   D

Before a period of time (*2,000 years*) the preposition *for* should be used.   ▲

B) Incorrect Inclusion or Omission of Prepositions

A preposition is used when one is not needed, or not used when one is needed.

▼   **Sample Items**

<u>According many</u> critics, Mark Twain's novel *Huckleberry Finn* is his
$\qquad$ A

<u>greatest</u> work, and is <u>one of the</u> greatest American <u>novels</u> ever written.
    B   C   D

The preposition *to* has been omitted from the phrase *According to*.

<u>Some</u> of the <u>most of</u> spectacular waterfalls <u>in the</u> eastern
    A   B   C

United States <u>are found in</u> the Pocono Mountains of Pennsylvania.
                    D

The preposition *of* should not be used in this phrase. (When *most* means "majority," it can be used in the phrase *most of the*. "Most of the people agree . . . ," for example. However, in this sentence, *most* is part of the superlative form of the adjective *spectacular*, and so cannot be used with *of*.)   ▲

Exercise 39.1

Focus: Identifying correct and incorrect preposition choice.

Directions: Underline the prepositions that correctly complete the sentences below. The first one is done as an example.

1. (<u>For</u>/To) an injection to be effective (on/<u>against</u>) tetanus, it must be administered (by/<u>within</u>) seventy-two hours (<u>of</u>/for) the injury.

2. Wage rates depend (in/on) part (from/on) the general prosperity (of/for) the economy.

3. The invention (of/for) the hand-cranked freezer opened the door (of/to) commercial ice cream production, and (for/since) then, the ice-cream industry has grown (in/into) a four-billion-dollar-a-year industry.

4. (At/On) the time (of/in) the Revolutionary War, the North American colonies were merely a long string (with/of) settlements (along/among) the Atlantic Coast (between/from) Maine and Georgia.

5. The probability (of/for) two people (in/on) a group (of/for) ten people having birthdays (in/on) the same day is about one (in/of) twenty.

6. Showboats were floating theaters that tied up (at/to) towns (in/on) the Ohio and Mississippi rivers to bring entertainment and culture (to/at) the people (on/in) the frontier.

7. Scrimshaw, the practice (of/for) carving ornate designs (in/on) ivory, was first practiced (by/of) sailors working (by/with) sail needles while (in/on) long sea voyages.

8. Assateague Island, (off/of) the coast (off/of) Virginia, is famous (for/to) its herds (of/with) wild ponies.

9. (In/On) order (for/to) an object to be visible, light must travel (from/for) that object (at/to) a person's eyes.

10. (In/On) the 1930's and 1940's, when train travel was (on/at) its peak, passengers could look forward (for/to) wonderful meals (on/at) trains.

11. (In/Since) the 1960's, op art, which was based (in/on) scientific theories (of/for) optics, employed patterns (of/in) lines and colors that seemed to change shape as the viewer looked (on/at) them.

12. The first national convention devoted (for/to) the issue (of/with) women's rights, organized partly (of/by) Elizabeth Cady Stanton, was held (in/on) her hometown (in/of) Seneca Falls, New York, (in/on) 1848.

13. (In/Since) 1716 a party (of/for) explorers led (by/with) Lieutenant Governor Spotswood (of/in) Virginia tried (in/on) vain to find a route (through/of) the Appalachian Mountains.

14. Dolphins rely (in/on) echolocation, a form (of/for) navigation similar (with/to) the sonar systems used (on/at) submarines.

15. Analytical geometry, (in/on) which algebraic ideas are used (for/to) the description (of/for) geometric objects, has been (in/on) use (in/since) the seventeenth century.

Exercise 39.2

Focus: Identifying and correcting errors involving the inclusion or omission of prepositions.

Directions: If there is a preposition unnecessarily included in a sentence, mark that sentence *X* and underline the preposition. If there is a preposition incorrectly omitted from a sentence, mark that sentence *X*, underline the word before and after the missing preposition, and write the correct preposition on the line at the end of the sentence. If the sentence is correctly written, mark that sentence *C*. The first one is done as an example.

___*X*___ 1. <u>According polls</u> taken throughout the twentieth century, Lincoln and Washington are the preeminent American presidents. _____*to*_____

_____ 2. Today, many varieties of fruit are available all year thanks improved storage and shipping techniques. _____

_____ 3. The origin of the Moon remains a mystery. _____

_____ 4. Traffic jams can cause of pollution, delays, and short tempers. _____

_____ 5. The Sun's rays heat the Earth's surface, on which then radiates the heat into the air. _____

_____ 6. A warm-blooded animal is one that keeps the same body temperature regardless the air temperature. _____

_____ 7. Charlie Parker, considered by many the greatest improviser in the history of jazz, influenced many other jazz musicians. _____

_____ 8. Most of people are aware of the need to visit dentists regularly. _____

_____ 9. Muscle fibers are attached bones by tendons. _____

_____ 10. In his essay "Self-Reliance," Ralph W. Emerson told to his readers why they should not depend on the ideas of others. _____

_____ 11. The crayfish is a freshwater crustacean related the lobster. _____

_____ 12. Charles Goren was an expert the game of bridge. _____

_____ 13. Stomata are the tiny openings in the leaves of plants through which oxygen and carbon dioxide pass. _____

_____ 14. Ducks have small oil glands by which keep their feathers oily and repel water. _____

_____ 15. The tail of a comet always points away the Sun. _____

_____ 16. Lichens grow in extreme environments in where no other plants can exist.
_____

_____ 17. Not all of waterfalls are formed in the same way. _____

_____ 18. The pulmonary artery carries blood from the right side the heart to the lungs.
_____

_____ 19. In addition to the twelve constellations of the zodiac, thirty other constellations were familiar people of ancient times. _____

_____ 20. Rainbows always appear in that part of the sky opposite the Sun. _____

Exercise 39.3

Focus: Identifying and correcting preposition errors. (Note: One or two items in this exercise do _not_ focus on preposition errors. These are marked in the answer key with an asterisk.)

Directions: Decide which of the four underlined words or phrases—(A), (B), (C), or (D)—would not be considered correct, and write the letter of that expression in the blank at the beginning of the sentence. Then, in the blank at the end of the sentence, write a correction for the underlined phrase. The first one is done as an example.

___A___ 1. Water polo is a game in which is played in the water by two teams, each with seven
              A   B C   D
         players. ____which____

_____ 2. Dynamics is a branch of physics that deals for the relationship between motion
             A   B   C
         and force . _____
         D

_____ 3. Many of radio stations began broadcasting baseball games during the 1920's.
            A   B   C   D
         _____

_____ 4. The economy of Maine is based to a great extent in its forests, which cover eighty
            A   B   C
         percent of its surface area. _____
         D

_____ 5. The removal of waste materials is essential to all forms of live . _____
            A   B   C   D

_____ 6. John Diefenbaker, Prime Minister of Canada during 1957 to 1963, is given much of the
                     A   B C
         credit for the adoption of the Canadian Bill of Rights. _____
           D

_____ 7. The first stage on the manufacturing of all types of clothing is the cutting of the
              A   B C   D
         material. _____

_____ 8. All of the wheat grown throughout the world belongs one of fourteen species.
                 A   B   C   D

_____

_____ 9. There are approximately 600 different species of trees native of the continental United
                            A   B   C   D

States. _____

_____ 10. Waterwheels, which appeared on the fourth century B.C., were probably the first
                            A   B   C

machines not powered by humans or animals. _____
                                D

_____ 11. Since centuries, Southwestern Indian tribes have valued turquoise and have used it
                 A   B   C

in jewelry. _____
         D

_____ 12. Loggerhead turtles lay thousands eggs at a single time, but only a few of the offspring
                                        A   B   C

survive to adulthood. _____
            D

_____ 13. In nowadays, commercial bakeries use complex, automated machines, but the basic
                 A

principles of baking have changed little for thousands of years. _____
              B   C   D

_____ 14. It takes over four years for light from the nearest star reaching the earth. _____
                    A   B   C   D

_____ 15. In the mid-1900's, an increasing number of jobs in the United States have involved the
                 A   B   C

handling of information. _____
            D

LESSON 40

ERRORS WITH ARTICLES

Like errors with prepositions, errors with articles are sometimes hard to catch. This is partly because of the complexity of the article system in English, and partly because articles, like prepositions, are "small words" and one's eye tends to skip over errors involving these words.

The basic uses of articles are explained in the chart:

Indefinite Articles *a* and *an*	Definite Article *the*	No Article (ø)
A or *an* is used before singular nouns when one does not have a specific person, place, thing, or concept in mind:	*The* is used before singular, plural, and non-count nouns when one has a specific person, place, thing, or concept in mind:	No article is used before non-count nouns or plural nouns when one does not have specific persons, places, things, or concepts in mind:
an orange	the orange	ø orange
a chair	the oranges	ø oranges
	the fruit	ø fruit
	the chair	ø chair
	the chairs	ø chairs
	the furniture	ø furniture

The indefinite article *a* is used before words that begin with a consonant sound (*a chair, a book*); *an* is used before words that begin with a vowel sound (*an orange, an ocean liner*). Before words that begin with the letters *h-* and *u-*, either *a* or *an* can be used, depending on the pronunciation of the words.

Vowel Sounds	Consonant Sounds
an honor	a hat
an umbrella	a university

There are also some specific rules for using (or not using) articles that you should be aware of.

■ An indefinite article can be used to mean "one." It can also be used to mean "per."

> a half, a quarter, a third, a tenth
> a mile a minute (one mile per minute)
> an apple a day (one apple per day)

■ A definite article is used when there is only one example of the thing or person, or when the identify of the thing or person is clear.

> *The Moon* went behind some clouds.   (There's only one Moon.)
> Please open *the door*.   (You know which door I mean.)

■ A definite article is usually used before these expressions of time and position.

the morning	the front	the beginning
the afternoon	the back	the middle
the evening*	the center	the end
	the top	
the past	the bottom	
the present		
the future		

*No article is used in the expression "at night."

■ A definite article comes before a singular noun that is used as a representative of an entire class of things. This is especially common with the names of animals, trees, inventions, musical instruments, and parts of the body.

> *The tiger* is the largest cat.
> My favorite tree is *the oak*.
> The Wright Bothers invented *the airplane*.
> *The oboe* is a woodwind instrument.
> *The heart* pumps blood.

■ A definite article is used before expressions with an ordinal number. No article is used before expressions with cardinal numbers.

the first	one
the fourth chapter	Chapter Four
the seventh volume	Volume Seven

■ A definite article is used before decades and centuries.

the 1930's	the 1800's
the fifties	the twenty-first century

■ A definite article is usually used before superlative forms of adjectives.

the widest river	the most important decision

■ A definite article is used in quantity expressions in this pattern: quantifier + *of* + *the* + noun.

many of the textbooks	not much of the paper
some of the water	most of the students
all of the people	a few of the photographs

These expressions can also be used without the phrase *of the*.

many textbooks	not much paper
some water	most students
all people	a few photographs

■ A definite article is used before the name of a group of people or a nationality. No article is used before the name of a language.

> *The Swedish* are proud of their ancestors, *the Vikings*.
> She learned to speak *Swedish* when she lived in Stockholm.

■ A definite article is used when an adjective is used without a noun to mean "people who are . . . ."

> Both the young and the old will enjoy this movie.
> The poor have many problems.

- A definite article is usually used before a non-count noun or a plural noun when it is followed by a modifier. No article is used when these nouns appear alone.

  > *The rice* that I bought today is in the bag.
  > *Rice* is a staple in many countries.
  > *Trees* provide shade.
  > *The trees* in this park are mostly evergreens.

- A definite article is used before the name of a field of study followed by an *of* phrase. If a field is used alone, or is preceded by an adjective, no article is used.

the literature of the twentieth century	literature
the history of the United States	American history

- Definite articles are used before the "formal" names of nations, states, and cities. (These usually contain *of* phrases.) No articles are used before the common names of nations, states, and cities.

the United States of America	America
the state of Montana	Montana
the city of Philadelphia	Philadelphia

- Definite articles are used before most plural geographic names: the names of groups of lakes, mountains, and islands. No article is used before the names of individual lakes, mountains, and islands.

the Great Lakes	Lake Powell
the Rocky Mountains	Mount Washington
the Hawaiian Islands	Long Island

In the Written Expression section, there are three main types of errors involving articles:

A) Incorrect Article Choice

One of the most common errors is the use of *a* in place of *an* or vice versa. Fortunately, this is also the easiest type of error to detect. Another error is *a* or *an* used in place of *the*, or *the* in place of *a* or *an*.

▼ **Sample Items**

> $\underset{A}{\underline{A \text{ eclipse}}}$ of $\underset{B}{\underline{\text{the Sun}}}$ may be $\underset{C}{\underline{\text{either}}}$ total or $\underset{D}{\underline{\text{partial}}}$.

An must be used before a noun beginning with a vowel sound such as *eclipse*.

> Rose Bird was $\underset{A}{\underline{a \text{ first}}}$ woman in $\underset{B}{\underline{\text{the history}}}$ of California $\underset{C}{\underline{\text{to serve}}}$
>
> on $\underset{D}{\underline{\text{the}}}$ State Supreme Court.

In a phrase with an ordinal number (such as *first*) the definite article *the* must be used. ▲

B) Incorrect Omission or Inclusion of an Article

Sometimes an article is used when none is needed, or one is omitted when one is required.

▼   **Sample Items**

Slag consists of <u>waste</u> materials and impurities <u>which</u>
                 A   B

<u>rise to top</u> of <u>melted metals</u>.
   C   D

The definite article *the* should not be omitted from the phrase *to the top of*.

<u>The most</u> asteroids <u>are</u> beyond <u>the</u> orbit of <u>the planet</u> Mars.
   A   B   C   D

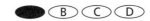

Definite article are used only before quantity expressions that contain *of* phrases. (*Most asteroids* or *Most of the asteroids* are both correct in this sentence.)   ▲

C) Use of a Definite Article in Place of a Possessive

A definite article may be incorrectly used in place of a possessive word—*its*, *his*, *her*, or *their*.

▼   **Sample Item**

The Ozark Mountains <u>of</u> Arkansas <u>are</u> <u>famous</u> for <u>the</u> rugged beauty.
                       A   B   C   D

The should correctly read *their* because the sentence refers to the beauty belonging to the Ozark Mountains.   ▲

Exercise 40.1

Focus: Identifying the correct and incorrect use of articles.

Directions: Underline the forms that correctly complete the sentence. The first one is done as an example.

1. Only about (the one/<u>one</u>) percent of (<u>the water</u>/water) on Earth is (the fresh/<u>fresh</u>) water.

2. (The mineral/Mineral) phosphate is (the most/most) common ingredient of all types of (the fertilizers/fertilizers).

3. (The/A) process of refining minerals requires (a/an) huge amount of (an electrical/electrical) energy.

4. (A humor/Humor) runs through (the American/American) literature from (the earliest/earliest) times until (the present/present).

5. (The ozone/Ozone) layer acts as (a/an) umbrella against (the most/most) of (the Sun's/Sun's) dangerous rays.

6. In (the early/early) 1800's, Sequoia, (a Cherokee/Cherokee) leader, created (the/a) first written form of (a North/North) American Indian language.

7. (The Goddard/Goddard) family of (the New/New) England produced some of (the/a) finest furniture made in (the United/United) States in (the seventeenth/seventeenth) century.

8. (The popcorn/Popcorn) has (a/the) same food value as any other kind of (a corn/corn).

9. One of (the most/most) important tools for (a research/research) in (the social/social) science is (a well-written/well-written) questionnaire.

10. Native to (the American/American) West, (the/a) coyote came east early in (the twentieth/twentieth) century when (its/the) chief natural competitor, (the/a) wolf, died out.

11. (The nineteenth/Nineteenth) century astronomer Alvin G. Clarke built hundreds of (the refracting/refracting) telescopes during (the/his) lifetime.

12. (The Hawaiian/Hawaiian) Islands are among (the most/most) geographically isolated islands in (the world/world).

Exercise 40.2

Focus: Identifying and correcting errors with articles. (Note: One or two items in this exercise do not focus on article errors. These are marked in the answer key with an asterisk.)

Directions: Decide which of the four underlined words or phrases—(A), (B), (C), or (D)—would not be considered correct, and write the letter of the expression in the blank. Then, in the line at the end of the sentence, write a correction for the underlined phrase. The first one is done as an example.

___A___ 1. The most butterfly eggs are coated with a sticky substance that holds them to plants .
         A   B   C   D

      ___Most___

_____ 2. A number of large insurance companies have the headquarters in Hartford,
           A   B   C   D

      Connecticut. _____

_____ 3. To be effective, an advertisement must first attract an attention . _____
             A   B   C   D

_____ 4. Virgin Islands National Park features a underwater preserve with coral reefs and colorful
                                     A   B   C

      tropical fish . _____
          D

_____ 5. Arthritis, a painful swelling of the joints, is often associated with elderly people, but
                     A   B   C

      can afflict young as well. _____
             D

_____ 6. Wilmington is an only large city in the state of Delaware. _____
                        A   B   C   D

_____ 7. About the third of the Earth's land surface is covered by relatively flat plains.
                 A   B   C   D

_____

_____ 8. In the 1920's, gasoline companies began giving away free road maps to the customers.
                  A   B   C   D

_____

_____ 9. The Tropic of Cancer is imaginary line that marks the northern boundary of the Earth's
                A   B   C   D

tropical zone. _____

_____ 10. Hereford cows are one of most common breeds of cattle raised for beef. _____
                 A   B   C   D

_____ 11. American soprano Kathleen Battle taught music in elementary school before beginning
                                              A   B

the career as a professional singer. _____
     C   D

_____ 12. In 1891 first state law to help local communities pay for highways was passed in New
                   A   B   C   D

Jersey. _____

_____ 13. Lumber is dried and seasoned in an heated chamber called a dry kiln. _____
                 A   B   C   D

_____ 14. Grandfather Mountain, highest mountain in the Blue Ridge mountain range, is in
                                  A   B   C   D

North Carolina. _____

_____ 15. The term "baritone" refers to the range of male voices that lies between tenor to bass.
                A   B   C   D

_____

_____ 16. It was around 1925 that accurate, convenient system for recording the choreography of
                  A   B   C

ballet was developed. _____
     D

_____ 17. Richard Byrd was the first person in the history to fly over the North Pole.
                        A   B   C   D

       _____

_____ 18. At beginning of the Civil War, Matthew Brady was authorized to accompany
              A   B

       the Union Army and take photographs. _____
              C   D

_____ 19. In 1878 in San Francisco, Kate Wiggins open the first kindergarten on the West Coast.
                        A   B   C   D

       _____

_____ 20. The tulip tree, the tallest broadleaf plant in the eastern United States, may reach height
              A   B   C   D

       of over 200 feet. _____

LESSON 41

ERRORS WITH COMPARATIVES AND SUPERLATIVES

Most adjectives have three forms: the absolute (the basic adjective form), the comparative, and the superlative. Comparatives are used to show that one item has more of some quality than another does.

> George is *taller* than his brother.

Superlatives are used to show that one item in a group of three or more has the greatest amount of some quality.

> He was the *tallest* man in the room.

The chart explains how comparatives and superlatives are formed:

	Absolute	Comparative	Superlative
One-syllable adjectives	warm	warmer	the warmest
Two-syllable adjectives ending with -*y*	funny	funnier	the funniest
Other two-syllable adjectives	common	more common	the most common
Adjectives with three or more syllables	important	more important	the most important

Some two-syllable adjectives have two correct forms of both the comparative and the superlative:

narrower	clever	polite
more narrow	more clever	more polite
narrowest	cleverest	politest
most narrow	most clever	most polite

A "negative" comparison can be expressed with the words *less* and *least*. *Less* and *least* are used no matter how many syllables an adjective has.

less bright	less expensive
the least bright	the least expensive

The absolute form of a few adjectives ends in -*er* (*tender, bitter, slender, clever,* and so on). Don't confuse these with the comparative forms (*more bitter* or *bitterer,* for example).

Many adverbs also have comparative and superlative forms. The comparative and superlative forms of all -*ly* adverbs are formed with *more* and *most*.

more brightly	more importantly
most brightly	most importantly

A few adjectives and adverbs have irregular comparative and superlative forms:

Irregular Comparatives and Superlatives		
good/well	better	the best
bad/badly	worse	the worst
far	farther	the farthest
	further	the furthest

(*Far* has two comparative and superlative forms, depending on how the word is used, but the distinction between these two forms will not be tested.)

There are two main types of errors involving comparatives and superlatives:

A) Incorrect Choice of the Three Forms

Any of the three forms—absolute, comparative, or superlative—may be incorrectly used in place of one of the other forms.

▼ **Sample Items**

Basketball <u>is played</u> at a <u>much</u> <u>fast</u> pace than <u>baseball</u>.
         A   B   C   D

The comparative form *faster* is needed because two concepts—the pace of basketball and the pace of baseball—are being compared.

The <u>deep</u> oceans <u>contain</u> some of the <u>stranger</u> of all <u>living</u> creatures.
   A   B   C   D

This sentence does not compare two groups; a superlative form (*strangest*) is required. ▲

B) Incorrect Forms of Comparatives and Superlatives

Incorrect forms such as *more bigger* or *most hot* may appear.

▼ **Sample Item**

The <u>most small</u> vessels in the circulatory <u>system</u> <u>are</u> capillaries.
      A   B   C D

The correct form is *smallest* because *small* is a one-syllable adjective. ▲

Exercise 41

Focus: Identifying and correcting errors in comparatives and superlatives.

Directions: If the underlined form is correct, mark the sentence *C*. If the underlined form is incorrect, mark the sentence *X* and write a correction for the underlined form in the blank at the end of the sentence. The first one is done as an example.

  _X_   1. The period is probably <u>the most easiest</u> punctuation mark to use. __the easiest__

  _____   2. When metal replaced wood in the construction of ships' hulls, <u>more strong and large</u> ships could be built. _____

  _____   3. Charcoal is <u>the most commonly</u> used cooking fuel in the world. _____

_____ 4. Soft solder melts at a <u>low</u> temperature than ordinary solder. _____

_____ 5. Many of the nation's <u>most important</u> documents are stored in the National Archives Building in Washington, D.C. _____

_____ 6. The surfboards used twenty-five years ago were <u>more heavier</u> than the ones used by surfers today. _____

_____ 7. Few American politicians have spoken <u>more eloquently</u> than William Jennings Bryan. _____

_____ 8. Subterranean termites are the <u>more destructive</u> type of termites in the United States. _____

_____ 9. Prince Edward Island is the <u>less</u> populous of Canada's ten provinces. _____

_____ 10. During a depression, economic conditions are far <u>worst</u> than they are during a recession. _____

_____ 11. One of <u>the most basic</u> American contributions to technology was the so-called "American system" of interchangeable machine parts. _____

_____ 12. The horse chestnut has a stronger, <u>bitter</u> taste than other chestnuts. _____

_____ 13. Chicago's Field Museum is one of the largest and <u>better-known</u> natural history museums in the United States. _____

_____ 14. Baltimore has one of the world's <u>most finest</u> natural harbors. _____

_____ 15. The Kennedy-Nixon race of 1960 was <u>the closest</u> presidential election of the twentieth century. _____

_____ 16. The finback whale is the fastest of all whales, and only the blue whale is <u>largest</u>. _____

_____ 17. The cello is shorter and <u>more slender</u> than the double bass. _____

_____ 18. Oil floats on water because oil is <u>less denser</u> than water. _____

LESSON 42

ERRORS IN WORD ORDER

Most word-order errors in Written Expression consist of two words in reverse order. Some of the most common examples of this type of error are given below:

Error	Example	Correction
Noun + adjective	drivers careful	careful drivers
Noun + possessive	clothing women's	women's clothing
Main verb + auxiliary	finished are	are finished
Adjective + adverb	a basic extremely idea	an extremely basic idea
Verb + subject (in an indirect question or other *wh-* clause)	Tell me where is it. I spoke to John when was he here.	Tell me where it is. I spoke to John when he was here.
Preposition/adverb clause marker + adverb	after immediately	immediately after
Participle + adverb	baked freshly bread	freshly baked bread
Relative pronoun + preposition	the house which in she lives	the house in which she lives
adverb, adjective, participle, or quantifier + *almost*	totally almost late almost finished almost all almost	almost totally almost late almost finished almost all
too much + adjective	too much heavy	much too heavy
enough + adjective*	enough good	good enough

Enough can correctly be used before nouns: *enough money, enough time. Enough* may also be used before an adjective when the adjective comes before a noun. (There weren't *enough good seats* at the concert.)

▼ **Sample Items**

Goods such as flowers fresh and seafood are often shipped by air.
   A   B   C   D

The adjective *fresh* must come before the noun *flowers: fresh flowers.*

Visitors to Vancouver often comment on how beautiful its
                   A   B

setting is and on how clean is it.
  C   D

The correct word order is subject + verb: *it is.* ▲

Exercise 42.1

Focus: Identifying and correcting word order in sentences.

Directions: If the word order of the underlined form is correct, mark the sentence *C*. If the word order is incorrect, mark the sentence *X* and write a correction in the blank at the end of the sentence.

___X___ 1. The Douglas fir is the <u>source chief</u> of lumber in the state of Oregon. __*chief source*__

_____ 2. The painted turtle is a <u>colored brightly</u>, smooth-shelled turtle. _____

_____ 3. Trained in Europe, John Sargent became <u>an extremely successful</u> portrait painter in the United States. _____

_____ 4. Insects lived on the Earth <u>before long</u> the first mammal appeared. _____

_____ 5. The freezing point is the temperature <u>which at</u> a liquid becomes a solid. _____

_____ 6. Ammonia, a compound of nitrogen and hydrogen, has many <u>industrial uses</u>.
_____

_____ 7. The Atlantic coastline of the United States is about 400 <u>longer miles</u> than the Gulf coastline. _____

_____ 8. Zoos provide an opportunity to study a wide range of animals, often in their <u>habitats natural</u>. _____

_____ 9. A test pilot tries out new kinds of aircraft to determine if <u>are they</u> safe. _____

_____ 10. The air of the upper atmosphere is just <u>enough dense</u> to ignite meteors by friction.
_____

_____ 11. More pigs are raised in Iowa than in <u>other any</u> state. _____

_____ 12. Cirrus clouds are composed <u>entirely almost</u> of ice crystals. _____

_____ 13. Many sailboats are equipped with small engines for times when there is not <u>enough wind</u>. _____

_____ 14. Prior to the 1940's, most runways were <u>too much</u> short for long-distance airplanes to take off from, so many long-distance aircraft were seaplanes. _____

_____ 15. Margaret Wise Brown was a successful author of <u>books children's</u>. _____

Exercise 42.2

Focus: Identifying errors involving word order. (Note: One or two items in this exercise do *not* focus on word-order errors. These are marked in the answer key with an asterisk.)

Directions: Decide which of the four underlined words or phrases—(A), (B), (C), or (D)—would not be considered correct, and write the letter of the expression in the blank. Then, in the line at the end of the sentence, write the correction for the underlined phrase. The first one is done as an example.

___C___ 1. During <u>pioneer times</u>, the Allegheny Mountains <u>were</u> a <u>barrier major</u> to <u>transportation</u>.
                 A   B   C   D

    __*major barrier*__

_____ 2. In Philadelphia's Franklin Institute, there is a working model of a human heart
$\qquad\qquad\quad$ A $\qquad$ B $\qquad\qquad$ C

enough large for visitors to walk through. _____
$\quad$ D

_____ 3. The task of the cartographer is to represent the Earth's surface at a reduced greatly scale.
$\qquad\quad$ A $\qquad\qquad\qquad$ B $\qquad\qquad\qquad$ C $\qquad\qquad$ D

_____

_____ 4. Mutualism is a relationship between animal species which in both benefit.
$\qquad\qquad\qquad$ A $\qquad\qquad$ B $\qquad$ C $\qquad$ D

_____

_____ 5. To grow properly, a tree must be well-suited to the area where is it planted.
$\qquad\quad$ A $\qquad\qquad$ B $\qquad$ C $\qquad\qquad\qquad$ D

_____ 6. The development of transistors made possible it to reduce the size of many
$\qquad\quad$ A $\qquad\qquad\qquad$ B $\qquad\qquad$ C

electronic devices. _____
$\quad$ D

_____ 7. Twelve drawings usually have to be prepared for second each of animated film.
$\qquad\qquad\qquad$ A $\qquad\qquad$ B $\qquad$ C $\qquad$ D

_____

_____ 8. Today many garden vegetables have few resemblance to the wild plants from which
$\qquad\qquad\quad$ A $\qquad\qquad$ B $\qquad\qquad$ C $\qquad$ D

they came. _____

_____ 9. Sloths are moving slow, shaggy mammals that are often seen hanging upside down from
$\qquad\qquad\quad$ A $\qquad\qquad\qquad$ B $\qquad\qquad$ C

tree limbs. _____
$\quad$ D

_____ 10. Carbohydrates as such sugar or starches are important energy sources for
$\qquad\qquad\qquad$ A $\qquad\qquad$ B $\qquad\qquad$ C

humans and animals. _____
$\quad$ D

_____ 11. On nights when is the sky clear and the air calm, the Earth's surface rapidly radiates heat
$\qquad\qquad\qquad$ A $\qquad\qquad$ B $\qquad\qquad$ C $\qquad$ D

into the atmosphere. _____

_____ 12. Frank Lloyd Wright is known for his original highly methods of harmonizing buildings
$\qquad\qquad\qquad$ A $\qquad\qquad$ B $\qquad\qquad$ C

with their surroundings. _____

_____ 13. Some algae <u>are microscopic</u> and consist of <u>one only</u> cell, but others are <u>large plants</u>
         A B C

         containing <u>many cells</u>. _____
         D

_____ 14. A <u>fully grown</u> <u>male mountain lion</u> may <u>be</u> eight <u>long feet</u>. _____
         A B C D

_____ 15. Stone fruits are fruits <u>such as</u> peaches and plums <u>in which</u> a hard pit <u>surrounded is</u> by
         A B C

         <u>soft pulp</u>. _____
         D

_____ 16. Job enrichment is a <u>technique used</u> to increase <u>satisfaction workers'</u> by <u>giving them</u>
         A B C

         <u>more responsibilities</u>. _____
         D

_____ 17. The first <u>permanent European</u> settlement in <u>what is now</u> Mississippi <u>was a</u>
         A B C

         <u>center trading</u> in Biloxi. _____
         D

_____ 18. <u>In the early</u> 1800's, a <u>dispute developed</u> among geologists <u>how about</u> <u>rocks are</u> formed.
         A B C D

         _____

_____ 19. Most <u>country music</u> songs are <u>deeply personal</u> and <u>deal with</u> themes of love, <u>lonely</u>, and
         A B C D

         separation. _____

_____ 20. An umbra is a <u>shadow's darkest</u> central part <u>from which</u> <u>is light</u> <u>totally excluded</u>.
         A B C D

         _____

LESSON 43

ERRORS WITH CONJUNCTIONS

You may encounter errors with either **correlative conjunctions** or **coordinate conjunctions.**

A) Errors with Correlative Conjunctions

Correlative conjunctions are two-part conjunctions. Errors usually involve an incorrect combination of the two parts, such as *neither . . . or* or *not only. . . . and.* Anytime you see a sentence containing correlative conjunctions, you should be on the lookout for this type of error. This is an easy error to spot!

Correlative Conjunctions
either . . . or
neither . . . nor
both . . . and
not only . . . but also
whether . . . or

Another error is the use of *both . . . and* to join three elements.

▼ Sample Items

X rays <u>have</u> important <u>applications</u>, not only in medicine
     A   B

<u>and</u> in <u>industry</u>.
 C   D

The correct pattern is *not only . . . but also.*

<u>The</u> air <u>that</u> surrounds <u>our planet</u> is <u>both odorless</u>,
 A   B   C   D

colorless, and invisible.

Because *both . . . and* can be used to join only two elements, the word *both* must be eliminated to correct the sentence. ▲

B) Errors with Coordinate Conjunctions

The conjunction *and* is correctly used to show addition; *or* is used to show choice between alternatives; *but* is used to show contrast or opposition.

▼ **Sample Item**

Brakes and clutches <u>serve</u> very different <u>functions</u>
              A   B

in an automobile, <u>and</u> their principles of operation
                              C

are <u>nearly</u> the same.
     D

The first clause discusses how brakes and clutches are different; the second clause discusses how they are the same. Therefore, the conjunction joining them must show contrast. Choice (C) should read *but*. ▲

Exercise 43

Focus: Identifying and correcting errors involving conjunctions.

Directions: If the underlined form is correct, mark the sentence *C*. If the underlined form is incorrect, mark the sentence *X* and write a correction for the underlined form in the blank at the end of the sentence. The first one is done as an example.

___X___ 1. Model airplanes can be guided <u>both</u> by control wires or by radio transmitters.
      ____*either*____

_____ 2. Information in a computer can be lost because it is no longer stored or because it is stored <u>but</u> cannot be retrieved. _____

_____ 3. John Lancaster Spaulding was not only a religious leader <u>and also</u> a social reformer. _____

_____ 4. Although fish can hear, they have neither external ears <u>or</u> eardrums. _____

_____ 5. In all animals, whether simple <u>and</u> complex, enzymes aid in the digestion of food. _____

_____ 6. The two most common methods florists use to tint flowers are the spray method <u>or</u> the absorption method. _____

_____ 7. Beekeepers can sell <u>either</u> the honey and the beeswax that their bees produce. _____

_____ 8. The alloys brass <u>and</u> bronze both contain copper as their principal metals. _____

_____ 9. The human brain is often compared to a computer, <u>and</u> such an analogy can be misleading. _____

_____ 10. Rust both corrodes the surface of metal <u>but also</u> weakens its structure. _____

_____ 11. A work of science fiction generally uses scientific discoveries and advanced technology, either real <u>or</u> imaginary, as part of its plot. _____

_____ 12. Community theater <u>both</u> provides entertainment for local audiences but also furnishes a creative outlet for amateurs interested in drama. _____

_____ 13. The heron is a long-legged wading bird that preys on <u>both frogs</u>, fish, and eels. _____

_____ 14. For over twenty years after winning the World Chess Championship in 1972, Bobby Fischer played in <u>either</u> a tournament nor an exhibition game. _____

_____ 15. Designing fabric requires not only artistic talent but also a knowledge of fiber <u>and</u> of textile machinery. _____

ANSWER SHEET
MINI-TEST 7: WRITTEN EXPRESSION

1. A B C D   10. A B C D   19. A B C D
2. A B C D   11. A B C D   20. A B C D
3. A B C D   12. A B C D   21. A B C D
4. A B C D   13. A B C D   22. A B C D
5. A B C D   14. A B C D   23. A B C D
6. A B C D   15. A B C D   24. A B C D
7. A B C D   16. A B C D   25. A B C D
8. A B C D   17. A B C D
9. A B C D   18. A B C D

MINI-TEST 7: WRITTEN EXPRESSION

Directions: The sentences below have four underlined words or phrases, (A), (B), (C), and (D). You must identify the one underlined expression that must be changed for the sentence to be correct. Then find the number of the question on your answer sheet and fill in the space corresponding to the letter. Then mark the appropriate answer either in the blanks next to the items or on the answer sheet above.

Time: 15 minutes

_____ 1. Commercial bakeries <u>can make</u> thousands of <u>loaves</u> of bread <u>on one time</u> by <u>using</u>
                                    A   B   C   D
automated equipment.

_____ 2. North America is <u>a</u> <u>third</u> <u>largest of the</u> seven <u>continents</u>.
                             A   B   C   D

_____ 4. <u>The astronomer</u> George Hale was <u>a pioneer</u> <u>in the art</u> of <u>photograph</u> the Sun.
               A   B   C   D

_____ 5. Trucks <u>can be</u> used <u>transport</u> <u>a wide</u> <u>variety</u> of cargoes.
                       A   B   C   D

_____ 6. Pikes Peak, <u>named for</u> explorer Zebulon Pike, is Colorado's <u>most famous</u> <u>but</u> not its
                            A   B   C
<u>most highest</u> mountain.
       D

_____ 7. Identical colors <u>may appear</u> <u>to be</u> quite different when <u>are they</u> viewed <u>against</u> different
                                A   B   C   D
backgrounds.

_____ 8. Oceanography is not <u>a single</u> science <u>and</u> rather a group of disciplines <u>with</u> a common
                                       A   B   C

<u>focus</u>.
D

_____ 9. <u>Until</u> 1960, Maine was unique in that <u>it held</u> presidential and congressional elections <u>on</u>
       A   B   C

September, two months <u>earlier</u> than the rest of the nation.
                           D

_____ 10. Snowshoes permit a person <u>walking</u> on snow without <u>sinking</u> into it because <u>they</u>
                                   A   B   C

distribute <u>the person's</u> weight over a wide area.
           D

_____ 11. Fuel injection engines <u>employ</u> injectors <u>instead</u> a carburetor <u>to spray</u> fuel <u>into</u> the
                              A   B   C   D

cylinders.

_____ 12. <u>Ocean</u> currents have <u>a enormous</u> effect <u>on life</u> <u>on this planet</u>.
        A   B   C   D

_____ 13. Hydraulic elevators are <u>still used</u> in some <u>old</u> buildings, but <u>all almost</u> new buildings are
                                       A   B   C

<u>equipped with</u> electrical elevators.
            D

_____ 14. Diaries <u>and</u> journals <u>writing</u> during colonial times provide <u>the best</u> records of <u>that era</u>.
                   A   B   C   D

_____ 15. Frequently, the <u>combination of</u> several spices will <u>result of</u> a more <u>pleasing</u> flavor <u>than</u>
                                 A   B   C   D

the use of just one.

_____ 16. Gold topaz is <u>much</u> <u>rare</u> <u>than</u> either white or <u>blue</u> topaz.
                      A   B   C   D

_____ 17. A mosaic is <u>picture</u> <u>made</u> from small bits of <u>colored</u> glass <u>or</u> tile.
                    A   B   C   D

_____ 18. Reclamation is <u>the successful</u> attempt <u>to make</u> deserts, marshlands, or other unusable
                               A   B

land <u>suitable</u> of farming or <u>building</u>.
          C   D

_____ 19. A <u>successful</u> salesperson <u>must have</u> an intuitive <u>understanding</u> of <u>psychology human</u>.
           A   B   C   D

_____ 20. The University of Wisconsin was the first school to make a serious effort teach students
                                              A   B   C

public administration.
        D

_____ 21. Some underground water is enough safe to drink, but all surface water must be treated.
            A   B   C   D

_____ 22. A feeding animal will usually allow competitors approaching only within a certain
            A   B   C

distance, the boundaries of which are called its feeding territory.
                            D

_____ 23. Most familiar type of pump in use today is the piston pump.
            A   B   C   D

_____ 24. The term "forgetting" refers to the loss, whether temporary and long-term, of material
            A   B   C

that has previously been learned.
D

_____ 25. Dieticians urge people to eat the banana a day to get enough potassium in their diet.
                              A   B   C   D

MINI-LESSONS FOR SECTION 2
Preposition Use

It is important for the Structure and especially the Written Expression parts of the test that you be familiar with the correct usage of prepositions. The mini-lessons for this section consist of lists of prepositions in combination with other words and in various set expressions. The exercises allow you to practice using these prepositions in sentences. Cover the lists with a piece of paper as you complete the exercises.

Mini-Lesson 2.1
Adjectives/Participles + Prepositions, Part A

acceptable to	characteristic of	eligible for
accustomed to	close to	equal to
adequate for	composed of	equipped with
afraid of	contrary to	essential to/for
aware of	dependent on	familiar with
based on	different from	famous for
capable of	disappointed in/with	

Exercise: Fill in the blanks in the sentences below with the correct prepositions. The first one is done as an example.

1. The Medical Center is close ___to___ campus.

2. I was disappointed _____ the grade I received on my last essay.

3. Now that she has graduated, Anne is no longer dependent _____ her parents for financial support.

4. Catherine became accustomed _____ spicy foods when she was traveling.

5. Table salt is composed _____ two elements, sodium and chlorine.

6. Is your bicycle equipped _____ a light?

7. This computer isn't capable _____ running that software.

8. Bluegrass music is somewhat different _____ other types of country music.

9. Washington State is famous _____ its apples.

10. Was your choice of research topic acceptable _____ your instructor?

11. People who are afraid _____ heights are called acrophobes.

12. Water is essential _____ all life.

13. Were you aware _____ the regulation against smoking in this area?

14. Tepees are characteristic _____ the Indian tribes of the Great Plains.

15. Will this office be adequate _____ your needs?

16. I'm not familiar _____ that song.

17. One meter is approximately equal _____ a yard.

18. This movie is based _____ a true story.

19. This summer, he'll be eligible _____ a three-week vacation.

20. What he said is contrary _____ common sense.

Mini-Lesson 2.2
Adjectives/Participles + Prepositions, Part B

free of	next to	related to
independent of	opposed to	relevant to
inferior to	opposite of*	satisfied with
married to	perfect for	suitable for
native to	possible for	surprised at/by
necessary for/to	preferable to	typical of

Opposite of is used for words or concepts that are completely different, such as *large* and *small*. When *opposite* means "across from," it is not used with *of*. "The bank is *opposite* the post office on Cedar Street."

Exercise: Fill in the blanks in the sentences below with the correct prepositions.

1. The art museum is located next _____ the museum of natural history on State Street.

2. Many vegetables, including tomatoes, potatoes, and corn, are native _____ the New World.

3. This style of architecture is typical _____ the colonial period.

4. Oxygen, fuel, and heat are all necessary _____ combustion.

5. Two people would find this apartment too crowded, but it's perfect _____ one.

6. These tools are inferior _____ the ones I usually use.

7. Were you surprised _____ the grade you received?

8. The opposite _____ *old fashioned* is *modern*.

9. House cats are distantly related _____ lions and tigers.

10. Is this type of soil suitable _____ growing tomatoes?

11. The point that Murray brought up wasn't really relevant _____ the discussion.

12. Organically raised crops are free _____ chemical pesticides and herbicides.

13. A grade of A- is preferable _____ one of B+.

14. If you're not satisfied _____ your essay, then I suggest that you rewrite it.

15. Abolitionists were people who were opposed _____ the practice of slavery.

16. The United States became independent _____ England in 1776.

17. Is it possible _____ me to get an appointment sometime next week?

18. President James Madison was married _____ one of the most famous of all first ladies, Dolley Madison.

Mini-Lesson 2.3
Nouns + Prepositions

approach to	exception to	origin of
attention to	experience with	part of
cause of	expert on	price of
component of	form of	probability of
contribution to	group of	quality of
cure for	improvement in	reason for
decrease in	increase in	reliance on
demand for	influence on	result of
effect of/on*	interest in	solution to
example of	native of	supply of

*effect + of + cause
effect + on + thing or person affected
(The effect *of* heat *on* rocks. . .)

Exercise: Fill in the blanks in the sentences below with the correct prepositions.

1. A decrease _____ the supply _____ a good usually results in an increase _____ the price _____ that good.

2. Once scientists fully understand the cause _____ a disease, it becomes easier for them to find a cure _____ it.

3. Professor Lyle noticed a distinct improvement _____ the quality _____ her students' work.

4. It is believed that sunspots have an influence _____ the Earth's weather patterns.

5. Have you had much experience _____ computers?

6. I'm sorry; I wasn't paying close attention _____ what you said.

7. The professor gave us several examples _____ that phenomenon.

8. Do you know the reason _____ the delay?

9. Interest _____ physical fitness increased during the 1980's.

10. The Dorothy Chandler Pavilion is part _____ the Los Angeles Music Center.

11. Linguists have many theories about the origin _____ language.

12. This is an exception _____ the general rule.

13. What approach should I take _____ this problem?

14. The Ivy League is a group _____ eight prestigious universities in the Northeast.

15. People's reliance _____ automobiles as their chief form _____ transportation has increased over the years.

16. I've tried and tried, but I simply can't find a solution _____ this dilemma.

17. The demand _____ personal computers continues to grow.

18. Only a native _____ the United States can serve as President.

19. Economists don't agree on what effects government spending has _____ the economy.

20. Margaret Knight designed some of the components _____ the rotary engine.

Mini-Lesson 2.4
Verbs + Prepositions

account for	compete with	insist on
adjust to	concentrate on	interfere with
agree with/on*	consist of	participate in
attach to	contribute to	plan on
attribute to	cooperate with	refer to
begin with	deal with	rely on
believe in	depend on	result in
belong to	devote to	search for
combine with	engage in	

Agree with is used with people.
Agree on is used with an issue, plan, etc.
(I *agreed with* Mary *on* that issue.)

Exercise: Fill in the blanks in the sentences below with the correct prepositions.

1. Do you belong _____ any campus clubs or organizations?

2. Cytology is the branch of biology that deals _____ the structure, form, and life of cells.

3. Maybe you should begin your speech _____ some jokes.

4. Let's concentrate _____ solving this problem before we discuss the other ones.

5. People want friends they can rely _____ .

6. Most essays consist _____ an introduction, a body, and a conclusion.

7. We didn't plan _____ such a long delay.

8. If you are engaged _____ any extracurricular activities, you should mention that fact on your résumé.

9. Iron combines _____ oxygen to form rust.

10. After several hours of discussion, the council finally agreed _____ a plan.

11. The accident resulted _____ several minor injuries.

12. Storms on the Sun can interfere _____ radio broadcasts on the Earth.

13. By the late 1940's, television had begun to seriously compete _____ radio for audience and advertisers.

14. That theatrical company can always be depended _____ to deliver a good performance.

15. James didn't have any trouble adjusting _____ the climate in Atlanta because he'd grown up in the South.

16. William insists _____ getting up early, even on weekends.

17. What does this symbol refer _____ ?

18. Occupational physicians search _____ the causes of injury and sickness at the workplace.

19. Many companies participated _____ the trade fair.

20. How do you account _____ this discrepancy?

21. Do you believe _____ any superstitions?

22. Workaholics devote too much of their time _____ their jobs.

Mini-Lesson 2.5
Phrasal Prepositions

according to	due to	on account of
ahead of	except for	prior to
along with	in favor of	regardless of
because of	in spite of	thanks to
by means of	instead of	together with

Exercise: Fill in the blanks in the sentences below with the correct prepositions.

1. Work on the new highway will be finished ahead _____ schedule.

2. _____ spite _____ the warnings, Phil dove off the cliff.

3. The chairman, along _____ his staff, attended the conference.

4. According _____ my dictionary, you're mispronouncing that word.

5. Prior _____ her wedding, Nicole's last name was Brooks.

6. Are you _____ favor _____ that amendment or against it?

7. _____ account _____ a lack of funds, the university library will now close at nine instead _____ at eleven.

8. Sunsets may appear more colorful because _____ air pollution.

9. Due _____ a computer error, $100,000 was transferred into Judy's checking account.

10. Regardless _____ the final score, I'm sure this will be an exciting game.

11. Glider pilots can actually increase their altitude _____ means _____ hot air currents called thermals.

12. Thanks _____ the financial aid he received, he was able to attend the university.

Mini-Lesson 2.6
In, On, and *At,* Part A

Expressions of Time

	+ century (*in the eighteenth century*)
	+ decade (*in the 1990's*)
	+ year (*in 1975*)
in	+ season (*in the summer*)
	+ month (*in July*)
	+ parts of the day (*in the morning, in the evening, in the afternoon*)

on	+ days of the week (*on Wednesday*)
	+ dates (*on October 7*)

at	+ time of day (*at 6 P.M.; at noon*)
	+ night

Expressions of Place

in +
+ continent (*in Africa*)
+ country (*in Mexico*)
+ state (*in Pennsylvania*)
+ city (*in Los Angeles*)
+ building (*in the bank*)
+ room (*in the auditorium*)
+ *the world*

on +
+ street (*on Maxwell Street*)
+ floor of a building (*on the fourth floor*)
+ *Earth*

at +
+ address (*at 123 Commonwealth Avenue*)

Exercise: Fill in the blanks in the sentences below with the preposition *in*, *on*, or *at*.

1. John F. Kennedy was the first President of the United States to be born _____ the twentieth century.
2. Fruit trees generally bloom _____ April or May.
3. Gettysburg, the greatest battle ever fought _____ North America, took place _____ July 1863.
4. I like to shower _____ the morning, but my roommate likes to shower _____ night.
5. The President lives _____ the White House, which is located _____ 1600 Pennsylvania Avenue _____ Washington, D.C.
6. Many advertising agencies are located _____ Madison Avenue _____ New York City.
7. Jazz was so popular _____ the 1920's that the decade is sometimes called the Jazz Age.
8. Leaves turn red and gold _____ the autumn.
9. Most college football games are played _____ Saturdays.
10. Both Washington and Lincoln were born _____ February. Washington was born _____ February 22, Lincoln _____ February 12.
11. About 90% of all the people _____ New Jersey live _____ cities.
12. The New Year is celebrated _____ midnight _____ January 1.
13. Dean Hughes' office is _____ the Administration Building _____ the third floor.
14. Quebec is the largest province _____ Canada.
15. The First World War ended _____ 11 A.M. _____ the eleventh day _____ the eleventh month _____ 1918.

Mini-Lesson 2.7

In, On, and *At,* Part B

The prepositions *in, on,* and *at* are also used in a number of set expressions:

in a book/magazine	on a bus/train/etc.	at best/worst
newspaper	on fire	at birth
in charge (of)	on the other hand	at death
in common (with)	on purpose	at first/last
in danger (of)	on radio/television	at least/most
in detail	on the whole	at the moment
in existence		at once
in the front/middle/back		at the peak (of)
in general		at present
in part		at random
in the past/future		
in practice		
in a row		
in style		
in theory		

Exercise: Fill in the blanks in the sentences below with the preposition *in, on,* or *at.*

1. Did you hear that news _____ television or read it _____ the newspaper?

2. The members of a jury are chosen _____ random from a list of voters.

3. Videophones are not practical _____ present, but they may be _____ the near future.

4. Mr. Grigsby is _____ charge of the marketing department.

5. Please come here _____ once.

6. I'm sure he didn't break the window _____ purpose.

7. Air travel is _____ its peak _____ the summer.

8. _____ the whole, I enjoyed the movie, but there were a few scenes I didn't like.

9. Mark is a good friend, but we don't have much _____ common.

10. Claudia has gotten so many speeding tickets that she's _____ danger of losing her driver's license.

11. The story _____ the magazine described the incident _____ great detail.

12. There is _____ least one vowel in virtually every English word.

13. Five oak trees were planted _____ a row _____ front of the school.

14. This type of music is no longer _____ style.

15. _____ general, I found zoology to be an easier subject than botany.

16. The American Constitution has been _____ existence for over two hundred years.

17. Like many other baby birds, ducklings are blind _____ birth.

18. This book is based _____ part on fact.

19. The ship was _____ fire.

20. _____ theory, this idea is quite difficult to understand; _____ the other hand, it is quite simple _____ practice.

Mini-Lesson 2.8

Other Prepositions

By is often used with forms of communication and transportation:

> *by car, by plane, by phone, by express mail*

(Note: If the noun is plural or is preceded by a determiner, the preposition *in* or *on* must be used: *in cars, on a boat, on the telephone, in a taxi*.)

By is also used with a gerund to show how an action happened:

> How did you get an appointment with Dr. Blish?
> *By calling* his secretary.

With is used to indicate the idea of accompaniment or possession:

> Melanie came to the party *with her friend*.
> He wanted a house *with a garage*.

Without indicates the opposite relationship:

> Melanie came to the party *without her friend*.
> He bought a house *without a garage*.

With also indicates that an instrument was used to perform an action:

> He opened the door *with a key*.

Without indicates the opposite relationship:

> He opened the door *without a key*.

By and *for* are also used in the following expressions:

by chance	for example
by far	for free
by hand	for now

For is sometimes used to show purpose; it means "to get."

> She went to the store *for toothpaste and shampoo*.

Exercise: Fill in the blanks in the sentences below with the correct prepositions.

1. Magnetic compasses are not very useful on ships _____ steel hulls.
2. Penicillin was discovered more or less _____ chance.
3. Legal aid organizations provide legal advice for poor people for small fees or _____ free.
4. Alaska is _____ far the largest state.
5. Amoebas are so small that they can't be seen _____ a microscope.
6. Fruits, vegetables, and other agricultural products are generally shipped _____ truck.
7. Semaphore operators communicate _____ using flags.
8. The most expensive rugs are made _____ hand.
9. Ice hockey is played _____ a hard rubber disk called a puck.
10. They traveled to the island _____ a boat.

Guide to Reading Comprehension

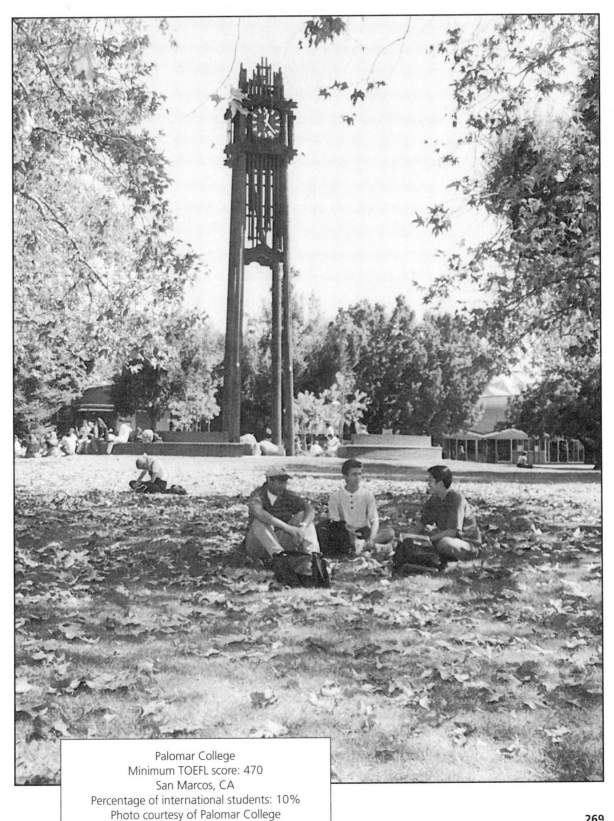

Palomar College
Minimum TOEFL score: 470
San Marcos, CA
Percentage of international students: 10%
Photo courtesy of Palomar College

About Reading Comprehension

This part of the exam tests your ability to read and answer questions about passages written in formal English. It usually contains five passages (seven on the long form). After each passage there are usually from eight to twelve questions referring to that passage for a total of fifty questions (seventy-five on the long form). The passages vary in length from about seven lines to about thirty-five.

In July 1995, Section 3 of TOEFL changed somewhat. The first part of the section, which consisted of thirty individual vocabulary items, was eliminated. More vocabulary-in-context items have been added. These ask about the meaning of words in the passages. The passages have become somewhat longer, and the time limit has been extended by ten minutes.

▼ Sample Items

       Like mammals, birds claim their own territories. A bird's territory may be small or large. Some birds claim only their nest and the area right around it,
(line)   while others claim far larger territories that include
(5)   their feeding areas. Gulls, penguins, and other waterfowl nest in huge colonies, but even in the biggest colonies, each male and his mate have small territories of their own immediately around their nests.
       Male birds defend their territory chiefly against other
(10)   males of the same species. In some cases, a warning call or threatening pose may be all the defense needed, but in other cases, intruders may refuse to leave peacefully.

1. What is the main topic of this passage?
   (A) Birds that live in colonies
   (B) How birds defend their territory
   (C) The behavior of birds
   (D) Territoriality in birds

Choice (A) deals with particular types of birds—gulls, penguins, and others—but the passage concerns all birds. Choice (B) deals only with the concept of defending a territory. This is the topic of the second paragraph, but not of the passage as a whole. Choice (C) is too general; there are many types of bird behavior that this passage does not examine. Choice (D) is best, because all the aspects of the passage deal with some factors of birds' territories.

2. According to the passage, male birds defend their territories primarily against
   (A) female birds
   (B) birds of other species
   (C) males of their own species
   (D) carnivorous mammals

Lines 9–10 state that male birds "defend their territories chiefly against other males of the same species." There is no mention in the passage of any of the other options.

3. It can be inferred from the passage that gulls and penguins
   (A) do not claim a feeding area as part of their territories
   (B) share their territories with many other birds
   (C) leave their colonies during their nesting season
   (D) do not build nests

The passage says that birds which claim their feeding areas have large territories compared to those which do not. Birds living in colonies have "small territories . . . immediately around their nests," indicating that their feeding areas would not be part of their territories. Choice (B) contradicts lines 7–8, which state that "each male and his mate . . . have small territories of their own." Choice (C) is unlikely because the passage indicates that these birds' nests are part of large colonies; they would not leave during nesting season. Choice (D) is incorrect because these birds' nests are part of their territories.

4. In line 3, the word "it" refers to
   (A) a nest
   (B) an area
   (C) a bird
   (D) a territory

Substitute all four answer choices for the word *it* in line 3; as you'll see, only (A) is a logical choice.

5. The word "intruders" in line 12 is closest in meaning to
   (A) invaders
   (B) youngsters
   (C) defenders
   (D) guests

It is clear from the passage that the "intruders" mentioned in this line are male birds that "refuse to leave peacefully." Of the four answer choices, only "invaders" (persons or creatures that attack from the outside) could be substituted for the word "intruders" with no major change in meaning. ▲

The Passages

The passages cover a wide range of topics, but in general can be classified as follows:

1. **Science and technology (40%)**   Includes astronomy, geology, chemistry, physics, mathematics, zoology, botany, medicine, engineering, mechanics, and so on.

2. **North American history, government, geography, and culture (20%)**

3. **Art (15%)**   Includes literature, painting, architecture, dance, drama, and so on.

4. **Social science (10%)**   Includes anthropology, economics, psychology, urban studies, sociology, and so on.

5. **Biography (15%)**

Some passages may be classified in more than one way. For example, a biography might be about the life of a historical figure, an artist, or a scientist.

If there is a national context for any of the passages, it is American or occasionally Canadian. Therefore, if a passage is about history, it will be about the history of the United States or Canada.

Although the passages deal with various topics, the style in which they are written is similar, and they usually follow fairly simple patterns of organization.

The vocabulary used in the Reading Comprehension portion is fairly sophisticated. There will almost certainly be words that you do not recognize. Sometimes you can guess the meaning of these words by context. However, it is not necessary to understand all the vocabulary in the passages in order to answer the questions.

The Questions

The main types of questions asked can be categorized as shown below:

Type of Question/ Percentage on Test	Explanation	Example
Main Idea/ Main Topic/ Main Purpose (10%)	These ask you to identify an answer choice that correctly summarizes the author's main idea, the subject of the whole passage, or the author's reason for writing the passage.	"What is the main idea of the passage?" "What is the passage primarily about?" "Why did the author write the passage?"
Factual Questions (24%)	These ask you to locate and identify answers to questions about specific information and details in the passage.	"According to the passage, where did . . . ?" "According to the author, why did . . . ?" "Which of the following is true, according to the passage?"
Negative Questions (9%)	These ask which of the answer choices is NOT discussed in the passage.	"Which of the following is NOT true about . . ." "All of the following are true EXCEPT . . ."
Scanning Questions (4%)	These ask you to find the place in the passage where some topic is mentioned.	"Where in the passage does the author first discuss . . ."
Inference Questions (12%)	These ask you to draw conclusions based on information in the passage.	"The author implies that which of the following is true?" "Which of the following can be inferred from the passage?"

Vocabulary-in-Context Questions (26%)	These ask you identify the meaning of a word or phrase as used in the passage.	"The word '——' in line 5 is closest in meaning to . . ."
Reference Questions (10%)	These ask you to identify the noun to which a pronoun or other expression refers.	"The word "it" in line 15 refers to . . ." "In line 20, the word "there" refers to which of the following?"

There are a few other types of questions that are occasionally asked about the readings. These make up the remaining 5% of the question types.

About half the Reading items have **closed stems;** they begin with direct questions. The others have **open stems;** they begin with incomplete sentences.

> Closed Stem
> Which of the following is the main topic of the passage?

> Open Stem
> The main topic of the passage is

The Answer Choices

For all questions in this part, the four options are equally grammatical and, in most cases, would be equally logical choices for someone who has not carefully read the passage. Incorrect choices are generally based on information that is found in the passage, but does not correctly answer the question.

What Is the Best Way to Approach the Passages?

First, take a quick look at the questions (*not* at the answer choices) to see what will be asked about. Try to keep these in the back of your mind as you read the passage. Then read the article at a comfortable speed. Try *not* to read one word at a time, like this:

> A   bird's   territory   may   be   small   or   large.   Some   birds   claim   only   their
> nest   and   the   area   right   around   it.

Word-by-word reading slows you down and interferes with your comprehension. Try to read in units of thought. In other words, group words into related phrases.

> A bird's territory   may be   small or large.   Some birds
> claim only their nest   and the area   right around it.

The paragraph is the primary unit of meaning in all reading. Most passages consist of from one to five paragraphs. If you can form a clear idea of what each paragraph is about, you can put these ideas together and come up with the main idea of the entire passage. The main idea of each paragraph is often contained in one sentence, called the topic sentence. Try to locate topic sentences. Often, the topic sentence is the first sentence of a paragraph, but it may also be the last sentence. Occasionally, a paragraph has no topic sentence; the topic is stated indirectly.

If there is more than one paragraph in the passage, try to understand the relationship between the paragraphs. Form a mental "map" of the passage. Watch for words that signal special relationships and transitions, such as *however, therefore, first, next, then,* and so on.

What Is the Best Way to Answer the Questions?

It depends on the type of question. The best tactics for answering each type of question are given in the next five lessons. In the exercises, you will read passages similar to the ones found on actual TOEFL tests to develop the reading skills needed to do well on this section.

Are There Any "Secrets" for Finding Answers in the Passage Quickly?

Sometimes you can use "line-number" questions to help find the information you need. Look at this sequence of questions:

1. What is the main topic of this passage?

2. The word "_____" in line 4 is closest in meaning to which of the following?

3. According to the passage, when was . . .?

4. What can be inferred from the passage about . . .?

5. The word "they" in line 11 refers to . . .

Because the order of specific questions follows the order of the passage, you know that the information needed to answer questions 3 and 4 is found between lines 4 and 11.

What Are Some Important Factors in Scoring High on This Section?

Timing is an important factor. Most test-takers find this the hardest to complete because reading the passages takes up so much time. Near the end of the test, you may realize that you won't have enough time to finish. Don't panic! When there are only about four or five minutes remaining, this is what you should do: If you have not read one of the passages, skim it over very quickly to get the main idea. Answer the first question about it (which will probably be a main idea or topic question). Then answer any of the questions that provide line numbers (vocabulary-in-context and reference questions) because these require less time to locate the information you need. Then answer any remaining questions, referring back to the passage as little as possible. If you can't find the information needed to answer the question in about ten seconds, just pick the choice that seems the most logical. Then, in the last few seconds, fill in any empty blanks with your "guess answer."

On the other hand, if you *do* finish the test before time is called, go back and work on items that you had trouble with the first time. Don't just sit back and relax, and don't turn back to Sections 1 or 2.

Concentration is another important factor. This is the last section of the test. It's also the longest and, for some people, the most difficult. You may be starting to get tired. However, you've got to maintain your concentration until the end of the test and not waste any time.

What Is the Best Way to Prepare for This Part of TOEFL?

After completing the exercises in the *Guide* and taking the practice tests in this book, read as much on your own as you can. A recent study showed that **extracurricular reading** (reading done outside of classes) was the single most important factor in improving overall TOEFL scores. Material from textbooks, magazines, newspapers, and encyclopedias will be useful. You might also want to try writing TOEFL-style questions about passages that you read. This technique not only increases your comprehension, but it also helps you think like the people who write TOEFL tests.

Strategies for Section 3

- As with the other sections, be familiar with the directions and examples for Section 3 so that you can begin work immediately.

- For each passage, begin by briefly looking over the questions (but not the answer choices). Try to keep these questions in mind during your reading.

- Read each passage at a comfortable speed.

- Answer the questions, referring to the passage when necessary.

- Eliminate answers that are clearly wrong or do not answer the questions. If more than one option remains, guess.

- Mark difficult or time-consuming answers so that you can come back to them later if you have time. Erase all these marks before the end of the test.

- Don't spend more than about 10 minutes on any one reading and the questions about it.

- When only a few minutes remain, **don't** start guessing blindly. Skim the remaining passage or passages quickly; then answer the first question in each set. Then answer any questions with line numbers. After that, read the remaining questions, and if you can't find the answer quickly, choose the one that seems most logical to you.

- When there are only a few seconds left, fill in all remaining blanks with your guess letter.

Sample Reading Comprehension Test

Time: 55 minutes

This section of the test measures your ability to understand the meaning of words and to comprehend written materials.

Directions: The remainder of this section contains several passages, each followed by a number of questions. Read the passages and, for each question, choose the *one* best answer—(A), (B), (C), or (D)—based on what is stated in the passage or on what can be inferred from the passage. Then fill in the space on your answer sheet that matches the letter of the answer that you have selected.

Read the following passage:

Like mammals, birds claim their own territories. A
bird's territory may be small or large. Some birds
claim only their nest and the area right around it,
(line)   while others claim far larger territories that include
(5)   their feeding areas. Gulls, penguins, and other waterfowl
nest in huge colonies, but even in the biggest colonies,
each male and his mate have small territories of their
own immediately around their nests.
Male birds defend their territory chiefly against other
(10)   males of the same species. In some cases, a warning call
or threatening pose may be all the defense needed, but in
other cases, intruders may refuse to leave peacefully.

Example I   Sample Answer

What is the main topic of this passage?

(A) Birds that live in colonies
(B) Birds' mating habits
(C) The behavior of birds
(D) Territoriality in birds

The passage mainly concerns the territories of birds. You should fill in (D) on your answer sheet.

Example II   Sample Answer

       According to the passage, male birds defend
       their territory primarily against

       (A) female birds
       (B) birds of other species
       (C) males of their own species
       (D) mammals

The passage states that "Male birds defend their territory chiefly against other males of the same species." You should fill in (C) on your answer sheet.

    As soon as you understand the directions, begin work on this part.

Go on to the next page ➤

Questions 1–12

The technology of the North American colonies did not differ strikingly from that of Europe, but in one respect, the colonists enjoyed a great advantage. Especially by comparison with
(line) Britain, Americans had a wonderfully plentiful supply of wood.
(5)   The first colonists did not, as many people imagine, find an entire continent covered by a climax forest. Even along the Atlantic seaboard, the forest was broken at many points. Nevertheless, all sorts of fine trees abounded, and through the early colonial period, those who pushed westward encountered new
(10)   forests. By the end of the colonial era, the price of wood had risen slightly in eastern cities, but wood was still extremely abundant.

The availability of wood brought advantages that have seldom been appreciated. Wood was a foundation of the economy. Houses
(15)   and all manner of buildings were made of wood to a degree unknown in Britain. Secondly, wood was used as a fuel for heating and cooking. Thirdly, it was used as the source of important industrial compounds, such as potash, an industrial alkali; charcoal, a component of gunpowder; and tannic acid, used for
(20)   tanning leather.

The supply of wood conferred advantages but had some negative aspects as well. Iron at that time was produced by heating iron ore with charcoal. Because Britain was so stripped of trees, she was unable to exploit her rich iron mines. But the American
(25)   colonies had both iron ore and wood; iron production was encouraged and became successful. However, when Britain developed coke smelting, the colonies did not follow suit because they had plenty of wood and besides, charcoal iron was stronger than coke iron. Coke smelting led to technological innovations and was
(30)   linked to the emergence of the Industrial Revolution. In the early nineteenth century, the former colonies lagged behind Britain in industrial development because their supply of wood led them to cling to charcoal iron.

1. What does the passage mainly discuss?

   (A) The advantages of using wood in the colonies
   (B) The effects of an abundance of wood on the colonies
   (C) The roots of the Industrial revolution
   (D) The difference between charcoal iron and coke iron

Go on to the next page ➤

2. The word "strikingly" in line 2 is closest in meaning to

(A) realistically
(B) dramatically
(C) completely
(D) immediately

3. Which of the following is a common assumption about the forests of North America during the colonial period?

(A) They contained only a few types of trees.
(B) They existed only along the Atlantic seaboard.
(C) They had little or no economic value.
(D) They covered the entire continent.

4. The use of the word "abounded" in line 8 indicates that the trees were

(A) present in large numbers
(B) restricted to certain areas
(C) cut down
(D) cultivated

5. According to the passage, by the end of the colonial period, the price of wood in eastern cities

(A) rose quickly because wood was becoming scarce
(B) was much higher than it was in Britain
(C) was slightly higher than in previous years
(D) decreased rapidly because of lower demand for wood

6. What can be inferred about houses in Britain during the period written about in the passage?

(A) They were more expensive than American houses.
(B) They were generally built with imported materials.
(C) They were typically smaller than homes in North America.
(D) They were usually built from materials other than wood.

7. Why does the author mention gunpowder in line 19

(A) To illustrate the negative aspects of some industrial processes
(B) To give an example of a product made from wood compounds
(C) To remind readers that the Colonial era ended in warfare
(D) To suggest that wood was not the only important product of the Colonies

8. The word "conferred" in line 21 is closest in meaning to

(A) consulted
(B) gathered
(C) provided
(D) restricted

9. The phrase "follow suit" in line 27 means

(A) do the same thing
(B) make an attempt
(C) have the opportunity
(D) take a risk

10. According to the passage, why was the use of coke smelting advantageous?

(A) It led to advances in technology.
(B) It was less expensive than wood smelting.
(C) It produced a stronger type of iron than wood smelting.
(D) It stimulated the demand for wood.

11. The phrase "cling to" in line 33 is closest in meaning to

(A) try to develop
(B) avoid
(C) continue to use
(D) reconsider

Go on to the next page

10. According to the passage, why was the use of coke smelting advantageous?
    (A) It led to advances in technology.
    (B) It was less expensive than wood smelting.
    (C) It produced a stronger type of iron than wood smelting.
    (D) It stimulated the demand for wood.

11. The phrase "cling to" in line 33 is closest in meaning to
    (A) try to develop
    (B) avoid
    (C) continue to use
    (D) reconsider

12. Where in the passage does the author begin to discuss in detail the disadvantages that an abundant supply of wood brought to the colonies?

    (A) Lines 1–3
    (B) Lines 5–7
    (C) Lines 13–14
    (D) Lines 21–22

Go on to the next page ➡

Questions 13–22

The Peales were a distinguished family of American artists.
Charles Willson Peale is best remembered for his portraits of
leading figures of the American Revolution. He painted portraits
(line) of Franklin and Jefferson, and over a dozen of George Washington.
(5)   His life-size portrait of his sons Raphaelle and Titian was so
realistic that George Washington reportedly once tipped his hat
to the figures in the picture.

Charles Willson Peale gave up painting in his middle age and
devoted his life to the Peale Museum, which he founded in
(10)   Philadelphia. The world's first popular museum of art and natural
science, it featured paintings by Peale and his family as well as
displays of animals in their natural settings. Peale found the
animals himself and devised a method of taxidermy to make the
exhibits more lifelike. The museum's most popular display was
(15)   the skeleton of a mastodon—a huge, extinct elephant—which Peale
unearthed on a New York farm in 1801.

Three of Peale's seventeen children were also famous artists.
Raphaelle Peale often painted still lifes of flowers, fruit, and
cheese. His works show the same luminosity and attention to
(20)   detail that the works of the Dutch masters show. In the late
eighteenth century, however, portraiture was the rage, and so
Raphaelle Peale found few buyers for his still lifes at the time.
His brother Rembrandt studied under his father and painted
portraits of many noted people, including one of George
(25)   Washington. Another brother, Rubens Peale, painted mostly
landscapes and portraits.

James Peale, the brother of Charles Willson Peale, specialized
in miniatures. His daughter Sarah Miriam Peale was probably the
first professional female portrait painter in America.

13. What is the main topic of the passage?

(A) The life of Charles Willson Peale
(B) Portraiture in the 18th century
(C) The Peale Museum
(D) A family of artists

14. The author probably mentions that Washington "tipped his hat to the figures in the painting" (lines 6-7) to indicate that

(A) Charles Willson Peale's painting was very lifelike
(B) Washington respected Charles Willson Peale's work
(C) Washington was friendly with Raphaelle and Titian Peale
(D) the painting of the two brothers was extremely large

15. The word "settings" in line 12 is closest in meaning to which of the following?

(A) Environments
(B) Categories
(C) Positions
(D) Requirements

Go on to the next page

15. The word "settings" in line 12 is closest in meaning to which of the following?

    (A) Environments
    (B) Categories
    (C) Positions
    (D) Requirements

16. For which of the following terms does the author give a definition in the second paragraph?

    (A) Natural science
    (B) Skeleton
    (C) Taxidermy
    (D) Mastodon

17. Which of the following questions about the Peale Museum does the passage NOT supply enough information to answer?

    (A) Who found and prepared its animal exhibits?
    (B) In what city was it located?
    (C) Where did its most popular exhibit come from?
    (D) In what year was it founded?

18. The word "unearthed" in line 16 is closest in meaning to

    (A) displayed
    (B) dug up
    (C) located
    (D) looked over

19. Which of the following words could best be substituted for the word "rage" in line 21

    (A) Fashion
    (B) Anger
    (C) Conflict
    (D) Desire

20. According to the passage, Rembrandt Peale and his father both painted

    (A) miniatures
    (B) portraits of George Washington
    (C) paintings of flowers, fruit, and cheese
    (D) pictures of animals

21. Which of the following is NOT one of the children of Charles Willson Peale?

    (A) Titian Peale
    (B) Rubens Peale
    (C) Raphaelle Peale
    (D) Sarah Miriam Peale

22. The author's attitude toward the Peales is generally

    (A) envious
    (B) puzzled
    (C) admiring
    (D) disappointed

Go on to the next page ➤

Questions 23–34

(line)   According to the best evidence gathered by space probes and
astronomers, Mars is an inhospitable planet, more similar to
Earth's Moon than to Earth itself—a dry, stark, seemingly
lifeless world. Mars' air pressure is equal to Earth's at an
(5)   altitude of 100,000 feet. The air there is 95% carbon dioxide.
Mars has no ozone layer to screen out the Sun's lethal radiation.
Daytime temperatures may reach above freezing, but because the
planet is blanketed by the mere wisp of an atmosphere, the heat
radiates back into space. Even at the equator, the temperature
(10)   drops to -50°C (-60°F) at night. Today there is no liquid water,
although valleys and channels on the surface show evidence of
having been carved by running water. The polar ice caps are made
of frozen water and carbon dioxide, and water may be frozen in
the ground as permafrost.
(15)   Despite these difficult conditions, certain scientists believe
that there is a possibility of transforming Mars into a more
Earth-like planet. Nuclear reactors might be used to melt frozen
gases and eventually build up the atmosphere. This in turn could
create a "greenhouse effect" that would stop heat from radiating
(20)   back into space. Liquid water could be thawed to form a polar
ocean. Once enough ice has melted, suitable plants could be
introduced to build up the level of oxygen in the atmosphere so
that, in time, the planet would support animal life from Earth
and even permanent human colonies. "This was once thought to be
(25)   so far in the future as to be irrelevant," said Christopher
McKay, a research scientist at the National Aeronautics and Space
Administration. "But now it's starting to look practical. We
could begin work in four or five decades."
The idea of "terra-forming" Mars, as enthusiasts call it, has
(30)   its roots in science fiction. But as researchers develop a more
profound understanding of how Earth's ecology supports life, they
have begun to see how it may be possible to create similar
conditions on Mars. Don't plan on homesteading on Mars any time
soon, though. The process could take hundreds or even thousands
of years to complete, and the cost would be staggering.

23. With which of the following is the passage
primarily concerned?

(A) The possibility of changing the Martian
environment
(B) The challenge of interplanetary travel
(C) The advantages of establishing colonies
on Mars
(D) The need to study the Martian ecology

Go on to the next page

24. The word "stark" in line 3 is closest in meaning to

    (A) harsh
    (B) unknown
    (C) dark
    (D) distant

25. The word "there" in line 5 refers to

    (A) a point 100 miles above the Earth
    (B) the Earth's Moon
    (C) Mars
    (D) outer space

26. Which of the following does the author NOT list as a characteristic of the planet Mars that would make colonization difficult?

    (A) There is little liquid water.
    (B) Daytime temperatures are dangerously high.
    (C) The Sun's rays are deadly.
    (D) Nighttime temperatures are extremely low.

27. According to the passage, the Martian atmosphere today consists mainly of

    (A) carbon dioxide
    (B) oxygen
    (C) ozone
    (D) water vapor

28. It can be inferred from the passage that the "greenhouse effect" mentioned in line 19 is

    (A) the direct result of nuclear reactions
    (B) the cause of low temperatures on Mars
    (C) caused by the absence of green plants
    (D) a possible means of warming Mars

29. The word "suitable" in line 21 is closest in meaning to

    (A) resistant
    (B) altered
    (C) appropriate
    (D) native

30. According to Christopher McKay, the possibility of transforming Mars

    (A) could occur only in science fiction stories
    (B) will not begin for hundreds, even thousands, of years
    (C) is completely impractical
    (D) could be started in 40 to 50 years

31. As used in line 29, the term "terra-forming" refers to

    (A) a process for adapting plants to live on Mars
    (B) a means of transporting materials through space
    (C) a method of building housing for colonists on Mars
    (D) a system of creating Earth-like conditions on other planets

32. The phrase "more profound" in lines 30–31 is closest in meaning to

    (A) deeper
    (B) more practical
    (C) more up-to-date
    (D) brighter

Go on to the next page ➡

33. According to the article, the basic knowledge needed to transform Mars comes from

    (A) the science of astronomy
    (B) a knowledge of Earth's ecology
    (C) data from space probes
    (D) science fiction stories

34. The word "staggering" in line 35 is closest in meaning to

    (A) astonishing
    (B) restrictive
    (C) increasing
    (D) unpredictable

Go on to the next page

Questions 35–43

Another critical factor that plays a part in susceptibility to colds is age. A study done by the University of Michigan School of Public Health revealed particulars that seem to hold true for (line) the general population. Infants are the most cold-ridden group, (5) averaging more than six colds in their first year. Boys have more colds than girls up to age three. After the age of three, girls are more susceptible than boys, and teenage girls average three colds a year to boys' two.

The general incidence of colds continues to decline into (10) maturity. Elderly people who are in good health have as few as one or two colds annually. One exception is found among people in their twenties, especially women, who show a rise in cold infections, because people in this age group are most likely to have young children. Adults who delay having children until (15) their thirties and forties experience the same sudden increase in cold infections.

The study also found that economics plays an important role. As income increases, the frequency at which colds are reported in the family decreases. Families with the lowest income suffer (20) about a third more colds than families at the upper end. Lower income generally forces people to live in more cramped quarters than those typically occupied by wealthier people, and crowding increases the opportunities for the cold virus to travel from person to person. Low income may also adversely influence diet. (25) The degree to which poor nutrition affects susceptibility to colds is not yet clearly established, but an inadequate diet is suspected of lowering resistance generally.

35. The paragraph that precedes this passage most probably deals with

(A) minor diseases other than colds
(B) the recommended treatment of colds
(C) a factor that affects susceptibility to colds
(D) methods of preventing colds among elderly people

36. Which of the following is closest in meaning to the word "particulars" in line 3?

(A) Minor errors
(B) Specific facts
(C) Small distinctions
(D) Individual people

37. What does the author claim about the study discussed in the passage?

(A) It contains many inconsistencies.
(B) It specializes in children.
(C) It contradicts the results of earlier studies in the field.
(D) Its results apparently are relevant for the population as a whole.

Go on to the next page ➤

38. It may be inferred from the passage that which of the following groups of people is most likely to catch colds?

    (A) Infant boys
    (B) Young girls
    (C) Teenage boys
    (D) Elderly women

39. There is information in the second paragraph of the passage to support which of the following conclusions?

    (A) Men are more susceptible to colds than women.
    (B) Children infect their parents with colds.
    (C) People who live in a cold climate have more colds than those who live in a warm one.
    (D) People who don't have children are more susceptible to colds than those who do.

40. The phrase "people in this age group" (line 13) refers to

    (A) infants
    (B) people in their twenties
    (C) people in their thirties and forties
    (D) elderly people

41. The author's main purpose in writing the last paragraph of the passage was to

    (A) explain how cold viruses are transmitted
    (B) prove that a poor diet causes colds
    (C) discuss the relationship between income and frequency of colds
    (D) analyze the distribution of income among the people in the study

42. The word "cramped" in line 21 is closest in meaning to

    (A) cheap
    (B) crowded
    (C) depressing
    (D) simple

43. The author's tone in this passage could best be described as

    (A) neutral
    (B) humorous
    (C) tentative
    (D) critical

Go on to the next page

Questions 44–50

About fifty years ago, plant physiologists set out to grow
roots by themselves in solutions in laboratory flasks. The
scientists found that the nutrition of isolated roots was quite
(line)   simple. They required sugar and the usual minerals and vitamins.
(5)   However, they did not require organic nitrogen compounds. These
roots got along fine on mineral inorganic nitrogen. Roots are
capable of making their own proteins and other organic compounds.
These activities by roots require energy, of course. The process
of respiration uses sugar to make the high energy compound ATP,
(10)   which drives the biochemical reactions. Respiration also requires
oxygen. Highly active roots require a good deal of oxygen.
The study of isolated roots has provided an understanding of
the relationship between shoots and roots in intact plants. The
leaves of the shoots provide the roots with sugar and vitamins,
(15)   and the roots provide the shoots with water and minerals. In
addition, roots can provide the shoots with organic nitrogen
compounds. This comes in handy for the growth of buds in the
early spring when leaves are not yet functioning. Once leaves
begin photosynthesizing, they produce protein, but only mature
(20)   leaves can "export" protein to the rest of the plant in the form
of amino acids.

44. What is the main topic of the passage?
   (A) The relationship between a plant's
       roots and its shoots
   (B) What can be learned by growing roots
       in isolation
   (C) How plants can be grown without roots
   (D) What elements are necessary for the
       growth of plants

45. The word "themselves" in line 2 refers to
   (A) plant physiologists
   (B) solutions
   (C) laboratory flasks
   (D) roots

46. According to the passage, what is ATP?
   (A) A biochemical process
   (B) The tip of a root
   (C) A chemical compound
   (D) A type of plant cell

47. The word "intact" in line 13 is closest in
    meaning to
   (A) mature
   (B) wild
   (C) whole
   (D) tiny

48. The use of the phrase "comes in handy" in
    line 17 indicates that the process is
   (A) useful
   (B) predictable
   (C) necessary
   (D) successful

Go on to the next page

48. The use of the phrase "comes in handy" in line 17 indicates that the process is
    (A) useful
    (B) predictable
    (C) necessary
    (D) successful

49. It can be inferred from the passage that, in the early spring, the buds of plants
    (A) "export" protein in the form of amino acids
    (B) do not require water
    (C) have begun photosynthesizing
    (D) obtain organic compounds from the roots

50. Which of the following best describes the organization of the passage?
    (A) The results of two experiments are compared.
    (B) A generalization is made, and several examples of it are given.
    (C) The findings of an experiment are explained.
    (D) A hypothesis is presented, and several means of proving it are suggested.

THIS IS THE END OF THE SAMPLE READING COMPREHENSION SECTION.

IF YOU FINISH BEFORE THE TIME LIMIT, GO BACK AND CHECK YOUR WORK.

STOP   STOP   STOP   STOP   STOP   STOP

LESSON 44

OVERVIEW QUESTIONS

A) Main Idea, Main Topic, and Main Purpose Questions

After almost every passage, the first question is an **overview question** about the main idea, main topic, or main purpose of a passage. **Main idea questions** ask you to identify the most important thought in the passage. Answer choices are complete sentences.

Sample Questions

- What is the main idea of the passage?
- The primary idea of the passage is . . .
- Which of the following best summarizes the author's main idea?

When there is not a single, readily identified main idea, **main topic questions** may be asked. These ask you what the passage is generally "about." Answer choices are noun phrases.

Sample Questions

- The main topic of the passage is . . .
- What does the passage mainly discuss?
- The passage is primarily concerned with . . .

Main purpose questions ask *why* an author wrote a passage. The answer choices for these questions usually begin with infinitives.

Sample Questions

- The author's purpose in writing is to . . .
- What is the author's main purpose in the passage?
- The main point of this passage is to . . .
- Why did the author write the passage?

Sample Answer Choices

- To define . . .
- To discuss . . .
- To illustrate . . .
- To distinguish between
  _____ and _____

- To relate . . .
- To propose . . .
- To support the idea that . . .
- To compare _____ and
  _____

Don't answer the initial overview question about a passage until you have answered the other questions. The process of answering the detail questions may give you a clearer idea of the main idea, topic, or purpose of the passage.

The correct answers for main idea, main topic, and main purpose questions correctly summarize the main points of the passage; they must be more general than any of the supporting ideas or details, but not so general that they include ideas outside the scope of the passages.

Distractors for this type of question have one of these characteristics:

1. They are too specific.

2. They are too general.

3. The are incorrect according to the passage.

4. They are irrelevant (unrelated) to the main idea of the passage.

If you're not sure of the answer for one of these questions, go back and quickly scan the passage. You can usually infer the main idea, main topic, or main purpose of the entire passage from an understanding of the main ideas of the paragraphs that make up the passage and the relationship between them.

B) Other Overview Questions

A number of other questions are asked that require an overall understanding of the passage. These are often the last question in a set of questions.

Tone questions ask you to determine the author's feelings about the topic by the language that he or she uses in writing the passage. Look for vocabulary that indicates if the author's feelings are positive, negative, or neutral.

Sample Questions

- What tone does the author take in writing this passage?
- The tone of this passage could best be described as . . .

Sample Answer Choices

■ Positive	■ Negative	■ Neutral
■ Favorable	■ Critical	■ Objective
■ Optimistic	■ Unfavorable	■ Impersonal
■ Amused	■ Angry	
■ Pleased	■ Defiant	
■ Respectful	■ Worried	
■ Humorous	■ Outraged	

If you read the following sentences in passages, would the tone of those passages most likely be positive or negative?

A) That was just the beginning of a *remarkable* series of performances by this *brilliant* actress.

B) Despite some minor problems, this device has a number of *admirable* features.

C) This practice is *a waste of time and money*.

D) At the time his poems were first published, they were very popular, but today most critics find them *simplistic and rather uninteresting*.

The italicized words in sentences A) and B) show a positive tone; in C) and D), the italicized words indicate a negative attitude. Notice that sentence B) contains negative words ("minor problems"), but the overall meaning of the sentence is positive. Sentence D) contains positive language ("very popular"), but overall, the tone is negative. (Words like *despite, but, although, however,* and similar words can "reverse" the tone of the passage.)

Most TOEFL Reading passages have a neutral tone, but sometimes an author may take a position for or against some point. However, answer choices that indicate strong emotion—*angry, outraged, sad,* and so forth—will seldom be correct.

Attitude questions are very similar to tone questions. Again, you must understand the author's opinion. The language that the author uses will tell you what his or her position is.

What is the author's attitude toward smoking on airplanes as expressed in the sentence below?

> Although some passengers may experience a slight discomfort from not smoking on long flights, their smoking endangers the health of all the passengers and crew.

The author opposes smoking during flights. He admits that there is some argument in favor of smoking—some passengers may feel discomfort—but this is not as important as the fact that smoking can be dangerous to everyone on the flight. The word *although* shows this.

Sample Questions

- What is the author's attitude toward . . .
- The author's opinion of _____ is best described as . . .
- The author's attitude toward _____ could best be described as one of . . .
- How would the author probably feel about . . .

Another type of attitude question presents four statements and asks how the author would feel about them.

- Which of the following recommendations would the author most likely support?
- The author would be LEAST likely to agree with which of the following statements?
- The author of the passage would most likely be in favor of which of the following policies?

Organization questions ask about the overall structure of a passage or about the organization of a particular paragraph.

Sample Question

- Which of the following best describes the organization of the passage?

Sample Answer Choices

- A general concept is defined, and examples are given.
- Several generalizations are presented, from which a conclusion is drawn.
- The author presents the advantages and disadvantages of _____.
- The author presents a system of classification for _____.
- Persuasive language is used to argue against _____.
- The author describes _____.
- The author presents a brief account of _____.
- The author compares _____ and _____.

Questions about previous or following paragraphs ask you to assume that the passage is part of a longer work: What would be the topic of the hypothetical paragraph that precedes or follows the passage? To find the topic of the previous paragraph, look for clues in the first line or two of the passage; for the topic of the following passage, look in the last few lines. Sometimes incorrect answer choices mention topics that have already been discussed in the passage.

Sample Questions

- With what topic would the following/preceding paragraph most likely deal?
- The paragraph prior to/after the passage most probably discusses . . .
- It can be inferred from the passage that the previous/next paragraph concerns . . .
- What most likely precedes/follows the passage?

Exercise 44.1

Focus: Identifying correct answers and recognizing distractors in main idea/main topic/main purpose questions.

Directions: Read the passages. Then mark each answer choice according to the following system:

S	Too specific
G	Too general
X	Incorrect
I	Irrelevant
C	Correct

The first one is done as an example.

There are two main types of cell division. Most cells are produced by a process called mitosis. In mitosis, a cell divides and forms two identical daughter cells, each with an identical number of chromosomes. Most one-celled creatures reproduce by this method, as do most of the cells in multi-celled plants and animals. Sex cells, however, are formed in a special type of cell division called meiosis. This process reduces the number of chromosomes in a sex cell to half the number found in other kinds of cells. Then, when sex cells unite, they produce a single cell with the original number of chromosomes.

1. What is the main topic of this passage?
   - _S_ (A) The method by which one-celled organisms reproduce
   - _C_ (B) A comparison between mitosis and meiosis
   - _X_ (C) Meiosis, the process by which identical cells are produced

The last gold rush belongs as much to Canadian history as it does to American. The discovery of gold along the Klondike River, which flows from Canada's Yukon Territory into Alaska, drew some 30,000 fortune hunters to the north. The Yukon became a territory, and its capital of the time, Dawson, would not have existed without the gold rush. The gold strike furnished material for a dozen of Jack London's novels. It inspired Robert Service to write "The Shooting of Dan McGrew" and other poems, and it provided the background for the wonderful Charlie Chaplin movie, *The Gold Rush*. It also marked the beginnings of modern Alaska.

2. This author's main purpose in writing is to
   - _____ (A) discuss the significance of mining in Canada and the United States
   - _____ (B) show the influence of the Klondike gold strike on the creative arts
   - _____ (C) point out the impact of the Klondike gold strike

The keystone arch was used by almost every early civilization. To build a keystone arch, stones are cut so that the opposite sides taper toward each other slightly. The upper and lower surfaces are carved so that when several stones are placed side by side, the upper and lower surfaces meet in smooth, continuous curves. Some form of scaffolding is built under the arch and shaped to accept the curved underside of the stones. Then the stones are fitted in place one by one. The keystone is the top center stone, the last to be dropped into position. Afterwards, the scaffolding is removed and the arch is self-supporting.

3. The passage mainly concerns the
   - _____ (A) basic principles of building keystone arches
   - _____ (B) uses of arches in modern architecture
   - _____ (C) role of scaffolding in building keystone arches

Circumstantial evidence is evidence not drawn from the direct observation of a fact. If, for example, there is evidence that a piece of rock embedded in a wrapped chocolate bar is the same type of rock found in the vicinity of the candy factory, and that rock of this type is found in few other places, then there is circumstantial evidence that the stone found its way into the candy during manufacture and suggests that the candy-maker was negligent. Despite a popular notion to look down on the quality of circumstantial evidence, it is of great usefulness if there is enough of it and if it is properly interpreted. Each circumstance, taken singly, may mean little, but a whole chain of circumstances can be as conclusive as direct evidence.

4. What is the author's main purpose in this passage?
   - _____ (A) To show that a manufacturer's negligence can be shown by direct evidence only
   - _____ (B) To define circumstantial evidence and show its usefulness
   - _____ (C) To demonstrate that circumstantial evidence can be very useful in science

The Northwest Ordinance was passed by Congress in 1787. It set up the government structure of the region north of the Ohio River and west of Pennsylvania, then called the Northwest Territory. It set the conditions under which parts of the Territory could become states having equality with the older states. But the ordinance was more than just a plan for government. The law also guaranteed freedom of religion and trial by jury in the Territory. It organized the Territory into townships of 36 square miles and ordered a school to be built for each township. It also abolished slavery in the Territory. The terms were so attractive that thousands of pioneers poured into the Territory. Eventually, the Territory became the states of Ohio, Indiana, Illinois, Michigan, and Wisconsin.

5. What is the main topic of this passage?
   _____ (A) The structure of government
   _____ (B) The provisions of an important law
   _____ (C) The establishment of schools in the Northwest Territory

The story of the motel business from 1920 to the start of World War II in 1941 is one of uninterrupted growth. Motels spread from the West and the Midwest all the way to Maine and Florida. They clustered along transcontinental highways such as U.S. routes 40 and 66 and along the north-south routes running up and down both the East and West coast. There were 16,000 motels by 1930 and 24,000 by 1940. The motel industry was one of the few industries that was not hurt by the Depression of the 1930's. Their cheap rates attracted travelers who had very little money.

6. What does the passage mainly discuss?
   _____ (A) How the Depression hurt U.S. motels
   _____ (B) The impact of transcontinental highways
   _____ (C) Two decades of growth for the motel industry

An old proverb states, "Beware of oak, it draws the stroke." This saying is handy during thunderstorm season. In general, trees with deep roots that tap into groundwater attract more lightning than do trees with shallow, drier roots. Oaks are around 50 times more likely to be struck than beeches. Spruces are nearly as safe as beeches. Pines are not as safe as these two, but are still much safer than oaks.

7. What is the author's main point?
   _____ (A) Old proverbs often contain important truths.
   _____ (B) Trees with shallow roots are more likely to avoid lightning than those with deep roots.
   _____ (C) The deeper a tree's roots, the safer it is during a thunderstorm.

Alternative history is generally classified as a type of science fiction, but it also bears some relation to historical fiction. This type of writing describes an imaginary world that is identical to ours up to a certain point in history, but at that point, the two worlds diverge; some important historical event takes place in one world but not in the other, and they go in different directions. Alternative histories might describe worlds in which the Roman Empire had never fallen, in which the Spanish Armada had been victorious, or in which the South had won the Civil War. Or they may suppose that some technology had been introduced earlier in the world's history than actually happened. For example: What if computers had been invented in Victorian times? Many readers find these stories interesting because of the way they stimulate the imagination and get them thinking about the phenomenon of cause and effect in history.

8. What is the main idea of this passage?
   _____ (A) Alternative histories describe worlds in which history has taken another course.
   _____ (B) Alternative histories are a type of historical novel.
   _____ (C) Science fiction writers have accurately predicted certain actual scientific developments.

Until the late 1700's, metal could not be turned on a lathe to make it uniformly smooth and round. The operator could not guide the cutting tool evenly by hand against the turning piece. This problem was solved by David Wilkinson of Pawtucket, Rhode Island. In 1798 he invented a machine in which the cutter was clamped into a movable slide that could be advanced precisely, by hand crank, parallel to the work. The slide rest, as it came to be called, has many uses. It permits the manufacture of parts so uniform that they can be interchanged. Without it, mass production would not have been possible. As it turns out, the great English machinist Henry Maudsley had developed nearly the same mechanism a few years before, but this was unknown to Wilkinson and does not diminish his accomplishment.

9. Why did the author write this passage?
_____ (A) To prove that Wilkinson's invention was based on Maudsley's
_____ (B) To demonstrate the importance of mass production to American society
_____ (C) To show the usefulness of Wilkinson's invention

Almost every form of transportation has given someone the idea for a new type of toy. After the Montgolfier brothers flew the first balloon, toy balloons became popular playthings. In the nineteenth century, soon after railroads and steamships were developed, every child had to have model trains and steamboats. The same held true for automobiles and airplanes in the early twentieth century. Toy rockets and missiles became popular at the beginning of the space age, and by the 1980's, there were many different versions of space-shuttle toys.

10. The main idea of this passage is that
_____ (A) inventors have been inspired by toys to build new forms of transportation
_____ (B) toy automobiles and airplanes were very popular in the early 1900's
_____ (C) toy design has followed developments in transportation

Exercise 44.2

Focus: Answering a variety of overview questions about short passages.

Directions: Read the passages and mark the best answer choice—(A), (B), (C), or (D). The first one is done as an example.

American folk music originated with ordinary people at a time when the rural population was isolated and music was not yet spread by radio, tapes, compact disks, or music videos. It was transmitted by oral tradition and is noted for its energy, humor, and emotional impact. The major source of early American folk songs was music from the British Isles, but songs from Africa as well as songs of the American Indians have a significant part in its heritage. Later settlers from other countries also contributed songs. In the nineteenth century, composer Stephen Foster wrote some of the most enduringly popular of all American songs, which soon became part of the folk tradition. Beginning in the 1930's, Woody Guthrie gained great popularity by adapting traditional melodies and lyrics and supplying new ones as well. In the 1950's and 1960's, singer-composers such as Pete Seeger, Bob Dylan, and Joan Baez continued this tradition by creating "urban" folk music. Many of these songs dealt with important social issues, such as racial integration and the war in Vietnam.

1. The primary purpose of this passage is to
__✔__ (A) trace the development of American folk music
_____ (B) explain the oral tradition
_____ (C) contrast the styles of folk musicians
_____ (D) point out the influence of social issues on "urban" folk music

Every scientific discipline tends to develop its own special language because it finds ordinary words inadequate, and psychology is no different. The purpose of this special jargon is not to mystify non-psychologists; rather, it allows psychologists to accurately describe the phenomena they are discussing and to communicate with each other effectively. Of course, psychological terminology consists in part of everyday words such as *emotion, intelligence,* and *motivation,* but psychologists use these words somewhat differently. For example, laymen use the term *anxiety* to mean nervousness or fear, but most psychologists reserve the term to describe a condition produced when one fears events over which one has no control.

2. The main topic of this passage is
   _____ (A) effective communication
   _____ (B) the special language of psychology
   _____ (C) two definitions of the word *anxiety*
   _____ (D) the jargon of science

Gifford Pinchot was the first professionally trained forester in the United States. After he graduated from Yale in 1889, he studied forestry in Europe. In the 1890's he managed the forest on the Biltmore estate in North Carolina (now Pisgah National Forest) and became the first to practice scientific forestry. Perhaps his most important contribution to conservation was persuading President Theodore Roosevelt to set aside millions of acres in the West as forest reserves. These lands now make up much of the national parks and national forests of the United States. Pinchot became the Chief Forester of the U.S. Forest Service in 1905. Although he held that post for only five years, he established guidelines that set forest policy for decades to come.

3. The passage primarily deals with
   _____ (A) Gifford Pinchot's work on the Biltmore Estate
   _____ (B) the practice and theory of scientific forestry
   _____ (C) the origin of national parks and national forests in the United States
   _____ (D) the contributions Gifford Pinchot made to American forestry

Off-Broadway theater developed in New York City in about 1950 as a result of dissatisfaction with conditions on Broadway. Its founders believed that Broadway was overly concerned with producing safe, commercially successful hit plays rather than drama with artistic quality. Off-Broadway producers tried to assist playwrights, directors, and performers who could not find work on Broadway. Off-Broadway theaters were poorly equipped, had limited seating, and provided few conveniences for audiences. But the originality of the scripts, the creativity of the performers, and the low cost of tickets made up for these disadvantages, and off-Broadway theater prospered. However, by the 1960's, costs began to rise and by the 1970's, off-Broadway theater was encountering many of the difficulties of Broadway and had lost much of its vitality. With its decline, a experimental movement called *off-off-Broadway* theater developed.

4. What is the main idea of this passage?
   _____ (A) After initial success, off-Broadway theater began to decline.
   _____ (B) Off-Broadway theaters produced many hit commercial plays.
   _____ (C) Theaters on Broadway were not well equipped.
   _____ (D) Off-Broadway plays were highly creative.

5. The paragraph that follows this passage most likely deals with
   _____ (A) the help off-Broadway producers provided directors, playwrights, and performers
   _____ (B) methods off-Broadway theaters used to cope with rising prices
   _____ (C) the development of off-off-Broadway theater
   _____ (D) the decline of Broadway theater

At the time of the first European contact, there were from 500 to 700 languages spoken by North American Indians. These were divided into some 60 language families, with no demonstrable genetic relationship among them. Some of these families spread across several of the seven cultural areas. The Algonquin family, for instance, contained dozens of languages and occupied a vast territory. Speakers of Algonquin languages included the Algonquins of the Eastern Woodland, the Blackfoots of the Plains, and the Wiyots and Yuroks of California. Other language families, like the Zuni family of the Southwest, occupied only a few square miles of area and contained only a single tribal language.

6. What is the main idea of this passage?
_____ (A) Each of the cultural areas was dominated by one of the language families.
_____ (B) The Zuni language is closely related to the Algonquin language.
_____ (C) There is considerable diversity in the size and the number of languages in language families of the North American Indians.
_____ (D) Contact with Europeans had an extraordinary effect on the languages of the Indian tribes of North America.

Other major changes in journalism occurred around this time. In 1846 Richard Hoe invented the steam cylinder rotary press, making it possible to print newspapers faster and cheaper. The development of the telegraph made possible much speedier collection and distribution of news. Also in 1846 the first wire service was organized. A new type of newspaper appeared around this time, one that was more attuned to the spirit and needs of the new America. Although newspapers continued to cover politics, they came to report more human interest stories and to record the most recent news, which they could not have done before the telegraph. New York papers and those of other northern cities maintained corps of correspondents to go into all parts of the country to cover newsworthy events.

7. The main purpose of the passage is to
_____ (A) present a brief history of American journalism
_____ (B) outline certain developments in mid-19th-century journalism
_____ (C) explain the importance of the steam cylinder rotary press
_____ (D) present some biographical information about Richard Hoe

8. What is the most probable topic of the paragraph preceding this one?
_____ (A) Other types of rotary presses
_____ (B) Alternatives to using wire services
_____ (C) Newspapers that concentrated on politics
_____ (D) Other developments in journalism

9. The tone of the passage could best be described as
_____ (A) objective
_____ (B) optimistic
_____ (C) angry
_____ (D) humorous

In the western third of North America, the convoluted folds of the Earth's surface and its fractured geologic structure tend to absorb the seismic energy of an earthquake. Even if an earthquake measuring 8.5 on the Richter scale struck Los Angeles, its force would fade by the time it reached San Francisco, some 400 miles away. But in the eastern two thirds of the continent the same energy travels more easily. The earthquake that struck New Madrid, Missouri, in 1811, estimated at 8 on the Richter scale, shook Washington, D.C., about 800 miles away, and was felt as far as Boston and Toronto.

10. Which of the following best expresses the main idea of this passage?
_____ (A) If a major earthquake strikes Los Angeles, it will probably damage San Francisco as well.
_____ (B) The New Madrid earthquake of 1811 was felt in Boston and Toronto.
_____ (C) The geology of the western United States is much more complex than that of the East.
_____ (D) Earthquakes travel farther in the East than in the West.

There has never been an adult scientist who has been half as curious as any child between the ages of four months and four years. Adults sometimes mistake this superb curiosity about everything as a lack of ability to concentrate. The truth is that children begin to learn at birth, and by the time they begin formal schooling at the age of five or six, they have already absorbed a fantastic amount of information, perhaps more, fact for fact, than they will learn for the rest of their lives. Adults can multiply by many times the knowledge children absorb if they appreciate this curiosity while simultaneously encouraging the children to learn.

11. With which of the following statements would the author probably agree?
_____ (A) Children lack the ability to concentrate.
_____ (B) Scientists have a much greater curiosity than children do.
_____ (C) The first few years of school are the most important ones for most children.
_____ (D) Adults can use children's intense curiosity to help children learn more.

12. The paragraph following this one most likely deals with
_____ (A) ways in which adults can help children learn by stimulating their curiosity
_____ (B) the learning habits of older children
_____ (C) the methods adult scientists use to study the curiosity of young children
_____ (D) ways in which adults can become as curious as children

Settlement houses were institutions established to improve living conditions in poor city neighborhoods in the late 1800's and early 1900's. They offered health, educational, recreational, and cultural activities. The first to open in the United States was University Settlement in New York City. It was established by the social reformer Stanton Coit in 1886. The most famous example was Hull House, established by the well-known reformer Jane Addams in Chicago in 1890. Settlement houses were usually staffed by idealistic young college graduates who were eager to improve the condition of the poor.

13. The passage mainly discusses
_____ (A) U.S. cities in the late nineteenth century
_____ (B) the idealism of college graduates
_____ (C) settlement houses in the late 1800's and early 1900's
_____ (D) the life of several American social reformers

The dancer Isadora Duncan was a daring, dynamic innovator in dance. While she was not very successful in teaching her highly personal style of dance to others, she taught a generation of dancers to trust their own forms of expression. She rebelled against the rigid, formal style of classical ballet. Inspired by the art of Greece, she usually danced barefoot in a loose, flowing Greek tunic. She found further inspiration in nature and used dance movements to mirror the waves of the sea and passing clouds.

Isadora Duncan was born in San Francisco in 1878. She gave her first performance in 1899. Early failures gave way to triumphant performances in Budapest, Berlin, London, and finally, in 1908, back in the United States. She lived in Europe most of her life, establishing dancing schools for children there. She died in 1927 near Nice, France, in a freak accident, her long scarf being caught in the wheel of an open sports car in which she was riding.

14. The author's attitude toward Isadora Duncan could best be described as one of
  _____ (A) displeasure
  _____ (B) admiration
  _____ (C) compassion
  _____ (D) amazement

15. Which of the following best describes the organization of the passage?
  _____ (A) The author first discusses Isadora Duncan's style of dance and then her life history.
  _____ (B) The first paragraph deals with Isadora Duncan's role as a teacher, the second her role as a performer.
  _____ (C) The author first discusses Isadora Duncan's shortcomings and then her positive points.
  _____ (D) First there is an analysis of Isadora Duncan's influences and then of her lasting contributions to dance.

Through the centuries, the dream of medieval alchemists was to discover how to turn lead and other "base" metals into gold. Some were fakes, but many were learned men with philosophical goals. Their quest was based on the ancient idea that all matter consists of different proportions of just four substances—earth, water, fire, and air. They believed that it was possible to adjust the proportions of the elements that made up lead by chemical means so that it turned into gold, a process called transmutation. Their experiments were concerned with finding the substance—which they called the *philosopher's stone*—that, when added to lead, would cause this astonishing change to take place. Alchemists also searched for the *elixir of life*, a substance that could cure diseases and prolong life. They failed on both counts. However, their techniques for preparing and studying chemicals helped lay the foundation for the modern science of chemistry.

16. Which of the following statements best summarizes the author's attitude toward medieval alchemists?
  _____ (A) Although they were all fakes, they made important contributions to science.
  _____ (B) Their discovery of the philosopher's stone was more important than the achievements of modern chemists.
  _____ (C) Although their theories were sound, they lacked the equipment needed to accomplish their goals.
  _____ (D) They were unable to realize their goals, but they helped prepare the way for modern chemistry.

Exercise 44.3

Focus: Understanding the meaning of multi-paragraph passages by identifying the main point of each of the paragraphs.

Directions: Read the following passages and the questions about them. Decide which of the choices best answers the question, and mark the answer. The first one is done as an example.

Questions 1–3

In most of Europe, farmers' homes and outbuildings are generally located within a village, and tools and animals are housed there. Every morning, the farmers and farm laborers leave their village to work their land or tend their animals in distant fields, and return to the village at the end of the day. Social life is thus centripetal; that is, it is focused around the community center, the village. Only in certain parts of Quebec has this pattern been preserved in North America.

Throughout most of North America, a different pattern was established. It was borrowed from northern Europe, but was pushed even further in the New World where land was cheap or even free.

It is a centrifugal system of social life, with large isolated farms whose residents go to the village only to buy goods and procure services. The independence associated with American farmers stems from this pattern of farm settlement. The American farmer is as free of the intimacy of the village as the urbanite.

1. The main topic of the first paragraph is
_____ (A) European farm products
_____ (B) social life in Quebec
__✔__ (C) the European pattern of rural settlement

2. The main topic of the second paragraph is
_____ (A) the relative isolation of North American farm families
_____ (B) the relationship between farmers and urbanites in North America
_____ (C) the low cost of farmland in North America

3. The main topic of the entire passage is
_____ (A) a comparison of farming in northern and southern Europe
_____ (B) the difference between farming in Quebec and the rest of North America
_____ (C) European influence on American agriculture
_____ (D) a contrast between a centripetal system of rural life and a centrifugal system

Questions 4–7

While fats have lately acquired a bad image, one should not forget how essential they are. Fats provide the body's best means of storing energy, far more efficient energy sources than either carbohydrates or proteins. They act as insulation against cold, as cushioning for the internal organs, and as lubricants. Without fats, there would be no way to utilize fat-soluble vitamins. Furthermore, some fats contain fatty acids that contain necessary growth factors and help with the digestion of other foods.

An important consideration of fat intake is the ratio of saturated fats to unsaturated fats. Saturated fats, which are derived from dairy products, animal fats, and tropical oils, increase the amount of cholesterol in the blood. Cholesterol may lead to coronary heart disease by building up in the arteries of the heart. However, unsaturated fats, derived from vegetable oils, tend to lower serum cholesterol if taken in a proportion twice that of saturated fats.

The consumption of a variety of fats is necessary, but the intake of too much fat may lead to a variety of health problems. Excessive intake of fats, like all nutritional excesses, is to be avoided.

4. What is the main idea of the first paragraph?
_____ (A) Fats have a bad image.
_____ (B) Fats serve important functions in the body.
_____ (C) Fats store food more efficiently than proteins or carbohydrates.

5. What is the main idea of the second paragraph?
_____ (A) Saturated fats may reduce cholesterol levels.
_____ (B) The consumption of any type of fat leads to heart disease.
_____ (C) Fats taken in the proper proportion may reduce serum cholesterol.

6. The main idea of the third paragraph is that
_____ (A) people are eating less and less fat today
_____ (B) fats should be gradually eliminated from the diet
_____ (C) excessive consumption of fats may be dangerous to one's health

7. With which of the following is the whole passage primarily concerned?
_____ (A) The role of fats in human health
_____ (B) The dangers of cholesterol
_____ (C) The benefits of fats in the diet
_____ (D) The importance of good nutrition

Questions 8–10

The term *weathering* refers to all the ways in which rock can be broken down. It takes place because minerals formed in a particular way (say at high temperatures, in the case of igneous rocks) are often unstable when exposed to various conditions. Weathering involves the interaction of the lithosphere (the earth's crust) with the atmosphere and hydrosphere (air and water). It occurs at different rates and in different ways, depending on the climactic and environmental conditions. But all kinds of weathering ultimately produce broken minerals and rock fragments and other products of the decomposition of stone.

Soil is the most obvious and, from the human point of view, the most important result of the weathering process. Soil is the weathered part of the Earth's crust that is capable of sustaining plant life. The character of soil depends on the nature of rock from which it is formed. It also depends on the climate and on the relative "age" of the soil. Immature soils are little more than broken rock fragments. Over time, immature soil develops into mature soil, which contains quantities of humus, formed from decayed plant matter. Mature soil is darker, richer in microscopic life, and more conducive to plant growth.

8. The first paragraph primarily describes
    _____ (A) the process by which rocks are broken down
    _____ (B) the weathering of igneous rocks
    _____ (C) gradual changes in the earth's weather patterns

9. The main topic of the second paragraph is
    _____ (A) a description of immature soil
    _____ (B) the growth of plants
    _____ (C) the evolution of soil

10. The main idea of the entire passage is that
    _____ (A) weathering breaks down rocks and leads to the development of soil
    _____ (B) soils may be classified as mature or immature
    _____ (C) the process of soil development is more important to humans than that of weathering
    _____ (D) the Earth's crust is constantly changing

Questions 11–15

The first Dutch outpost in New Netherlands was made at Fort Orange (now Albany) in 1624; it became a depot of the fur trade. But the most important settlement was at the southern tip of Manhattan, commanding the great harbor at the mouth of the Hudson River. Peter Minuit, first governor-general of New Netherlands, "purchased" title to the island from the Canarsie Indians for the equivalent of twenty-four dollars worth of trinkets. However, the Canarsie Indians might be described as tourists from Brooklyn; Minuit had to make a later payment to the group that was actually resident there.

In 1626 engineers from Holland arrived in Manhattan to construct Fort Amsterdam. Within its rectangular walls, permanent houses were built, replacing the thatched dwellings of the original Manhattanites. The fort became the nucleus of the town of New Amsterdam. Soon Manhattan had its first skyline: the solid outline of the fort, the flagstaff, the silhouette of a giant windmill, and the masts of trading ships.

The Dutch West India company established dairy farms in the vicinity of New Amsterdam. Each morning, the cattle were driven to the "Bouwerie" (now the Bowery), a large open common in the city. Just southwest of the Bouwerie was the Bowling Green, a level area where the burghers played ninepins, the ancestor of modern bowling. The Bowling Green became the site of a cattle fair where livestock were marketed; beer and sausage was available from booths; cheese, lace, and linen were sold by farmers' wives; and Indian women sold baskets and other handicrafts. These colorful gatherings and other aspects of everyday life in New Amsterdam are described in Washington Irving's rollicking book, *Diedrich Knickerbocker's History of New York.*

The last and most powerful governor-general of New Netherlands was Peter Stuyvesant, famous for his temper and his wooden leg. He annexed the Swedish colony of Delaware and ordered the streets of New Amsterdam laid out in an orderly manner and numbered. He did his best to obtain military and financial aid from Holland against the British. When the British sent emissaries demanding the surrender of the colony, he wanted to fight.

Four British warships, commanded by Colonel Richard Nicolls, sailed into the harbor in 1664. The fort was long out of repair, and there was a shortage of ammunition. Stuyvesant had no choice but to surrender. New Netherlands became the British colony of New York, and New Amsterdam became New York City.

11. What is the main topic of the first paragraph?
   _____ (A) The first Dutch settlement in New Netherlands
   _____ (B) Peter Minuit's acquisition of Manhattan
   _____ (C) Tourism in Manhattan

12. The second paragraph deals primarily with
   _____ (A) the establishment of Fort Amsterdam
   _____ (B) the skyline of Manhattan
   _____ (C) the thatched houses of the Indians

13. The third paragraph mainly describes
   _____ (A) aspects of everyday life in New Amsterdam
   _____ (B) the origin of the game of modern bowling
   _____ (C) Washington Irving's book about New Amsterdam

14. What does the fourth paragraph mainly discuss?
   _____ (A) The annexation of the Swedish colony of Delaware
   _____ (B) The ordering of the streets in New Amsterdam
   _____ (C) A description of Peter Stuyvesant and his accomplishments

15. What is the primary topic of the entire passage?
   _____ (A) A history of the British colony of New York
   _____ (B) The origin and importance of the Cattle Fair
   _____ (C) European colonization in the New World
   _____ (D) Forty years of Dutch rule in New Amsterdam

LESSON 45

FACTUAL QUESTIONS, NEGATIVE QUESTIONS, AND SCANNING QUESTIONS

A) Factual Questions

Factual questions ask about explicit facts and details given in the passage. They often contain one of the *wh-* question words: *who, what, when, where, why, how much.*

Factual questions often begin with the phrases "According to the passage, . . ." or "According to the author, . . ." When you see these phrases, you know that the information needed to answer the question is directly stated somewhere in the passage (unlike answers for inference questions).

To answer factual questions, you have to locate and identify the information that the question asks about. If you are not sure from your first reading where to look for specific answers, use the following **scanning** techniques:

- Focus on one or two key words as you read the stem of each question. Lock these words in your mind.
- Scan the passage looking for the key words or their synonyms. Look only for these words. Do *not* try to read every word of the passage.
- It may help to use the eraser end of your pencil as a pointer to focus your attention. Don't re-read the passage completely—just look for these words.
- When you find the key words in the passage, carefully read the sentence in which they occur. You may have to read the sentence preceding or following that sentence as well.
- Compare the information you read with the four answer choices.

The order of detail questions about a passage almost always follows the order in which ideas are presented in the passage. In other words, the information you need to answer the first detail question will usually come near the beginning of the passage; the information for the second will follow that, and so on. Knowing this should help you locate the information you need. You can also use line-number questions to locate the information needed to answer questions. See page 274.

Correct answers for detail questions are seldom the same, word for word, as information in the passage; they often contain synonyms and use different grammatical structures.

There are generally more factual questions—twelve to eighteen per Reading section—than any other type except (on some tests) vocabulary-in-context questions.

B) Negative Questions

These questions ask you to determine which of the four choices is not given in the passage. These questions contain the words NOT, EXCEPT, or LEAST (which are always capitalized).

- According to the passage, all of the following are true
  EXCEPT
- Which of the following is NOT mentioned in the passage?
- Which of the following is the LEAST likely . . .

Scan the passage to find the answers that ARE correct or ARE mentioned in the passage. Sometimes the three distractors are clustered in one or two sentences; sometimes they are scattered throughout the passage. The correct answer, of course, is the one that does not appear.

Negative questions often take more time than other questions. Therefore, you may want to guess and come back to these questions if you have time.

There are generally from three to six negative questions per Reading section.

C) Scanning Questions

These questions ask you to find where in the passage some particular information or transition is located. They are easy to identify: the answers are usually line numbers. They are usually easy to answer too. Scanning questions are often the last question in a set of questions about a passage. To answer these questions, use the same techniques for scanning given in Part A about factual questions.

Sample Questions

- In what line does the author shift his focus to _____?
- Where in the passage does the author first discuss _____?
- A description of _____ can be found in . . .
- Where in the passage does the author specifically stress _____?
- In what paragraph does the author first mention the concept of _____?

In each Reading section, there are generally from one to three scanning questions.

Exercise 45.1

Focus: Scanning passages to locate answers for factual and scanning questions.

Directions: For each question, locate that part of the passage in which the answer will probably be found, and write down the line numbers in the blank at the end of the passage. Don't worry about answering the question itself, only about finding the information. The first one is done as an example. Do these scanning exercises as fast as you can.

Questions 1–7

Antlers grow from permanent knoblike bones on a deer's skull. Deer use their antlers chiefly to fight for mates or for leadership of a herd. Among most species of deer, only the males have
(line)
(5)   antlers, but both male and female reindeer and caribou have antlers. Musk deer and Chinese water deer do not have antlers at all.

Deer that live in mild or cold climates lose their antlers each winter. New ones begin to grow the next spring. Deer that live in tropical climates may lose their antlers and grow new ones at
(10)   other times of year.

New antlers are soft and tender. Thin skin grows over the antlers as they develop. Short, fine hair on the skin makes it look like velvet. Full-grown antlers are hard and strong. The velvety skin dries up and the deer rubs the skin off by scraping
(15)   its antlers against trees. The antlers fall off several months later.

The size and shape of a deer's antlers depend on the animal's age and health. The first set grows when the deer is from one to two years old. On most deer, the first antlers are short and
(20)   straight. As deer get older, their antlers grow larger and form intricate branches.

1. How do deer primarily use their antlers? ___2-3___

2. In what way are reindeer and caribou different from other types of deer? _____

3. When do deer that live in temperate climates begin to grow their antlers? _____

4. According to the article, which of the following does the skin on deer's antlers most closely resemble? _____

5. Which of the following factors influences the size and shape of a deer's antlers? _____

6. At what age do deer get their first antlers? _____

7. What happens to a deer's antlers as the deer grow older? _____

Questions 8–13

The trumpet player Louis Armstrong, or Satchmo as he was usually called, was among the first jazz musicians to achieve international fame. He is known for the beautiful, clear tone of his trumpet playing and for his gruff, gravelly singing voice. He was one of the first musicians to sing in the scat (line) style, using rhythmic nonsense syllables instead of lyrics.

(5)   Armstrong was born into a poor family in New Orleans. He first learned to play the cornet at the age of 13, taking lessons while living in a children's home. As a teenager, he played in a number of local jazz bands in New Orleans' rollicking nightlife district, Storyville.

In 1922, Armstrong moved to Chicago to play in Joe "King" Oliver's band. Two years later, he joined Fletcher Henderson's band. Then, from 1925 to 1928, Armstrong made a series of records (10) with groups called the Hot Five, the Hot Seven, and the Savoy Ballroom Five. These records rank among the greatest recordings in the history of jazz. They include "Cornet Chop Suey," "Potato Head Blues," and "West End Blues."

Armstrong led a big band during the 1930's and 1940's, but in 1947 returned to playing with small jazz groups. He performed all over the world and made a number of hit records, such as "Hello, (15) Dolly" and "Mack the Knife." Armstrong also appeared in a number of movies, first in *New Orleans* in 1947, *High Society* in 1956, and *Hello, Dolly* in 1969.

8. What was Armstrong's nickname? _____

9. Which of the following phrases best describes Armstrong's singing voice? _____

10. Where did Armstrong first learn to play the cornet? _____

11. In what city was Joe "King" Oliver's band based? _____

12. During what period did Armstrong record some of jazz's greatest records? _____

13. What was the first movie Armstrong appeared in? _____

Questions 14–23

In 1862, during the Civil War, President Lincoln signed the Morrill Act. The measure was named for its sponsor, Congressman (later Senator) Justin S. Morrill of Vermont. Popularly called the Land Grant Act, it provided each state with 30,000 acres of public land for each senator and each (line) representative it had in Congress. It required that the land be sold, the proceeds invested, and the (5) income used to create and maintain colleges to teach agriculture and engineering.

Although not all states used the money as planned in the act, some thirty states did establish new institutions. Purdue University, the University of Illinois, Texas A & M, Michigan State, and the University of California all trace their roots to the Morrill Act. Eighteen states gave the money to existing state universities to finance new agricultural and engineering departments. A few gave their (10) money to private colleges. For example, Massachusetts used much of its funds to endow the Massachusetts Institute of Technology. One state changed its mind. Yale University was chosen to be funded in Connecticut, but farmers protested, and the legislature moved the assets to the University of Connecticut.

Most students chose to study engineering. Agriculture was not even considered a science until it (15) had been dignified by the work of research stations. These were established at land-grant institutions in 1887 by the Hatch Act. Gradually, universities broke away from the narrow functions Congress had assigned them and presented a full range of academic offerings, from anthropology to zoology.

Today there are some 69 land-grant institutions in all 50 states, the District of Columbia, and Puerto Rico. About one in five college students in the United States attends land-grant schools.

14. When was the Morrill Act signed? _____

15. Who sponsored the Morrill Act? _____

16. What position did the sponsor of the Morrill Act have at the time it was passed? _____

17. How much land did each state receive under the Morrill Act? _____

18. How many states used the money in the way it was intended by Congress? _____

19. Which of these states used its money to fund a private university? _____

20. Who objected to the way the Connecticut legislature initially decided to spend its funds? _____

21. What was one effect of the Hatch Act of 1887? _____

22. How many land-grant institutions are in operation at present? _____

23. What percent of college students in the United States currently attend land-grant institutions? _____

Exercise 45.2

Focus: Answering factual, negative, and scanning questions about reading passages.

Directions: Read the following passages and the questions about them. Decide which of the choices—(A), (B), (C), or (D)—best answers the question, and mark the answer. The first one is done as an example.

Questions 1–9

Mesa Verde is the center of the prehistoric Anasazi culture. It is located in the high plateau lands near Four Corners, where Colorado, Utah, New Mexico, and Arizona come together. This high ground is majestic but not forbidding. The climate is dry, but tiny streams trickle at the bottom of
(line) deeply cut canyons, where seeps and springs provided water for the Anasazi to irrigate their crops.
(5) Rich red soil provided fertile ground for their crops of corn, beans, squash, tobacco, and cotton. The Anasazi domesticated the wild turkey and hunted deer, rabbits, and mountain sheep.

For a thousand years the Anasazi lived around Mesa Verde. Although the Anasazi are not related to the Navajos, no one knows what these Indians called themselves, and so they are commonly referred to by their Navajo name, Anasazi, which means "ancient ones" in the Navajo language.
(10) Around 550 A.D., early Anasazi—then a nomadic people archaeologists call the Basketmakers— began constructing permanent homes on mesa tops. In the next 300 years, the Anasazi made rapid technological advancements, including the refinement of not only basket-making but also pottery-making and weaving. This phase of development is referred to as the Early Pueblo Culture.

By the Great Pueblo Period (1100–1300 A.D.), the Anasazi population swelled to over 5,000 and
(15) the architecturally ambitious cliff dwellings came into being. The Anasazi moved from the mesa tops onto ledges on the steep canyon walls, creating two- and three-story dwellings. They used sandstone blocks and mud mortar. There were no doors on the first floor and people used ladders to reach the first roof. All the villages had underground chambers called *kivas*. Men held tribal councils there and also used them for secret religious ceremonies and clan meetings. Winding paths, ladders, and steps
(20) cut into the stone led from the valleys below to the ledges on which the villages stood. The largest settlement contained 217 rooms. One might surmise that these dwellings were built for protection, but the Anasazi had no known enemies and there is no sign of conflict.

But a bigger mystery is why the Anasazi occupied these structures such a short time. By 1300, Mesa Verde was deserted. It is conjectured that the Anasazi abandoned their settlements because of
(25) drought, overpopulation, crop failure, or some combination of these. They probably moved southward and were incorporated into the pueblo villages that the Spanish explorers encountered two hundred years later. Their descendants still live in the Southwest.

1. The passage does NOT mention that the Anasazi hunted
   _____ (A) sheep
   ___✔___ (B) turkeys
   _____ (C) deer
   _____ (D) rabbits

2. The name that the Anasazi used for themselves
   _____ (A) means "basketmakers" in the Navajo language
   _____ (B) is unknown today
   _____ (C) was given to them by archaeologists
   _____ (D) means "ancient ones" in the Anasazi language

3. How long did the Early Pueblo Culture last?
   _____ (A) 200 years
   _____ (B) 300 years
   _____ (C) 550 years
   _____ (D) 1000 years

4. Where did the Anasazi move during the Great Pueblo Period?
   _____ (A) To settlements on ledges of canyon walls
   _____ (B) To pueblos in the south
   _____ (C) Onto the tops of the mesas
   _____ (D) Onto the floors of the canyons

5. According to the passage, the Anasazi buildings were made primarily of
   _____ (A) dried mud
   _____ (B) blocks of wood
   _____ (C) sandstone
   _____ (D) the skins of animals

6. According to the passage, the Anasazi entered their buildings on the ledges
   _____ (A) by means of ladders
   _____ (B) from underground chambers
   _____ (C) by means of stone stairways
   _____ (D) through doors on the first floor

7. According to the passage, *kivas* were used for all the following purposes EXCEPT
   _____ (A) clan meetings
   _____ (B) food preparation
   _____ (C) religious ceremonies
   _____ (D) tribal councils

8. According to the passage, the LEAST likely reason that the Anasazi abandoned Mesa Verde was
   _____ (A) drought
   _____ (B) overpopulation
   _____ (C) war
   _____ (D) crop failure

9. Where in the passage does the author mention specific accomplishments of the Basketmakers?
   _____ (A) Lines 7–9
   _____ (B) Lines 11–13
   _____ (C) Lines 14–15
   _____ (D) Lines 23–25

Questions 10–15

(line)

(5)

(10)

Dulcimers are musical instruments that basically consist of wooden boxes with strings stretched over them. In one form or another, they have been around since ancient times, probably originating with the Persian santir. Today there are two varieties: the hammered dulcimer and the Appalachian, or mountain dulcimer. The former is shaped like a trapezoid, has two or more strings, and is played with wooden mallets. It is the same instrument played in a number of Old World countries. The Appalachian dulcimer is classified by musicologists as a box zither. It is a descendant of the Pennsylvania Dutch scheitholt and the French epinette. Appalachian dulcimers are painstakingly fashioned by artisans in the mountains of West Virginia, Kentucky, Tennessee, and Virginia. These instruments have three or four strings and are plucked with quills or the fingers. They are shaped like teardrops or hourglasses. Heart-shaped holes in the sounding board are traditional. Most performers play the instruments while seated with the instruments in their laps, but others wear them around their necks like guitars or place them on tables in front of them. Originally used to play dance music, Appalachian dulcimers were popularized by performers such as John Jacob Niles and Jean Ritchie during the folk music revival of the 1960's.

10. According to the passage, a hammered dulcimer is made in the shape of
_____ (A) an hourglass
_____ (B) a heart
_____ (C) a trapezoid
_____ (D) a teardrop

11. According to the passage, which of the following is NOT an ancestor of the Appalachian dulcimer?
_____ (A) The box zither
_____ (B) The santir
_____ (C) The scheitholt
_____ (D) The epinette

12. According to the passage, how many strings does the Appalachian dulcimer have?
_____ (A) One or two
_____ (B) Three or four
_____ (C) Four or five
_____ (D) Six or more

13. According to the author, most performers play the Appalachian dulcimer
_____ (A) while sitting down
_____ (B) with the instrument strapped around their neck
_____ (C) while standing at a table
_____ (D) with wooden hammers

14. According to the author, what are John Jacob Niles and Jean Ritchie known for?
_____ (A) Playing dance music on Appalachian dulcimers
_____ (B) Designing Appalachian dulcimers
_____ (C) Helping to bring Appalachian dulcimers to the public's attention
_____ (D) Beginning the folk music revival of the 1960's

15. Where in the passage does the author describe the hammered dulcimer?
_____ (A) Lines 1–2
_____ (B) Lines 4–5
_____ (C) Lines 9–10
_____ (D) Lines 13–14

Questions 16–20

Humanitarian Dorothea Dix was born in Hampden, Maine, in 1802. At the age of 19, she established a school for girls, the Dix Mansion School, in Boston, but had to close it in 1835 due to her poor health. She wrote and published the first of many books for children in 1824. In 1841, Dix
(line)   accepted an invitation to teach classes at a prison in East Cambridge, Massachusetts. She was deeply
(5)   disturbed by the sight of mentally ill persons thrown in the jail and treated like criminals. For the next 18 months, she toured Massachusetts institutions where other mental patients were confined, and reported the shocking conditions she found to the state legislature. When improvements followed in Massachusetts, she turned her attention to the neighboring states and then to the West and South.
(10)   Dix's work was interrupted by the Civil War; she served as superintendent of women hospital nurses for the federal government.

Dix saw special hospitals for the mentally ill built in some 15 states. Although her plan to obtain public land for her cause failed, she aroused concern for the problem of mental illness all over the United States as well as in Canada and Europe.
(15)   Dix's success was due to her independent and thorough research, her gentle but persistent manner, and her ability to secure the help of powerful and wealthy supporters.

16. In what year was the Dix Mansion School closed?
    _____ (A) 1802
    _____ (B) 1824
    _____ (C) 1835
    _____ (D) 1841

17. Why did Dorothea Dix first go to a prison?
    _____ (A) She taught classes there.
    _____ (B) She was sent there by the state legislature.
    _____ (C) She was convicted of a crime.
    _____ (D) She was doing research for a book.

18. Where was Dorothea Dix first able to bring about reforms in the treatment of the mentally ill?
    _____ (A) Canada
    _____ (B) Massachusetts
    _____ (C) The West and South
    _____ (D) Europe

19. Dorothea Dix was NOT successful in her attempt to
    _____ (A) become superintendent of nurses
    _____ (B) publish books for children
    _____ (C) arouse concern for the mentally ill
    _____ (D) obtain public lands

20. At what point of the passage does the author discuss specific reasons for Dix's success?
    _____ (A) Lines 1-3
    _____ (B) Lines 4-5
    _____ (C) Lines 10-11
    _____ (D) Lines 15-16

Questions 21–26

(line)

(5)

(10)

(15)

A quilt is a bed cover made of squares of material pieced together. Each square consists of two layers filled with a layer of wool or cotton cloth, feathers, or down. Often, the squares are decorated with fancy stitches and designs. According to legend, the earliest pieced quilt was stitched in 1704 by Sarah Sedgewick Everett, wife of the governor of the Massachusetts colony. By 1774 George Washington was buying quilts in Belvoir, Virginia, to take back to Martha in Mount Vernon. As the frontier moved westward, quilting went along. In addition to sleeping under them, homesteaders kept out drafts by hanging quilts over doors and windows. And if the money ran out, quilts were used to pay debts.

For isolated pioneer women, quilts were a source of comfort. Mary Wilman, whose family moved to Texas from Missouri in 1890, recalled the first time she and her mother had to spend a week alone and a dust storm came up. "The wind blew for three days and the dust was so thick that you couldn't see the barn. My mother quilted all day, and she taught me how to quilt. If it hadn't been for quilting, I think we would have gone crazy."

Quilting provided an important social function for the women of the frontier as well. At quilting bees, women met to work on quilts and to share the latest news.

Today, however, the homely quilt has become a costly cultural phenomenon. The International Quilt Festival in Houston, Texas, the "world's fair of quilting," attracted only 2,500 people and displayed only 200 quilts when it began a dozen years ago. This year there were over 20,000 visitors and 5,000 quilts, some of which sold for as much as $50,000.

21. According to legend, who made the first American quilt?
_____ (A) Sarah Sedgewick Everett
_____ (B) the governor of the colony of Massachusetts
_____ (C) Martha Washington
_____ (D) Mary Wilman

22. Which of the following is NOT mentioned in the passage as one of the benefits of quilts for pioneers?
_____ (A) They could be used to pay debts.
_____ (B) They could be used to help insulate houses.
_____ (C) They could provide psychological comfort.
_____ (D) They could be worn as warm clothing.

23. According to the passage, what is a "quilting bee?"
_____ (A) A type of insect
_____ (B) A gathering where women socialized and made quilts
_____ (C) A type of quilt
_____ (D) A place where people buy and sell quilts

24. In what state is the International Quilt Festival held?
_____ (A) Massachusetts
_____ (B) Texas
_____ (C) Virginia
_____ (D) Missouri

25. How many quilts were displayed at the first International Quilt Festival?
_____ (A) 200
_____ (B) 2,500
_____ (C) 5,000
_____ (D) 20,000

26. Where in the passage does the author first begin to discuss the way in which the public's perception of quilts has changed in modern times?

_____ (A) Lines 6–8

_____ (B) Line 9

_____ (C) Lines 14–15

_____ (D) Line 16

Questions 27–32

(line)

(5)

(10)

Ambient divers, unlike divers who go underwater in submersible vehicles or pressure-resistant suits, are exposed to the pressure and temperature of the surrounding (*ambient*) water. Of all types of diving, the oldest and simplest is free diving. Free divers may use no equipment at all, but most use a face mask, foot fins, and a snorkel. Under the surface, free divers must hold their breath. Most free divers can descend only 30 to 40 feet, but some skilled divers can go as deep as 100 feet.

Scuba diving provides greater range than free diving. The word *scuba* stands for *self-contained underwater breathing apparatus*. Scuba divers wear metal tanks with compressed air or other breathing gases. When using open-circuit equipment, a scuba diver simply breathes air from the tank through a hose and releases the exhaled air into the water. A closed-circuit breathing device, also called a rebreather, filters out carbon dioxide and other harmful gases and automatically adds oxygen. This enables the diver to breathe the same air over and over.

In surface-supplied diving, divers wear helmets and waterproof canvas suits. Today, sophisticated plastic helmets have replaced the heavy copper helmets used in the past. These divers get their air from a hose connected to compressors on a boat. Surface-supplied divers can go deeper than any other type of ambient diver.

27. Ambient divers are ones who

_____ (A) can descend to extreme depths

_____ (B) use submersible vehicles

_____ (C) use no equipment

_____ (D) are exposed to the surrounding water

28. According to the passage, a free diver may use any of the following EXCEPT

_____ (A) a rebreather

_____ (B) a snorkel

_____ (C) foot fins

_____ (D) a mask

29. According to the passage, the maximum depth for free divers is around

_____ (A) 40 feet

_____ (B) 100 feet

_____ (C) 200 feet

_____ (D) 1,000 feet

30. When using closed-circuit devices, divers

_____ (A) exhale air into the water

_____ (B) hold their breath

_____ (C) breathe the same air over and over

_____ (D) receive air from the surface

31. According to the passage, surface-supplied divers today use helmets made from

_____ (A) glass

_____ (B) copper

_____ (C) plastic

_____ (D) canvas

32. Where in the passage does the author mention which type of diver can make the deepest descents?

    _____ (A) Lines 2–3
    _____ (B) Lines 6–8
    _____ (C) Lines 9–10
    _____ (D) Lines 14–15

LESSON 46

INFERENCE QUESTIONS AND PURPOSE QUESTIONS

A) Inference Questions

As in the Listening Comprehension section, there are questions in the Reading Comprehension section that require you to make **inferences.** The answers to these questions are not directly provided in the passage—you must "read between the lines." In other words, you must make conclusions based indirectly on information in the passage. Many test-takers find these questions the most difficult type of Reading question.

Inference questions may be phrased in a number of ways. Many of these questions contain some form of the words *infer* or *imply.*

- Which of the following can be inferred from the passage?
- It can be inferred from the passage that . . .
- The author implies that . . .
- Which of the following does the passage imply?
- Which of the following would be the most reasonable guess about _____?
- The author suggests that . . .
- It is probable that . . .

There will probably be from five to eight of these questions per Reading section.

▼   **Sample Item**

A star very similar to the Sun is one of the nearest stars to Earth. That star is Alpha Centauri, just 4.3 light-years away. Other than our own Sun, the nearest star to the Earth is a tiny red star, not visible without a telescope, called Proxima Centauri.

It can be inferred from this passage that
(A) Proxima Centauri is similar to the Earth's Sun.
(B) Proxima Centauri is the closest star to the Earth.
(C) Alpha Centauri is invisible from the Earth.
(D) Proxima Centauri is less than 4.3 light-years from the Earth.

Choice (A) is not a valid inference; Alpha Centauri is similar to the Sun, but Proxima Centauri is "a tiny red star." Choice (B) also cannot be inferred; the closest star to the Earth is our own Sun. Nor can (C) be inferred; Proxima Centauri is invisible, but there is no information as to whether Alpha Centauri is. Since Alpha Centauri is 4.3 light-years away, it can be inferred that Alpha Centauri, the closest star, is less than that.   ▲

B) Purpose Questions

These questions ask why the author of a passage mentions some piece of information, includes a quotation from a person or a study, or uses some particular word or phrase.

Sample Questions

- Why does the author mention _____?
- The author refers to _____ to indicate that . . .
- The author quotes _____ in order to show . . .
- The phrase _____ in line _____ is mentioned to illustrate the effect of . . .

Sample Answer Choices

- To strengthen the argument that _____
- To provide an example of _____
- To challenge the idea that _____
- To contradict _____
- To support the proposal to _____

There are usually from one to four purpose questions per Reading section.

Exercise 46.1

Focus: Identifying valid inferences based on sentences.

Directions: Read each sentence; then mark the one answer choice—(A), (B), or (C)—that is a valid inference based on that sentence. The first one is done as an example.

1. Cities founded around the turn of the eighteenth century, such as Williamsburg, Annapolis, and especially Philadelphia, were laid out on a regular grid with public squares, while cities laid out in the mid-seventeenth century, such as Boston, remain chaotic in their street plans to this day.
   - _____ (A) Philadelphia is today laid out more regularly than either Williamsburg or Annapolis.
   - __✔__ (B) Boston was not originally laid out according to a logical plan.
   - _____ (C) Philadelphia, Williamsburg, and Annapolis were founded before Boston.

2. When apple growers talk about new varieties of apples, they don't mean something developed last month, last year, or even in the last decade.
   - _____ (A) Apple growers haven't developed any new varieties in recent decades.
   - _____ (B) Some varieties of apples can be developed in a short time, but others take a long time.
   - _____ (C) New varieties of apples take many years to develop.

3. Blood cholesterol used to be thought of as a problem only for adults.
   - _____ (A) Blood cholesterol is no longer a problem for adults.
   - _____ (B) Only children have a problem with blood cholesterol.
   - _____ (C) Blood cholesterol affects both adults and children.

4. A metal-worker of 3,000 years ago would recognize virtually every step of the lost-wax process used to cast titanium for jet engines.
   - _____ (A) Titanium has been forged for thousands of years.
   - _____ (B) The lost-wax method of casting is very old.
   - _____ (C) Metal working has changed very little in 3,000 years.

5. There is more quartz in the world than any one kind of feldspar, but the feldspars as a group are five times more common than quartz.
   - _____ (A) One type of quartz is five times more plentiful than feldspar.
   - _____ (B) Quartz is less common than the feldspars.
   - _____ (C) The most common type of feldspar is as plentiful as quartz.

6. Compared with the rest of its brain, the visual area of a turtle's brain is comparatively small since turtles, like all other reptiles, depend on senses other than sight.
_____ (A) No reptile uses sight as its primary sense.
_____ (B) Animals that depend on sight all have larger visual areas in their brain than turtles do.
_____ (C) The visual areas of other reptile brains are comparatively smaller than those of turtles.

7. Contrary to popular belief, there is no validity to the stories one hears of initials carved in a tree by a young boy becoming elevated high above his head when he visits the tree as an old man.
_____ (A) Trees don't grow the way many people think they do.
_____ (B) If a child carves initials in a tree, it won't grow.
_____ (C) Over time, initials that are carved into a tree will be elevated.

8. Illegible handwriting does not indicate weakness of character, as even a quick glance at the penmanship of George Washington, Franklin D. Roosevelt, or John Kennedy reveals.
_____ (A) Washington, Roosevelt, and Kennedy all had handwriting that was difficult to read.
_____ (B) A person's handwriting reveals a lot about that person.
_____ (C) The author believes that Washington, Roosevelt, and Kennedy all had weak characters.

9. William Faulkner set many of his novels in and around an imaginary town, Jefferson, Mississippi, which he closely patterned after his hometown of Oxford, Mississippi.
_____ (A) William Faulkner wrote many of his novels while living in Jefferson, Mississippi.
_____ (B) The town of Oxford, Mississippi, exists only in Faulkner's novels.
_____ (C) Faulkner actually wrote about his hometown but did not use its real name.

10. Most fish take on, to a certain degree, the coloration of their natural surroundings, so it is not surprising that the fish inhabiting warm, shallow waters around tropical reefs are colored all the brilliant tints of the rainbow.
_____ (A) Tropical fish are unlike other fish because they take on the coloration of their environment.
_____ (B) Tropical fish are brightly colored because they inhabit warm waters.
_____ (C) Tropical reefs are brightly colored environments.

11. Although sheepherding is an older and more beloved occupation, shepherds never caught the attention of American filmmakers the way cowboys did.
_____ (A) There have been more American films about cowboys than about shepherds.
_____ (B) Films about shepherds were popular before films about cowboys.
_____ (C) Cowboys are generally younger than shepherds.

12. The Okefenokee Swamp is a fascinating realm that both confirms and contradicts popular notions of a swamp, because along with huge cypresses, dangerous quagmires, and dim waterways, the Okefenokee has sandy pine islands, sunlit prairies, and clear lakes.
_____ (A) People generally feel that swamps are fascinating places.
_____ (B) The Okefenokee has features that most people do not associate with swamps.
_____ (C) Most swamps do not have huge cypresses, dangerous quagmires, and dim waterways.

13. As an architect, Thomas Jefferson preferred the Roman style, as seen in the buildings of the University of Virginia, to the English style favored by Charles Bullfinch.
_____ (A) The architecture of the University of Virginia was influenced by the Roman style.
_____ (B) Bullfinch was an English architect.
_____ (C) Jefferson preferred to build in the English style of architecture.

14. In all cultures, gestures are used as a form of communication, but the same gestures may have very different meanings in different cultures.
_____ (A) No two cultures use the same gestures.
_____ (B) One gesture will never have the same meaning in two cultures.
_____ (C) A person from one culture may misunderstand the gestures used by a person from another culture.

15. Even spiders that do not build webs from silk use it for a variety of purposes, such as constructing egg sacs and nursery tents.

_____ (A) All spiders build webs.

_____ (B) Spiders that build webs don't build egg sacs or nursery tents.

_____ (C) Silk is used by all spiders.

Exercise 46.2

Focus: Recognizing valid inferences based on longer passages.

Directions: Read the passages. If the statements following the passages are valid inferences based on those passages, mark the items _I._ If the statements cannot be inferred from the passage, mark those items _X._ The first one is done as an example.

Questions 1–7

(line)

(5)

(10)

The term "neon light" was originally applied to a particular type of vapor lamp using the inert, colorless gas neon. A long tube was filled with neon, which then became luminous at low pressure when an electric current was passed through it. The lamp then emitted the characteristic reddish-orange light of neon. Today, the term "neon light" is given to lamps of this general type which may be filled with a variety of gases, depending on the color that is desired. Argon, for example, is used to produce blue light. Colors can also be altered by changing the color of the glass tube. The tubes must be quite long in all these lamps to produce light efficiently. As a result, high voltages are required. Neon tube lamps are not practical for indoor illumination, but they have found widespread outdoor use in glowing, colorful advertising signs.

__X__ 1. The inert gas neon is reddish-orange in color.

_____ 2. The meaning of the term "neon light" has changed over time.

_____ 3. Today's "neon lights" never actually contain neon.

_____ 4. All types of "neon lights" work on the same general principles.

_____ 5. When stimulated by electricity, different types of gas may produce different colors.

_____ 6. Modern "neon lights" are more efficient than those used in the past.

_____ 7. The primary market for neon lights is businesses rather than private households.

Questions 8–15

Natural flavorings and fragrances are often costly and limited in supply. For example, the vital ingredient in a rose fragrance is extracted from natural rose oil at a cost of thousands of
(line)   dollars a pound; an identical synthetic substance can be made for
(5)   1% of this cost. Since the early twentieth century, success in reproducing these substances has created a new industry that today produces hundreds of artificial flavors and fragrances.

Some natural fragrances are easily synthesized; these include vanillin, the aromatic ingredient in vanilla, and benzaldehyde,
(10)   the aromatic ingredient in wild cherries. Other fragrances, however, have dozens, even hundreds of components. Only recently has it been possible to separate and identify these ingredients by the use of gas chromatography and spectroscopy. Once the chemical identity is known, it is often possible to synthesize
(15)   them. Nevertheless, some complex substances, such as the aroma of fresh coffee, have still not been duplicated satisfactorily.

Many of the chemical compounds making up these synthetics are identical to those found in nature, and are as harmless or harmful as the natural substances. New products must be tested
(20)   for safety, and when used in food, must be approved by the U.S. Food and Drug Administration.

The availability of synthetic flavors and fragrances has made possible a large variety of products, from inexpensive beverages to perfumed soap to used cars with applied "new car odor."

_____ 8. Natural rose fragrance is 100 times more expensive to produce than artificial rose fragrance.

_____ 9. Vanillin is easier to synthesize than benzaldehyde.

_____ 10. In general, the more components there are in a fragrance, the harder it is to synthesize.

_____ 11. Once a substance has been chemically analyzed, it can always be easily synthesized.

_____ 12. Only recently has it been possible to satisfactorily synthesize the aroma of fresh coffee.

_____ 13. Not all synthetic flavors are harmless.

_____ 14. Synthesized substances must be tested for safety only if they are used in food.

_____ 15. Synthetic fragrances can be used to make a used car smell like a new one.

Questions 16–20

(line)

(5)

(10)

A legend is a popular type of folk tale. In some ways, legends resemble myths, another type of folk tale. But myths describe events from antiquity and usually deal with religious subjects, such as the birth of a god. Legends tell of recognizable people, places, and events and often take place in comparatively recent times. Some legends are based on real persons or events, but many are entirely fictional. The legends of the superhuman accomplishments of Paul Bunyan and Pecos Bill are imaginary, while the legends about Washington and Lincoln are mostly exaggerations of real qualities those two presidents had.

All societies have legends. Most legends began as stories about the heroes of a particular region, occupation, or ethnic group. For example, John Henry was a legendary hero of black Americans, and Casey Jones of railroad workers. Over time, however, these figures have become national heroes.

_____ 16. Both legends and myths can be classified as folk tales.

_____ 17. Myths generally take place in comparatively recent times.

_____ 18. The stories of Paul Bunyan and Pecos Bill are not true, but they are based on actual people.

_____ 19. Legends about Washington and Lincoln are not entirely fictional.

_____ 20. John Henry and Casey Jones are today well-known only by small groups of people.

Exercise 46.3

Focus: Answering inference and purpose questions.

Directions: Read the following passages and the questions about them. Decide which of the choices—(A), (B), (C), or (D)—best answers the question, and mark the answer. The first one is done as an example.

Questions 1–4

(line)

(5)

(10)

Pigeons have been taught to recognize human facial expressions, upsetting long-held beliefs that only humans had evolved the sophisticated nervous systems to perform such a feat. In recent experiments at the University of Iowa, eight trained pigeons were shown photographs of people displaying emotions of happiness, anger, surprise, and disgust. The birds learned to distinguish between these expressions. Not only that, but they were also able to correctly identify the same expressions on photographs of unfamiliar faces. Their achievement does not suggest, of course, that the pigeons had any idea what the human expressions meant.

Some psychologists have theorized that because of the importance of facial expression to human communication, humans developed special nervous systems capable of recognizing subtle expressions. The pigeons cast doubt on that idea, however.

(15)   In fact, the ability to recognize facial expressions of emotion
is not necessarily innate even in human babies, but may have to
be learned in much the same way pigeons learn. In experiments
conducted several years ago at the University of Iowa, it was
found that pigeons organize images of things into the same

(20)   logical categories that humans do.

None of this work would come as any surprise to Charles Darwin,
who long ago wrote about the continuity of mental development
from animals to humans.

1. From the passage, which of the following can be inferred about pigeons?
_____ (A) They can show the same emotions humans can.
_____ (B) They can understand human emotions.
_____ (C) They can only identify the expressions of people they are familiar with.
__✔__ (D) They have more sophisticated nervous systems than was once thought.

2. The passage implies that, at birth, human babies
_____ (A) have nervous systems capable of recognizing subtle expressions
_____ (B) can learn from pigeons
_____ (C) are not able to recognize familiar faces
_____ (D) may not be able to identify basic emotions through facial expressions

3. Why does the author mention the experiments conducted several years ago at the University of Iowa?
_____ (A) They proved that pigeons were not the only kind of animal with the ability to recognize facial expressions.
_____ (B) They were contradicted by more recent experiments.
_____ (C) They proved that the ability to recognize human expressions was not innate in human babies.
_____ (D) They showed the similarities between the mental organization of pigeons and that of humans.

4. If Charles Darwin could have seen the results of this experiment, his most probable response would have been one of
_____ (A) rejection
_____ (B) surprise
_____ (C) agreement
_____ (D) amusement

Questions 5–7

The spectacular eruptions of Old Faithful geyser in Yellowstone
National Park do not occur like clockwork. Before the earthquake
of 1959, eruptions came every 60 to 65 minutes; today they are as

(line)   little as 30 minutes or as much as 90 minutes apart. The geyser
(5)   usually gives a warning: a short burst of steam. Then a graceful
column rises up to 150 feet in the air. The water unfurls in the
sunlight with the colors of the rainbow playing across it.

This eruption is only the visible part of the spectacle. The
geyser is linked by an intricate plumbing network to some

(10)   extremely hot rocks. As water seeps into the underground system,
it is heated at the bottom like water in a tea kettle. But while
water in a kettle rises because of convection, the narrow tubes
of the geyser system prevent free circulation of the water. Thus,

(15) the water in the upper tubes is far cooler than the water
at the bottom. The weight of the water puts pressure on the
column, and this raises the boiling point of the water near the
bottom. Finally, the water in the upper part of the column warms
and expands, some of it welling out of the mouth of the geyser.
This decreases the pressure on the superheated water, which
(20) abruptly turns to steam. This in turn forces all the water and
vapor out of the geyser.

5. It can be inferred from the passage that the earthquake of 1959 made Old Faithful geyser erupt
_____ (A) more frequently
_____ (B) less regularly
_____ (C) more suddenly
_____ (D) less spectacularly

6. Why does the author mention a rainbow in line 7?
_____ (A) The column of water forms an arc in the shape of a rainbow.
_____ (B) In the sunlight, the column of water may produce the colors of the rainbow.
_____ (C) Rainbows can be seen quite frequently in Yellowstone National Park.
_____ (D) The rainbow, like the geyser, is an example of the beauty of nature.

7. The passage implies that Old Faithful would probably not erupt at all if
_____ (A) the tubes of the geyser system were much wider
_____ (B) the climate suddenly changed
_____ (C) there had not been an earthquake in 1959
_____ (D) the underground tubes were much longer

Questions 8–12

In 1881, a new type of weed began spreading across the northern
Great Plains. Unlike other weeds, the tumbleweed did not spend
its life rooted to the soil; instead it tumbled and rolled across
(line) fields in the wind. The weed had sharp, spiny leaves that could
(5) lacerate the flesh of ranchers and horses alike. It exploited the
vast area of the plains, thriving in regions too barren to
support other plants. With its ability to generate and
disseminate numerous seeds quickly, it soon became the scourge of
the prairies.
(10) To present-day Americans, the tumbleweed symbolizes the Old West.
They read the Zane Grey novels in which tumbleweeds drift across stark
western landscapes and see classic western movies in which tumbleweeds
share scenes with cowboys and covered wagons, and they assume that
these weeds were a permanent feature of the western plains. Yet just over
(15) a century ago, the tumbleweed was a newcomer. The first sign of the
invasion occurred in North and South Dakota in the late 1870's.
Farmers had noticed the sudden appearance of the new, unusual
weed. One group of immigrants, however, did not find the weed at
all unfamiliar. The tumbleweed, it turns out, was a native of
(20) southern Russia, where it was known as Tartar thistle. It was
imported to the United States by unknown means.

(25)

Frontier settlers gave the plants various names: saltwort, Russian cactus, and wind witch. But botanists at the Department of Agriculture preferred the designation *Russian thistle* as the plant's common name. However, these botanists had a much harder time agreeing on the plant's scientific name. Generally, botanists compare a plant to published accounts of similar plants, or to samples kept as specimens. Unfortunately, no book described the weed, and no samples existed in herbaria in the United States.

8. Which of the following can be inferred about tumbleweeds?
_____ (A) They have strong, deep roots.
_____ (B) They require a lot of care.
_____ (C) They reproduce efficiently.
_____ (D) They provided food for ranchers and animals.

9. The passage suggests that most present-day Americans
_____ (A) consider the tumbleweed beneficial
_____ (B) don't know when tumbleweeds came to North America
_____ (C) have never heard of tumbleweeds
_____ (D) believe tumbleweeds are newcomers to the United States

10. The author mentions the novels of Zane Grey and classic western movies (lines 11–12) because they
_____ (A) tell the story of the invasion of tumbleweeds
_____ (B) are sources of popular information about tumbleweeds
_____ (C) present unbelievable descriptions of tumbleweeds
_____ (D) were written long before tumbleweeds were present in the United States

11. It is probable that the "group of immigrants" mentioned in line 18
_____ (A) was from southern Russia
_____ (B) had lived in North and South Dakota for many years
_____ (C) imported tumbleweeds into the United States
_____ (D) wrote a number of accounts about tumbleweeds

12. From the passage it can be inferred that the botanists at the Department of Agriculture
_____ (A) could not find any tumbleweeds on the plains
_____ (B) gave the names saltwort, Russian cactus, and wind witch to the tumbleweed
_____ (C) could not decide on a common designation for the tumbleweed
_____ (D) found it difficult to classify the plant scientifically

Questions 13–17

(line)

(5)

(10)

For most modern airports, the major design problem is scale— how to allow adequate space on the ground for maneuvering wide-body jets while permitting convenient and rapid movement of passengers departing, arriving, or transferring from one flight to another.

Most designs for airport terminals take one of four approaches. In the linear plan, the building may be straight or curved. The passengers board aircraft parked next to the terminal. This plan works well for small airports that need to provide boarding areas for only a few aircraft at a time.

In the pier plan, narrow corridors or piers extend from a central building. This plan allows many aircraft to park next to the building. However, it creates long walking distances for passengers.

(15)   In the satellite plan, passengers board aircraft from small terminals that are separated from the main terminals. Passengers reach the satellites by way of shuttle trains or underground passageways that have shuttle trains or moving sidewalks.

         The transporter plan employs some system of transport to move

(20)   passengers from the terminal building to the aircraft. If buses are used, the passengers must climb a flight of stairs to board the aircraft. If mobile lounges are used, they can link up directly with the aircraft and protect passengers from the weather.

13. It can be inferred that scale would not pose a major design problem at airports if
   _____ (A) airports were larger
   _____ (B) aircraft did not need so much space to maneuver on the ground
   _____ (C) other forms of transportation were more efficient
   _____ (D) airplanes could fly faster

14. The linear plan would probably be best at
   _____ (A) a busy airport
   _____ (B) an airport used by many small aircraft
   _____ (C) an airport with only a few arrivals or departures
   _____ (D) an airport that serves a large city

15. The passage implies that the term "satellite plan" is used because
   _____ (A) satellites are launched and tracked from these sites
   _____ (B) small terminals encircle the main terminal like satellites around a planet
   _____ (C) the plan makes use of the most modern, high-technology equipment
   _____ (D) airports that make use of this plan utilize data from weather satellites

16. The passage suggests that shuttle trains transfer passengers to satellite terminals from
   _____ (A) the main terminal
   _____ (B) airplanes
   _____ (C) downtown
   _____ (D) other satellite terminals

17. It can be inferred that mobile lounges would be more desirable than buses when
   _____ (A) passengers are in a hurry
   _____ (B) flights have been delayed
   _____ (C) the weather is bad
   _____ (D) passengers need to save money

Questions 18–20

(line)

(5)

(10)

(15)

The sea has been rising relative to the land for at least 100 years, geologists say. During that same period, the Atlantic Coast has eroded an average of 2 to 3 feet per year, the Gulf Coast even faster. Many engineers maintain that seawalls and replenished beaches are necessary to protect the nation's shoreline. Too many people live or vacation in Miami Beach, Atlantic City, or Martha's Vineyard to allow their roads and buildings to simply fall into the sea.

The problem with seawalls is that they simply don't work. One study has shown that, in fact, seawalls accelerate the erosion of beaches.

Faced with the loss of their beaches, other communities have tried a simple but expensive solution: replace the lost sand. These replenishment programs, however, are costly and of dubious value. Another study has shown that only 10% of replenished beaches lasted more than 5 years.

18. It can be inferred from the passage that the author
_____ (A) opposes the use of both seawalls and beach replenishment
_____ (B) believes beach replenishment would be more effective than seawalls
_____ (C) opposes any actions to protect the shoreline
_____ (D) denies that beach erosion is a problem

19. Why does the author mention Miami Beach, Atlantic City, and Martha's Vinyard?
_____ (A) These are communities with seawalls.
_____ (B) These are communities that have implemented replenishment programs.
_____ (C) These are communities in danger of beach erosion.
_____ (D) These are communities which have lost roads and buildings to erosion.

20. The author quotes the two studies in the passage in order to
_____ (A) suggest that the sea is not rising as fast as was originally believed
_____ (B) strengthen the engineers' contention that seawalls and replenished beaches are necessary
_____ (C) propose two new solutions to beach erosion
_____ (D) support his own position

LESSON 47

VOCABULARY-IN-CONTEXT QUESTIONS

When ETS eliminated the first part of Section 3, which consisted of 30 discrete vocabulary items, it replaced them with an increased number of questions (from 12 to 18) about the vocabulary in the reading passages. Most test-takers find that, in general, it is easier to answer vocabulary questions based on the context of a passage that it is to answer questions about vocabulary in single, isolated sentences.

In vocabulary-in-context questions, you must determine which of four words or phrases can best substitute for a word or words in the passage.

Most of the questions ask about single words (usually nouns, verbs, adjectives, and adverbs). Some ask about two- or three-word phrases.

Sometimes two or more of the answer choices for these items might be "correct" definitions of the word that is asked about. In those cases, you must decide which is correct in the context of the passage.

There are a number of clues that can help you determine the meaning of an unknown word:

- **Synonyms**

    The first state to institute <u>compulsory</u> education was Massachusetts, which made it mandatory for students to attend school 12 weeks a year.

    The word *mandatory* is a synonym for the word *compulsory*.

- **Examples**

    Many gardeners use some kind of <u>mulch</u>, such as chopped leaves, peat moss, grass clippings, pine needles, or wood chips, in order to stop the growth of weeds and to hold in moisture.

    From the examples given, it is clear that *mulch* is plant matter.

- **Contrast**

    In the 1820's the Southern states supported improvements in the national transportation system, but the Northern states <u>balked</u>.

    Since the Southern states supported improvements, and since a word signaling contrast (*but*) is used, it is clear that the Northern states disagreed with this idea, and that the word *balked* must mean *objected* or *refused*.

- **General Context**

    In a desert, vegetation is so <u>scanty</u> as to be incapable of supporting any large human population.

    As is generally known, deserts contain little vegetation, so clearly the word *scanty* must mean *scarce* or *barely sufficient*.

When answering vocabulary-in-context questions, you must often depend on the general context of the sentence to help you choose the correct answer.

You should follow these steps to answer vocabulary-in-context items:

1. Look at the word being asked about and the four answer choices. If you are familiar with the word, guess which answer is correct. Do *not* mark your answer sheet yet.
2. Read the sentence in which the word appears. If you were familiar with the word and guessed at the answer, make sure that the word that you chose fits with the word as it is used in the sentence. If you were unfamiliar with the word, see if context clues in the sentence or in the sentences before or after help you guess the meaning.

3. If you are not sure which answer is correct, read the sentence with each of the four answer choices in place. Does one seem more logical, given the context of the sentence, than the other three? If not, do any seem illogical? (Those you can eliminate.)

4. If you're still not sure, make the best guess you can and go on.

▼ **Sample Items**

In Britain's North American colonies, university
trained physicians were at a premium. At the time of
the Revolution, there were probably only around 400 physicians
(line)   and some 3,000 practitioners who had on-the-job training as
(5)   barber-surgeons or physicians' apprentices. Whether
university trained or not, none had much knowledge of
the causes of disease, and the "cures" they often
recommended—bleeding, blistering, and the use of
violent purgatives—were at best ineffective and at
(10)   worst lethal.

1. The phrase "at a premium" in line 2 is closest in meaning to
   (A) well-paid
   (B) not very numerous
   (C) very experienced
   (D) not well-respected

The phrase "only around 400" indicates that there was a shortage of university-trained physicians.

2. Which of the following words could best be substituted for the word "lethal" in line 10?
   (A) Impractical
   (B) Brutal
   (C) Wonderful
   (D) Deadly

The phrase "at best ineffectual and at worst lethal" indicates that the correct answer must describe a situation much worse than ineffectual. Choices (A) and (C) don't create logical sentences when substituted for *lethal*. Choice (B), *brutal* (which means savage or violent), is more logical, but only choice (D) is synonymous with the word that is asked about. ▲

Exercise 47.1

Focus: Using context clues to answer vocabulary-in-context questions involving words with multiple definitions.

Directions: Read each item. Then mark the answer choice that could best be used in place of the underlined expression as it appears in the sentence.

1. The planet Mercury is visible to the <u>naked</u> eye but is not the easiest planet to spot.
   _____ (A) unclothed
   __✔__ (B) unaided
   _____ (C) unarmed

2. Every atlas has its own <u>legend</u>.
   _____ (A) mythical story
   _____ (B) famous person
   _____ (C) explanation of symbols

3. Above the snowline, any mountain hollow is permanently <u>occupied</u> with snow.
   _____ (A) filled
   _____ (B) busy

4. The glass factories of Toledo, Ohio, <u>boomed</u> after Michael Owens invented a process that turned out bottles by the thousands.
   _____ (A) exploded
   _____ (B) resounded
   _____ (C) prospered

5. Dr. René Dubos, a French physician who came to the United States in 1924, searched for substances that would <u>check</u> the growth of bacteria.
   _____ (A) restrict
   _____ (B) investigate

6. The root of the horseradish plant has a <u>biting</u> taste.
   _____ (A) chewing
   _____ (B) sharp
   _____ (C) sarcastic

7. The double-bass is shaped like a viola and has a deep, <u>rich</u> tone.
   _____ (A) valuable
   _____ (B) resonant
   _____ (C) abundant

8. A public library is a resource the entire community can <u>draw on</u>.
   _____ (A) illustrate
   _____ (B) approach
   _____ (C) use

9. A business <u>concern</u> with two or more owners is referred to as a partnership.
   _____ (A) firm
   _____ (B) worry

10. Table salt is <u>finer</u> than rock salt.
    _____ (A) made up of smaller particles
    _____ (B) of better quality
    _____ (C) freer of impurities

11. Shirley Jackson's sometimes <u>chilling</u>, sometimes hilarious stories were largely ignored by critics at the time they were published.
    _____ (A) freezing
    _____ (B) frightening

12. As a child, the sharpshooter Annie Oakley hunted <u>game</u> with such success that, by selling it, she was able to pay off the mortgage on her family's farm.
    _____ (A) animals
    _____ (B) athletic competition

13. All chimpanzees are extremely <u>curious</u> about their surroundings.
    _____ (A) strange
    _____ (B) inquisitive

14. Furniture design and manufacture were originally the work of individuals, but by the eighteenth century, many furniture makers had teams of artisans to help them <u>carry out</u> their plans.

_____ (A) transport

_____ (B) obey

_____ (C) implement

15. Samuel Latham Mitchell helped found Rutgers Medical College in New Jersey in 1826, and he produced several important <u>works</u> in chemistry and geology.

_____ (A) books

_____ (B) accomplishments

_____ (C) factories

Exercise 47.2

Focus: Answering vocabulary-in-context questions about words or phrases in reading passages.

Directions: Answer the questions about the vocabulary in the passages, and mark the words or phrases that are closest in meaning to the words or phrases that are asked about. The first one is done as an example.

Questions 1–11

(line)

(5)

(10)

(15)

(20)

      The Civil War created feverish manufacturing activity to supply critical material, especially in the North. When the fighting stopped, the stage was set for dramatic economic growth. Wartime taxes on production vanished, and the few taxes that remained leaned heavily on real estate, not on business. The population flow from farm to city increased, and the labor force it provided was buttressed by millions of newly arrived immigrants willing to work for low wages in the mills of the North and on the railroad crews of the Midwest and West.

      Government was nothing if not accommodating. It established tariff barriers, provided loans and grants to build a transcontinental railroad, and assumed a studied posture of nonintervention in private enterprise. The social Darwinism of British philosopher Herbert Spencer and American economist William Graham Summer prevailed. The theory was that business, if left to its own devices, would eliminate the weak and nurture the strong. But as business expanded, rivalry heated up. In the 1880's, five railroads operating between New York and Chicago were vying for traffic, and two more were under construction. As a result of the battle, the fare between the cities decreased to $1. The petroleum industry suffered from similar savage competition, and in the 1870's, many oil industries failed.

1. The word "feverish" in line 1 is closest in meaning to

__✔__ (A) extremely rapid

_____ (B) sickly and slow

_____ (C) very dangerous

_____ (D) understandable

2. Which of the following is closest in meaning to the word "critical" in line 2?

_____ (A) Industrial

_____ (B) Serious

_____ (C) Crucial

_____ (D) Insulting

3. The phrase "the stage was set" in line 3 is closest in meaning to which of the following?
   _____ (A) The play was over.
   _____ (B) The progress continued.
   _____ (C) The foundation was laid.
   _____ (D) The direction was clear.

4. The phrase "real estate" in line 5 refers to
   _____ (A) tools and machines
   _____ (B) actual income
   _____ (C) new enterprises
   _____ (D) land and buildings

5. The word "buttressed " in line 7 is closest in meaning to
   _____ (A) concerned
   _____ (B) supplemented
   _____ (C) restructured
   _____ (D) enriched

6. The word "accommodating" in line 10 is closest in meaning to
   _____ (A) persistent
   _____ (B) indifferent
   _____ (C) balanced
   _____ (D) helpful

7. Which of the following could best be substituted for the word "posture" in line 12?
   _____ (A) Stature
   _____ (B) Predicament
   _____ (C) Position
   _____ (D) Situation

8. The word "prevailed" in line 15 is closest in meaning to
   _____ (A) influenced
   _____ (B) triumphed
   _____ (C) premiered
   _____ (D) evolved

9. The phrase "left to its own devices" in lines 15–16 means
   _____ (A) forced to do additional work
   _____ (B) allowed to do as it pleased
   _____ (C) made to change its plans
   _____ (D) encouraged to produce more goods

10. The word "vying" in line 18 is closest in meaning to
    _____ (A) competing
    _____ (B) hoping
    _____ (C) arranging
    _____ (D) caring

11. The word "savage" in line 21 is closest in meaning to
    _____ (A) fierce
    _____ (B) growing
    _____ (C) surprising
    _____ (D) genuine

Questions 12–19

All birds have feathers, and all animals with feathers are birds. No other major group of animals is so easy to categorize. All birds have wings, too, but wings are not peculiar to birds.

(line)   Many adaptations are found in both feathers and wings. Feathers
(5)   form the soft down of geese and ducks, the long decorative plumes of ostriches, and the strong flight feathers of eagles and hawks. Wings vary from the short, broad ones of chickens, which seldom fly, to the long, slim ones of albatrosses, which spend almost all their lives soaring on air currents. In penguins, wings have been
(10)   modified into flippers and feathers into a waterproof covering. In kiwis, the wings are almost impossible to detect.

Yet diversity among birds is not so striking as it is among mammals. The difference between a hummingbird and a penguin is immense, but hardly as startling as that between a bat and a whale.
(15)   It is variations in details rather than in fundamental patterns that have been important in the adaptation of birds to many kinds of ecosystems.

12. The word "categorize" in line 2 is closest in meaning to
_____ (A) appreciate
_____ (B) comprehend
_____ (C) classify
_____ (D) visualize

13. Which of the following is closest in meaning to the phrase "peculiar to" in line 3?
_____ (A) Unusual for
_____ (B) Common to
_____ (C) Necessary for
_____ (D) Unique to

14. The word "slim" in line 8 is closest in meaning to
_____ (A) slender
_____ (B) powerful
_____ (C) graceful
_____ (D) soft

15. The word "detect" in line 11 is closest in meaning to
_____ (A) utilize
_____ (B) extend
_____ (C) observe
_____ (D) describe

16. Which of the following is closest in meaning to the word "diversity" in line 12?
_____ (A) Function
_____ (B) Heredity
_____ (C) Specialty
_____ (D) Variety

17. The word "hardly" in line 14 is closest in meaning to
_____ (A) definitely
_____ (B) not nearly
_____ (C) possibly
_____ (D) not always

18. The word "startling" in line 14 is closest in meaning to
_____ (A) initial
_____ (B) exciting
_____ (C) tremendous
_____ (D) surprising

19. The word "fundamental" in line 15 is closest in meaning to
_____ (A) basic
_____ (B) shifting
_____ (C) predictable
_____ (D) complicated

Questions 20–27

Manufactured in the tranquil New England town of Concord, New Hampshire, the famous Concord Coach came to symbolize the Wild West. Its rugged body and a suspension system of leather straps
(line)   could handle the hard jolts from rough roads. A journalist in
(5)   1868, describing a railroad shipment of 30 coaches bound for Wells, Fargo and Company, wrote, "They are splendidly decorated . . . the bodies red and the running parts yellow. Each door has a handsome picture, mostly landscapes, and no two coaches are exactly alike."

Wells, Fargo and Company was founded in 1852 to provide mail and
(10)   banking services for the gold camps of California and later won a monopoly on express services west of the Mississippi. A Wells, Fargo Concord Coach carried nine to fourteen passengers plus baggage and mail. The accommodations were by no means plush. However, the stagecoach was the swiftest method of travel through much of the Far West.

20. The word "tranquil" in line 1 is closest in meaning to
_____ (A) peaceful
_____ (B) bustling
_____ (C) industrial
_____ (D) tiny

21. The word "symbolize" in line 2 is closest in meaning to
_____ (A) recollect
_____ (B) fulfill
_____ (C) deny
_____ (D) represent

22. Which of the following could best substitute for the word "rugged" in line 3?
_____ (A) Streamlined
_____ (B) Roomy
_____ (C) Sturdy
_____ (D) Primitive

23. Which of the following is closest in meaning to the word "jolts" in line 4?
_____ (A) Signs
_____ (B) Shocks
_____ (C) Sights
_____ (D) Shots

24. The phrase "bound for" in line 5 is closest in meaning to
_____ (A) belonged to
_____ (B) destined for
_____ (C) built by
_____ (D) paid for

25. The word "splendidly" in line 6 is closest in meaning to
_____ (A) superbly
_____ (B) deliberately
_____ (C) specifically
_____ (D) slightly

26. The word "plush" in line 13 is closest in meaning to
_____ (A) normal
_____ (B) luxurious
_____ (C) memorable
_____ (D) unpleasant

27. Which of the following is closest in meaning to the word "swiftest" in line 14?
_____ (A) Most comfortable
_____ (B) Cheapest
_____ (C) Most direct
_____ (D) Fastest

Questions 28–35

(line)

(5)

(10)

The Hopi people of Arizona stress the institutions of family and religion in a harmonious existence which makes the self-sacrificing individual the ideal. The Hopi individual is trained to feel his or her responsibility to and for the Peaceful People—the Hopi's own term for themselves. Fighting, bullying, or attempting to surpass others bring automatic rebuke from the community.

Implicit in the Hopi view is an original and integrated theory of the universe. With this they organize their society in such a way to obtain a measure of security from a harsh and hazardous environment made up of human foes, famine, and plagues. They conceive of the universe—humans, animals, plants, and supernatural spirits—as an ordered system functioning under a set of rules known to them alone. These rules govern their behavior, emotions, and thoughts in a prescribed way.

28. The word "stress" in line 1 is closest in meaning to
_____ (A) emphasize
_____ (B) define
_____ (C) strain
_____ (D) persuade

29. Which of the following could best substitute for the word "harmonious" in line 2?
_____ (A) Cooperative
_____ (B) Dangerous
_____ (C) Philosophical
_____ (D) Exclusive

30. The word "term" in line 5 is closest in meaning to
_____ (A) era
_____ (B) name
_____ (C) area
_____ (D) law

31. The word "bullying" in line 5 is closest in meaning to
_____ (A) lying
_____ (B) organizing
_____ (C) entertaining
_____ (D) tormenting

32. Which of the following can replace the word "rebuke" in line 6 with the least change in meaning?
_____ (A) Prestige
_____ (B) Criticism
_____ (C) Reaction
_____ (D) Acknowledgment

33. Which of the following could best be substituted for the word "hazardous" in line 9?
_____ (A) Changing
_____ (B) Random
_____ (C) Familiar
_____ (D) Dangerous

34. The word "foes" in line 10 is closest in meaning to
_____ (A) fears
_____ (B) needs
_____ (C) enemies
_____ (D) failures

35. Which of the following is closest in meaning to the word "prescribed" in line 14?
_____ (A) Set
_____ (B) Disorderly
_____ (C) Legal
_____ (D) Compatible

Questions 36–42

(line)

(5)

Canadian researchers have discovered a set of genes that determine the lifespan of the common nematode, a type of worm. This finding sheds new light on the aging process that may eventually allow scientists to delay the inexorable process of aging and death.

By manipulating the newly discovered genes, the team at McGill University in Montreal was able to increase the lifespan of the nematode fivefold. Altering the genes apparently slowed the metabolism of the worms to a more leisurely pace. This in turn may

(10)

slow the accumulation of the DNA defects thought to cause aging. Although the causes of aging in humans are undoubtedly more involved, researchers are confident that the discoveries will provide invaluable clues about this heretofore mysterious process.

36. The word "determine" in line 2 is closest in meaning to
_____ (A) control
_____ (B) modify
_____ (C) estimate
_____ (D) shorten

37. Which of the following is closest in meaning to the phrase "sheds new light on" in line 3?
_____ (A) Contradicts what is known about
_____ (B) Gives new meaning to
_____ (C) Provides more information about
_____ (D) Calls more attention to

38. The word "inexorable" in line 4 is closest in meaning to
_____ (A) cruel
_____ (B) unstoppable
_____ (C) essential
_____ (D) incomprehensible

39. Which of the following could best be used in place of the phrase "more leisurely" in line 9?
_____ (A) More relaxed
_____ (B) Livelier
_____ (C) Easier
_____ (D) More irregular

40. The word "involved" in line 12 is closest in meaning to
_____ (A) committed
_____ (B) serious
_____ (C) apparent
_____ (D) complicated

41. Which of the following is closest in meaning to the word "clues" in line 13?
_____ (A) Plans
_____ (B) Secrets
_____ (C) Signals
_____ (D) Hints

42. The word "heretofore" in line 13 is closest in meaning to
_____ (A) universally
_____ (B) almost
_____ (C) previously
_____ (D) somewhat

LESSON 48

REFERENCE QUESTIONS

Reference questions ask what noun (called the **referent**) a pronoun or some other expression refers to. The correct answer is *not* always the noun that is closest to the pronoun in the passage. Incorrect choices are usually other nouns that appear in the passage. If you are unable to decide immediately which answer is correct, substitute the four choices for the word that is being asked about. Which one is the most logical substitute?

In general, reference questions tend to be the easiest type of reading question.

▼   **Sample Item**

There is a poisonous, plant-like animal called the anemone that lives among coral reefs. When small fish venture too close to the tentacles of these "living
(line)   flowers," they are stung and eaten. For unknown reasons,
(5)   the anemone makes an exception of the clownfish, which swims through its deadly tentacles in safety. When in danger, the clownfish dashes among the anemone's tentacles where other fish are afraid to follow. The clownfish even builds its nest where the anemone can protect it.

1. The word "they" in line 4 refers to
   - (A) coral reefs
   - (B) small fish
   - (C) tentacles
   - (D) flowers

Of the four choices, only "small fish" is a logical answer.

2. The word "it" in line 10 is a reference to the
   - (A) clownfish
   - (B) nest
   - (C) anemone
   - (D) exception

Only the word "nest" is a logical substitute for "it."   ▲

Exercise 48.1

Focus: Identifying the referents for pronouns and other expressions in sentences and very short passages.

Directions: Read the items. Decide which choice is the correct referent for the underlined word, and mark the answer. The first one is done as an example.

1. Detergents clean clothes by first removing particles of dirt from the fabric, then suspending the particles until <u>they</u> can be washed away.
   - _____ (A) clothes
   - __✔__ (B) particles of dirt
   - _____ (C) detergents

2. Wooly mammoths were hunted by big cats called sabertooth tigers, which also became extinct by the end of the last Ice Age. <u>They</u> were also hunted by early men armed with spears and clubs.
   _____ (A) sabertooth tigers
   _____ (B) early men
   _____ (C) wooly mammoths

3. X-rays allow art historians to examine paintings internally without damaging <u>them</u>.
   _____ (A) x-rays
   _____ (B) art historians
   _____ (C) paintings

4. There is a New England influence in southern Ohio, manifesting <u>itself</u> in white churches and village greens.
   _____ (A) a New England influence
   _____ (B) southern Ohio

5. Florists often refrigerate cut flowers to protect <u>their</u> fresh appearance.
   _____ (A) florists'
   _____ (B) flowers'

6. A flat kite needs a tail to supply drag and to keep the kite pointed toward the sky. A simple <u>one</u> consists of cloth strips tied end to end.
   _____ (A) kite
   _____ (B) tail
   _____ (C) sky

7. A number of sculptors have rejected the abstractions of minimalist artists. <u>These sculptors</u> have developed a style of extreme realism involving ordinary subjects.
   _____ (A) extreme realists
   _____ (B) minimalists

8. Water is an exception to many of nature's rules because of <u>its</u> unusual properties.
   _____ (A) nature's
   _____ (B) water's

9. Compound bows are popular with bow hunters, but <u>they</u> are not permitted in international archery competitions.
   _____ (A) bow hunters
   _____ (B) compound bows

10. Ropes are cords at least .15 inches in diameter and are made of three or more strands which are <u>themselves</u> formed of twisted yarns.
    _____ (A) yarns
    _____ (B) ropes
    _____ (C) strands
    _____ (D) cords

11. Grocers slice sides, quarters, and what are called primal cuts of beef into smaller pieces. <u>These pieces</u> are called retail cuts.
    _____ (A) smaller pieces
    _____ (B) sides, quarters, and primal cuts

12. Leaves are found on all deciduous trees, but <u>they</u> differ greatly in size and shape.
    _____ (A) trees
    _____ (B) leaves

13. Yasuo Kuniyashi was born in Japan in 1883 and studied art at the Los Angeles School of Art and Design. He also studied art in New York City, where he gave his first one-man show. In 1925 he moved from <u>there</u> to Paris where he was influenced by the works of Chagall and other artists.
    _____ (A) Japan
    _____ (B) Paris
    _____ (C) Los Angeles
    _____ (D) New York City

14. In the past, biologists considered mushrooms and other fungi as a type of non-green plant. Today, however, <u>they</u> are most commonly regarded as a separate kingdom of living things.
    _____ (A) mushrooms and other fungi
    _____ (B) biologists
    _____ (C) plants

15. William Dean Howells, a contemporary and friend of Mark Twain, wrote a number of books that realistically portrayed life on farms in Midwestern America. One of his followers, Hamlin Garland, was even more bitter in his criticism of rural America than <u>his mentor</u>.
    _____ (A) Hamlin Garland
    _____ (B) Mark Twain
    _____ (C) William Dean Howells

16. The Wisconsin Dells is a region where the Wisconsin River cuts through soft sandstone. The strange formations that have been carved out of the rocks there are a delight to tourists. <u>They</u> have names such as Devil's Elbow, Grand Piano, and Fat Man's Misery.
    _____ (A) strange formations
    _____ (B) tourists
    _____ (C) rocks

17. The lives of beetles are divided into four stages, as are <u>those</u> of wasps, ants, and butterflies.
    _____ (A) lives
    _____ (B) stages
    _____ (C) insects

18. After electron microscopes were invented, scientists found many new viruses. Some of <u>them</u> were round, some oval, and some corkscrew-shaped.
    _____ (A) electron microscopes
    _____ (B) viruses
    _____ (C) scientists

19. The detailed information in maps is now produced almost entirely from satellite photography rather than by ground surveying because <u>this method</u> is faster, cheaper, and more accurate.
    _____ (A) satellite photography
    _____ (B) ground surveying

20. An elephant is bigger than a mouse because it has trillions more cells, not because <u>its</u> cells are any bigger.
    _____ (A) a mouse's
    _____ (B) an elephant's

Exercise 48.2

Focus: Answering reference questions based on longer passages.

Directions: Read the following passages and the questions about them. Decide which of the choices—(A), (B), (C), or (D)—best answers the question, and mark the answer. The first one is done as an example.

Questions 1–6

(line)

(5)

(10)

(15)

(20)

> In addition to these various types of deep mining, several types of surface mining may be used when minerals lie relatively close to the surface of the Earth. One type is open-pit mining. The first step is to remove the overburden, the layers of rock and earth lying above the ore, with giant scrapers. The ore is broken up in a series of blasting operations. Power shovels pick up the pieces and load them into trucks or, in some cases, ore trains. These carry it up ramps to ground level. Soft ores are removed by drilling screws, called augers.
>
> Another type is called "placer" mining. Sometimes heavy metals such as gold are found in soil deposited by streams and rivers. The soil is picked up by a power shovel and transferred to a long trough. Water is run through the soil in the trough. This carries soil particles away with it. The metal particles are heavier than the soil and sink to the bottom, where they can be recovered.
>
> The finishing-off process of mining is called mineral concentration. In this process, the desired substances are removed from the waste in various ways. One technique is to bubble air through a liquid in which ore particles are suspended. Chemicals are added that make the minerals cling to the air bubbles. The bubbles rise to the surface with the mineral particles attached, and they can be skimmed off and saved.

1. The word "them" in line 7 refers to
_____ (A) power shovels
_____ (B) layers of rock and earth
_____ (C) giant scrapers
__✔__ (D) pieces of ore

2. To which of the following does the word "These" in line 8 refer?
_____ (A) Ramps
_____ (B) Trucks or ore trains
_____ (C) Augers
_____ (D) Blasting operations

3. The phrase "Another type" in line 10 is a reference to another type of
_____ (A) deep mining
_____ (B) ore
_____ (C) metal
_____ (D) surface mining

4. The word "This" in line 13 refers to
_____ (A) a power shovel
_____ (B) gold
_____ (C) running water
_____ (D) a long trough

5. In line 17, the phrase "this process" refers to
_____ (A) surface mining
_____ (B) the depositing of soil
_____ (C) mineral concentration
_____ (D) placer mining

6. The word "they" in line 22 refers to the
_____ (A) processes
_____ (B) air bubbles
_____ (C) chemicals
_____ (D) minerals

Questions 7–10

(line)

(5)

(10)

(15)

Mount Rainier, the heart of Mt. Rainier National Park, is the highest mountain in the state of Washington and in the Cascade Range. The mountain's summit is broad and rounded. It is 14,410 feet above sea level and has an area of about one square mile. Numerous steam and gas jets occur around the crater, but the volcano has been sleeping for many centuries.

Mount Rainier has a permanent ice cap and extensive snow fields, which give rise to over forty glaciers. These feed swift streams and tumbling waterfalls that race through the glacial valleys. Forests extend to 4,500 feet. There are alpine meadows between the glaciers and the forests which contain beautiful wild flowers. The Nisqually Glacier is probably the ice region that is most often explored by visitors. Paradise Valley, where hotel accommodations are available, perches on the mountain's slope at 5,400 feet. The Wonderland Trail encircles the mountain. Its 90-mile length can be covered in about a week's time.

7. To which of the following does the word "It" in line 3 refer?
_____ (A) Mt. Rainier
_____ (B) The summit
_____ (C) The Cascade range
_____ (D) The national park

8. The word "These" in line 8 refers to which of the following?
_____ (A) Snow fields
_____ (B) Steam and gas jets
_____ (C) Glaciers
_____ (D) Streams and waterfalls

9. The word "which" in line 11 refers to
_____ (A) forests
_____ (B) wild flowers
_____ (C) alpine meadows
_____ (D) glacial valleys

10. What does the word "Its" in line 15 refer to?
_____ (A) The trail's
_____ (B) An ice region's
_____ (C) The mountain's
_____ (D) A week's

Questions 11–15

(line)

(5)

(10)

(15)

Some people associate migration mainly with birds. Birds do travel vast distances, but mammals also migrate. An example is the caribou, reindeer that graze on the grassy slopes of northern Canada. When the weather turns cold, they travel south until spring. Their tracks are so well-worn that they are clearly visible from the air. Another migrating mammal is the Alaska fur seal. These seals breed only in the Pribilof Islands in the Bering Sea. The young are born in June and by September are strong enough to go with their mothers on a journey of over 3,000 miles. Together they swim down the Pacific Coast of North America. The females and young travel as far as southern California. The males do not journey so far. They swim only to the Gulf of Alaska. In the spring, males and females all return to the islands, and there the cycle begins again. Whales are among the greatest migrators of all. The humpback, fin, and blue whales migrate thousands of miles each year from the polar seas to the tropics. Whales eat huge quantities of tiny plants and animals (called plankton). These are most abundant in cold polar waters. In winter, the whales move to warm waters to breed and give birth to their young.

11. The phrase "An example" in line 2 refers to an example of a
   _____ (A) migratory mammal
   _____ (B) place where animals migrate
   _____ (C) bird
   _____ (D) person who associates migration with birds

12. In line 5, the word "Their" is a reference to the
   _____ (A) caribou's
   _____ (B) grassy slopes'
   _____ (C) birds'
   _____ (D) seals'

13. To what does the word "They" in line 12 refer?
   _____ (A) female seals
   _____ (B) young seals
   _____ (C) the islands
   _____ (D) male seals

14. In line 14, the word "there" refers to
   _____ (A) the Gulf of Alaska
   _____ (B) the Pribilof Islands
   _____ (C) southern California
   _____ (D) the Pacific Coast of North America

15. The word "These" in line 18 refers to
   _____ (A) three types of whales
   _____ (B) tiny plants and animals
   _____ (C) polar seas
   _____ (D) warm waters

Questions 16–19

(line)
(5)

Design is the arrangement of materials to produce certain effects. Design plays a role in visual arts and in the creation of commercial products as well. Designers are concerned with the direction of lines, the size of shapes, and the shading of colors. They arrange these patterns in ways that are satisfying to viewers. There are various elements involved in creating a pleasing design.

(10)

Harmony, or *balance*, can be obtained in a number of ways. It may be either symmetrical (in balance) or asymmetrical (out of balance, but still pleasing to the eye). Or a small area may balance a large area if it has an importance to the eye (because of color or treatment) which equals that of the larger area.

(15)

Contrast is the opposite of harmony. The colors red and orange harmonize, since orange contains red. A circle and oval harmonize, as they are both made up of curved lines. But a short line does not harmonize with a long line. It is in contrast.

(20)

Unity occurs when all the elements in a design combine to form a consistent whole. Unity resembles balance. A design has balance if its masses are balanced, or if its tones and colors harmonize. But unity differs from balance because it implies that balanced elements work together to form harmony in the design as a whole.

16. The word "They" in line 5 refers to
_____ (A) designers
_____ (B) lines, shapes, and colors
_____ (C) directions, size, and shape
_____ (D) visual arts

17. The word "that" in line 12 is used as a reference to
_____ (A) a color
_____ (B) an area
_____ (C) importance
_____ (D) balance

18. The word "It" in line 16 is used as a reference to
_____ (A) a circle
_____ (B) the color red
_____ (C) a long line
_____ (D) a short line

19. In line 20, the word "it" refers to
_____ (A) unity
_____ (B) balance
_____ (C) a design
_____ (D) a consistent whole

Questions 20–22

(line)

(5)

Although they had been used to haul freight and passengers between the Eastern seaboard and the Ohio Valley since 1812, wagon trains were first used extensively in the 1820's on the Santa Fe Trail. Long trains of covered wagons drawn by oxen or mules carried manufactured goods to trade for fur, gold, and silver in Santa Fe. The independent traders who pooled their resources to form these trains elected a captain and several lieutenants who commanded the parallel columns in which the wagons usually moved. They enforced the rules, selected the routes, and designated stopping places.

20. To what does the word "they" in line 1 refer?
    _____ (A) the Eastern Seaboard and the Ohio Valley
    _____ (B) wagon trains
    _____ (C) freights and passengers
    _____ (D) oxen and mules

21. The word "their" in line 6 refers to the
    _____ (A) covered wagons'
    _____ (B) oxen and mules'
    _____ (C) independent traders'
    _____ (D) captain and lieutenants'

22. To what does the word "They" in line 9 refer?
    _____ (A) The leaders
    _____ (B) The traders
    _____ (C) The parallel columns
    _____ (D) The stopping places

Questions 23–26

(line)

(5)

(10)

(15)

In most of the earliest books for children, illustrations were an afterthought. But in the Caldecott "toy books," pictures were as important as the few lines of copy, and they occupied far more space. One can almost read the nursery rhymes from the dramatic action in the pictures.

Since then, thousands of successful picture books have been published in the United States and in many countries around the world. In the best, the text and illustrations seem to complement each other perfectly. Often one person is the author and illustrator—for example, Robert McCloskey (*Make Way for Ducklings*) and Arnold Loebel (*Frog and Toad Together*). Many others have been produced by an author-artist team, as in *The Happy Lion*, written by Louise Fatio and illustrated by Roger Duvoisin.

Wordless picture books have also become popular. With a little help, three- or four-year-olds can follow the sequence of events and they can understand the stories suggested in them. One of the most delightful examples of a wordless book is Jan Ormerod's *Sunshine*.

(20)   American publishers have also drawn on artists from other countries whose original, imaginative works have brought their different visions to American children's book illustration. Among them are Leo Lionni from Italy, Feoddor Rojankowski from Russia, and Taro Yashima from Japan.

23. The word "they" in line 3 refers to
    _____ (A) the earliest books for children
    _____ (B) lines of copy
    _____ (C) the Caldecott "toy books"
    _____ (D) pictures

24. The phrase "the best" in line 8 refers to the best
    _____ (A) picture books
    _____ (B) illustrations
    _____ (C) authors
    _____ (D) nursery rhymes

25. The word "they" in line 17 refers to
    _____ (A) delightful examples
    _____ (B) events
    _____ (C) 3- and 4-year-olds
    _____ (D) wordless picture books

26. The word "their" in line 22 refers to
    _____ (A) American publishers'
    _____ (B) original, imaginative works'
    _____ (C) artists'
    _____ (D) American children's

ANSWER SHEET
MINI-TEST 8: READING COMPREHENSION

1. (A) (B) (C) (D)   11. (A) (B) (C) (D)   21. (A) (B) (C) (D)
2. (A) (B) (C) (D)   12. (A) (B) (C) (D)   22. (A) (B) (C) (D)
3. (A) (B) (C) (D)   13. (A) (B) (C) (D)   23. (A) (B) (C) (D)
4. (A) (B) (C) (D)   14. (A) (B) (C) (D)   24. (A) (B) (C) (D)
5. (A) (B) (C) (D)   15. (A) (B) (C) (D)   25. (A) (B) (C) (D)
6. (A) (B) (C) (D)   16. (A) (B) (C) (D)   26. (A) (B) (C) (D)
7. (A) (B) (C) (D)   17. (A) (B) (C) (D)   27. (A) (B) (C) (D)
8. (A) (B) (C) (D)   18. (A) (B) (C) (D)   28. (A) (B) (C) (D)
9. (A) (B) (C) (D)   19. (A) (B) (C) (D)   29. (A) (B) (C) (D)
10. (A) (B) (C) (D)   20. (A) (B) (C) (D)   30. (A) (B) (C) (D)

31. (A) (B) (C) (D)   41. (A) (B) (C) (D)
32. (A) (B) (C) (D)   42. (A) (B) (C) (D)
33. (A) (B) (C) (D)   43. (A) (B) (C) (D)
34. (A) (B) (C) (D)   44. (A) (B) (C) (D)
35. (A) (B) (C) (D)   45. (A) (B) (C) (D)
36. (A) (B) (C) (D)   46. (A) (B) (C) (D)
37. (A) (B) (C) (D)   47. (A) (B) (C) (D)
38. (A) (B) (C) (D)   48. (A) (B) (C) (D)
39. (A) (B) (C) (D)   49. (A) (B) (C) (D)
40. (A) (B) (C) (D)   50. (A) (B) (C) (D)

MINI-TEST 8: READING COMPREHENSION

Directions: In this mini-test, there are several passages, each followed by a number of questions.
Read the passages and, for each question, choose the *one* best answer, (A), (B), (C), or (D).
All of your answers should be based on what is stated or implied in the passages. Then mark
the appropriate answer either in the blanks next to the items or on the answer sheet above.

Questions 1–12

	Humans have struggled against weeds since the beginnings of
	agriculture. Marring our gardens is one of the milder effects of
	weeds—any plants that thrive where they are unwanted. They clog
(line)	waterways, destroy wildlife habitats, and impede farming. Their
(5)	spread eliminates grazing areas and accounts for one-third of all
	crop loss. They compete for sunlight, nutrients, and water with
	useful plants.

The global need for weed control has been answered mainly by the
chemical industry. Its herbicides are effective and sometimes
(10) necessary, but some pose serious problems, particularly if misused.
Toxic compounds threaten animal and public health when they
accumulate in food plants, ground water, and drinking water. They
also harm workers who apply them.

In recent years, the chemical industry has introduced several
(15) herbicides that are more ecologically sound. Yet new chemicals
alone cannot solve the world's weed problems. Hence, scientists are
exploring the innate weed-killing powers of living organisms,
primarily insects and microorganisms.

The biological agents now in use are harmless to humans and
are environmentally benign. They can be chosen for their
(20) ability to attack selected targets and leave crops and other plants
untouched. In contrast, some of the most effective chemicals kill
virtually all the plants they come in contact with, sparing only
those that are naturally resistant or have been genetically
modified for resistance. Furthermore, a number of biological agents
(25) can be administered only once, after which no added applications
are needed. Chemicals typically must be used several times per
growing season.

1. With what topic does this passage primarily deal?
   _____ (A) The importance of the chemical industry
   _____ (B) The dangers of toxic chemicals
   _____ (C) Advantages of biological agents over chemical ones
   _____ (D) A proposal to ban the use of all herbicides

2. The word "Marring" in line 2 is closest in meaning to
   _____ (A) spoiling
   _____ (B) dividing
   _____ (C) replacing
   _____ (D) planting

3. The word "clog" in line 3 is closest in meaning to
   _____ (A) drain
   _____ (B) float on
   _____ (C) obstruct
   _____ (D) grow along

4. Which of the following terms does the author define in the first paragraph?
   _____ (A) Grazing areas
   _____ (B) Weeds
   _____ (C) Wildlife habitats
   _____ (D) Nutrients

5. With which of the following statements about the use of chemical agents as herbicides would the author most likely agree?
   _____ (A) It should be increased.
   _____ (B) It has become more dangerous recently.
   _____ (C) It is safe but inefficient.
   _____ (D) It is occasionally required.

6. Which of the following is NOT given as an advantage of biological agents over chemical herbicides?
_____ (A) They are less likely to destroy desirable plants.
_____ (B) They are safer for workers.
_____ (C) They are more easily available.
_____ (D) They do not have to be used as often.

7. Which of the following is closest in meaning to the word "Hence" in line 16?
_____ (A) In addition
_____ (B) Consequently
_____ (C) Subsequently
_____ (D) In contrast

8. The word "innate" in line 17 is closest in meaning to
_____ (A) natural
_____ (B) effective
_____ (C) organic
_____ (D) active

9. According to the passage, biological agents consist mainly of
_____ (A) insects and microorganisms
_____ (B) useful plants
_____ (C) weeds
_____ (D) herbicides

10. The word "those" in line 23 refers to
_____ (A) chemicals
_____ (B) targets
_____ (C) plants
_____ (D) agents

11. The word "applications" in line 25 could best be replaced by which of the following?
_____ (A) Requests
_____ (B) Special purposes
_____ (C) Treatments
_____ (D) Qualifications

12. Which of the following best describes the organization of the passage?
_____ (A) A general idea is introduced, and several specific examples are given.
_____ (B) A recommendation is analyzed and rejected.
_____ (C) A problem is described, and possible solutions are discussed.
_____ (D) Two possible causes for a phenomenon are compared.

Questions 13–21

          West Side Story is a musical tragedy based on William Shakespeare's play *Romeo and Juliet*. It is set in the early 1950's, when gang warfare in big cities led to injuries and even

(line)
(5)
death. *West Side Story* transforms the Montagues and Capulets of Shakespeare's play into feuding street gangs, the Jets and the Sharks, one consisting of newly arrived Puerto Ricans and the other of native-born New Yorkers. The plot, tightly choreographed by Jerome Robbins, tells the story of the love of Maria, a Puerto Rican, for Tony, who, while attempting to stop a street fight, kills

(10)
Maria's brother and is ultimately killed himself. Leonard

Bernstein's musical score is brilliant, and Stephen Sondheim, making his Broadway debut, reveals a remarkable talent for writing lyrics. Among the hit songs of the play are "Tonight," "Maria," "America," and "I Feel Pretty."

(15)   The play opened on September 26, 1957. It ran for 734 performances, toured for 10 months, and then returned to New York for an additional 246 performances. A film version was released in 1961, and a successful New York revival opened in 1980.

13. The author's attitude toward the play is generally
_____ (A) regretful
_____ (B) critical
_____ (C) emotional
_____ (D) favorable

14. According to the passage, when does the action of the play *West Side Story* take place?
_____ (A) In Shakespeare's time
_____ (B) In the early 1950's
_____ (C) In 1957
_____ (D) In 1980

15. It can be inferred from the passage that the Capulets and Montagues
_____ (A) were rival groups in Shakespeare's play
_____ (B) were 1950's street gangs
_____ (C) fought against the Jets and Sharks
_____ (D) were groups of actors, dancers, and singers

16. The word "feuding" in line 5 is closest in meaning to
_____ (A) growing
_____ (B) hostile
_____ (C) organized
_____ (D) criminal

17. Which of the following is closest in meaning to the word "ultimately" in line 10?
_____ (A) Accidentally
_____ (B) Immediately
_____ (C) Eventually
_____ (D) Savagely

18. According to the article, the words to the songs of *West Side Story* were written by
_____ (A) Jerome Robbins
_____ (B) Leonard Bernstein
_____ (C) William Shakespeare
_____ (D) Stephen Sondheim

19. The word "score" in line 11 could best be replaced by which of the following?
_____ (A) Talent
_____ (B) Music
_____ (C) Performance
_____ (D) Dialogue

20. During its initial appearance in New York, how many times was *West Side Story* performed?
_____ (A) 10
_____ (B) 26
_____ (C) 246
_____ (D) 734

21. Where in the passage is the basic story of *West Side Story* summarized?
_____ (A) Lines 1-4
_____ (B) Lines 7-10
_____ (C) Lines 13-14
_____ (D) Lines 15-17

Questions 22–33

(line)

(5)

(10)

(15)

(20)

About 8,000 people looked over the horseless carriages on November 3, 1900, the opening day of the New York Auto Show, and the first opportunity for the automobile industry to show off its wares to a sizable audience.

By happenstance, the number of people at the show equalled the entire car population at that time. At that time, 10 million bicycles and an unknown number of horse-and-buggies provided the prime means of transportation. Only about 4,000 cars were assembled in the United States in 1900, and only a quarter of those were gasoline powered. (The rest ran on steam or electricity.)

After viewing the cars made by 32 car makers, the show's audience favored electric cars because they were quiet. The risk of a boiler explosion turned people away from steamers, and the gasoline powered cars produced smelly fumes. The Duryea Motor Wagon Company, which launched the American auto industry in 1892, offered an additive designed to mask the smell of the naphtha that it burned.

The prices were not that different from what they are today. Most cost between $800 and $1,500, or roughly $11,000 to $18,500 in today's prices. Many of the 1900 models were cumbersome—the Gasmobile, the Franklin, and the Orient, for example, steered with tillers like boats rather than with steering wheels.

The black-tie audience at the show viewed the display more as a social outing than as the extravaganzas that auto shows were about to become.

22. Approximately how many cars were there in the United States in 1900?
_____ (A) 4,000
_____ (B) 8,000
_____ (C) 10 million
_____ (D) An unknown number

23. Which of the following is closest in meaning to the phrase "By happenstance" as used in line 5?
_____ (A) Generally
_____ (B) For example
_____ (C) Coincidentally
_____ (D) By design

24. Approximately how many of the cars assembled in the year 1900 were gasoline powered?
_____ (A) 32
_____ (B) 1,000
_____ (C) 2,000
_____ (D) 4,000

25. According to the passage, people at the 1900 New York Auto Show favored cars powered by
_____ (A) electricity
_____ (B) naphtha
_____ (C) gasoline
_____ (D) steam

26. The word "fumes" in line 14 is closest in meaning to
_____ (A) fuels
_____ (B) grains
_____ (C) fires
_____ (D) gases

27. Which of the following is closest in meaning to the word "launched" in line 15?
_____ (A) Joined
_____ (B) Designed
_____ (C) Initiated
_____ (D) Anticipated

28. The purpose of the additive mentioned in line 16 was to
_____ (A) increase the speed of cars
_____ (B) make engines run more efficiently
_____ (C) hide offensive smells
_____ (D) make cars look better

29. What was the highest price asked for a car at the 1900 New York Auto Show in the dollars of that time?
_____ (A) $800
_____ (B) $1,500
_____ (C) $11,300
_____ (D) $18,500

30. The word "cumbersome" in line 20 is closest in meaning to
_____ (A) clumsy
_____ (B) inexpensive
_____ (C) fragile
_____ (D) inconvenient

31. Which of the following is NOT mentioned in the passage as steering with a tiller rather than with a steering wheel?
_____ (A) A Franklin
_____ (B) A Duryea
_____ (C) An Orient
_____ (D) A Gasmobile

32. The passage implies that the audience viewed the 1900 New York Auto Show primarily as
_____ (A) a formal social affair
_____ (B) a chance to buy automobiles at low prices
_____ (C) an opportunity to learn how to drive
_____ (D) a chance to invest in one of thirty-two automobile manufacturers

33. It can be inferred from the passage that auto shows held after 1900
_____ (A) were more formal
_____ (B) involved fewer manufacturers
_____ (C) were more spectacular
_____ (D) involved less expensive cars

Questions 34–41

(line)

(5)

(10)

When drawing human figures, children often make the head too large for the rest of the body. A recent study offers some insights into this common disproportion in children's illustrations. As part of the study, researchers asked children between four and seven years old to make several drawings of men. When they drew front views of male figures, the size of the heads was markedly enlarged. However, when the children drew rear views of men, the size of the heads was not so exaggerated. The researchers suggest that children draw bigger heads when they know they must leave room for facial details. Therefore, the odd head size in children's illustrations is a form of planning, and not an indication of a poor sense of scale.

34. The main subject of the passage is
_____ (A) what the results of an experiment revealed
_____ (B) how children learn to draw
_____ (C) how researchers can gather data from works of art
_____ (D) what can be done to correct a poor sense of scale

35. It can be inferred that, during the research project, the children drew
_____ (A) pictures of men from different angles
_____ (B) figures without facial expression
_____ (C) sketches of both men and women
_____ (D) only the front view of men

36. The word "they" in line 6 refers to
_____ (A) researchers
_____ (B) men
_____ (C) illustrations
_____ (D) children

37. The word "markedly" in line 7 is closest in meaning to
_____ (A) modestly
_____ (B) noticeably
_____ (C) merely
_____ (D) newly

38. The findings of the experiment described in the passage would probably be of LEAST interest to which of the following groups?
_____ (A) Teachers of art to children
_____ (B) Commercial artists
_____ (C) Experts in child development
_____ (D) Parents of young children

39. The word "odd" in line 10 is closest in meaning to
_____ (A) unusual
_____ (B) huge
_____ (C) average
_____ (D) expected

40. The word "scale" in line 12 is closest in meaning to
_____ (A) measurement
_____ (B) proportion
_____ (C) balance
_____ (D) property

41. The passage provides information to support which of the following conclusions?

_____ (A) Children under the age of seven do not generally have a good sense of scale.

_____ (B) With training, young children can be taught to avoid disproportion in their art.

_____ (C) Children enlarge the size of the head because they sense that it is the most important part of the body.

_____ (D) Children plan ahead when they are drawing pictures.

Questions 42–50

	Georgia O'Keeffe was born in Sun Prairie, Wisconsin, in 1887. She studied art in Chicago and New York from 1904 to 1908. Beginning as an advertising illustrator, she supported herself until 1918 by
(line)	teaching in various schools and colleges in Texas. After that date,
(5)	she devoted herself entirely to painting. Her paintings were first exhibited in 1916 at "291," an experimental art gallery in New York City owned by Alfred Steiglitz which was frequented by some of the most influential artists of the time. O'Keeffe married Steiglitz in 1924.
(10)	O'Keeffe's early paintings were mostly abstract designs. In the 1920's she produced depictions of flowers and precise cityscapes of New York City. Whether painting flowers or buildings, she captured their beauty by intuitively magnifying their shapes and simplifying their details.
(15)	O'Keeffe's style changed dramatically in 1929 during a visit to New York Mexico. She was enchanted by the stark but beautiful landscapes under the bright Southwestern sun, and she then adopted her characteristic style. Thereafter, she most often painted desert landscapes, often with the blanched skull of a longhorn in the
(20)	foreground.
	O'Keeffe's paintings were exhibited annually at several New York galleries until 1946, and she is represented in the permanent collections of most major American museums. In her later years, she settled in Taos, New Mexico, becoming the dean of Southwestern painters and one of the best known of American artists.

42. The author's main purpose in writing this passage was to

_____ (A) criticize Georgia O'Keeffe's style of painting

_____ (B) discuss the early successes of an important American artist

_____ (C) compare abstract art and landscape art

_____ (D) give the highlights of Georgia O'Keeffe's artistic career

43. According to the article, where did Georgia O'Keeffe receive her formal art training?

_____ (A) Sun Prairie, Wisconsin

_____ (B) Chicago and New York

_____ (C) Texas

_____ (D) Taos, New Mexico

44. The expression "that date" in line 4 refers to

_____ (A) 1887

_____ (B) 1908

_____ (C) 1916

_____ (D) 1918

45. The word "frequented" in line 7 is closest in meaning to
_____ (A) visited
_____ (B) supported
_____ (C) founded
_____ (D) favored

46. The word "intuitively" in line 13 is closest in meaning to
_____ (A) deliberately
_____ (B) defiantly
_____ (C) instinctively
_____ (D) instructively

47. Which of the following had the greatest influence on changing O'Keeffe's style of painting?
_____ (A) A trip to the Southwest
_____ (B) Alfred Steiglitz's photographs
_____ (C) Her job as an advertising illustrator
_____ (D) Meeting influential artists

48. The word "blanched" in line 19 is closest in meaning to
_____ (A) shattered
_____ (B) prominent
_____ (C) whitened
_____ (D) inexplicable

49. Which of the following became the most common subject of O'Keeffe's paintings after 1929?
_____ (A) City scenes
_____ (B) Desert scenes
_____ (C) Flowers
_____ (D) Abstract patterns

50. It can be inferred from the passage that, in her later years, O'Keeffe
_____ (A) continued to be successful
_____ (B) returned to New York City
_____ (C) could not match the successes of her early career
_____ (D) took up photography

MINI-LESSONS FOR SECTION 3
Vocabulary Building

These mini-lessons consist of lists of over 500 words and their synonyms as well as practice exercises. Although vocabulary is no longer tested in discrete items in Part 3, there are vocabulary-in-context questions in the Reading Comprehension section. These exercises will improve your ability to use context to choose the word that best fits into a sentence.

Mini-Lesson 3.1

abandon *v.*   desert, leave behind
able *adj.*   capable, qualified, fit
abolish *v.*   end, eliminate
abrupt *adj.*   sudden, hasty, unexpected
acclaim *v.*   applaud, praise, honor
             n.   praise, applause, honor
acrid *adj.*   bitter, sharp, biting
adapt *v.*   adjust, modify
adept *adj.*   skillful, expert
adhere *v.*   stick, cling
admonish *v.*   warn, caution, advise
adorn *v.* decorate
advent *n.*   coming, arrival
adverse *adj.*   hostile, negative, contrary
affluent *adj.*   rich, wealthy, prosperous, well-to-do
aggravate *v.*   (1) annoy, irritate
                    (2) intensify, worsen
aggregate *adj.*   entire, total, combined
agile *adj.*   graceful, nimble, lively
ailment *n.*   sickness, illness
allot *v.*   divide, distribute
amazing *adj.*   astonishing, astounding, surprising, startling
amiable *adj.*   agreeable, congenial, pleasant
anticipate *v.*   foresee, expect, predict
anxious *adj.*   (1) worried, nervous, apprehensive
                    (2) eager, avid
appraise *v.*   evaluate, estimate, assess
apt *adj.*   (1) appropriate, suitable, correct, relevant, proper
             (2) likely, prone
arduous *adj.*   difficult, exhausting
arid *adj.*   dry, barren
aroma *n.*   fragrance, smell, odor, scent
artificial *adj.*   synthetic, imitation, manmade
astonishing *adj.*   surprising, amazing, astounding
astute *adj.*   intelligent, clever, perceptive
attain *v.*   accomplish, achieve
augment *v.*   supplement, increase, strengthen, expand
austere *adj.*   strict, harsh, severe, stern
authentic *adj.*   genuine, true
aversion *n.*   dislike, hostility, fear
awkward *adj.*   clumsy

Exercise: Complete the following sentences by filling in the blanks with vocabulary item (A), (B), or (C) according to the context of the sentences. The first one is done as an example.

1. Penicillin can have an ____A____ effect on a person who is allergic to it.
   (A) adverse   (B) anxious   (C) awkward

2. Burning rubber produces an _____ smoke.
   (A) austere   (B) arid   (C) acrid

3. Rationing is a system for _____ scarce resources.
   (A) allotting   (B) adapting   (C) appraising

4. Anthrax is generally an _____ of sheet and cattle, but may also be transmitted to humans.
   (A) ailment   (B) aroma   (C) aversion

5. The head of an academic department at a university should be not only a distinguished scholar but also an _____ administrator.
   (A) agile   (B) able   (C) abrupt

6. Mountain climbing is an _____ sport.
   (A) austere   (B) arduous   (C) anxious

7. Turtles _____ their eggs after they lay them and never see their young.
   (A) abandon   (B) appraise   (C) adorn

8. Scholarships allow some students from less _____ families to attend college.
   (A) artificial   (B) affluent   (C) amiable

9. Jewelers are sometimes asked to _____ jewelry for insurance purposes.
   (A) attain   (B) abandon   (C) appraise

10. Acrobats must be extremely _____.
    (A) awkward   (B) affluent   (C) agile

11. In a domed stadium such as Seattle's King Dome, natural grass cannot be grown. _____ turf is used on the playing field.
    (A) Artificial   (B) Arid   (C) Austere

12. Southern Arizona has an _____ climate.
    (A) arid   (B) astute   (C) acrid

13. A person suffering from claustrophobia has an _____ to confined spaces.
    (A) ailment   (B) aversion   (C) acclaim

14. I didn't care for the play because it ended so _____.
    (A) amiably   (B) abruptly   (C) anxiously

15. The ballerina was _____ for her wonderful performances.
    (A) augmented   (B) anticipated   (C) acclaimed

Mini-Lesson 3.2

baffle *v.*   confuse, puzzle, mystify
balmy *adj.*   mild, warm
ban *v.*   prohibit, forbid
bar *v.*   prevent, obstruct, block
barren *adj.*   sterile, unproductive, bleak, lifeless
barter *v.*   trade, exchange
beckon *v.*   summon, call, signal
belligerent *adj.*   hostile, aggressive
beneficial *adj.*   helpful, useful, advantageous
benevolent *adj.*   benign, kind, compassionate
bias *n.*   prejudice, leaning
blanched *adj.*   whitened, pale, bleached
bland *adj.*   mild, tasteless, dull
blatant *adj.*   flagrant, obvious, overt
blend *v.*   mix, mingle, combine
     n.   mixture, combination
bloom *v.*   blossom, flower, flourish
blunder *v.*   make a mistake
     n.   error, mistake
blunt *adj.*   (1) unsharpened, dull
     (2) rude, abrupt, curt
blurry *adj.*   unfocused, unclear, indistinct
bold *adj.*   brave, courageous
bolster *v.*   support, sustain
bond *v.*   join, connect
     n.   tie, link, connection
boom *v.*   expand, prosper
     n.   expansion, prosperity, growth
brace *v.*   support, reinforce
brilliant *adj.*   (1) bright, shiny, radiant, dazzling
     (2) talented, gifted, intelligent
brisk *adj.*   (1) lively, quick, vigorous
     (2) cool, chilly, invigorating
brittle *adj.*   fragile, breakable, weak
bulky *adj.*   huge, large, clumsy

Exercise: Complete the following sentences by filling in the blanks with vocabulary item (A), (B), or (C) according to the context of the sentences.

1. Most flowers _____ in the spring.
   (A) blend   (B) brace   (C) bloom

2. The Virgin Islands, located in the Caribbean, have a _____ climate.
   (A) blurry   (B) brittle   (C) balmy

3. Before currency came into use, people used the _____ system, exchanging goods directly for goods.
   (A) barter   (B) blunder   (C) bias

4. The airline _____. It sent me to Atlanta but my luggage to Montreal.
   (A) beckoned   (B) bartered   (C) blundered

5. People with ulcers must eat _____ foods.
   (A) bold   (B) bland   (C) bulky

6. Steel is not as _____ as cast iron; it doesn't break as easily.
   (A) brisk   (B) brittle   (C) brilliant

7. Some people feel that violent sports such as boxing should be _____ because they are too dangerous.
   (A) banned   (B) bloomed   (C) braced

8. Many people think of deserts as _____ regions, but many species of plants and animals have adapted to life there.
   (A) bland   (B) barren   (C) balmy

9. An autocratic ruler who serves his people well is sometimes called a _____ dictator.
   (A) blatant   (B) belligerent   (C) benevolent

10. Robert Goddard was a _____ pioneer in the field of rocketry.
    (A) brilliant   (B) balmy   (C) brisk

11. I enjoy taking walks on _____ autumn mornings.
    (A) barren   (B) brisk   (C) blurry

12. The victim was apparently struck by a club or some other _____ object.
    (A) bland   (B) brittle   (C) blunt

Mini-Lesson 3.3

calamity *n.*   disaster, catastrophe
capable *adj.*   competent, able, efficient, skillful
carve *v.*   cut, sculpt, slice
casual *adj.*   (1) informal, relaxed
                    (2) accidental, chance
caustic *adj.*   biting, harsh, sarcastic
cautious *adj.*   careful, alert, prudent
celebrated *adj.*   distinguished, famous, prominent
charming *adj.*   delightful, lovely, attractive
cherish *v.*   appreciate, esteem, treasure
choice *n.*   selection, option
        adj.   exceptional, superior
cite *v.*   quote, mention, refer to, list
clash *v.*   argue, dispute, quarrel
        n.   argument, conflict, dispute
classify *v.*   categorize
clever *adj.*   smart, sharp, witty, bright
cling *v.*   stick, adhere, hold
clumsy *adj.*   awkward, inept
coax *v.*   persuade, urge
colossal *adj.*   huge, enormous, gigantic
commence *v.*   begin, initiate, start
commerce *n.*   trade, business
commodity *n.*   good, product, merchandise
compel *v.*   force, require, coerce
competent *adj.*   adept, skillful, capable, able

Exercise: Complete the following sentences by filling in the blanks with vocabulary item (A), (B), or (C) according to the context of the sentences.

1. The Red Cross provides relief in case of _____ such as floods, earthquakes, and hurricanes.
   (A) challenges   (B) commodities   (C) calamities

2. Spoken language is generally more _____ than written language.
   (A) casual   (B) capable   (C) cautious

3. When writing research papers, writers must _____ the sources they use.
   (A) coax   (B) cite   (C) clash

4. Monkeys are _____ as primates.
   (A) compelled   (B) classified   (C) coaxed

5. _____ remarks can offend people.
   (A) Casual   (B) Caustic   (C) Clever

6. Sculptors use hammers and chisels to _____ statues out of stone.
   (A) clash   (B) compel   (C) carve

7. The Space Age _____ in October 1957 when Sputnik, the first artificial satellite, was launched by the Soviet Union.
   (A) commenced   (B) coaxed   (C) cited

8. Workers must be very _____ when dealing with toxic substances.
   (A) caustic   (B) casual   (C) cautious

9. In seaside communities, building sites that have a view of the ocean are considered _____.
   (A) choice   (B) clever   (C) competent

10. With the growth of international _____, the economies of the world have become more interdependent.
    (A) commodity   (B) commerce   (C) choice

11. The Lincoln Memorial features a _____ statue of the sixteenth president.
    (A) colossal   (B) caustic   (C) casual

12. Corn, cotton, sugar, and many other goods are bought and sold in _____ markets.
    (A) clash   (B) commerce   (C) commodity

Mini-Lesson 3.4

complement *v.*   supplement, complete
                    n.   supplement, addition
compliment *v.*   praise, flatter, commend
                    n.   praise, flattery, commendation
comprehensive *adj.*   complete, thorough, exhaustive
compulsory *adj.*   necessary, obligatory, mandatory
concede *v.*   admit, acknowledge, recognize
concise *adj.*   brief, short, abbreviated
concrete *adj.*   tangible, specific, real, perceptible
congregate *v.*   assemble, gather
conspicuous *adj.*   noticeable, obvious, prominent
contemplate *v.*   think about, ponder, speculate
controversial *adj.*   disputable, debatable
convenient *adj.*   accessible, available, handy
cope with *v.*   deal with, manage, handle
copious *adj.*   abundant, ample, plentiful
cordial *adj.*   congenial, warm, friendly
courteous *adj.*   polite, refined, gracious
covert *adj.*   secret, hidden
cozy *adj.*   (1) comfortable, warm
            (2) friendly, intimate, close
crave *v.*   desire, long for, hope for
crooked *adj.*   (1) curved, twisted, zigzag
              (2) dishonest, corrupt
crucial *adj.*   critical, decisive, key
crude *adj.*   (1) rude, impolite, vulgar
            (2) unprocessed, raw, unrefined
cruel *adj.*   brutal, vicious, ruthless
cryptic *adj.*   secret, hidden, mysterious
curb *v.*   restrict, limit, control
curious *adj.*   (1) inquisitive
              (2) odd, strange, unusual
curt *adj.*   abrupt, blunt, impolite

Exercise: Complete the following sentences by filling in the blanks with vocabulary item (A), (B), or (C) according to the context of the sentences.

1. The use of seat belts is _____ in many states; failure to wear them may result in fines.
   (A) covert   (B) cruel   (C) compulsory

2. Every summer, bears from all over southern Alaska _____ along the McNeil River.
   (A) crave   (B) curb   (C) congregate

3. An abstract is a _____ form of an academic article. Many journals publish abstracts so readers can decide if it is worthwhile to read the full version of the article.
   (A) concise   (B) comprehensive   (C) concrete

4. Before 1754, Britain and the North American colonies had a _____ relationship, but after that, their relationship became strained.
   (A) conspicuous   (B) cozy   (C) curt

5. Automatic teller machines provide a _____ means of banking twenty-four hours a day.
   (A) cordial   (B) crooked   (C) convenient

6. Lombard Street in San Francisco, which zigzags its way up Nob Hill, is known as the most _____ street in the world.
   (A) controversial   (B) crooked   (C) cryptic

7. A good writer supports his or her generalizations with _____ examples.
   (A) concrete   (B) curious   (C) crude

8. Many hunters wear orange and other bright colors in order to be as _____ as possible, and therefore avoid being shot by other hunters by mistake.
   (A) covert   (B) cruel   (C) conspicuous

9. Movie directors use music to _____ the action on the screen.
   (A) contemplate   (B) complement   (C) compliment

10. Workers in the service sector should be trained to act as _____ as possible.
    (A) crudely   (B) courteously   (C) curtly

Mini-Lesson 3.5

damp *adj.*   moist, wet, humid
daring *adj.*   bold, courageous, brave
dazzling *adj.*   shining, sparkling, blinding, bright
declare *v.*   announce, proclaim
deem *v.*   believe, consider, regard, judge
defective *adj.*   flawed, faulty, broken, malfunctioning
defiant *adj.*   rebellious, insubordinate
delicate *adj.*   exquisite, fragile
delightful *adj.*   charming, attractive, enchanting
delusion *n.*   illusion, dream, fantasy
demolish *v.*   tear down, destroy, wreck, raze
dense *adj.*   thick, solid
desist *v.*   stop, cease, discontinue
device *n.*   instrument, tool, mechanism
devise *v.*   invent, plan, figure out
dim *adj.*   unclear, faint, indistinct
din *n.*   noise, clamor, commotion
dire *adj.*   desperate, grievous, serious
dismal *adj.*   gloomy, depressing, dreary
disperse *v.*   scatter, distribute, spread
dispute *n.*   argument, quarrel, debate, clash, feud
distinct *adj.*   discrete, separate, different
distinguished *adj.*   celebrated, notable, famous, well-known
divulge *v.*   reveal, admit, disclose
dogged *adj.*   stubborn, determined, persistent
dominate *v.*   rule, control, govern
dot *v.*   are located in, are scattered around
     n.   spot, point
downfall *n.*   collapse, ruin, destruction
doze *v.*   sleep, nap
drawback *n.*   disadvantage, weakness, flaw
dreary *adj.*   dismal, gloomy, bleak
drench *v.*   wet, soak
drowsy *adj.*   sleepy, tired
dubious *adj.*   doubtful, skeptical, uncertain
durable *adj.*   lasting, enduring, resistant
dwell *v.*   live, reside, inhabit
dwelling *n.*   house, home, residence
dwindle *v.*   decrease, diminish
dynamic *adj.*   energetic, forceful, active, vibrant

Exercise: Complete the following sentences by filling in the blanks with vocabulary item (A), (B), or (C) according to the context of the sentences.

1. The snow on the mountaintop was _____ in the bright morning sun.
   (A) dazzling   (B) dogged   (C) dim

2. A person who has been accused of a crime cannot be forced to _____ any information that is self-incriminating.
   (A) divulge   (B) desist   (C) disperse

3. Roses have a _____ beauty.
   (A) dense   (B) delicate   (C) dire

4. An odometer is a _____ for measuring distance.
   (A) device   (B) delusion   (C) dwelling

5. The amount of open space has _____ as more and more land is developed.
   (A) dominated   (B) dwindled   (C) dispersed

6. A _____ battery can cause an electrical device to malfunction.
   (A) dogged   (B) durable   (C) defective

7. Richard Bird and his pilot Floyd Bennet undertook a _____ flight to the North Pole in May of 1926.
   (A) daring   (B) defiant   (C) distinct

8. Steep, round hills called knobs _____ southern Indiana.
   (A) demolish   (B) dot   (C) dwell

9. Artists Nathaniel Currier and J. Merritt Ives produced some _____ prints of nineteenth century New England scenes which collectors prize for their charm.
   (A) dreary   (B) dim   (C) delightful

10. Economists define _____ goods as ones intended to last more than four months.
    (A) durable   (B) dense   (C) delicate

11. One cause of the American Revolution was a _____ over taxation.
    (A) drawback   (B) delusion   (C) dispute

12. Florida has a humid climate. Summers there are particularly hot and _____.
    (A) dynamic   (B) damp   (C) dogged

Mini-Lesson 3.6

eerie *adj.* strange, odd, unusual, frightening
elderly *adj.* old, aged
elegant *adj.* sophisticated, polished
eligible *adj.* suitable, qualified, acceptable
eminent *adj.* celebrated, distinguished, famous
emit *v.* send out, discharge
enchanting *adj.* delightful, charming, captivating
encounter *v.* meet, find, come across
　　　　　 n. meeting, confrontation
endeavor *n.* attempt, venture
endorse *v.* authorize, approve, support
enhance *v.* intensify, amplify, strengthen
ensue *v.* follow, result
entice *v.* lure, attract, tempt
era *n.* period, age, stage
essential *adj.* critical, vital, crucial, key
esteem *v.* cherish, honor, admire
evade *v.* escape, avoid, elude
exhaustive *adj.* thorough, complete, comprehensive
exhilarating *adj.* exciting, thrilling, stimulating
extravagant *adj.* excessive, lavish

fable *n.* story, tale
fabled *adj.* legendary, mythical, famous
facet *n.* aspect, point, feature
faint *adj.* dim, pale, faded, indistinct
falter *v.* hesitate, waver
fancy *adj.* decorative, ornate, elaborate
fasten *v.* attach, secure
fatal *adj.* mortal, lethal, deadly
fatigue *v.* tire, exhaust
　　　　 n. exhaustion, weariness
faulty *adj.* flawed, inferior
feasible *adj.* possible
feeble *adj.* weak, fragile, frail
ferocious *adj.* fierce, savage, violent
fiery *adj.* (1) blazing, burning
　　　　 (2) passionate, fervent
fitting *adj.* suitable, proper, apt, appropriate
flagrant *adj.* blatant, obvious
flaw *n.* defect, imperfection, fault
flee *v.* escape, go away, elude
flimsy *adj.* fragile, frail, weak, feeble
forego *v.* abandon, give up
foremost *adj.* chief, principal, leading
fragment *n.* particle, piece, bit
fragrant *adj.* aromatic, scented
fraudulent *adj.* false, deceptive, deceitful
fundamental *adj.* basic, integral, elemental
fusion *n.* blend, merger, union
futile *adj.* useless, pointless, vain

Exercise: Complete the following sentences by filling in the blanks with vocabulary items (A), (B), or (C) according to the context of the sentences.

1. In 1906 much of San Francisco was destroyed by an earthquake and the fires that _____.
   (A) evaded   (B) ensued   (C) encountered

2. The writer H. P. Lovecraft wrote many _____ stories about the supernatural.
   (A) essential   (B) eerie   (C) exhilarating

3. A new _____ of aviation began in 1947 when Chuck Yeager became the first pilot to fly faster than the speed of sound.
   (A) fable   (B) endeavor   (C) era

4. Vance Packard's book *The Hidden Persuaders* deals with the tactics advertisers use to _____ . consumers.
   (A) endorse   (B) entice   (C) enhance

5. Riding a roller coaster is an _____ experience.
   (A) exhilarating   (B) elegant   (C) exhaustive

6. Before the plane takes off, passengers must _____ their seat belts.
   (A) flee   (B) emit   (C) fasten

7. In the United States, citizens are _____ to vote at the age of eighteen.
   (A) essential   (B) elderly   (C) eligible

8. Barracudas are _____ predators, sometimes called the "tigers" of tropical waters.
   (A) elegant   (B) futile   (C) ferocious

9. Certain gases such as neon _____ light when exposed to an electrical current.
   (A) emit   (B) evade   (C) esteem

10. People make more mistakes when they are _____ than when they are fresh.
    (A) exhaustive   (B) eminent   (C) fatigued

11. A _____ in a jewel makes it less valuable.
    (A) fragment   (B) facet   (C) flaw

12. Honeysuckle is a shrub that has _____ white or yellowish blossoms.
    (A) flagrant   (B) fragrant   (C) exhilarating

Mini-Lesson 3.7

gala *adj.*   festive, happy, joyous
gap *n.*   break, breach, opening
garrulous *adj.*   talkative
gaudy *adj.*   showy, flashy, ostentatious
genial *adj.*   pleasant, cordial, agreeable
gentle *adj.*   mild, kind, considerate
genuine *adj.*   authentic, real, valid
glitter *v.*   sparkle, shine, glisten
glory *n.*   grandeur, majesty, fame
gorgeous *adj.*   attractive, beautiful
graphic *adj.*   clear, explicit, vivid
grasp *v.*   (1) grab, seize, grip
              (2) understand
grave *adj.*   serious, grievous, solemn, somber
gregarious *adj.*   sociable, friendly
grim *adj.*   severe, dreary, bleak, somber
grip *v.*   hold, grasp, seize
grueling *adj.*   exhausting, difficult
gullible *adj.*   innocent, naive, trusting, credulous

hamper *v.*   delay, obstruct, hinder, block
haphazard *adj.*   random, chance, aimless, unplanned
hardship *n.*   difficulty, trouble
harm *v.*   injure, damage
harmony *n.*   accord, agreement, peace
harness *v.*   control, use
harsh *adj.*   severe, rough, strict
hasty *adj.*   quick, rushed, hurried
hazardous *adj.*   dangerous, risky
heed *v.*   obey, listen to, mind, follow
hinder *v.*   block, obstruct, hamper
hoist *v.*   lift, raise, pick up
hue *n.*   color, tint, shade
huge *adj.*   enormous, giant, colossal, immense
hurl *v.*   pitch, throw, fling

Exercise: Complete the following sentences by filling in the blanks with vocabulary item (A), (B), or (C) according to the context of the sentences.

1. During the construction of skyscrapers, cranes are used to _____ building materials to the upper floors.
   (A) hurl   (B) harness   (C) hoist

2. The twenty-six mile-long Boston Marathon is a _____ foot race.
   (A) gorgeous   (B) grueling   (C) hasty

3. Dams can _____ the power of rivers, but they may also destroy their beauty.
   (A) heed   (B) harness   (C) hurl

4. The more facets a diamond has, the more it _____.
   (A) glitters   (B) harms   (C) hinders

5. Many people celebrate the New Year with _____ parties.
   (A) gala   (B) grueling   (C) haphazard

6. Think it over for a while; don't make a _____ decision.
   (A) genuine   (B) gullible   (C) hasty

7. Bad weather _____ the rescue crews trying to locate the life rafts.
   (A) hampered   (B) grasped   (C) harnessed

8. Gorillas look ferocious but are actually quite _____ creatures.
   (A) gaudy   (B) gentle   (C) gorgeous

9. Con artists are criminals who take advantage of _____ people by tricking them and taking their money.
   (A) garrulous   (B) grim   (C) gullible

10. Working with toxic materials is a _____ occupation.
    (A) hazardous   (B) genial   (C) haphazard

11. Most minnows are tiny fish, but squaw fish, which can weigh as much as 30 pounds, are actually _____ minnows.
    (A) gregarious   (B) gaudy   (C) huge

12. At first, the results of the experiment seemed _____, but finally a pattern emerged.
    (A) haphazard   (B) grave   (C) genuine

Mini-Lesson 3.8

idea *n.* concept, notion, thought
ideal *n.* model, standard
     adj. perfect, model, standard
idle *adj.* (1) inactive, unused, inert
        (2) lazy
illusion *n.* fantasy, delusion
imaginary *adj.* unreal, fantastic, fictitious
imaginative *adj.* creative, original, clever
immense *adj.* huge, enormous, massive, colossal
impair *v.* damage, injure, spoil
impartial *adj.* fair, unbiased, neutral
implement *v.* realize, achieve, put into practice, execute
         n. tool, utensil, instrument
incessant *adj.* constant, ceaseless, continuous
increment *n.* increase, amount
indifferent *adj.* uncaring, apathetic, unconcerned
indigenous *adj.* native
indispensable *adj.* necessary, essential, vital, critical
indistinct *adj.* unclear, blurry, hazy
induce *v.* persuade, convince, coax
inept *adj.* incompetent, awkward, clumsy
inexorable *adj.* unstoppable
infamous *adj.* notorious, shocking
infinite *adj.* limitless, endless, boundless
infinitesimal *adj.* tiny, minute, minuscule
ingenious *adj.* brilliant, imaginative, clever, inventive
ingenuous *adj.* naive, trusting
inhabit *v.* live, dwell, reside, populate
inhibit *v.* control, limit, restrain
initial *adj.* original, first, beginning, introductory
innate *adj.* natural, inborn
intense *adj.* powerful, heightened, concentrated
intricate *adj.* complicated, complex, involved
irate *adj.* angry, furious, upset

jagged *adj.* rough, rugged, uneven, irregular
jeopardy *n.* danger, hazard, risk, threat
jolly *adj.* joyful, happy, cheerful, jovial
jolt *v.* shock, jar, shake up, surprise
   n. blow, surprise, shock

keen *adj.* (1) sharp
         (2) shrewd, clever, bright
         (3) eager, enthusiastic
key *adj.* principal, crucial, important
knack *n.* skill, ability, aptitude, talent

Exercise: Complete the following sentences by filling in the blanks with vocabulary item (A), (B), or (C) according to the context of the sentences.

1. Many people feel that Hawaii has an almost _____ climate.
   (A) idle   (B) impartial   (C) ideal

2. A plow is a farm _____ used to break up soil and prepare the land for planting.
   (A) increment   (B) knack   (C) implement

3. A laser uses a synthetic ruby to concentrate light into an extremely _____ high-energy beam.
   (A) intense   (B) indistinct   (C) imaginary

4. Jesse James was an _____ outlaw, well-known as a bank robber and gunfighter.
   (A) inept   (B) ingenuous   (C) infamous

5. Antibiotics _____ the growth of bacteria.
   (A) inhabit   (B) jolt   (C) inhibit

6. Optical _____ deceive the eye with tricks of perception.
   (A) illusions   (B) ideals   (C) increments

7. Stockholders may be too _____ to vote in corporate elections, so they let management vote for them by proxy.
   (A) infamous   (B) indifferent   (C) ingenious

8. The heavily populated states of Ohio, Pennsylvania, Illinois, and Michigan are _____ states for any candidate in a presidential election.
   (A) initial   (B) impartial   (C) key

9. A virus is so _____ that it can be seen only with an electron microscope.
   (A) infinite   (B) imaginary   (C) infinitesimal

10. The _____ character Falstaff is one of Shakespeare's finest comic creations.
    (A) keen   (B) jolly   (C) irate

11. Anyone can learn basic cooking skills; you don't need a special _____.
    (A) knack   (B) idea   (C) implement

12. Alcohol _____ one's ability to drive.
    (A) jolts   (B) impairs   (C) induces

13. The _____ people of Australia were called Aborigines by the English settlers.
    (A) indigenous   (B) ingenuous   (C) innate

14. The rhinoceros has a poor sense of sight but _____ sense of smell.
    (A) an impartial   (B) an inept   (C) a keen

15. The equator is _____ line running around the center of the Earth.
    (A) an imaginative   (B) a jagged   (C) an imaginary

16. A glacier's progress is slow but _____.
    (A) inexorable   (B) impartial   (C) infinite

Mini-Lesson 3.9

lack *v.*   need, require, not have
    n.   shortage, absence, scarcity
lag *v.*   fall behind, go slowly
lavish *adj.*   luxurious, plentiful, abundant
lax *adj.*   careless, negligent, loose
legendary *adj.*   mythical, fabled, famous
legitimate *adj.*   proper, authentic, valid
lethargic *adj.*   slow, listless, sluggish, lazy
likely *adj.*   probable, plausible
linger *v.*   remain, stay
link *v.*   join, connect, fasten, bind
    n.   connection, tie
long *v.*   desire, wish for
lucid *adj.*   clear, plain, understandable
lull *v.*   soothe, calm, quiet
    n.   pause, break
lure *v.*   attract, tempt, entice
lurid *adj.*   shocking, sensational, graphic
lurk *v.*   prowl, sneak, hide
luster *n.*   shine, radiance, brightness
luxurious *adj.*   lavish, elegant, plush

magnificent *adj.*   majestic, impressive, splendid
magnitude *n.*   size, extent, amount
mandatory *adj.*   necessary, obligatory, compulsory
mar *v.*   damage, ruin, deface, spoil
memorable *adj.*   unforgettable, impressive, striking
mend *v.*   fix, repair
mild *adj.*   gentle, moderate, calm
mingle *v.*   blend, combine, mix
minute *adj.*   tiny, minuscule, infinitesimal
monitor *v.*   observe, watch
moral *adj.*   honorable, ethical
morale *n.*   spirit, confidence, attitude
murky *adj.*   unclear, cloudy
mysterious *adj.*   puzzling, strange
mythical *adj.*   legendary, imaginary, fictional

Exercise: Complete the following sentences by filling in the blanks with vocabulary item (A), (B), or (C) according to the context of the sentences.

1. It's difficult for scuba divers to see when the water is _____.
   (A) murky   (B) lucid   (C) magnificent

2. In most cultures, it is traditional to prepare _____ meals to celebrate holidays.
   (A) lurid   (B) lethargic   (C) lavish

3. Parents often sing to children to _____ them to sleep.
   (A) lurk   (B) mingle   (C) lull

4. Julius Caesar is known not only for his military and political skills but also for his _____, informative writing.
   (A) lucid   (B) lurid   (C) lethargic

5. A cobbler _____ damaged shoes.
   (A) mars   (B) mends   (C) lacks

6. One of the _____ exhibits of Impressionist art is found at the Art Institute of Chicago.
   (A) mildest   (B) most memorable   (C) most lucid

7. The USO is a service organization which entertains U.S. troops and improves their _____.
   (A) morale   (B) luster   (C) lack

8. Quarks are _____ particles that are believed to be the fundamental unit of matter.
   (A) massive   (B) minute   (C) mythical

9. Some people like to _____ after dinner over coffee and dessert.
   (A) lag   (B) long   (C) linger

10. Paperback novels in the 1940's and 1950's often had _____ covers to attract readers' attention.
    (A) lurid   (B) murky   (C) legitimate

11. One problem caused by a rising crime rate is a _____ of space in prisons.
    (A) lag   (B) lack   (C) link

12. The _____ lumberjack Paul Bunyan and his giant blue ox Babe are two of the most famous characters in American folklore.
    (A) legendary   (B) moral   (C) minute

Mini-Lesson 3.10

negligible *adj.* unimportant, trivial
nimble *adj.* graceful, agile
notable *adj.* remarkable, conspicuous, striking
notify *v.* inform
notion *n.* idea, concept, thought
notorious *adj.* infamous, disreputable
novel *adj.* new, innovative

objective *n.* goal, purpose, aim
  adj. fair, impartial, unbiased, neutral
oblong *adj.* oval
obscure *adj.* unfamiliar, ambiguous, little-known
obsolete *adj.* antiquated, out-of-date, outmoded
odd *adj.* strange, unusual, peculiar, curious
offspring *n.* young, children, descendants
ominous *adj.* threatening, menacing, dangerous
opulent *adj.* luxurious, plush, affluent
ornamental *adj.* ornate, decorative, elaborate
outgoing *adj.* (1) open, friendly
    (2) departing, leaving
outlook *n.* (1) opinion, view
    (2) prospect, forecast
outstanding *adj.* excellent, exceptional, notable, well-known
overall *adj.* general, comprehensive
overcast *adj.* cloudy, gloomy
overcome *v.* subdue, defeat, overwhelm
overlook *v.* ignore, disregard, neglect
oversee *v.* supervise, manage, direct
oversight *n.* error, mistake, omission
overt *adj.* open, obvious
overtake *v.* catch up with, reach
overwhelm *v.* (1) astonish, astound, surprise
    (2) inundate, overcome, engulf
    (3) conquer, defeat, overpower

Exercise: Complete the following sentences by filling in the blanks with vocabulary item (A), (B), or (C) according to the context of the sentences.

1. Who should be _____ in case you are involved in an accident?
   (A) overlooked   (B) notified   (C) overtaken

2. Many of the world's most _____ restaurants are located in luxury hotels.
   (A) outgoing   (B) opulent   (C) overt

3. The black clouds of a gathering thunderstorm look quite _____.
   (A) ominous   (B) negligible   (C) overcast

4. Pulitzer Prizes are awarded to _____ journalists, novelists, poets, and other writers.
   (A) objective   (B) outstanding   (C) notorious

5. An _____ plant is cultivated chiefly for its beauty.
   (A) opulent   (B) obscure   (C) ornamental

6. Franklin D. Roosevelt was able to _____ his physical handicaps; he didn't permit them to interfere with his living a vigorous life.
   (A) oversee   (B) overcome   (C) overtake

7. The poetry of Ezra Pound is sometimes difficult to understand because it contains so many _____ references.
   (A) notable   (B) obscure   (C) objective

8. The Bessemer Process was once the most common method of making steel, but today this process is considered _____.
   (A) odd   (B) novel   (C) obsolete

9. Gregarious people are friendly and _____.
   (A) overcast   (B) nimble   (C) outgoing

10. The town planning commission said that their financial _____ for the next fiscal year was optimistic; they expect increased tax revenues.
    (A) outlook   (B) oversight   (C) notion

11. The new play was so successful that the demand for tickets was _____.
    (A) odd   (B) overwhelming   (C) negligible

12. A book's table of contents provides readers with an _____ idea of what the book is about.
    (A) outgoing   (B) overt   (C) overall

13. Because ultraviolet light from the Sun can penetrate clouds, it is possible to get a sunburn on an _____ day.
    (A) obscure   (B) overcast   (C) opulent

14. Although the accident appeared serious, only a _____ amount of damage was done.
    (A) novel   (B) notable   (C) negligible

Mini-Lesson 3.11

pace *n.* rate, speed
painstaking *adj.* careful, conscientious, thorough
pale *adj.* white, colorless, faded, blanched
paltry *adj.* unimportant, minor, trivial
particle *n.* piece, bit, fragment
path *n.* trail, track, way, route
peculiar *adj.* (1) strange, odd, puzzling
        (2) distinctive, characteristic, unique, special
penetrate *v.* enter, go through, pierce, puncture
perceive *v.* observe, sense, notice
peril *n.* danger, hazard, risk, threat
perpetual *adj.* constant, endless, eternal
perplexing *adj.* puzzling, mystifying, confusing
pierce *v.* penetrate, puncture, stab
plausible *adj.* likely, credible, believable
plead *v.* appeal, beg
plush *adj.* opulent, luxurious, elegant
ponder *v.* consider, think about, reflect on
portion *n.* share, part, section, segment
postpone *v.* delay, put off, defer
potent *adj.* strong, powerful, effective
pounce *v.* jump, leap, spring
precious *adj.* expensive, costly, rare
precise *adj.* accurate, exact, definite
premier *adj.* (1) first, opening, earliest, initial
        (2) chief, leading, foremost
pressing *adj.* urgent, crucial, compelling
pretext *n.* excuse, pretense, justification
prevail *v.* succeed, win, triumph
prevalent *adj.* common, widespread, popular
prior *adj.* earlier, preceding, former
probe *v.* investigate, inquire into
procure *v.* obtain, acquire, secure
profound *adj.* important, significant, deep
profuse *adj.* plentiful, abundant
prompt *adj.* punctual, timely
prosper *v.* flourish, thrive, succeed
provoke *v.* (1) irritate, anger, annoy
        (2) cause, trigger
prudent *adj.* careful, sensible, cautious
pulverize *v.* crush, grind, powder
pungent *adj.* (1) bitter, harsh, biting, sharp
        (2) spicy, sour, tart
pursue *v.* chase, follow, seek
puzzling *adj.* mystifying, confusing, baffling

Exercise: Complete the following sentences by filling in the blanks with vocabulary item (A), (B), or (C) according to the context of the sentences.

1. Turquoise is not valuable enough to be classified as a _____ stone.
   (A) perpetual   (B) pale   (C) precious

2. Employers often require job applicants to have _____ experience in the field.
   (A) premier   (B) prior   (C) plush

3. Hospitals define *urgent care* as medical care given to somewhat less _____ medical problems than emergency care.
   (A) perplexing   (B) pressing   (C) prudent

4. Tool makers must have the ability to work very _____ in order to meet exact specifications.
   (A) precisely   (B) profoundly   (C) plausibly

5. NASA _____ the launch of space vehicles on account of bad weather or technical problems.
   (A) ponders   (B) postpones   (C) probes

6. _____ of dust in the air may trigger allergies in some people.
   (A) Portions   (B) Pretexts   (C) Particles

7. The Appalachian Trail, extending from Maine to Georgia, is the longest continuous hiking _____ in the world.
   (A) pace   (B) peril   (C) path

8. When a tiger spots its prey, it crouches down and then _____.
   (A) pleads   (B) ponders   (C) pounces

9. X-rays cannot _____ lead.
   (A) provoke   (B) penetrate   (C) pursue

10. Morphine, a form of synthetic heroin, is a _____ painkiller.
    (A) potent   (B) pungent   (C) paltry

11. Sherlock Holmes, a fictional detective, solved many _____ crimes.
    (A) puzzling   (B) prevalent   (C) prompt

12. Mallows are wildflowers that grow _____ in prairies, woods, and marshes.
    (A) profusely   (B) profoundly   (C) preciously

13. Certain spices give foods a _____ taste.
    (A) prudent   (B) pungent   (C) pale

14. Trade with Britain and the West Indies allowed colonial seaports such as Boston to _____.
    (A) postpone   (B) provoke   (C) prosper

15. A _____ investor never takes unnecessary financial risks.
    (A) perplexing   (B) prudent   (C) premier

Mini-Lesson 3.12

quaint *adj.*   charming, picturesque, curious, old-fashioned
quake *v.*   shiver, shake, tremble
quandary *n.*   problem, dilemma, predicament
quarrel *n.*   argument, dispute, disagreement
quest *n.*   search, journey, venture

radiant *adj.*   bright, shiny, glowing
ragged *adj.*   torn, tattered, worn
range *n.*   scope, extent, spectrum
      v.   (1) extend, vary, fluctuate
         (2) roam, wander
rash *adj.*   thoughtless, careless, reckless
raw *adj.*   (1) uncooked
         (2) unprocessed, unrefined, crude
raze *v.*   demolish, level, knock down
recede *v.*   retreat, go back, subside, withdraw
reckless *adj.*   careless, rash
recollect *v.*   recall, remember
recount *v.*   narrate, tell
refine *v.*   improve, process, purify
refuge *n.*   shelter, haven, retreat
rehearse *v.*   practice, train, go over
reliable *adj.*   dependable, trustworthy
relish *v.*   enjoy, savor, like
remedy *n.*   treatment, cure
remnant *n.*   remainder, balance, fragment
remote *adj.*   isolated, distant
renowned *adj.*   famous, celebrated, notable
resent *v.*   dislike, take offense at
retract *v.*   withdraw, pull back
riddle *n.*   puzzle, mystery
rigid *adj.*   (1) stiff, unbending
         (2) harsh, severe, strict
rip *v.*   tear, cut, slash
ripe *adj.*   mature, developed, grown, ready
risky *adj.*   dangerous, hazardous, treacherous
roam *v.*   travel, wander, range
rough *adj.*   (1) uneven, jagged, rugged
         (2) difficult
         (3) impolite
route *n.*   way, course, path, road
rudimentary *adj.*   elementary, fundamental, primitive
rugged *adj.*   (1) jagged, rough, uneven
         (2) strong, sturdy
rumor *n.*   gossip, hearsay, story
rural *adj.*   agricultural
ruthless *adj.*   cruel, brutal, vicious

Exercise: Complete the following sentences by filling in the blanks with vocabulary item (A), (B), or (C) according to the context of the sentences.

1. Motorists can be fined for driving _____ .
   (A) recklessly   (B) reliably   (C) ruthlessly

2. Millions of bison once _____ the plains of North America.
   (A) recollected   (B) ripped   (C) roamed

3. Musicians have to _____ before performing.
   (A) rehearse   (B) resent   (C) recount

4. At the end of the Ice Age, glaciers began to _____ .
   (A) quake   (B) raze   (C) recede

5. Big Sur, a wild section of California's coastline, is known for its _____ beauty.
   (A) ragged   (B) rash   (C) rugged

6. Wetlands provide _____ for many species of birds, reptiles, mammals, and amphibians.
   (A) riddles   (B) refuge   (C) rumors

7. The pirate Blackbeard had a reputation for being a harsh, _____ man.
   (A) ruthless   (B) quaint   (C) reliable

8. Wrecking balls are used to _____ buildings.
   (A) rip   (B) quake   (C) raze

9. The northernmost section of the Rocky Mountains, the Brooks Range, is located in a _____ section of Alaska.
   (A) remote   (B) reliable   (C) radiant

10. Dogs can hear a greater _____ of sounds than humans.
    (A) remnant   (B) quandary   (C) range

11. Patent medicine salesmen have claimed to have _____ for all types of ailments, from cancer to baldness to the common cold.
    (A) remedies   (B) quandaries   (C) riddles

12. Visitors to Vermont delight in the beautiful scenery and picturesque villages and enjoy staying in some of the _____ country inns there.
    (A) rudimentary   (B) ragged   (C) quaint

13. _____ materials have less economic value than processed materials.
    (A) Raw   (B) Rash   (C) Renowned

14. Many medieval stories dealt with _____ , such as the story of the search for the Grail.
    (A) quarrels   (B) quandaries   (C) quests

15. The Tennessee Valley Authority helped bring cheap electricity to farmers in the _____ South.
    (A) reliable   (B) rural   (C) rugged

Mini-Lesson 3.13

salvage *v.* save, rescue, recover, retrieve
scale *v.* climb
       n. (1) range, spectrum
           (2) proportion
scarce *adj.* rare, sparse
scatter *v.* disperse, spread
scent *n.* aroma, fragrance, odor, smell
scrap *v.* abandon, get rid of
     n. piece, fragment
seasoned *adj.* experienced, veteran
secluded *adj.* hidden, isolated, secret
sensational *adj.* thrilling, exciting, shocking
serene *adj.* quiet, peaceful, calm, tranquil
sever *v.* cut, slice off, break
severe *adj.* (1) harsh, strict, austere
             (2) undecorated, plain
shatter *v.* break, smash, fragment
sheer *adj.* (1) steep, sharp, abrupt
          (2) transparent, thin, filmy
shimmer *v.* shine, glow, glisten, gleam
shred *v.* rip up, tear up
shrewd *adj.* clever, sly
shrill *adj.* piercing, high-pitched
shun *v.* avoid, stay away from
shy *adj.* timid, reserved
significant *adj.* important, vital, major
signify *v.* symbolize, stand for, indicate
sketch *v.* draw
      n. drawing, picture, diagram
slender *adj.* thin, slim, slight
sluggish *adj.* slow, listless, lazy, lethargic
sly *adj.* cunning, clever, shrewd
soak *v.* wet, drench, saturate
solace *n.* comfort, consolation, relief
somber *adj.* serious, grave, solemn
sort *v.* classify, categorize
    n. type, kind, variety
sound *n.* noise
      adj. safe, solid, secure

Exercise: Complete the following sentences by filling in the blanks with vocabulary item (A), (B), or (C) according to the context of the sentences.

1. Skunks use a pungent _____ as their first line of defense.
   (A) scent   (B) scrap   (C) sound

2. One of the most popular peaks for mountain climbers to _____ is El Capitan in Yosemite National Park.
   (A) scale   (B) soak   (C) shun

3. Foxes are not particularly rare, but they are not often seen because they are so _____.
   (A) sluggish   (B) somber   (C) shy

4. The Civil Rights Act of 1964 was a particularly _____ piece of legislation.
   (A) serene   (B) significant   (C) slender

5. _____ workers are more valuable to employers than beginners.
   (A) Shrill   (B) Seasoned   (C) Sluggish

6. The Shakers were a strict religious group that _____ all types of pleasure.
   (A) scrapped   (B) shunned   (C) sketched

7. Denver's plan to build a subway system was _____ in the 1970's.
   (A) scattered   (B) sorted   (C) scrapped

8. Even after a ship has sunk, its cargo can often be _____.
   (A) severed   (B) shattered   (C) salvaged

9. Some economists believe that the best way to get a _____ economy moving again is to cut taxes.
   (A) sensational   (B) sluggish   (C) shrewd

10. Government bonds and blue-chip stocks are _____ investments.
    (A) sound   (B) shy   (C) scarce

11. If a person's spinal cord is _____, paralysis results.
    (A) soaked   (B) severed   (C) salvaged

12. Silk is a _____ fabric.
    (A) sheer   (B) shrewd   (C) slender

Mini-Lesson 3.14

span *v.* extend, bridge, connect
    n. length, extent, range
spawn *v.* generate, create, produce
    n. offspring, descendants
specific *adj.* definite, particular, exact
specimen *n.* example, sample
spectacular *adj.* dramatic, sensational, impressive
spell *n.* interval, period, time
spirited *adj.* lively, energetic, vigorous
splendid *adj.* excellent, superb, wonderful
spoil *v.* (1) ruin, mar
       (2) decay, deteriorate, decompose, rot
spot *v.* locate, find, see
    n. (1) location, site
       (2) mark, stain, speck
spur *v.* stimulate, impel, encourage, provoke
    n. inducement, stimulus
stable *adj.* steady, secure, stationary, fixed
stage *v.* present, put on
    n. grade, step, level, phase
stain *v.* color, tint, discolor, dye
    n. spot, mark, blemish
stale *adj.* (1) old, dry
       (2) dull, trite, uninteresting
stall *v.* halt, delay, put off
stately *adj.* dignified, grand, magnificent, elegant
steep *adj.* sheer, perpendicular
stern *adj.* firm, severe, strict, harsh
strife *n.* conflict, dispute, struggle
strive *v.* attempt, try
struggle *v.* fight, argue, dispute
    n. conflict, strife, battle, effort
stubborn *adj.* rigid, uncompromising, obstinate
sturdy *adj.* strong, rugged, well-built
subsequent *adj.* later, succeeding, following, ensuing
subtle *adj.* indirect, suggestive, implied
suitable *adj.* appropriate, correct, apt
summit *n.* peak, apex, zenith
sundry *adj.* miscellaneous, diverse, various
superb *adj.* excellent, splendid
supplant *v.* replace, substitute for
supple *adj.* pliable, flexible, bendable
sway *v.* (1) wave, rock, swing, bend
       (2) persuade, influence
sweeping *adj.* complete, exhaustive, general, comprehensive
swift *adj.* fast, quick, rapid
swivel *v.* rotate, spin, turn

Exercise: Complete the following sentences by filling in the blanks with vocabulary item (A), (B), or (C) according to the context of the sentences.

1. High pressure cells may bring brief warm _____ even in the middle of winter.
   (A) struggles   (B) spells   (C) spans

2. The _____ cliffs of the Na Pali Coast of Kauai Island, Hawaii, rise some 4,000 feet from the sea.
   (A) still   (B) steep   (C) subtle

3. The process of refining oil involves a number of _____.
   (A) specimens   (B) spots   (C) stages

4. In high winds, skyscrapers will _____ slightly.
   (A) swivel   (B) sway   (C) stall

5. Severe thunderstorms may _____ tornadoes.
   (A) spot   (B) spawn   (C) span

6. The snow-covered _____ of Mount Hood is the highest point in the state of Oregon.
   (A) spur   (B) summit   (C) span

7. D. W. Griffith was the first director of _____ films. These were movies made on a colossal scale.
   (A) specific   (B) suitable   (C) spectacular

8. Cheetahs are the _____ of all land mammals, with top speeds of up to 70 miles per hour.
   (A) stalest   (B) subtlest   (C) swiftest

9. Salt can be used to keep meat from _____.
   (A) struggling   (B) spoiling   (C) stalling

10. Because they must be able to break a path through icebound waters, icebreakers have to be very _____ boats.
    (A) stern   (B) sturdy   (C) supple

11. Most people who divorce _____ remarry.
    (A) specifically   (B) subsequently   (C) stubbornly

12. A roadbed supplies a _____ base for a highway.
    (A) stable   (B) sundry   (C) sweeping

13. The geographical center of the North American continent is a _____ near Balta, North Dakota.
    (A) spot   (B) stage   (C) summit

14. Many medical tests require a blood _____.
    (A) spell   (B) specimen   (C) stain

15. Because of their protective coloration, ghost crabs are hard to _____.
    (A) spur   (B) spawn   (C) spot

Mini-Lesson 3.15

tact *n.* diplomacy, discretion, poise
tale *n.* story
tame *v.* domesticate, master
      adj. docile, domesticated, gentle
tamper (with) *v.* interfere (with)
tangle *v.* knot, twist
tart *adj.* sour, tangy, piquant
taunt *v.* insult, mock, torment
tedious *adj.* boring, dull, tiresome
telling *adj.* effective, convincing, forceful
temperate *adj.* mild, moderate
tempting *adj.* alluring, attractive, enticing
tender *adj.* (1) delicate, soft
         (2) gentle, loving
         (3) sore, painful
thaw *v.* melt
thorough *adj.* complete, comprehensive
thoroughfare *n.* street, boulevard
thrifty *adj.* economical, inexpensive
thrilling *adj.* exciting, stimulating, stirring
thrive *v.* prosper, flourish
thwart *v.* prevent, impede, obstruct
tidings *n.* news, message
tilt *v.* incline, slope
timid *adj.* fearful, shy, retiring
tint *v.* color, hue, shade, tone
    n. color, stain, dye
tiresome *adj.* tedious, dull, boring
toil *v.* labor, work
    n. exertion, labor, work
tolerant *adj.* patient, impartial, open-minded
torment *v.* taunt, abuse, bully
torrent *n.* flood, deluge
tow *v.* haul, draw, pull, drag
toxic *adj.* poisonous, noxious
trait *n.* characteristic, feature, quality
treacherous *adj.* dangerous, hazardous
trickle *n.* drip, leak
triumph *n.* victory, success, achievement
    v. win, succeed, prevail
trivial *adj.* unimportant, minor
trying *adj.* demanding, difficult, troublesome
tug *v.* pull, draw

Exercise: Complete the following sentences by filling in the blanks with vocabulary item (A), (B), or (C) according to the context of the sentences.

1. Citric acid gives citrus fruit their _____ taste.
   (A) temperate   (B) toxic   (C) tart

2. The use of robots and automated machinery has eliminated certain _____ factory jobs.
   (A) tedious   (B) thrilling   (C) timid

3. One should never buy food or medicine if the packaging has obviously been _____.
   (A) tangled   (B) thwarted   (C) tampered with

4. Alfred Hitchcock directed a number of _____ psychological dramas; among the most exciting are *Psycho* and *North by Northwest*.
   (A) timid   (B) trivial   (C) thrilling

5. Tides are caused by the _____ of the Moon's gravity.
   (A) tangle   (B) torrent   (C) tug

6. Many people find chocolate _____.
   (A) tempting   (B) tender   (C) temperate

7. Peachtree Street is the main _____ in Atlanta.
   (A) triumph   (B) thoroughfare   (C) tilt

8. In her book *Silent Spring*, Rachel Carson wrote about insecticides and their _____ effects on animal life.
   (A) tiresome   (B) tender   (C) toxic

9. In the desert, dry creek beds may turn into raging _____ after heavy rainstorms.
   (A) trickles   (B) torrents   (C) toils

10. Barley can be grown almost anywhere in the temperate zone. Unlike most other grains, it even _____ at high altitudes.
    (A) tampers   (B) thrives   (C) thaws

11. _____ such as hair color and eye color are inherited genetically from one's parents.
    (A) Traits   (B) Triumphs   (C) Tints

12. Washington Irving collected and interpreted many famous old _____, including the legends of Rip Van Winkle and the Headless Horseman.
    (A) tales   (B) tidings   (C) traits

Mini-Lesson 3.16

ultimate *adj.* (1) conclusive, definite, final
                  (2) maximum, highest, best
unbearable *adj.* intolerable, agonizing
uncouth *adj.* impolite, rude, vulgar
undertake *v.* try, attempt
ungainly *adj.* awkward, unskillful
uniform *adj.* consistent, regular
unique *adj.* singular, one of a kind, special
unruly *adj.* unmanageable, disorganized, disorderly
unsound *adj.* defective, faulty, unsafe
uphold *v.* support, sustain
upkeep *n.* maintenance
uproar *n.* disorder, disturbance, commotion
urge *v.* encourage, advise, implore
urgent *adj.* pressing, compelling
utensil *n.* tool, implement, device
utter *v.* say, speak
      adj. total, absolute, complete

vacant *adj.* empty, unoccupied
vague *adj.* unclear, uncertain, ambiguous
vain *adj.* (1) useless, pointless
            (2) conceited, proud
valid *adj.* genuine, authentic, legitimate
vanish *v.* disappear
variable *adj.* changeable, shifting
vast *adj.* huge, enormous, extensive, immense
venomous *adj.* poisonous
verbose *adj.* talkative, wordy
verge *n.* brink, edge, threshold
vessel *n.* (1) container, bottle
              (2) ship
vex *v.* irritate, anger, annoy
viable *adj.* (1) alive, living
              (2) feasible, practical, possible
vicinity *n.* area, proximity, zone
vigorous *adj.* dynamic, energetic, spirited
vital *adj.* critical, crucial, key, essential
vivid *adj.* clear, distinct, graphic
vow *v.* promise, pledge, swear
      n. oath, promise, pledge

Exercise: Complete the following sentences by filling in the blanks with vocabulary item (A), (B), or (C) according to the context of the sentences.

1. To be fair, laws must be _____ applied to all persons.
   (A) urgently   (B) vaguely   (C) uniformly

2. The rattlesnake is the most common _____ snake in the United States.
   (A) ungainly   (B) venomous   (C) variable

3. The League of Women Voters _____ all citizens to vote.
   (A) urges   (B) vexes   (C) upholds

4. In his novel *The Red Badge of Courage*, Stephen Crane _____ describes a Civil War battle.
   (A) vividly   (B) uniformly   (C) vitally

5. An Erlenmeyer flask is a glass _____ used in chemistry labs.
   (A) vessel   (B) vow   (C) verge

6. Aerobics is _____ form of exercise.
   (A) a viable   (B) an uncouth   (C) a vigorous

7. A metropolitan area consists of a central city and any suburban areas in its _____.
   (A) vicinity   (B) vessel   (C) upkeep

8. Special police tactics are required to deal with riots or _____ crowds.
   (A) ungainly   (B) unruly   (C) unsound

9. The kidneys play a _____ role in maintaining health by removing impurities from the bloodstream.
   (A) vivid   (B) viable   (C) vital

10. The myth of Narcissus tells the story of a handsome but _____ young man who stares at his reflection in a pool of water for so long that he turns into a flower.
    (A) vain   (B) ungainly   (C) verbose

11. The fork has been used as an eating _____ since at least the twelfth century.
    (A) vessel   (B) utensil   (C) verge

12. The Great Plains cover _____ area.
    (A) a vast   (B) a viable   (C) an ultimate

Mini-Lesson 3.17

wage *n.*   salary, pay, earnings
wander *v.*   roam, travel, range
wane *v.*   shrink, decrease, decline
ware *n.*   good, merchandise
warp *v.*   deform, bend, twist
wary *adj.*   careful, cautious, alert
weary *adj.*   tired, exhausted, fatigued
well-to-do *adj.*   rich, wealthy, affluent
wholesome *adj.*   healthy, nutritious, beneficial
wicked *adj.*   evil, corrupt, immoral
widespread *adj.*   extensive, prevalent, sweeping
wily *adj.*   crafty, cunning, shrewd
wise *adj.*   astute, prudent, intelligent
withdraw *v.*   retreat, pull out, remove
wither *v.*   dry, shrivel, wilt
withhold *v.*   reserve, retain, hold back
witty *adj.*   comic, clever, amusing
woe *n.*   trouble, distress, sorrow
wonder *v.*   think about, speculate, ponder
          n.   marvel, miracle
wound *v.*   injure, hurt
          n.   injury

yearn *v.*   desire, crave, want
yield *v.*   (1) give up, surrender
                (2) produce, supply
          n.   production, output, crop

zealous *adj.*   enthusiastic, eager
zenith *n.*   peak, tip, apex
zone *n.*   area, vicinity, region

Exercise: Complete the following sentences by filling in the blanks with vocabulary item (A), (B), or (C) according to the context of the sentences.

1. If boards become wet, they may _____.
   (A) wither   (B) yield   (C) warp

2. Whole grains and fresh fruit and vegetables are _____ foods.
   (A) wicked   (B) wholesome   (C) well-to-do

3. You must be _____ when buying a used car; be sure the engine is in good condition.
   (A) weary   (B) zealous   (C) wary

4. In the past, many salesmen tried to sell their _____ door- to-door.
   (A) wares   (B) woes   (C) yields

5. Humorist Will Rogers wrote many _____ newspaper columns.
   (A) wily   (B) weary   (C) witty

6. Congress sets the minimum _____, which is the lowest amount of money workers may be paid per hour.
   (A) wage   (B) yield   (C) zone

7. Intelligent policies are needed so that public funds are used _____.
   (A) wholesomely   (B) zealously   (C) wisely

8. Fertilizers can increase farmers' _____.
   (A) wonders   (B) yields   (C) woes

9. Some superstitions are familiar to many cultures. For example, there is a _____ belief that black cats bring bad luck.
   (A) widespread   (B) wily   (C) wicked

10. A green belt is a parklike _____ around a city in which no development is permitted.
    (A) zenith   (B) wound   (C) zone

Guide to the Test of Written English (TWE)

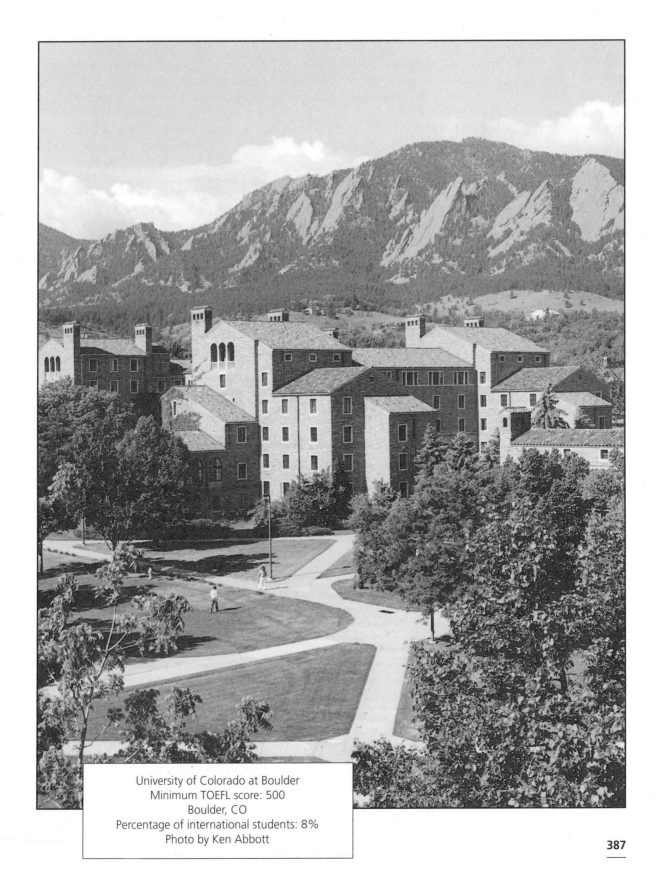

University of Colorado at Boulder
Minimum TOEFL score: 500
Boulder, CO
Percentage of international students: 8%
Photo by Ken Abbott

About the Test of Written English

Introduction

The TWE is given before the other three sections of TOEFL. It is currently given five times a year: in February, May, August, September, and October. There is no additional fee required to take TWE. This part of the test was added at the request of a number of universities that wanted an assessment of their prospective students' writing skills.

TWE differs from the rest of TOEFL in that it is **productive.** Instead of choosing one of four answer choices, you must write your own short essay. TWE consists of a single essay topic called a **prompt**; there is no choice as to what to write about. You have thirty minutes in which to write an essay based on the prompt. A typical TWE answer is about 200 to 300 words long and is divided into four or five paragraphs.

The most common type of TWE prompt asks you to write a contrast/opinion essay. In this type of essay, you must contrast two points of view, then defend one of those positions. Another type of essay asks you to select some development, invention, or phenomenon and explain its importance. Essay prompts that ask you to interpret the information given in a graph or chart are no longer given. Prompts are carefully chosen to avoid anything controversial, upsetting, or unfair to a particular group.

At ETS, your essay is read by at least two trained readers who score it "holistically." In other words, the essay is not judged according to individual errors you might make but by the overall organization, development, clarity, and effectiveness of your writing. The score is based on a scale of 1 to 6; half-point scores (5.5, 4.5, and so on) are also given. The scoring system ETS uses is similar to the one that follows. (You can use this chart to estimate your TWE score when you take the TWE Practice Tests.)

Score	Explanation of Score
6	Strongly indicates the ability to write a well-organized, well-developed, and logical essay. Specific examples and details support the main ideas. All the elements of the essay are unified and cohesive. A variety of sentence structures are used successfully, and sophisticated vocabulary is employed. Grammatical errors are infrequent, but a few minor mistakes may occur.
5	Indicates the ability to write an organized, developed, and logical essay. The main ideas are adequately supported by examples and details. Sentence structure may be less varied than that of a level 6 essay, and vocabulary less sophisticated. Some grammatical errors will appear.
4	Indicates a moderate ability to write an acceptable essay. Although main ideas may be adequately supported, weaknesses in organization and development will be apparent. Sentence structure and vocabulary may lack sophistication or be used inappropriately. Grammatical errors may be frequent.
3	Indicates some minimal ability in writing an acceptable essay, but involves serious weaknesses in organization and development. Significant sentence-structure and vocabulary problems occur, and there are frequent grammatical errors that sometimes make the writer's ideas difficult to comprehend.
2	Indicates the inability to write an acceptable essay. Organization and development are very weak or nonexistent. Lacks unity and cohesion. Few if any specific details may be given in support of the writer's ideas. If details are given, they may seem inappropriate. Significant and frequent errors in grammar occur throughout the essay. Writer may not have fully understood the essay topic.
1	Strongly indicates the inability to write an acceptable essay. No apparent development or organization. Sentences may be brief and fragmentary and unrelated to one another. Significant grammatical errors occur throughout the essay and make it difficult to

understand any of the author's ideas. Writer may have completely misunderstood the essay topic.

OFF   Did not write on the topic assigned.

1NR   Did not write the essay.

The average score TWE score is between 3.5 and 4.0. TWE is scored separately from the rest of the test and has no effect on your overall TOEFL score.

IMPORTANT: Don't take TWE if you don't need to! Many universities that require TOEFL scores do NOT require TWE scores. There is no way to cancel your TWE score without canceling your TOEFL score, and a low TWE score may have a negative effect on your application *even though you were not required to take the test.* If you are certain that you won't need a TWE score, then try to sign up for a test administration when TWE is not given if at all possible.

Following are two sample TWE prompts and essays that respond to those prompts. (Note: These essays are based on composite student essays. They have been edited to correct errors in grammar and mechanics.)

Sample TWE Prompt A

Some people believe that money spent on space research benefits all of humanity. Others take the opposite view and say that money for this type of research is wasted. Discuss these two positions, using examples. Tell which view you agree with and explain why.

<u>Notes</u>

<u>Intro:</u> Space research + 50 years:
            expensive—$ well spent or wasted?

– ideas	+ ideas
costs billions; also human resources; no real benefits	consumer products; e.g., PC's, freeze-dried foods, pacemakers
e.g., trip to Moon only brought back rocks	weather & communication satellites
many important uses for this $ on Earth:	scientific knowledge about planets, Moon, even Earth
e.g., education environment housing	

<u>Conclu:</u> As shown, many benefits—also, human race needs challenge just as individuals do—therefore, space research is worth all the money spent

For over fifty years, a number of nations have been involved in the exploration of outer space. This research has been very costly, of course. Has this money been well-spent or wasted?

Some people believe that all or most space research should be eliminated because of its incredible expense, not only in terms of money, but also in terms of scientific and human resources. These people point out the fact that it cost billions of dollars to send astronauts to the Moon, but all they brought back were some worthless rocks. These people say that the money and effort now being wasted in outer space could be spent on more important projects right here on Earth, such as providing housing for homeless people, improving the education system, saving the environment, and finding cures for diseases.

However, other people believe that space research has provided many benefits to humanity. They point out that hundreds of useful products, from personal computers to heart pacemakers to freeze-dried foods, are the direct or indirect results of space research. They say that weather and communication satellites, which are also products of space programs, have benefited people all over the globe. In addition to these practical benefits, supporters of the space program point to the scientific knowledge that has been acquired about the Sun, the Moon, the planets, and even our own Earth as a result of space research.

I agree with those people who support space research and want it to continue. Space research, as shown, has already brought many benefits to humanity. Perhaps it will bring even more benefits in the future, ones that we can't even imagine now. Moreover, just as individual people need challenges to make their lives more interesting, I believe the human race itself needs a challenge, and I think that the peaceful exploration of outer space provides just such a challenge.

Notice that in the first sample TWE, the writer organized the essay in the following way:

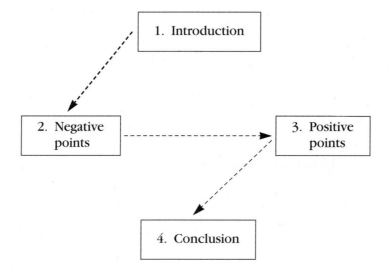

Sample TWE Prompt B

Developments in transportation such as the invention of the automobile have had an enormous impact on modern society. Choose another development in transportation that you think is of great importance. Give reasons for your selection.

<u>Notes</u>

<u>Intro:</u> One of most important develop is internat'l jet transport—since '50's—because of speed & rel. low costs, has changed way people think

<u>Speed:</u> 100 yrs ago, took weeks to cross ocean: today, few hrs—this has changed people's concept of space—world smaller

<u>Low costs:</u> In past, only wealthy could travel comfortably; poor people had to save for years—today, more and more people can travel: businessmen
                                               students
                                               tourists

<u>Conclusion:</u> countries no longer so isolated; people think of world as they used to think of their own hometowns

I believe that one of the most important developments in transportation has been the development of international jet transport. Since this style of transportation appeared in the 1950's, it has had some revolutionary effects. Because of the high speeds and the relatively low cost of this type of travel, it has changed the way people look at the world.

The most obviously important characteristic of jet travel is the high speed involved. A hundred years ago, it took weeks to cross the Atlantic or Pacific oceans by ship. Today, those same trips can be completed in a matter of hours. One can attend a meeting in Paris and have dinner in New York the same day. These amazing speeds have changed people's concepts of space. Today the world is much smaller than it was in the past.

Another important aspect of jet travel is its relatively low cost. An international journey one hundred years ago was extremely expensive. Only wealthy people could afford to travel comfortably, in first class. Poor people had to save for years to purchase a ticket, and the conditions in which they traveled were not very good. Today it is possible for more and more people in every country to travel in comfort. Thus it is possible for businesspeople to do business all over the world, for students to attend universities in other countries, and for tourists to take vacations anywhere in the world.

In conclusion, the speed and low cost of international jet travel have changed the world. Individual nations are not as isolated as they were in the past, and people now think of the whole planet as they once thought of their own hometowns.

Notice that the writer organized the second sample essay as follows:

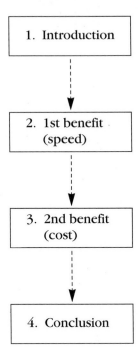

Ten Keys to Writing the TWE Essay

KEY #1: Budget your time carefully.

You have only a half-hour in which to complete your work. You should use your time more or less as shown below:

Reading and thinking about the prompt	2 minutes
Planning and taking notes	3 minutes
Writing the essay	22 minutes
Checking the essay	3 minutes

As with all parts of TOEFL, be familiar with the directions for TWE so that you don't have to waste time reading them.

KEY #2: Read the question carefully.

You must write on the prompt exactly as it is given, so be sure you understand it. If you write about another topic, you won't receive a score at all. If you don't completely address the topic, you will receive a lower score.

KEY #3: Brainstorm!

Before you begin to write, spend a minute or two just "brainstorming." Just think about the prompt and the best way to approach it. Remember: there is no "correct" answer for TWE. You can choose any position as long as you can adequately support it. While you're brainstorming, jot down your ideas in the section marked "NOTES".

KEY #4: Plan your essay before you write.

You don't have to write out a formal outline with Roman numerals, capital letters, and so on. However, you *should* make some notes. By following your notes, you can organize your essay *before* you write, leaving you free to concentrate on the task of writing.

When making notes, don't worry about writing complete, grammatical sentences; use abbreviations if possible. The point of taking notes is to simply get your ideas down on paper as quickly as possible.

KEY #5: Be sure your handwriting is as clear and legible as possible.

Handwriting that is hard to read may unconsciously prejudice the readers who are grading your essay. Be sure your handwriting is not too small or too large.

KEY #6: Follow a clear, logical organization.

All TWE essays should consist of three basic parts: an **introductory paragraph**, a **body** that consists of two or three paragraphs, and a **concluding paragraph**. You need to include all of these elements in your essay. The introduction states the main idea of the essay in one sentence called the **thesis statement** and may provide some background about that idea. The body develops the main idea brought up in the introduction. Specific examples are given to make the thesis statement seem stronger and more believable to the reader. The conclusion evaluates and summarizes the material that is in the body. It provides the reader with a sense of closure—the feeling that the essay is really finished, not that the writer simply ran out of time.

The exact plan of organization you use depends on the type of prompt you are given. The following patterns could be used for the two main types of prompt commonly given. Of course, these are not the only patterns that could be used in writing TWE essays, but they are effective plans for organizing your ideas.

Prompt Type A: Contrast/Opinion

Introduction:	Paragraph 1:	Present the two sides of the issue; give a brief amount of background information.
Body:	Paragraph 2:	Discuss the negative side of the issue; give examples.
	Paragraph 3:	Discuss the positive side of the issue; give examples.
Conclusion:	Paragraph 4:	Express you own opinion about the issue; give specific reasons for your decision.

Prompt Type B: Explain the Importance of a Development, Invention, or Phenomenon

Introduction:	Paragraph 1:	Explain what development you have chosen to write about, and why.
Body:	Paragraph 2:	Discuss one aspect of why this development is important; give examples.
	Paragraph 3:	Discuss another aspect of why this development is important; give examples.
Conclusion:	Paragraph 4:	Summarize the points made in paragraphs 2 and 3.

Now look back at the two TWE sample essays to see if they follow these patterns of organization.

KEY #7: Use concrete examples and specific reasons.

Whenever you make a general statement, you should support it with specific examples. Don't just say, "Computers are important to modern business." Give specific examples of how computers can benefit businesses. If you state an opinion, give reasons. Don't just say, "I believe television is harmful to children." Explain exactly why you think television hurts children.

KEY #8: Use signal words to indicate transitions.

Signal words can be used to join paragraph to paragraph and sentence to sentence. These words make your essay clearer and easier to follow. Some of these expressions and their meanings are given below.

Expressions Used to List Points, Examples, or Reasons

First example or reason
    First, . . .
    The first example is . . .
    The first reason for this is that . . .

Additional examples or reasons
    Second . . . (Third, Fourth)
    A second (third, fourth) example is that . . .
    Another example is . . .
    Another reason is that . . .
    In addition, . . .
    Furthermore, . . .
    Moreover, . . .

Final examples or reasons
    Finally, . . .

To give individual examples
    For example, . . .
    For instance, . . .
    To give a specific example, . . .
    X is an example of Y.

To show contrast
    However, . . .
    On the other hand, . . .
    Nevertheless, . . .

To show a conclusion
    Therefore, . . .
    Consequently, . . .

To show similarity
    Likewise, . . .
    Similarly, . . .

To begin a concluding paragraph
    In conclusion, . . .
    In summary, . . .

Examples of the Use of Signal Words

I agree with the idea of stricter gun control for a number of reasons. *First,* statistics show that guns are not very effective in preventing crime. *Second,* accidents involving guns frequently occur. *Finally,* guns can be stolen and later used in crimes.

I believe that a good salary is an important consideration when looking for a career. *However,* the nature of the work is more important to me. *Thus,* I would not accept a job that I did not find rewarding.

For me, the reasons for living in an urban area are stronger than the reasons for living in a rural community. *Therefore,* I agree with those people who believe it is an advantage to live in a big city.

Look back at the sample essays again. Did the authors use signal words to show transitions?

KEY #9: Use a variety of sentence types.

Good writing in English consists of a more or less equal balance between short, simple sentences consisting of only one clause and longer sentences containing two or more clauses. Therefore, make an effort to use sentences of various lengths.

You should also vary sentence structures. Begin some sentences with prepositional phrases or subordinate clauses.

Examples of various sentence types
Instead of . . .

I agree with this idea for several reasons.

Try . . .

For several reasons, I agree with this idea.

Instead of . . .

I support Idea A even though Idea B has some positive attributes.

Try . . .

Even though Idea B has some positive attributes, I support Plan A.

KEY #10: Check your essay for errors.

Allow a few minutes to proofread the essay. However, don't make any major changes at this time. Don't cross out long sections or try to add a lot of new material. Look for obvious errors in punctuation, spelling, and capitalization, as well as common grammatical mistakes: subject-verb agreement, wrong tense use, incorrect use of plurals, incorrect word forms, and so on. If you have ever taken a writing class in English, look at the corrections the teacher made on your papers to see what types of mistakes you commonly make, and look for these.

Three Practice TWE Tests

The following exams are very similar to actual TWE tests. Time yourself carefully while taking these practice tests. You can use the scoring chart on page 388 to estimate your score. If you are taking an English course, you may want to ask your English teacher to score your test and to make recommendations for improving your essay.

Practice TWE Directions

30 Minutes

1. When you are ready, turn the page and carefully read the essay prompt.

2. Before you begin writing, think about the prompt. You will probably want to make some notes to organize your thoughts. Use only the space marked NOTES to write notes or an outline.

3. Write on only *one* topic. If you do not write on the topic given, you will not receive a score.

4. Your essay should be clear and precise. Support your ideas with facts. The quality of your writing is of more importance than the quantity, but you will probably want to write more than one paragraph.

5. Begin your essay on the first line of the essay page. Use the next page if you need to. Write as neatly as possible. Don't write in large letters. Don't skip lines or leave large margins.

6. Check your essay after you have finished. Give yourself enough time to read over your essay and make minor revisions *before* the end of the exam.

7. After 30 minutes, stop writing and put your pencil down.

TWE Essay Prompt 1

Some people believe that advertising on television is generally beneficial to viewers. Others take the position that television advertising has primarily negative effects. Which position do you agree with? Explain your decision, using specific examples.

<u>NOTES</u>

Use this space for essay notes only. Write the final version of your essay on the next two pages.

Name:_____

Write your essay here.

_____

_____

_____

_____

_____

_____

_____

_____

_____

_____

_____

_____

_____

_____

_____

_____

_____

_____

_____

_____

_____

_____

_____

_____

_____

_____

_____

_____

_____

_____

TWE Essay Prompt 2

Some people say that university students should concentrate on their own field of study, and that all the classes they take should be closely related to that subject. Others believe that university students should get a general education, taking classes in many fields before concentrating on a single field. Discuss both points of view, using concrete examples. Which view do you support? Give reasons for your choice.

NOTES

Use this space for essay notes only. Write the final version of your essay on the next two pages.

Name:_____

Write your essay here.

_____

_____

_____

_____

_____

_____

_____

_____

_____

_____

_____

_____

_____

_____

_____

_____

_____

_____

_____

_____

_____

_____

_____

_____

_____

_____

_____

_____

_____

TWE Essay Prompt 3

Good, affordable housing is one of the factors that make a community a desirable place to live. Choose one other factor that you feel is important. Give specific reasons for your choice.

<u>NOTES</u>

Use this space for essay notes only. Write the final version of your essay on the next two pages.

Name:_____

Write your essay here.

_____
_____
_____
_____
_____
_____
_____
_____
_____
_____
_____
_____
_____
_____
_____
_____
_____
_____
_____
_____
_____
_____
_____
_____
_____
_____
_____
_____
_____
_____
_____
_____
_____
_____
_____

Three Complete Practice Tests

Students at Cornell University

About Taking the Practice Tests

One of the best ways to ensure success on TOEFL is to take realistic practice exams. The three tests in this book are accurate and up to date, reflecting the changes in format that ETS instituted in 1995. They duplicate actual exams in terms of format, content, and level of difficulty. They cover all the types of items that commonly appear on actual exams. All items have been pre-tested.

These tests can be used in the classroom or by self-study learners. In order to get the most from these practice tests, suggestions for both types of users are given below.

Using the Tests in the Classroom

- The test should be given under actual testing conditions—for example, desks should be arranged as they would be during a test, and no talking should be allowed. If possible, each test should be given in its entirety rather than section by section.
- Sections 2 and 3 should be carefully timed, and students should not work ahead.
- Students should mark answers on the answer sheets provided at the end of the book.
- An analysis and a discussion of all three parts of the exam is an important follow-up for the practice tests. These activities can be done as a class or in small groups. Test-takers should understand *why* a choice is correct.

Using the Tests for Self-Study

- Take each test all at one time rather than section by section.
- Use a watch to time yourself carefully during Sections 2 and 3. Do not go ahead to the next section even if you finish early. Do not give yourself extra time even if you haven't finished the section.
- Sit at a desk or table, not in an easy chair or on a sofa, and work away from distractions such as a television or a stereo.
- Mark your answers on the answer sheets rather than in the book.
- After completing the test, mark incorrect answers but do not write in the corrections. Instead, go back and answer these questions a second time.
- Read the explanations in the Written Expression section and the Reading Comprehension section for all items that you answer incorrectly.
- If you have time, take the entire test over again on another answer sheet. (You may want to make photocopies of the answer sheets in the back of the book before you begin.)
- Use the scoring charts in the back of this book to calculate your scores for each practice test.
- Keep track of your scores in the Personal Score Record in the Scoring section of this book. If you have consistently lower scores on one section of the test, you might want to review the corresponding section in the *Guide*.
- If you have enough time, take the entire test over on a separate answer sheet.

Scoring the Practice Tests

The level of difficulty varies slightly from one TOEFL test to another. ETS uses a statistical process called "test equating" to adjust each set of scores. The chart given here can only be used to determine a range of scores. ETS, of course, reports your score as a single number, not as a range.

After completing each test, obtain a raw score for each of the three sections by counting the number of correct answers in the three sections. Then look at the conversion chart to determine the range of scaled scores for each section. Add the three low scores from the range of scores for each section, then the three high scores. Multiply both totals by 10 and divide by 3. Your "actual" TOEFL score will lie somewhere in that range of numbers.

For example, suppose that you had 32 correct answers in Listening Comprehension, 29 in Structure and Written Expression, and 37 in Reading Comprehension:

	Raw Score (number correct)	Range of Scaled Scores (from conversion chart)
Section 1	32	49–50
Section 2	29	50–52
Section 3	37	53–54

49 + 50 + 53 = 152
50 + 52 + 54 = 156

152 × 10 = 1,520 ÷ 3 = 507
156 × 10 = 1,560 ÷ 3 = 520

Your score on the practice test would be between 507 and 520.

SCORE CONVERSION CHART					
Section 1		Section 2		Section 3	
Raw Scores	Range of Scaled Scores	Raw Scores	Range of Scaled Scores	Raw Scores	Range of Scaled Scores
48–50	65–68	39–40	64–68	48–50	65–67
45–47	57–64	36–38	60–64	45–47	57–64
42–44	55–57	34–35	57–59	42–44	56–57
39–41	54–55	31–33	53–56	39–41	55–56
36–38	52–54	29–30	50–52	36–38	53–54
33–35	50–52	27–28	49–50	33–35	51–52
30–32	49–50	24–26	48–49	30–32	50–51
27–29	47–48	21–23	46–48	27–29	48–49
24–26	45–47	18–20	43–45	24–26	46–47
21–23	44–45	15–17	39–42	21–23	44–45
18–20	42–44	12–14	36–38	18–20	42–44
15–17	39–41	9–11	32–35	15–17	39–41
12–14	36–38	6–8	28–32	12–14	36–38
9–11	33–36	3–5	24–27	9–11	33–36
6–8	29–32	0–2	20–23	6–8	29–32
3–5	25–28			3–5	25–28
0–2	23–24			0–2	21–24

Personal Score Record

Practice Test 1

Section 1 Range of Scores	Section 2 Range of Scores	Section 3 Range of Scores	Total Range of Scores

Practice Test 2

Section 1 Range of Scores	Section 2 Range of Scores	Section 3 Range of Scores	Total Range of Scores

Practice Test 3

Section 1 Range of Scores	Section 2 Range of Scores	Section 3 Range of Scores	Total Range of Scores

Practice Test 1

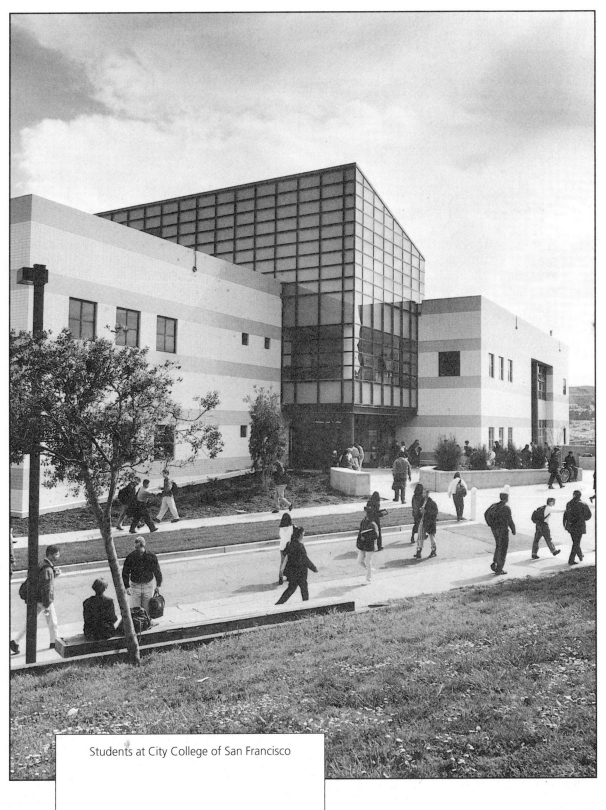

Students at City College of San Francisco

Listening Comprehension

This section tests your ability to comprehend spoken English. It is divided into three parts, each with its own directions. You are *not* permitted to turn the page during the reading of the directions or to take notes at any time.

Part A

Directions: Each item in this part consists of a brief conversation involving two speakers. Following each conversation, a third voice will ask a question. You will hear the conversations and questions only once, and they will *not* be written out.

When you have heard each conversation and question, read the four answer choices and select the *one*—(A), (B), (C), or (D)—that best answers the question based on what is directly stated or on what can be inferred. Then fill in the space on your answer sheet that matches the letter of the answer that you have selected.

Here is an example.

You will hear:

Sample Answer

You will read: (A) Open the window.
(B) Move the chair.
(C) Leave the room.
(D) Take a seat.

From the conversation you find out that the woman thinks the man should put the chair over by the window. The best answer to the question, "What does the woman think the man should do?" is (B), "Move the chair." You should fill in (B) on your answer sheet.

1. (A) She doesn't have an appointment.
   (B) Her problem is complicated.
   (C) She must live somewhere else.
   (D) Her apartment isn't far away.

2. (A) She can use his phone if she wants.
   (B) There's no charge for phone calls.
   (C) His phone is out of order too.
   (D) She can call him later if she likes.

3. (A) He couldn't find it.
   (B) It was too hard to solve.
   (C) It was simpler than he'd thought.
   (D) He solved it even though it was hard.

4. (A) Cleaned up after cooking.
   (B) Forgot to put the pots and pans away.
   (C) Went out in a terrible storm.
   (D) Put some plants in the kitchen.

5. (A) He studied forestry in school.
   (B) He worked in a forest.
   (C) He read a lot of books about them.
   (D) His father taught him.

6. (A) How many pages he must write.
   (B) What Professor Barclay discussed.
   (C) How long the class lasted.
   (D) When the paper is due.

7. (A) She doesn't like any music except classical.
   (B) There is some classical music she doesn't like.
   (C) She likes classical music, but she can't play it.
   (D) Classical music doesn't interest her at all.

8. (A) He was too busy to take it.
   (B) He did well on it.
   (C) He left some questions unanswered on it.
   (D) He took it two times.

9. (A) Breaking the glass.
   (B) Warming the lid.
   (C) Hitting the lid.
   (D) Filling the jar.

10. (A) It was too expensive.
    (B) She bought it at the shop next door.
    (C) It was given to her as a gift.
    (D) She paid very little for it.

11. (A) She doesn't want to discuss the traffic.
    (B) She didn't have to go downtown today.
    (C) She was in the traffic herself.
    (D) She thinks the traffic was better today.

12. (A) The classes aren't interesting.
    (B) Classes have been canceled.
    (C) The weather is pleasant.
    (D) It isn't very sunny today.

13. (A) Gary thanked her for the tape player.
    (B) She wants her tape player back.
    (C) She's glad Gary is finally here.
    (D) Gary can keep her tape player.

14. (A) Stay inside and read it.
    (B) Look in it for advertisements for umbrellas.
    (C) Cover her head with it.
    (D) Throw it away.

15. (A) She originally supported Margaret.
    (B) She can no longer support Ed.
    (C) Ed has dropped out of the race.
    (D) She's not interested in the election.

Go on to the next page

1 1 1 1 1 1 1 1 1 1 1

16. (A) She and her brother painted the apartment.
    (B) Her brother owes her some money.
    (C) Her brother painted the apartment by himself.
    (D) She painted her brother's apartment.

17. (A) Give him a map.
    (B) Cut his hair for him.
    (C) Drive him to the lake.
    (D) Show him another route.

18. (A) Hanging it.
    (B) Buying it.
    (C) Painting it.
    (D) Framing it.

19. (A) Borrow Stephanie's computer.
    (B) Get her own computer.
    (C) Save some money.
    (D) Stay home and complete her assignment.

20. (A) He doesn't need to practice anymore.
    (B) His team has won a lot of games.
    (C) He doesn't want to play volleyball.
    (D) His team needs to improve.

21. (A) She seems to be feeling better.
    (B) She has quite an imagination.
    (C) She takes beautiful pictures.
    (D) She's too sick to go out.

22. (A) Lou has been here once before.
    (B) They'll start when Lou arrives.
    (C) The meeting has already started.
    (D) Everyone is getting hungry.

23. (A) She thinks they're reasonably priced.
    (B) She doesn't like them at all.
    (C) She'd buy them if she had enough money.
    (D) She doesn't need them, but she still likes them.

24. (A) To improve his game quickly.
    (B) To take more lessons.
    (C) To train with a professional.
    (D) To teach people to play tennis.

25. (A) Wrap the present.
    (B) Play a game.
    (C) Point out a problem.
    (D) End the discussion.

26. (A) He wants to buy some books.
    (B) Two of the books are the same.
    (C) He needs some matches.
    (D) The couple is a good match.

27. (A) Neither street goes downtown.
    (B) California Street is better than Oak Street.
    (C) There's not enough time to go downtown.
    (D) He can take either street.

28. (A) It was hard to hear.
    (B) It wasn't true.
    (C) It was surprising.
    (D) It wasn't very interesting.

29. (A) The handle on the suitcase is broken.
    (B) His hands are already full.
    (C) The luggage is too heavy for him.
    (D) He'll be happy to help.

30. (A) She had to prepare for an exam.
    (B) She'd passed the physics test.
    (C) She was going camping.
    (D) She'd dropped the physics class.

Go on to the next page

Part B

Directions: This part of the test consists of extended conversations between two speakers. After each of these conversations, there are a number of questions. You will hear each conversation and question only once, and the questions are *not* written out.

When you have heard the question, read the four answer choices and select the *one*—(A), (B), (C), or (D)—that best answers the question based on what is directly stated or on what can be inferred. Then fill in the space on your answer sheet that matches the letter of the answer that you have selected.

Don't forget: During actual exams, taking notes or writing in your test book is *not* permitted.

1 1 1 1 1 1 1 1 1 1 1

31. (A) They are both studying social anthropology.
    (B) Both of them are going to the museum on Saturday.
    (C) They both have the same teacher.
    (D) Both of them have studied anthropology before.

32. (A) In the morning.
    (B) In the afternoon.
    (C) In the evening.
    (D) Only on Saturday.

33. (A) Relationships between parents and children.
    (B) The tools used by ancient people.
    (C) Leadership in contemporary society.
    (D) Marriage customs.

34. (A) He found it uninteresting.
    (B) He found it useful.
    (C) He found it fascinating.
    (D) He found it difficult.

35. (A) At a university.
    (B) At a television station.
    (C) At a newspaper office.
    (D) At a hospital.

36. (A) He needs a well-paying position.
    (B) He was told to by a professor.
    (C) He wants the experience.
    (D) He recently lost another job.

37. (A) Drama.
    (B) Journalism.
    (C) Telecommunications.
    (D) Medicine.

38. (A) Talk to Ms. Wagner.
    (B) Drop a class.
    (C) Change his major.
    (D) Complete a form.

Go on to the next page ➤

Part C

Directions: This part of the test consists of several talks, each given by a single speaker. After each of these talks, there are a number of questions. You will hear each talk and question only once, and the questions are *not* written out.

    When you have heard each question, read the four answer choices and select the *one*—(A), (B), (C), or (D)—that best answers the question based on what is directly stated or on what can be inferred. Then fill in the space on your answer sheet that matches the letter of the answer that you have selected.

    Here is an example.

    You will hear:

    Now here is a sample question.

    You will hear:

Sample Answer

You will read: (A) Philosophy.
                (B) Meteorology.
                (C) Astronomy.
                (D) Photography.

The lecture concerns a lunar eclipse, a topic that would typically be discussed in an astronomy class. The choice that best answers the question, "In what course is this lecture probably being given?" is (C), "Astronomy." You should fill in (C) on your answer sheet.

    Here is another sample question.

    You will hear:

Sample Answer

You will read: (A) The Earth's shadow moves across the Moon
                (B) Clouds block the view of the Moon.
                (C) The Moon moves between the Earth and the Sun.
                (D) The Sun can be observed without special equipment.

1 **1** **1** **1** **1** **1** **1** **1** **1** **1** **1** **1**

From the lecture you learn that a lunar eclipse occurs when the Earth moves between the Sun and the Moon and the shadow of the Earth passes across the Moon. The choice that best answers the question, "According to the speaker, which of the following occurs during a lunar eclipse?" is (A), "The Earth's shadow moves across the Moon."

Don't forget: During actual exams, taking notes or writing in your test book is *not* permitted.

1 1 1 1 1 1 1 1 1 1 1 1

39. (A) A football game.
    (B) Jet transportation.
    (C) The *Hindenburg* disaster.
    (D) Lighter-than-air craft.

40. (A) Early twentieth century airships.
    (B) Blimps.
    (C) Jet aircraft.
    (D) Modern airships.

41. (A) The age of zeppelins ended in disaster there.
    (B) It was there that the first blimp was designed.
    (C) Helium was first substituted for hydrogen there.
    (D) It was there that the last zeppelin was built.

42. (A) They would be safer.
    (B) They would use less fuel.
    (C) They would be faster.
    (D) They could fly higher.

43. (A) The Uniform Time Act.
    (B) The role of daylight saving time in wartime.
    (C) Ways to save energy.
    (D) The history of daylight saving time.

44. (A) In the spring.
    (B) In the summer.
    (C) In the fall.
    (D) In the winter.

45. (A) As confusing.
    (B) As innovative.
    (C) As amusing.
    (D) As wasteful.

46. (A) To standardize daylight saving time.
    (B) To establish year-round daylight saving time.
    (C) To abolish daylight saving time.
    (D) To shorten daylight saving time.

47. (A) A program the city is starting.
    (B) The uses of recycled materials.
    (C) A proposed schedule.
    (D) A recent newspaper article.

48. (A) Newspapers.
    (B) Aluminum cans.
    (C) Plastic bottles.
    (D) Glass containers.

49. (A) The north.
    (B) The east.
    (C) The south.
    (D) The central.

50. (A) Look in the local newspaper.
    (B) Keep listening to radio.
    (C) Stop by the recycling center.
    (D) Call the radio station.

THIS IS THE END OF SECTION 1, LISTENING COMPREHENSION.

STOP WORK ON SECTION 1.

Structure and Written Expression

Time: 25 minutes

This section tests your ability to recognize grammar and usage suitable for standard written English. This section is divided into two parts, each with its own directions.

Structure

Directions: Items in this part are incomplete sentences. Following each of these sentences, there are four words or phrases. You should select the *one* word or phrase—(A), (B), (C), or (D)—that best completes the sentence. Then fill in the space on your answer sheet that matches the letter of the answer that you have selected.

Example I

Pepsin _____ an enzyme used in digestion.

(A) that
(B) is
(C) of
(D) being

Sample Answer

Ⓐ ● Ⓒ Ⓓ

This sentence should properly read "Pepsin is an enzyme used in digestion." You should fill in (B) on your answer sheet.

Example II

_____ large natural lakes are found in the state of South Carolina.

(A) There are no
(B) Not the
(C) It is not
(D) No

Sample Answer

Ⓐ Ⓑ Ⓒ ●

This sentence should properly read "No large natural lakes are found in the state of South Carolina." You should fill in (D) on your answer sheet.

As soon as you understand the directions, begin work on this part.

Go on to the next page ➤

② ② ② ② ② ② ② ② ② ② ②

1. _____ team sports require cooperation.
   (A) Of all
   (B) They are all
   (C) All
   (D) Why are all

2. Anyone who has ever pulled weeds from a garden _____ roots firmly anchor plants to the soil.
   (A) is well aware of
   (B) is well aware that
   (C) well aware
   (D) well aware that

3. Centuries of erosion have exposed _____ rock surfaces in the Painted Desert of northern Arizona.
   (A) in colors of the rainbow
   (B) colored like a rainbow
   (C) rainbow-colored
   (D) a rainbow's coloring

4. The higher the temperature of a molecule, _____ .
   (A) the more energy it has
   (B) than it has more energy
   (C) more energy has it
   (D) it has more energy

5. Frontier surgeon Ephraim MacDonald had to perform operations _____ anesthesia.
   (A) no
   (B) not having
   (C) without
   (D) there wasn't

6. _____ young, chimpanzees are easily trained.
   (A) When are
   (B) When
   (C) They are
   (D) When they

7. A person of _____ age may suffer from defects of vision.
   (A) every
   (B) some
   (C) certain
   (D) any

8. _____ have settled, one of their first concerns has been to locate an adequate water supply.
   (A) Wherever people
   (B) There are people who
   (C) Whether people
   (D) People

9. If a bar magnet is _____, the two pieces form two complete magnets, each with a north and south pole.
   (A) broken
   (B) broke
   (C) breaking
   (D) break

10. The type of plant and animal life living in and around a pond depends on the soil of the pond, _____, and the pond's location.
    (A) what the quality of the water is
    (B) how is the water quality
    (C) the quality of the water
    (D) what is the water quality

11. Clifford Holland, _____ civil engineer, was in charge of the construction of the first tunnel under the Hudson River.
    (A) he was a
    (B) a
    (C) being a
    (D) who, as a

Go on to the next page

2 2 2 2 2 2 2 2 2 2 2 2

12. _____ parrots are native to tropical regions is untrue.
    (A) That all
    (B) All
    (C) Why all
    (D) Since all

13. A major concern among archaeologists today is the preservation of archaeological sites, _____ are threatened by development.
    (A) of which many
    (B) many of them
    (C) which many
    (D) many of which

14. In 1775 Daniel Boone opened the Wilderness Trail and made _____ the first settlements in Kentucky.
    (A) possibly it was
    (B) as possible
    (C) possible
    (D) it possible

15. Rarely _____ seen far from water.
    (A) spotted turtles
    (B) spotted turtles are
    (C) have spotted turtles
    (D) are spotted turtles

Go on to the next page ➜

Written Expression

Directions: The items in this part have four underlined words or phrases—(A), (B), (C), and (D). You must identify the *one* underlined expression that must be changed for the sentence to be correct. Then find the number of the question on your answer sheet and fill in the space corresponding to the letter of the answer that you have selected.

Example I   Sample Answer

Lenses may <u>to have</u> either <u>concave</u> <u>or</u> convex <u>shapes</u>.
          A   B   C   D

This sentence should read "Lenses may have either concave or convex shapes." You should therefore select answer (A).

Example II   Sample Answer

<u>When</u> painting a fresco, an artist <u>is applied</u> paint <u>directly</u> to the damp plaster <u>of a wall</u>.
A   B   C   D

This sentence should read "When painting a fresco, an artist applies paint directly to the damp plaster of a wall." You should therefore select answer (B).

As soon as you understand the directions, begin work on this section.

Go on to the next page ➤

2 2 2 2 2 2 2 2 2 2 2 2

16. Ceramics can be harder, <u>light</u>, and more <u>resistant</u> to <u>heat</u> than <u>metals</u>.
                A   B   C   D

17. <u>Not everyone</u> realizes <u>that</u> the <u>most largest</u> organ of the <u>human</u> body is the skin.
         A   B   C   D

18. Mold is <u>extremely</u> <u>destruction</u> to <u>books</u> in <u>a library</u>.
             A   B   C   D

19. Sidney Lanier <u>achieved</u> fame both <u>as a poet</u> <u>or</u> as a symphony <u>musician</u>.
                A   B   C   D

20. The <u>horses</u> used <u>play</u> polo are not of any <u>special</u> breed or of any <u>definite</u> size.
         A   B   C   D

21. A tapestry <u>consists of</u> a foundation weave, called the warp, <u>which across</u> are passed different
               A   B

    colored threads, called the weft, forming decorative <u>patterns</u>.
      C   D

22. The <u>works</u> of early American woodcarvers had <u>many</u> artistic qualities, but these craftsmen
         A   B

    probably <u>did not</u> think of <u>them</u> as artists.
           C   D

23. Perhaps mankind's <u>first</u> important <u>musical</u> influence <u>were</u> the songs of <u>birds</u>.
               A   B   C   D

24. The techniques of science and <u>magic</u> are quite <u>different</u>, but their basic aims—<u>to understand</u>
                       A   B   C

    and control nature—<u>they are</u> very similar.
                  D

25. It was in a cave near Magdalena, New Mexico, <u>when</u> the <u>oldest</u> <u>known</u> ears of cultivated corn
                                        A   B   C

    were <u>discovered</u>.
         D

26. The fossil remains of <u>much</u> extinct <u>mammals</u> have been <u>found</u> in the tar pits at Rancho La Brea
                  A   B   C

    <u>in</u> Los Angeles.
     D

27. Sharks <u>can detect</u> minute <u>electrical</u> discharges <u>coming</u> from <u>its</u> prey.
          A   B   C   D

Go on to the next page ➤

28. A dark nebula consists of <u>a cloud of</u> interstellar dust <u>enough dense</u> <u>to obscure</u> the stars
$\qquad\qquad\qquad\qquad\quad$ A $\qquad\qquad\qquad\qquad\qquad\quad$ B $\qquad\qquad\quad$ C

<u>beyond</u> it.
D

29. <u>Commercially</u> honey is heated and <u>filtered</u> in order to <u>stabilize</u> and clarify <u>it</u>.
$\quad$ A $\qquad\qquad\qquad\qquad\qquad\qquad$ B $\qquad\qquad\qquad\qquad$ C $\qquad\qquad\quad$ D

30. The <u>various</u> parts of the body require <u>so</u> different <u>surgical</u> skills that <u>many</u> surgical specialties
$\qquad\quad$ A $\qquad\qquad\qquad\qquad\qquad\quad$ B $\qquad\qquad\quad$ C $\qquad\qquad\qquad$ D

have developed.

31. One reason birds <u>have been</u> so successful is <u>because of</u> their <u>able</u> to escape from danger
$\qquad\qquad\qquad\qquad$ A $\qquad\qquad\qquad\qquad\qquad$ B $\qquad\qquad$ C

<u>quickly</u>.
D

32. The <u>wood</u> of the rosewood tree is used <u>to do</u> fine <u>musical</u> instruments.
$\qquad$ A $\qquad\qquad\qquad\qquad\qquad\quad$ B $\quad$ C $\qquad$ D

33. Chemical engineering is based <u>on</u> the <u>principles</u> of physics, <u>chemists</u>, and <u>mathematics</u>.
$\qquad\qquad\qquad\qquad\qquad$ A $\qquad$ B $\qquad\qquad\qquad$ C $\qquad\qquad$ D

34. Ballet performers <u>must be</u> believable <u>actors</u> and actresses <u>as well as</u> <u>experts</u> dancers.
$\qquad\qquad\qquad$ A $\qquad\qquad\qquad$ B $\qquad\qquad\qquad$ C $\qquad$ D

35. Venus, <u>the second</u> planet <u>from</u> the Sun, is <u>exactly almost</u> the <u>same size as</u> the Earth.
$\qquad\qquad$ A $\qquad\qquad$ B $\qquad\qquad\qquad$ C $\qquad\qquad$ D

36. P. T. Barnum opened <u>his own</u> circus in 1871 and <u>become</u> the <u>most famous</u> showman of his
$\qquad\qquad\qquad\qquad$ A $\qquad\qquad\qquad\qquad\qquad$ B $\qquad\qquad$ C

<u>time</u>.
D

37. The way a child <u>plays with</u> other children reveals <u>a lots</u> about <u>the child's</u> emotional
$\qquad\qquad\qquad$ A $\qquad\qquad\qquad\qquad\qquad$ B $\qquad\qquad$ C

<u>development</u>.
D

38. Sheep <u>have been</u> <u>domesticated</u> for <u>over</u> 5,000 <u>years ago</u>.
$\qquad$ A $\qquad\qquad$ B $\qquad\qquad$ C $\qquad\qquad$ D

Go on to the next page ➡

39. Chemical compounds <u>with</u> barium, cobalt, and strontium <u>are</u> responsible <u>to</u> many of the vivid

       A   B   C

<u>colors</u> in fireworks.
  D

40. Duke University in North Carolina <u>has</u> an outstanding <u>collecting</u> of documents <u>concerning</u>

                              A   B   C

Southern <u>history</u>.
           D

THIS IS THE END OF SECTION 2.

IF YOU FINISH BEFORE THE TIME LIMIT, CHECK YOUR WORK ON SECTION 2 ONLY.

DO NOT READ OR WORK ON ANY OTHER SECTION OF THE TEST.

Reading Comprehension

Time: 55 minutes

This section of the test measures your ability to comprehend written materials.

Directions: This section contains several passages, each followed by a number of questions. Read the passages and, for each question, choose the *one* best answer—(A), (B), (C), or (D)—based on what is stated in the passage or on what can be inferred from the passage. Then fill in the space on your answer sheet that matches the letter of the answer that you have selected.

▼ **Read the following passage:**

Like mammals, birds claim their own territories. A
bird's territory may be small or large. Some birds
claim only their nest and the area right around it,
(line)   while others claim far larger territories that include
(5)   their feeding areas. Gulls, penguins, and other waterfowl
nest in huge colonies, but even in the biggest colonies,
each male and his mate have small territories of their
own immediately around their nests.
Male birds defend their territory chiefly against other
(10)   males of the same species. In some cases, a warning call
or threatening pose may be all the defense needed, but in
other cases, intruders may refuse to leave peacefully.

Example I   Sample Answer

What is the main topic of this passage?

(A) Birds that live in colonies
(B) Birds' mating habits
(C) The behavior of birds
(D) Territoriality in birds

The passage mainly concerns the territories of birds. You should fill in (D) on your answer sheet.

Example II   Sample Answer

According to the passage, male birds defend their
territory primarily against

(A) female birds
(B) birds of other species
(C) males of their own species
(D) mammals

The passage states that "Male birds defend their territory chiefly against other males of the same species." You should fill in (C) on your answer sheet.

As soon as you understand the directions, begin work on this section.

Questions 1–11

The Sun today is a yellow dwarf star. It is fueled by
thermonuclear reactions near its center that convert hydrogen to
helium. The Sun has existed in its present state for about 4
(line)   billion, 600 million years and is thousands of times larger than
(5)   the Earth.

By studying other stars, astronomers can predict what the rest
of the Sun's life will be like. About 5 billion years from now,
the core of the Sun will shrink and become hotter. The surface
temperature will fall. The higher temperature of the center will
(10)   increase the rate of thermonuclear reactions. The outer regions of
the Sun will expand approximately 35 million miles, about the
distance to Mercury, which is the closest planet to the Sun. The
Sun will then be a red giant star. Temperatures on the Earth will
become too hot for life to exist.
(15)   Once the Sun has used up its thermonuclear energy as a red giant,
it will begin to shrink. After it shrinks to the size of the Earth,
it will become a white dwarf star. The Sun may throw off huge
amounts of gases in violent eruptions called nova explosions as it
changes from a red giant to a white dwarf.
(20)   After billions of years as a white dwarf, the Sun will have used
up all its fuel and will have lost its heat. Such a star is called
a black dwarf. After the Sun has become a black dwarf, the Earth
will be dark and cold. If any atmosphere remains there, it will
have frozen onto the Earth's surface.

1. What is the primary purpose of this passage?
   (A) To alert people to the dangers posed by the Sun
   (B) To discuss conditions on Earth in the far future
   (C) To present a theory about red giant stars
   (D) To describe changes that the Sun will go through

2. The word "fueled" in line 1 is closest in meaning to
   (A) powered
   (B) bombarded
   (C) created
   (D) propelled

3. The word "state" in line 3 is closest in meaning to
   (A) shape
   (B) condition
   (C) location
   (D) size

Go on to the next page

4. It can be inferred from the passage that the Sun
   (A) is approximately halfway through its life as a yellow dwarf
   (B) has been in existence for 10 billion years
   (C) is rapidly changing in size and brightness
   (D) will continue as a yellow dwarf for another 10 billion years

5. What will probably be the first stage of change as the Sun becomes a red giant?
   (A) Its core will cool off and use less fuel.
   (B) Its surface will become hotter and shrink.
   (C) It will throw off huge amounts of gases.
   (D) Its center will grow smaller and hotter.

6. When the Sun becomes a red giant, what will conditions be like on Earth?
   (A) Its atmosphere will freeze and become solid.
   (B) It will be enveloped in the expanding surface of the Sun.
   (C) It will become too hot for life to exist.
   (D) It will be nearly destroyed by nova explosions.

7. As a white dwarf, the Sun will be
   (A) the same size as the planet Mercury
   (B) thousands of times smaller than it is today
   (C) around 35 million miles in diameter
   (D) cold and dark

8. According to the passage, which of the following best describes the sequence of stages that the Sun will probably pass through?
   (A) Yellow dwarf, white dwarf, red giant, black giant
   (B) Red giant, white dwarf, red dwarf, nova explosion
   (C) Yellow dwarf, red giant, white dwarf, black dwarf
   (D) White dwarf, red giant, black dwarf, yellow dwarf

9. The phrase "throw off" in line 17 is closest in meaning to
   (A) eject
   (B) burn up
   (C) convert
   (D) let in

10. The word "there" in line 23 refers to
    (A) our own planet
    (B) the outer surface of the Sun
    (C) the core of a black dwarf
    (D) the planet Mercury

11. Which of the following best describes the tone of the passage?
    (A) Alarmed
    (B) Pessimistic
    (C) Comic
    (D) Objective

Go on to the next page ➤

Questions 12–23

It is said that George Washington was one of the first to realize how important the building of canals would be to the nation's development. In fact, before he became President, he headed the

(line)
(5) first company in the United States to build a canal which was to connect the Ohio and Potomac rivers. It was never completed, but it showed the nation the feasibility of canals. As the country expanded westward, settlers in western New York, Pennsylvania, and Ohio needed a means to ship goods. Canals linking natural waterways seemed to offer an effective solution.

(10) In 1791 engineers commissioned by the state of New York investigated the possibility of a canal between Albany on the Hudson River and Buffalo on Lake Erie, which would link the Great Lakes area with the Atlantic seacoast. It would avoid the mountains that served as a barrier to canals from the Delaware

(15) and Potomac rivers.

The first attempt to dig the canal, to be called the Erie Canal, was made by private companies, but only a comparatively small portion was built before the project was halted for lack of funds. The cost of the project was an estimated five million dollars, an

(20) enormous amount for those days. There was some on-again-off-again Federal funding, but the War of 1812 put an end to this. In 1817 DeWitt Clinton was elected Governor of New York and persuaded the state to finance and build the canal. It was completed in 1825, costing two million dollars more than expected.

(25) The canal rapidly lived up to its sponsors' faith, quickly paying for itself through tolls. It was far more economical than any other form of transportation at the time. It permitted trade between the Great Lake region and East Coast, robbing the Mississippi River of much of its traffic. It allowed New York to supplant Boston,

(30) Philadelphia, and other Eastern cities as the chief center of both domestic and foreign commerce. Cities sprang up along the canal. It also contributed in a number of ways to the North's victory over the South in the Civil War.

An expansion of the canal was planned in 1849. Increased traffic

(35) would undoubtedly have warranted its construction had it not been for the development of the railroads.

12. Why does the author most likely mention George Washington in the first paragraph?
   (A) He was President at the time the Erie Canal was built.
   (B) He was involved in pioneering efforts to build canals.
   (C) He successfully opened the first canal in the United States.
   (D) He commissioned engineers to study the possibility of building the Erie Canal.

Go on to the next page

13. The word "feasibility" in line 6 is closest in meaning to
    (A) profitability
    (B) difficulty
    (C) possibility
    (D) capability

14. According to the passage, the Erie Canal connected the
    (A) Potomac and Ohio rivers
    (B) Hudson River and Lake Erie
    (C) Delaware and Potomac rivers
    (D) Atlantic Ocean and the Hudson River

15. Which of the following is closest in meaning to the word "comparatively" in line 17?
    (A) Relatively
    (B) Contrarily
    (C) Incredibly
    (D) Considerably

16. The phrase "on-again-off-again" in line 20 could be replaced by which of the following with the least change in meaning?
    (A) Intermittent
    (B) Unsolicited
    (C) Ineffectual
    (D) Gradual

17. The completion of the Erie Canal was financed by
    (A) the state of New York
    (B) private companies
    (C) the federal government
    (D) DeWitt Clinton

18. The actual cost of building the Erie Canal was
    (A) five million dollars
    (B) less than had been estimated
    (C) seven million dollars
    (D) more than could be repaid

19. The word "tolls" in line 26 is closest in meaning to which of the following?
    (A) Jobs
    (B) Grants
    (C) Links
    (D) Fees

Go on to the next page

20. Which of the following is NOT given in the fourth paragraph as an effect of the building of the Erie Canal?
    (A) It allowed the East Coast to trade with the Great Lakes area.
    (B) It took water traffic away from the Mississippi River.
    (C) It helped determine the outcome of the Civil War.
    (D) It established Boston and Philadelphia as the most important centers of trade.

21. What can be inferred about railroads in 1849 from the information in the last paragraph?
    (A) They were being planned but had not yet been built.
    (B) They were seriously underdeveloped.
    (C) They had begun to compete with the Erie Canal for traffic.
    (D) They were weakened by the expansion of the canal.

22. The word "warranted" in line 35 is closest in meaning to
    (A) guaranteed
    (B) justified
    (C) hastened
    (D) prevented

23. At what point in the passage does the author focus on the beginning of construction of the Erie Canal?
    (A) Lines 3–5
    (B) Lines 10–13
    (C) Lines 16–18
    (D) Lines 25–26

Questions 24–33

(line)

(5)

(10)

(15)

It's a sound you will probably never hear, a sickened tree sending out a distress signal. But a group of scientists has heard the cries, and they think some insects also hear the trees and are drawn to them like vultures to a dying animal.

Researchers with the U.S. Department of Agriculture's Forest Service fastened sensors to the bark of parched trees and clearly heard distress calls. According to one of the scientists, most drought-stricken trees transmit their plight in the 50- to 500-kilohertz range. (The unaided human ear can detect no more than 20 kilohertz.) Red oak, maple, white pine, and birch all make slightly different sounds in the form of vibrations at the surface of the wood.

The scientists think that the vibrations are created when the water columns inside tubes that run the length of the tree break, a result of too little water flowing through them. These fractured columns send out distinctive vibration patterns. Because some

Go on to the next page

insects communicate at ultrasonic frequencies, they may pick up the
trees' vibrations and attack the weakened trees. Researchers are
now running tests with potted trees that have been deprived of

(20)   water to see if the sound is what attracts the insects. "Water-
stressed trees also smell differently from other trees, and they
experience thermal changes, so insects could be responding to
something other than sound," one scientist said.

24. Which of the following is the main topic of the passage?
   (A) The vibrations produced by insects
   (B) The mission of the U.S. Forest Service
   (C) The effect of insects on trees
   (D) The sounds made by distressed trees

25. The word "them" in line 4 refers to
   (A) trees
   (B) scientists
   (C) insects
   (D) cries

26. The word "parched" in line 6 is closest in meaning to which of the following?
   (A) Burned
   (B) Dehydrated
   (C) Recovered
   (D) Fallen

27. The word "plight" in line 8 is closest in meaning to
   (A) signal
   (B) condition
   (C) need
   (D) agony

28. It can be inferred from the passage that the sounds produced by the trees
   (A) serve as a form of communication with other trees
   (B) are the same no matter what type of tree produces them
   (C) cannot be heard by the unaided human ear
   (D) fall into the 1–20 kilohertz range

29. The word "fractured" in line 15 is closest in meaning to
   (A) long
   (B) blocked
   (C) hollow
   (D) broken

30. Which of the following could be considered a cause of the trees' distress signals?
   (A) Torn roots
   (B) Attacks by insects
   (C) Experiments by scientists
   (D) Lack of water

Go on to the next page

31. In line 17, the phrase "pick up" could best be replaced by which of the following?
    (A) Perceive
    (B) Lift
    (C) Transmit
    (D) Attack

32. All of the following are mentioned as possible factors in drawing insects to weakened trees EXCEPT
    (A) thermal changes
    (B) smells
    (C) sounds
    (D) changes in color

33. It can be inferred that, at the time the passage was written, research concerning the distress signals of trees
    (A) had been conducted many years earlier
    (B) had been unproductive up to then
    (C) was continuing
    (D) was no longer sponsored by the government

Questions 34–41

> (line)
> (5)
>
> (10)
>
> The concepts of analogy and homology are probably easier to exemplify than to define. When different species are structurally compared, certain features can be described as either analogous or homologous. For example, flight requires certain rigid aeronautical principles of design, yet birds, bats, and insects have all conquered the air. The wings of all three types of animals derive from different embryological structures, but they perform the same functions. In this case, the flight organs of these creatures can be said to be analogous. In contrast, features that arise from the same structures in the embryo but are used in different functions are said to be homologous. The pectoral fins of a fish, the wings of a bird, and the forelimbs of a mammal are all homologous structures. They are genetically related in the sense that both the forelimb and the wing evolved from the fin.

34. Which of the following best describes the organization of the passage?
    (A) A contrast is drawn between two concepts by means of examples.
    (B) A general concept is introduced, examples are given, and a conclusion is offered.
    (C) Two definitions of the same concept are compared.
    (D) Two proposals are suggested and support for both is offered.

35. According to the passage, the concepts of analogy and homology are
    (A) difficult to understand
    (B) easier to understand through examples than through definitions
    (C) impossible to explain
    (D) simple to define but hard to apply

Go on to the next page

36. The word "rigid" in line 4 is closest in meaning to
    (A) inflexible
    (B) ideal
    (C) unnatural
    (D) steep

37. According to the information provided in the passage, which of the following would most probably be considered analogous?
    (A) A shark's fin and a tiger's claws
    (B) A man's arms and a bird's wings
    (C) A monkey's tail and an elephant's tail
    (D) A spider's legs and a horse's legs

38. According to the passage, one way in which homologous organs differ from analogous organs is that they
    (A) are genetically related
    (B) are only found in highly developed animals
    (C) perform the same general functions
    (D) come from different embryological structures

39. As used throughout the passage, the term "structures" most nearly means
    (A) buildings
    (B) features of an animal's anatomy
    (C) organizational principles
    (D) units of grammar

40. The word "sense" in line 13 is closest in meaning to
    (A) feeling
    (B) logic
    (C) meaning
    (D) perception

41. Where in the passage does the author first focus his discussion on the concept of homology?
    (A) Lines 2-4
    (B) Lines 6-8
    (C) Lines 9-11
    (D) Lines 13-14

Questions 42–50

Probably the most famous film commenting on twentieth century technology is *Modern Times*, made in 1936. Charlie Chaplin was motivated to make the film by a reporter who, while interviewing him, happened to describe working conditions in industrial
(line)
(5)
Detroit. Chaplin was told that healthy young farm boys were lured

Go on to the next page

to the city to work on automotive assembly lines. Within four or five years, these young men's health was destroyed by the stress of work in the factories.

(10) The film opens with a shot of a mass of sheep making their way down a crowded ramp. Abruptly the scene shifts to a scene of factory workers jostling one another on their way to a factory. However, the rather bitter note of criticism in the implied comparison is not sustained. It is replaced by a gentler note of satire. Chaplin prefers to entertain rather than lecture.

(15) Scenes of factory interiors account for only about one-third of the footage of *Modern Times*, but they contain some of the most pointed social commentary as well as the most comic situations. No one who has seen the film can ever forget Chaplin vainly trying to keep pace with the fast-moving conveyor belt, almost losing his

(20) mind in the process. Another popular scene involves an automatic feeding machine brought to the assembly line so that workers need not interrupt their labor to eat. The feeding machine malfunctions, hurling food at Chaplin, who is strapped into his position on the assembly line and cannot escape. This serves to illustrate people's

(25) utter helplessness in the face of machines that are meant to serve their basic needs.

Clearly, *Modern Times* has its faults, but it remains the best film treating technology within a social context. It does not offer a radical social message, but it does accurately reflect the

(30) sentiments of many who feel they are victims of an over-mechanized world.

42. The author's main purpose in writing this passage is to
   (A) criticize the factory system of the 1930's
   (B) analyze an important film
   (C) explain Chaplin's style of acting
   (D) discuss how film reveals the benefits of technology

43. According to the passage, Chaplin got the idea for the film *Modern Times* from
   (A) a newspaper article
   (B) a scene in a movie
   (C) a job he had once held
   (D) a conversation with a reporter

44. The word "abruptly" in line 10 is closest in meaning to
   (A) suddenly
   (B) mysteriously
   (C) finally
   (D) predictably

Go on to the next page ➤

45. It can be inferred from the passage that two-thirds of the film *Modern Times*
    (A) is completely unforgettable
    (B) takes place outside a factory
    (C) is more critical than the other third
    (D) entertains the audience more than the other third

46. Which of the following could best replace the phrase "losing his mind" in lines 19–20?
    (A) Getting fired
    (B) Doing his job
    (C) Going insane
    (D) Falling behind

47. The word "This" in line 24 refers to which of the following?
    (A) The machine
    (B) The food
    (C) The assembly line
    (D) The scene

48. According to the passage, the purpose of the scene involving the feeding machine is to show people's
    (A) ingenuity
    (B) adaptability
    (C) helplessness
    (D) independence

49. The word "utter" in line 25 is closest in meaning to which of the following?
    (A) Notable
    (B) Complete
    (C) Regrettable
    (D) Necessary

50. The author would probably be LEAST likely to use which of the following words to describe the film *Modern Times*?
    (A) Revolutionary
    (B) Entertaining
    (C) Memorable
    (D) Satirical

THIS IS THE END OF THE SAMPLE READING COMPREHENSION SECTION.

IF YOU FINISH BEFORE THE TIME LIMIT,

GO BACK AND CHECK YOUR WORK IN THIS SECTION ONLY.

THERE IS NO TEST MATERIAL ON THIS PAGE.

Practice Test 2

Students at Palomar College

Listening Comprehension

This section tests your ability to comprehend spoken English. It is divided into three parts, each with its own directions. You are *not* permitted to turn the page during the reading of the directions or to take notes at any time.

Part A

Directions: Each item in this part consists of a brief conversation involving two speakers. Following each conversation, a third voice will ask a question. You will hear the conversations and questions only once, and they will *not* be written out.

When you have heard each conversation and question, read the four answer choices and select the *one*—(A), (B), (C), or (D)—that best answers the question based on what is directly stated or on what can be inferred. Then fill in the space on your answer sheet that matches the letter of the answer that you have selected.

Here is an example.

You will hear:

Sample Answer

You will read: (A) Open the window.
(B) Move the chair.
(C) Leave the room.
(D) Take a seat.

From the conversation you find out that the woman thinks the man should put the chair over by the window. The best answer to the question, "What does the woman think the man should do?" is (B), "Move the chair." You should fill in (B) on your answer sheet.

1. (A) The plane hasn't taken off yet.
   (B) The cost of flying has increased.
   (C) More flights will soon be scheduled.
   (D) He hasn't changed his vacation plans.

2. (A) All of the books are cheap.
   (B) None of the books is required.
   (C) Half of the books should be returned.
   (D) Only four of the books are expensive.

3. (A) It will probably rain this afternoon.
   (B) She likes to watch the rain come down.
   (C) She'll play golf even if it rains.
   (D) It has rained a lot lately.

4. (A) Nearly all of the students can meet.
   (B) The meeting time must be changed.
   (C) Only Lisa will be at the library.
   (D) Lisa dropped the class on Friday.

5. (A) He walked so far that he was
       exhausted.
   (B) He was wearing shorts on his hike.
   (C) He encountered some wild animals in
       the woods.
   (D) He should get some comfortable hiking
       shoes.

6. (A) He intends to see Michelle.
   (B) Michelle may visit him anytime.
   (C) He has to return some money to
       Michelle.
   (D) Michelle owes him some money.

7. (A) Buying some red chairs.
   (B) Renting a bigger auditorium.
   (C) Moving chairs from the auditorium.
   (D) Getting more chairs.

8. (A) He can't read the sign.
   (B) He didn't make the sign.
   (C) He didn't sign his name.
   (D) He doesn't like the sign.

9. (A) Housing near campus is getting
       cheaper and cheaper.
   (B) She doesn't need to live close to
       campus.
   (C) It's not easy to find inexpensive
       housing near campus.
   (D) The man could find housing if he
       looked carefully.

10. (A) To a game.
    (B) To buy tickets.
    (C) To get some groceries.
    (D) To a party.

11. (A) The bucket has been broken.
    (B) The water was spilled.
    (C) They still need more money.
    (D) They have run out of time.

12. (A) He is kind.
    (B) He is impolite.
    (C) He is somewhat busy.
    (D) She doesn't want to say.

13. (A) It's not surprising that Tony went
        fishing.
    (B) He already knew Tony had caught only
        one fish.
    (C) He doesn't think Tony is a good
        fisherman.
    (D) Tony usually catches a lot of fish.

14. (A) Don't complete the form.
    (B) Don't waste time.
    (C) Take a form.
    (D) There's no hurry.

15. (A) He is telling her the truth.
    (B) He's never been to Seattle.
    (C) He has visited Seattle once.
    (D) She's only spoken to him once.

16. (A) Disapproved of her plan.
    (B) Watered Lily's plants.
    (C) Traveled overseas.
    (D) Caught colds.

17. (A) It should have been turned up.
    (B) The people across town enjoyed it.
    (C) It's extremely popular.
    (D) It was much too loud.

18. (A) It was quite relaxing.
    (B) The weather wasn't good.
    (C) It was unexpectedly busy.
    (D) It was perfectly planned.

Go on to the next page

19. (A) The lab is generally locked on Saturday mornings.
    (B) The man doesn't have a key to the lab.
    (C) Something strange happened in the lab on Saturday.
    (D) The lab should never be locked.

20. (A) He needs the insurance no matter how much it costs.
    (B) There are other types of insurance he should buy.
    (C) The man doesn't have enough money to buy insurance.
    (D) The cost of insurance is becoming more reasonable.

21. (A) She's an art student.
    (B) She's afraid of flying.
    (C) She did well on the test.
    (D) She got her pilot's license.

22. (A) An elevator.
    (B) A television.
    (C) An automobile.
    (D) A telephone.

23. (A) Meg's sister took it to the cleaner's.
    (B) Meg cleaned it.
    (C) Meg wore it to class.
    (D) Meg's sister borrowed it.

24. (A) They must go to an orientation session.
    (B) They are not new students.
    (C) They won't be allowed to register.
    (D) They were given the wrong schedule.

25. (A) He doesn't mind moving.
    (B) His brother won't move for two weeks.
    (C) He'd rather not help his brother move.
    (D) His brother decided not to move.

26. (A) She has a coin like his.
    (B) She knows a lot about coins.
    (C) She thinks the coin is worthless.
    (D) She's never seen this type of coin.

27. (A) Its lyrics are hard to understand.
    (B) It needs a stronger melody.
    (C) It has become very popular.
    (D) Its melody is hard to forget.

28. (A) He hadn't been smiling.
    (B) His picture hadn't been taken.
    (C) It wasn't a good picture.
    (D) The woman wouldn't show him the picture.

29. (A) They're always expensive.
    (B) They haven't been cleaned.
    (C) They're inexpensive now.
    (D) There aren't any available.

30. (A) From college.
    (B) Through her roommate.
    (C) From the reception.
    (D) Through her sister.

Go on to the next page

Part B

Directions: This part of the test consists of extended conversations between two speakers. After each of these conversations, there are a number of questions. You will hear each conversation and question only once, and the questions are *not* written out.

When you have heard the questions, read the four answer choices and select the *one*—(A), (B), (C), or (D)—that best answers the question based on what is directly stated or on what can be inferred. Then fill in the space on your answer sheet that matches the letter of the answer that you have selected.

Don't forget: During actual exams, taking notes or writing in your test book is *not* permitted.

31. (A) At a newspaper.
    (B) At an advertising agency.
    (C) At a furniture store.
    (D) At a real estate office.

32. (A) A two-bedroom apartment.
    (B) A sofa.
    (C) A chair.
    (D) A roommate.

33. (A) Her phone number.
    (B) The location of the apartment.
    (C) The best time to call her.
    (D) Her first name.

34. (A) $5.
    (B) $15.
    (C) $30.
    (D) $250.

35. (A) From a newspaper advertisement.
    (B) From a magazine article.
    (C) From a television program.
    (D) From an automobile dealer.

36. (A) To warn of dangers.
    (B) To explain traffic regulations.
    (C) To wake up drivers who are falling asleep.
    (D) To give directions.

37. (A) He has a good sense of direction.
    (B) He owns a "smart" car.
    (C) He doesn't know how to drive.
    (D) He doesn't know the way to the woman's house.

38. (A) He got lost.
    (B) He ran out of gas.
    (C) He was in an accident.
    (D) His car broke down.

Go on to the next page

Part C

Directions: This part of the test consists of several talks, each given by a single speaker. After each of these talks, there are a number of questions. You will hear each talk and question only once, and the questions are *not* written out.

When you have heard each question, read the four answer choices and select the *one*—(A), (B), (C), or (D)—that best answers the question based on what is directly stated or on what can be inferred. Then fill in the space on your answer sheet that matches the letter of the answer that you have selected.

Here is an example.

You will hear:

Now here is a sample question.

You will hear:

Sample Answer

You will read: (A) Philosophy.
(B) Meteorology.
(C) Astronomy.
(D) Photography.

The lecture concerns a lunar eclipse, a topic that would typically be discussed in an astronomy class. The choice that best answers the question, "In what course is this lecture probably being given?" is (C), "Astronomy." You should fill in (C) on your answer sheet.

Here is another sample question.

You will hear:

Sample Answer

You will read: (A) The Earth's shadow moves across the Moon.
(B) Clouds block the view of the Moon.

From the lecture you learn that a lunar eclipse occurs when the Earth moves between the Sun and the Moon and the shadow of the Earth passes across the Moon. The choice that best answers the question, "According to the speaker, which of the following occurs during a lunar eclipse?" is (A), "The Earth's shadow moves across the Moon."

Don't forget: During actual exams, taking notes or writing in your test book is *not* permitted.

39. (A) To present an award.
    (B) To say goodbye to Professor Callaghan.
    (C) To explain computer models.
    (D) To welcome a new college president.

40. (A) An administrator.
    (B) A faculty member.
    (C) A chancellor of the college.
    (D) A graduate student.

41. (A) Computer science.
    (B) History.
    (C) Economics.
    (D) Political science.

42. (A) Two.
    (B) Four.
    (C) Six.
    (D) Eight.

43. (A) A bicycle racer.
    (B) A radio announcer.
    (C) A coach.
    (D) A television reporter.

44. (A) The benefits of bicycle commuting.
    (B) Local traffic problems.
    (C) A series of bicycle races.
    (D) The American university system.

45. (A) On the college campus.
    (B) On downtown streets.
    (C) In Woodland Park.
    (D) In the nearby countryside.

46. (A) Take part in the race.
    (B) Travel to the country.
    (C) Avoid the downtown area.
    (D) Ride a bicycle.

47. (A) In an art history class.
    (B) In a painter's studio.
    (C) In a photography class.
    (D) In an art museum.

48. (A) A famous person.
    (B) A beautiful landscape.
    (C) An empty phone booth.
    (D) Geometric shapes.

49. (A) They are very valuable.
    (B) They are quite large.
    (C) They are highly abstract.
    (D) They are extremely lifelike.

50. (A) Paint pictures.
    (B) Write papers.
    (C) View some slides.
    (D) Discuss their reactions.

THIS IS THE END OF SECTION 1, LISTENING COMPREHENSION.

STOP WORK ON SECTION 1.

2 Structure and Written Expression

Time: 25 minutes

This section tests your ability to recognize grammar and usage suitable for standard written English. This section is divided into two parts, each with its own directions.

Structure

Directions: Items in this part are incomplete sentences. Following each of these sentences, there are four words or phrases. You should select the *one* word or phrase—(A), (B), (C), or (D)—that best completes the sentence. Then fill in the space on your answer sheet that matches the letter of the answer that you have selected.

Example I

Pepsin _____ an enzyme used
in digestion.

(A) that
(B) is
(C) of
(D) being

Sample Answer

(A) ● (C) (D)

This sentence should properly read "Pepsin is an enzyme used in digestion." You should fill in (B) on your answer sheet.

Example II

_____ large natural lakes are found
in the state of South Carolina.

(A) There are no
(B) Not the
(C) It is not
(D) No

Sample Answer

(A) (B) (C) ●

This sentence should properly read "No large natural lakes are found in the state of South Carolina." You should fill in (D) on your answer sheet.

As soon as you understand the directions, begin work on this part.

2 2 2 2 2 2 2 2 2 2 2

1. Sharp knives are actually safer to use _____.
   (A) as dull ones
   (B) as ones that are dull
   (C) than dull ones
   (D) that are dull ones

2. Daniel Webster, Thaddeus Stevens, and many others _____ prominent in public life began their careers by teaching school.
   (A) they became
   (B) once they became
   (C) became
   (D) who became

3. As coal mines became deeper, the problems of draining water, bringing in fresh air, and _____ to the surface increased.
   (A) transporting ore
   (B) to transport ore
   (C) how ore is transported
   (D) ore is transporting

4. _____ because of the complexity of his writing, Henry James never became a popular writer, but his works are admired by critics and other writers.
   (A) It may be
   (B) Perhaps
   (C) Besides
   (D) Why is it

5. Piedmont glaciers are formed _____ several valley glaciers join and spread out over a plain.
   (A) by
   (B) when
   (C) from
   (D) that

6. As late as 1890, Key West, with a population of 18,000, _____ Florida's largest city.
   (A) that was
   (B) to be
   (C) was
   (D) it was

7. A mastery of calculus depends on _____ of algebra.
   (A) an understanding
   (B) is understood
   (C) to understand
   (D) understand

Go on to the next page

2 2 2 2 2 2 2 2 2 2 2 2

8. _____ he was not a musician himself, Lawrence Hammond developed an electronic keyboard instrument called the Hammond organ.
(A) Although
(B) That
(C) Despite
(D) For

9. Agnes De Mille's landmark musical play *Oklahoma!* was _____ of story, music, and dance.
(A) successfully combined
(B) a successful combination
(C) to combine successfully
(D) successful combining

10. _____ single dialect of American English has ever become dominant.
(A) No
(B) Not only a
(C) Not
(D) Nor a

11. In 1837 the University of Michigan became the first state university _____ by a board of regents elected by the voters of the state.
(A) under the control
(B) it was controlled
(C) being controlled
(D) to be controlled

12. Indoor heating systems have made _____ for people to live and work comfortably in temperate climates.
(A) it is possible
(B) possible
(C) it possible
(D) possibly

13. Certain fish eggs contain droplets of oil, _____ to float on the surface of the water.
(A) allowing them
(B) allows them
(C) they are allowed
(D) this allows them

14. Considered America's first great architect, _____.
(A) many of the buildings at Harvard University were designed by Henry Hobson Richardson
(B) Henry Hobson Richardson designed many of the buildings at Harvard University
(C) Harvard University has many buildings that were designed by Henry Hobson Richardson
(D) it was Henry Hobson Richardson who designed many of the buildings at H_____

Written Expression

Directions: The items in this part have four underlined words or phrases—(A), (B), (C), and (D). You must identify the *one* underlined expression that must be changed for the sentence to be correct. Then find the number of the question on your answer sheet and fill in the space corresponding to the letter of the answer that you have selected.

This sentence should read "Lenses may have either concave or convex shapes." You should therefore select answer (A).

This sentence should read "When painting a fresco, an artist applies paint directly to the damp plaster of a wall." You should therefore select answer (B).

As soon as you understand the directions, begin work on this section.

16. Dreams are <u>commonly</u> <u>made up of</u> <u>either</u> visual and <u>verbal images</u>.
              A   B   C   D

17. The *Yale Daily News* is <u>oldest than</u> any <u>other</u> college newspaper <u>still</u> <u>in operation</u> in the
                    A   B   C   D

    United States.

18. Mary Rinehart was <u>a pioneer</u> in the <u>field</u> of <u>journalist</u> <u>in the early</u> twentieth century.
                   A   B   C   D

19. The Dave Brubek Quartet, one of <u>the most popular</u> jazz bands of the 1950's, had a <u>particularly</u>
                                A   B

    loyal <u>following</u> on <u>campuses college</u>.
           C   D

20. <u>In the</u> architecture, a <u>capital</u> is <u>the top</u> portion of a <u>column</u>.
        A   B   C   D

21. Today, successful farmers are experts not only in <u>agriculture</u>, <u>but also</u> in <u>market</u>, finance, and
                                             A   B   C

    <u>accounting</u>.
       D

22. In the <u>early</u> days of jet development, jet engines <u>used</u> great <u>numbers</u> of <u>fuel</u>.
           A   B   C   D

23. Georgia has <u>too</u> many types of <u>soil</u> that <u>virtually</u> any temperate-zone crop can be grown <u>there</u>.
               A   B   C   D

24. The sum of <u>all</u> chemical reactions in <u>an organism's</u> living cells <u>are</u> called <u>its</u> metabolism.
             A   B   C   D

25. River <u>transportation</u> in the United States <u>consists</u> <u>primarily</u> of barges <u>pull</u> by towboats.
             A   B   C   D

26. <u>Most modern</u> barns are <u>both insulated</u>, ventilated, and <u>equipped with</u> <u>electricity</u>.
          A   B   C   D

27. <u>Many</u> bridges in New England <u>were covered</u> with wooden roofs to protect <u>it</u> from
        A   B   C

    <u>rain and snow</u>.

2 2 2 2 2 2 2 2 2 2 2 2

28. It is their <u>nearly perfect</u> crystal structure <u>that gives</u> diamonds their <u>hardness</u>, brilliance, and
          A   B   C

    <u>transparent</u>.
        D

29. Needles are <u>simple-looking</u> tools, <u>but</u> they are <u>very relatively</u> difficult <u>to make</u>.
                        A   B   C   D

30. Ducks are <u>less</u> susceptible <u>to</u> infection <u>than</u> <u>another</u> types of poultry.
                    A   B   C   D

31. <u>Unlike</u> competitive <u>running</u>, race walkers must always keep some portion of <u>their</u> feet
         A   B   C

    <u>in contact with</u> the ground.
            D

32. One of the <u>most beautiful</u> botanical <u>gardens</u> in the United States is the <u>wildly</u> and lovely
                      A   B   C

    Magnolia Gardens <u>near</u> Charleston, South Carolina.
                          D

33. Composer John Cage used many <u>unusual</u> objects as <u>instrument</u> in his music, <u>including</u>
                                        A   B   C

    cowbells, flower pots, <u>tin cans</u>, and saw blades.
                                D

34. Woody Guthrie wrote <u>thousands</u> of songs during <u>the lifetime</u>, many of <u>which</u> became classic
                            A   B   C

    <u>folk songs</u>.
        D

35. Runner Wilma Rudolph <u>win</u> three gold medals at the <u>1960</u> Olympics, and <u>she set the</u>
                            A   B   C

    <u>world record</u> for the 100-meter dash in 1961.
        D

36. Some critics <u>have called</u> Theodore Dreiser's book *Sister Carrie* <u>a first</u> modern novel <u>because</u>
                      A   B   C

    it broke <u>so many</u> traditions.
                  D

37. Abigail Adams' <u>letters</u> <u>to</u> her husband <u>present</u> a graphic picture of the <u>age which</u> she lived,
                        A   B   C   D

<u>Go on to the next page</u> ➔

38. Viscosity is a measurement <u>describing</u> the <u>relative</u> difficulty or <u>easy</u> <u>with which</u> liquids flow.
                                              A   B   C   D

39. <u>More than</u> 10,000 years ago, glaciers <u>moved</u> across the Minnesota region four <u>time</u>, leveling
        A   B   C

    <u>most of</u> the land.
      D

40. The <u>discover</u> of gold and silver in the rugged <u>mountains</u> of Nevada in 1858 <u>attracted</u> many
          A   B   C

    fortune-seekers <u>to that area</u>.
                    D

THIS IS THE END OF SECTION 2.

IF YOU FINISH BEFORE THE TIME LIMIT, CHECK YOUR WORK ON SECTION 2 ONLY.

DO NOT READ OR WORK ON ANY OTHER SECTION OF THE TEST.

3 Reading Comprehension

Time: 55 minutes

This section of the test measures your ability to comprehend written materials.

Directions: This section contains several passages, each followed by a number of questions. Read the passages and, for each question, choose the *one* best answer—(A), (B), (C), or (D)—based on what is stated in the passage or on what can be inferred from the passage. Then fill in the space on your answer sheet that matches the letter of the answer that you have selected.

▼ Read the following passage:

       Like mammals, birds claim their own territories. A
bird's territory may be small or large. Some birds
claim only their nest and the area right around it,
(line)   while others claim far larger territories that include
(5)   their feeding areas. Gulls, penguins, and other waterfowl
nest in huge colonies, but even in the biggest colonies,
each male and his mate have small territories of their
own immediately around their nests.
       Male birds defend their territory chiefly against other
(10)   males of the same species. In some cases, a warning call
or threatening pose may be all the defense needed, but in
other cases, intruders may refuse to leave peacefully.

Example I   Sample Answer

What is the main topic of this passage?

(A) Birds that live in colonies
(B) Birds' mating habits
(C) The behavior of birds
(D) Territoriality in birds

The passage mainly concerns the territories of birds. You should fill in (D) on your answer sheet.

Example II

Sample Answer

Ⓐ Ⓑ ● Ⓓ

According to the passage, male birds defend
their territory primarily against

(A) female birds
(B) birds of other species
(C) males of their own species
(D) mammals

The passage states that "Male birds defend their territory chiefly against other males of the same species." You should fill in (C) on your answer sheet.

As soon as you understand the directions, begin work on this section.

Questions 1–11

The time when humans crossed the Arctic land bridge from
Siberia to Alaska seems remote to us today, but actually
represents a late stage in the prehistory of humans, an era when
(line)   polished stone implements and bows and arrows were already being
(5)   used, and dogs had already been domesticated.

When these early migrants arrived in North America, they found
the woods and plains dominated by three types of American
mammoths. These elephants were distinguished from today's
elephants mainly by their thick, shaggy coats and their huge,
(10)   upward-curving tusks. They had arrived on the continent hundreds
of thousands of years before their human followers. The
wooly mammoth in the North, the Columbian mammoth in middle North
America, and the imperial mammoth of the South, together with
their distant cousins the mastodons, dominated the land. Here, as
(15)   in the Old World, there is evidence that humans hunted these
elephants, as shown by the numerous spear points found with
mammoth remains.

Then, at the end of the Ice Age, when the last glaciers had
retreated, there was a relatively sudden and widespread
(20)   extinction of elephants. In the New World, both mammoths and
mastodons disappeared. In the Old World, only Indian and African
elephants survived.

Why did the huge, seemingly successful mammoths disappear?
Were humans connected with their extinction? Perhaps, but at
(25)   that time, although they were cunning hunters, humans were still
widely scattered and not very numerous. It is difficult to see
how they could have prevailed over the mammoth to such an extent.

1. With which of the following is the passage primarily concerned?
   (A) Migration from Siberia to Alaska
   (B) Techniques used to hunt mammoths
   (C) The prehistory of humans
   (D) The relationship between man and mammoth in the New World

2. The word "implements" in line 4 is closest in meaning to
   (A) tools
   (B) ornaments
   (C) houses
   (D) carvings

3. The phrase "these early migrants" in line 6 refers to
   (A) mammoths
   (B) humans
   (C) dogs
   (D) mastodons

Go on to the next page

4. Where were the imperial mammoths the dominant type of mammoth?
   (A) In Alaska
   (B) In the central portion of North America
   (C) In the southern part of North America
   (D) In South America

5. It can be inferred that when humans crossed into the New World, they
   (A) had previously hunted mammoths in Siberia
   (B) had never seen mammoths before
   (C) brought mammoths with them from the Old World
   (D) soon learned to use dogs to hunt mammoths

6. Which of the following could best substitute for the word "remains" in line 17?
   (A) Bones
   (B) Drawings
   (C) Footprints
   (D) Spear points

7. The word "seemingly" in line 23 is closest in meaning to
   (A) tremendously
   (B) apparently
   (C) formerly
   (D) obviously

8. The passage supports which of the following conclusions about mammoths?
   (A) Humans hunted them to extinction.
   (B) The freezing temperatures of the Ice Age destroyed their food supply.
   (C) The cause of their extinction is not definitely known.
   (D) Competition with mastodons caused them to become extinct.

9. The word "cunning" in line 25 is closest in meaning to
   (A) clever
   (B) determined
   (C) efficient
   (D) cautious

10. Which of the following is NOT true about prehistoric humans at the time of the mammoths' extinction?
    (A) They were relatively few in number.
    (B) They knew how to use bows and arrows.
    (C) They were concentrated in a small area.
    (D) They were skilled hunters.

11. Which of the following types of elephants does the author discuss in the most detail in the passage?
    (A) The mastodon
    (B) Th

Questions 12–23

(line)

(5)

(10)

(15)

(20)

(25)

Just before and during World War I, a number of white musicians came to Chicago from New Orleans playing in an idiom they had learned from blacks in that city. Five of them formed what eventually became known as the Original Dixieland Band. They moved to New York in 1917 and won fame there. That year they recorded the first phonograph record identified as jazz.

The first important recording by black musicians was made in Chicago in 1923 by King Oliver's Creole Jazz Band, a group that featured some of the foremost jazz musicians of the time, including trumpet player Louis Armstrong. Armstrong's dynamic trumpet style became famous worldwide. Other band members had played in Fate Marable's band, which traveled up and down the Mississippi River entertaining passengers on riverboats.

The characteristics of this early type of jazz, known as Dixieland jazz, included a complex interweaving of melodic lines among the cornet or trumpet, clarinet, and trombone, and a steady chomp-chomp beat provided by the rhythm section, which included the piano, bass, and drums. Most bands used no written notations, preferring arrangements agreed on verbally.

Improvisation was an indispensable element. Even bandleaders such as Duke Ellington, who provided his musicians with written arrangements, permitted them plenty to freedom to improvise when playing solos.

In the late 1920's, the most influential jazz artists in Chicago were members of small bands such as the Wolverines. In New York, the trend was toward larger groups. These groups played in revues, large dance halls, and theaters. Bands would become larger still during the next age of jazz, the Swing era.

12. What is the main topic of this passage?
    (A) The early history of jazz
    (B) The music of World War I
    (C) The relationship of melody and rhythm in jazz
    (D) The New York recording industry in the 1920's

13. The word "idiom" in line 2 is closest in meaning to
    (A) slang
    (B) tempo
    (C) tune
    (D) style

14. The musicians who made the earliest jazz recordings were originally from
    (A) New Orleans
    (B) Chicago
    (C) New York
    (D) Mississippi

Go on to the next page

15. When was the first important recording by black jazz musicians made?
    (A) In 1917
    (B) In 1923
    (C) In the late 1920's
    (D) In the early 1930's

16. According to the passage, Louis Armstrong was a member of which of the following?
    (A) The Original Dixieland Band
    (B) Fate Marable's riverboat band
    (C) King Oliver's Creole Jazz Band
    (D) The Wolverines

17. The word "steady" in line 17 is closest in meaning to
    (A) constant
    (B) basic
    (C) urgent
    (D) happy

18. According to the passage, which of the following instruments helped provide the beat for Dixieland jazz?
    (A) The cornet
    (B) The piano
    (C) The trombone
    (D) The clarinet

19. Duke Ellington is given as an example of a bandleader who
    (A) could not read music
    (B) did not value improvisation
    (C) discouraged solo performances
    (D) used written arrangements

20. Which of the following phrases would be LEAST likely to be applied to Dixieland jazz?
    (A) Relatively complex
    (B) Highly improvisational
    (C) Rhythmic and melodic
    (D) Carefully planned

21. According to the passage, who were the Wolverines?
    (A) A band that played in large dance halls
    (B) A New York group
    (C) A Swing band
    (D) A small group

22. The author provides the most detailed description of early jazz music in the
    (A) first paragraph
    (B) second paragraph

23. The paragraph following this one most likely deals with
    (A) the music of small bands
    (B) the Swing era
    (C) music that influenced Dixieland Jazz
    (D) other forms of music popular in the 1920's

Questions 24–32

	A pioneering study by Donald Appleyard made the astounding
	discovery that a sudden increase in the volume of traffic through
	an area affects people in the way that a sudden increase in crime
(line)	does. Appleyard observed this by finding three blocks of houses
(5)	in San Francisco that looked much alike and had the same kind of
	middle-class and working-class residents, with approximately the
	same ethnic mix. The difference was that only 2,000 cars a day
	ran down Octavia Street (LIGHT street, in Appleyard's
	terminology) while Gough Street (MEDIUM street) was used by 8,000
(10)	cars daily, and Franklin Street (HEAVY street) had around 16,000
	cars a day. Franklin Street often had as many cars in an hour as
	Octavia Street had in a day.
	Heavy traffic brought with it danger, noise, fumes, and soot,
	directly, and trash secondarily. That is, the cars didn't bring
(15)	in much trash, but when trash accumulated, residents seldom
	picked it up. The cars, Appleyard determined, reduced the amount
	of territory residents felt responsible for. Noise was a constant
	intrusion into their homes. Many Franklin Street residents
	covered their doors and windows and spent most of their
(20)	time in the rear of their houses. Most families with children had
	already left.
	Conditions on Octavia Street were much different. Residents
	picked up trash. They sat on their front steps and chatted with
	neighbors. They had three times as many friends and twice
(25)	as many acquaintances as the people on Franklin.
	On Gough Street, residents said that the old feeling of
	community was disappearing as traffic increased. People were
	becoming more and more preoccupied with their own lives. A
	number of families had recently moved, and more were considering
(30)	it. Those who were staying expressed deep regret at the
	destruction of their community.

24. The word "astounding" in line 1 is closest in meaning to
    (A) startling
    (B) disappointing
    (C) dubious
    (D) alternative

Go on to the next page

25. The three streets mentioned in this passage are different in that
    (A) they are in different cities
    (B) the residents are of different ethnic backgrounds
    (C) they have varying amounts of traffic
    (D) the income levels of the residents vary considerably

26. Approximately how many cars use Franklin Street daily?
    (A) 2,000
    (B) 8,000
    (C) 16,000
    (D) 20,000

27. All of the following are direct results of heavy traffic EXCEPT
    (A) increased amounts of trash
    (B) greater danger to residents
    (C) more pollution
    (D) more vibrations

28. The author's main purpose in the second paragraph is to
    (A) discuss the problems of trash disposal
    (B) point out the disadvantages of heavy traffic
    (C) propose an alternate system of transportation
    (D) suggest ways to cope with traffic problems

29. On which street is there the most social interaction?
    (A) Octavia Street
    (B) Gough Street
    (C) Franklin Street
    (D) There is no significant social interaction on any of the three streets.

30. The word "chatted" in line 23 is closest in meaning to
    (A) joked
    (B) talked
    (C) argued
    (D) walked

31. Which of the following is NOT a statement you would expect from a resident of Gough Street?
    (A) People on this street are unhappy because the neighborhood is deteriorating.
    (B) People on this street think mostly of themselves.
    (C) People on this street have more and more space for which they feel responsible.
    (D) A number of people are preparing to leave this street.

32. In what order does the author present detailed discussions of the three streets?
    (A) LIGHT, MEDIUM, HEAVY
    (B) HEAVY, MEDIUM, LIGHT
    (C) HEAVY, LIGHT, MEDIUM
    (D) LIGHT, HEA

Questions 33–42

Rachel Carson was born in 1907 in Springsdale, Pennsylvania. She studied biology at college and zoology at Johns Hopkins University, where she received her master's degree in 1933. In 1936 (line) she was hired by the U.S. Fish and Wildlife Service, where she (5) worked most of her life.

Carson's first book, *Under the Sea Wind,* was published in 1941. It received excellent reviews, but sales were poor until it was reissued in 1952. In that year she published *The Sea Around Us,* which provided a fascinating look beneath the ocean's (10) surface, emphasizing human history as well as geology and marine biology. Her imagery and language had a poetic quality. Carson consulted no fewer than 1,000 printed sources. She had voluminous correspondence and frequent discussions with experts in the field. However, she always realized the limitations of her (15) non-technical readers.

In 1962 Carson published *Silent Spring,* a book that sparked considerable controversy. It proved how much harm was done by the uncontrolled, reckless use of insecticides. She detailed how they poison the food supply of animals, kill birds and fish, and (20) contaminate human food. At the time, spokesmen for the chemical industry mounted personal attacks against Carson and issued propaganda to indicate that her findings were flawed. However, her work was vindicated by a 1963 report of the President's Science Advisory Committee.

33. The passage mainly discusses Rachel Carson's work
    (A) as a researcher
    (B) at college
    (C) at the U.S. Fish and Wildlife Service
    (D) as a writer

34. According to the passage, what did Carson primarily study at Johns Hopkins University?
    (A) Oceanography
    (B) History
    (C) Literature
    (D) Zoology

35. When she published her first book, Carson was closest to the age of
    (A) 26
    (B) 29
    (C) 34
    (D) 45

Go on to the next page ➔

36. It can be inferred from the passage that in 1952, Carson's book *Under the Sea Wind*
    (A) was outdated
    (B) became more popular than her other books
    (C) was praised by critics
    (D) sold many copies

37. Which of the following was NOT mentioned in the passage as a source of information for *The Sea Around Us*?
    (A) Printed matter
    (B) Talks with experts
    (C) A research expedition
    (D) Letters from scientists

38. Which of the following words or phrases is LEAST accurate in describing *The Sea Around Us*?
    (A) Highly technical
    (B) Poetic
    (C) Fascinating
    (D) Well-researched

39. The word "reckless" in line 18 is closest in meaning to
    (A) unnecessary
    (B) limited
    (C) continuous
    (D) irresponsible

40. According to the passage, *Silent Spring* is primarily
    (A) an attack on the use of chemical preservatives in food
    (B) a discussion of the hazards insects pose to the food supply
    (C) a warning about the dangers of misusing insecticides
    (D) an illustration of the benefits of the chemical industry

41. The word "flawed" in line 22 is closest in meaning to
    (A) faulty
    (B) deceptive
    (C) logical
    (D) offensive

42. Why does the author of the passage mention the report of the President's Science Advisory Committee (lines 23–24)?
    (A) To provide an example of government propaganda
    (B) To support Carson's ideas
    (C) To indicate a growing government concern with the environment
    (D) To validate the chemical industry's claims

Questions 43–50

(line)

(5)

(10)

(15)

(20)

What is meant by the term *economic resources*? In general, these are all the natural, man-made, and human resources that go into the production of goods and services. This obviously covers a lot of ground: factories and farms, tools and machines, transportation and communication facilities, all types of natural resources, and labor. Economic resources can be broken down into two general categories: property resources—land and capital—and human resources—labor and entrepreneurial skills.

What do economists mean by *land*? Much more than the non-economist. Land refers to all natural resources that are usable in the production process: arable land, forests, mineral and oil deposits, and so on. What about capital? Capital goods are all the man-made aids to producing, storing, transporting, and distributing goods and services. Capital goods differ from consumer goods in that the latter satisfy wants directly, while the former do so indirectly by facilitating the production of consumer goods. It should be noted that *capital* as defined here does not refer to money. Money, as such, produces nothing.

The term *labor* refers to the physical and mental talents of humans used to produce goods or services (with the exception of a certain set of human talents, entrepreneurial skills, which will be considered separately because of their special significance). Thus the services of a factory worker or an office worker, a ballet dancer or an astronaut all fall under the general heading of labor.

43. What is the author's main purpose in writing this passage?
(A) To explain the concept of labor
(B) To criticize certain uses of capital
(C) To contrast capital goods and consumer goods
(D) To define economic resources

44. In lines 3–4, the author uses the expression "This obviously covers a lot of ground . . ." to indicate that
(A) the factories and farms discussed in the passage are very large
(B) economic resources will be discussed in great depth
(C) the topic of economic resources is a broad one
(D) land is an important concept in economics

45. When non-economists use the term "land," its definition
(A) is much more general than when economists use it
(B) is much more restrictive than when economists use it
(C) changes from place to place
(D) includes all types of natural resources

Go on to the next page

46. The word "arable" in line 11 is closest in meaning to
    (A) dry
    (B) fertile
    (C) developed
    (D) open

47. The phrase "the latter" in line 15 refers to
    (A) economists
    (B) non-economists
    (C) capital goods
    (D) consumer goods

48. Which of the following could be considered a capital good as defined in the passage?
    (A) A railroad
    (B) Money
    (C) A coal deposit
    (D) Human skills

49. The word "heading" in line 24 is closest in meaning to
    (A) direction
    (B) practice
    (C) category
    (D) utility

50. The skills of all the following could be considered examples of labor, as defined in the passage, EXCEPT
    (A) artists and scientists
    (B) workers who produce services, not goods
    (C) office workers
    (D) entrepreneurs

THIS IS THE END OF THE SAMPLE READING COMPREHENSION SECTION.

IF YOU FINISH BEFORE THE TIME LIMIT,

GO BACK AND CHECK YOUR WORK IN THIS SECTION ONLY.

Practice Test 3

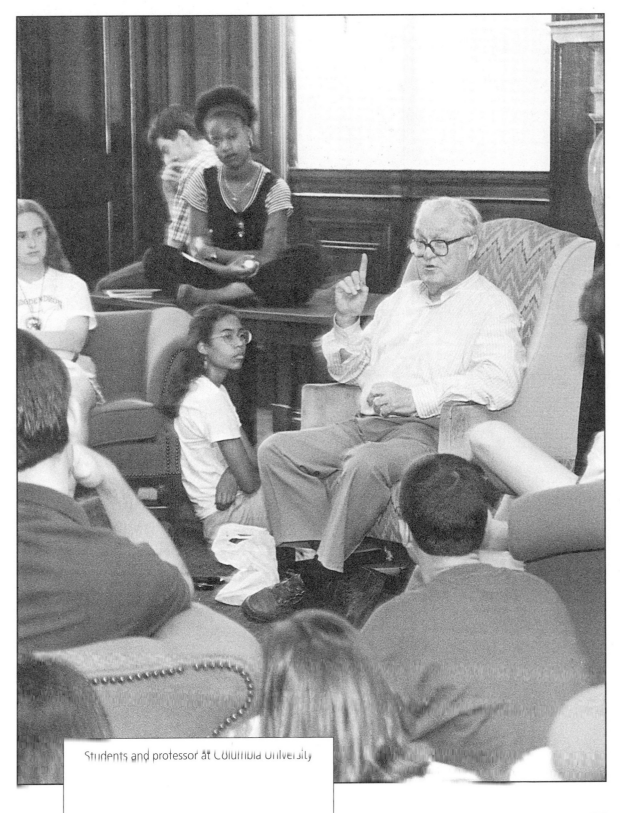

Students and professor at Columbia University

Listening Comprehension

This section tests your ability to comprehend spoken English. It is divided into three parts, each with its own directions. You are *not* permitted to turn the page during the reading of the directions or to take notes at any time.

Part A

Directions: Each item in this part consists of a brief conversation involving two speakers. Following each conversation, a third voice will ask a question. You will hear the conversations and questions only once, and they will *not* be written out.

When you have heard each conversation and question, read the four answer choices and select the *one*—(A), (B), (C), or (D)—that best answers the question based on what is directly stated or on what can be inferred. Then fill in the space on your answer sheet that matches the letter of the answer that you have selected.

Here is an example.

You will hear:

Sample Answer

You will read: (A) Open the window.
(B) Move the chair.
(C) Leave the room.
(D) Take a seat.

From the conversation you find out that the woman thinks the man should put the chair over by the window. The best answer to the question, "What does the woman think the man should do?" is (B), "Move the chair." You should fill in (B) on your answer sheet.

1. (A) She broke the window herself.
   (B) She repaired the broken window.
   (C) She was able to get the widow open.
   (D) She hurt herself on the broken glass.

2. (A) The golf tournament made it famous.
   (B) It's grown a lot lately.
   (C) It can't be found without a map.
   (D) Very few people there play golf.

3. (A) Where she got her information.
   (B) How the copy was made.
   (C) Who painted the picture.
   (D) Why the copy was made.

4. (A) Groceries.
   (B) A used car.
   (C) Gasoline.
   (D) Medicine.

5. (A) She read it again and again.
   (B) She covered it up.
   (C) She read every page of it.
   (D) She ripped its cover off.

6. (A) He can no longer play.
   (B) He's played every day for years.
   (C) His playing has improved.
   (D) He played quite well.

7. (A) He needs to get more camping
       equipment.
   (B) He is an experienced camper.
   (C) He is taking too much equipment.
   (D) He shouldn't go camping for such a
       long time.

8. (A) Try to get elected mayor.
   (B) Attend a class.
   (C) Interview the mayor.
   (D) Apply for a job.

9. (A) She was mistaken about Professor
       Leguin.
   (B) She just returned from San Francisco.
   (C) She doesn't know what the professor
       looks like.
   (D) She's an admirer of Professor Leguin.

10. (A) He's speaking a language they don't
        know.
    (B) He doesn't have a microphone.
    (C) He's speaking much too quickly.
    (D) He's using a defective microphone.

11. (A) It's near the elevator.
    (B) He doesn't know where it is.
    (C) It's on another floor.
    (D) The directory doesn't list it.

12. (A) She's heard it only a few times.
    (B) She doesn't get to listen to it very
        often.
    (C) She once liked it, but she's heard
        enough.
    (D) She enjoys it very much.

13. (A) It's no wonder that she had to work.
    (B) It wasn't busy because of the weather.
    (C) She was very busy at work.
    (D) The snow made her late for work.

14. (A) He doesn't have any money left either.
    (B) The club is looking for some new
        members.
    (C) He can lend the woman some money.
    (D) It doesn't cost much to join the club.

15. (A) He doesn't enjoy receptions.
    (B) He uses his computer a lot.
    (C) His computer isn't working.
    (D) He will definitely attend.

16. (A) Only one person in the group is older
        than he.
    (B) His group is almost the oldest.
    (C) He's the youngest person in the group.
    (D) He appears only in the second
        photograph.

17. (A) Pancakes are not his favorite dish.
    (B) His pancakes don't taste very good.
    (C) He never makes enough pancakes.
    (D) He can't cook many dishes.

Go on to the next page

$$\boxed{1} \quad \boxed{1} \quad \boxed{1} \quad \boxed{1} \quad \boxed{1} \quad \boxed{1} \quad \boxed{1} \quad \boxed{1} \quad \boxed{1} \quad \boxed{1} \quad \boxed{1} \quad \boxed{1}$$

18. (A) She disagrees with the man.
    (B) She doesn't know Professor Bryant.
    (C) She thinks Professor Bryant is fair too.
    (D) She doesn't understand the man's remark.

19. (A) In a few days.
    (B) Before they eat.
    (C) During lunch.
    (D) When lunch is over.

20. (A) The woman would enjoy the mountain scenery.
    (B) The weather has been hot this month.
    (C) The weather in the mountains is unusual.
    (D) The woman probably doesn't like cool weather.

21. (A) It has exceptionally good service.
    (B) It has excellent food.
    (C) The service there is disappointing.
    (D) Everything there is great.

22. (A) If his name sounds familiar.
    (B) If she's spoken to him on the phone.
    (C) If he's a musician.
    (D) If she likes his name.

23. (A) He thought other science courses would be harder.
    (B) It's a required class for all students.
    (C) He's studied geology before.
    (D) It was the only science course open to him.

24. (A) He's never been to the zoo.
    (B) He's seen only one bear.
    (C) He's never seen a bear in the wild.
    (D) There weren't any bears at that zoo.

25. (A) When she will answer the questions.
    (B) Where she drove.
    (C) What kind of car she has.
    (D) Why she asked so many questions.

26. (A) He thinks it will be better than the old one.
    (B) He's anxious for it to be completed.
    (C) He's worried that it's not long enough.
    (D) He feels that it shouldn't have been built.

27. (A) Where he's studying.
    (B) What subject he's studying.
    (C) How long he's been in Europe.
    (D) When he's returning.

28. (A) Charlotte wouldn't be attending graduate school.
    (B) Charlotte had gotten a scholarship.
    (C) Graduate school wouldn't start until September.
    (D) Scholarships were easy to get.

29. (A) He paid it today for the first time.
    (B) He pays it on the last day of the month.
    (C) He pays it after it's due.
    (D) He's planning to pay it tomorrow.

30. (A) The debate involved only a few issues.
    (B) Many people changed their plans.
    (C) A lot of people attended.
    (D) The debate lasted longer than expected.

Part B

Directions: This part of the test consists of extended conversations between two speakers. After each of these conversations, there are a number of questions. You will hear each conversation and question only once, and the questions are *not* written out.

When you have heard the questions, read the four answer choices and select the *one*—(A), (B), (C), or (D)—that best answers the question based on what is directly stated or on what can be inferred. Then fill in the space on your answer sheet that matches the letter of the answer that you have selected.

Don't forget: During actual exams, taking notes or writing in your test book is *not* permitted.

31. (A) Because it was cheap.
    (B) Because it is in such good condition.
    (C) Because it is a collector's item.
    (D) Because he can re-sell it at a high price.

32. (A) In the 1930's.
    (B) In the 1940's.
    (C) In the 1950's.
    (D) In the 1960's.

33. (A) Replace its engine.
    (B) Enter it in some shows.
    (C) Take it on a long drive.
    (D) Re-sell it for more money.

34. (A) At a conference hall.
    (B) At an art gallery.
    (C) At an airport.
    (D) At a hotel.

35. (A) To attend a conference.
    (B) To see the planetarium.
    (C) To change planes.
    (D) To go sightseeing.

36. (A) She recently went there.
    (B) It's not a very good one.
    (C) There's one in her hometown.
    (D) It will be closed when she's free.

37. (A) On foot and by boat.
    (B) By car and on foot.
    (C) By air and by car.
    (D) By car and by bus.

1 1 1 1 1 1 1 1 1 1 1

Part C

Directions: This part of the test consists of several talks, each given by a single speaker. After each of these talks, there are a number of questions. You will hear each talk and question only once, and the questions are *not* written out.

When you have heard each question, read the four answer choices and select the *one*—(A), (B), (C), or (D)—that best answers the question based on what is directly stated or on what can be inferred. Then fill in the space on your answer sheet that matches the letter of the answer that you have selected.

Here is an example.

You will hear:

Now here is a sample question.

Sample Answer

You will read: (A) Philosophy.
(B) Meteorology.
(C) Astronomy.
(D) Photography.

The lecture concerns a lunar eclipse, a topic that would typically be discussed in an astronomy class. The choice that best answers the question, "In what course is this lecture probably being given?" is (C), "Astronomy." You should fill in (C) on your answer sheet.

Here is another sample question:

You will hear:

Sample Answer

You will read: (A) The Earth's shadow moves across the Moon.
(B) Clouds block the view of the Moon.
(C) The Moon moves between the Earth and the Sun.
(D) The Sun can be observed without special equipment.

From the lecture you learn that a lunar eclipse occurs when the Earth moves between the Sun and the Moon and the shadow of the Earth passes across the Moon. The choice that best answers the

1 1 1 1 1 1 1 1 1 1 1

38. (A) Tourists.
    (B) Professional dancers.
    (C) Students.
    (D) Traditional musicians.

39. (A) It will be different from the ones usually
        performed in Hawaii today.
    (B) It will involve women wearing grass
        skirts.
    (C) It will involve only male dancers.
    (D) It was once performed for great
        Hawaiian leaders.

40. (A) They prohibited it.
    (B) They sponsored it.
    (C) They proposed some small changes
        in it.
    (D) They exported it to other islands.

41. (A) Attend a live performance.
    (B) Go on a tour.
    (C) Perform a dance.
    (D) Watch a video.

42. (A) To discuss a weather phenomenon.
    (B) To explain how to drive during storms.
    (C) To describe supercooled water.
    (D) To warn gardeners of the danger of
        hail.

43. (A) Because of its size.
    (B) Because of its color.
    (C) Because of its layers.
    (D) Because of its weight.

44. (A) As a drop of supercooled water.
    (B) As a snowflake.
    (C) As a particle of dust.
    (D) As a ball of ice.

45. (A) In the spring.
    (B) In the summer.
    (C) In the fall.
    (D) In the winter.

46. (A) New theories about the origin of
        language.
    (B) How to teach grammar to children.
    (C) Mistakes children sometimes make.
    (D) The stages of children's language
        learning.

47. (A) "Koo, Koo."
    (B) "Da-da."
    (C) "More milk!"
    (D) "Na-na."

48. (A) Between four and eight months.
    (B) Between one year and eighteen
        months.
    (C) Between two and three years.
    (D) Between three and four years.

49. (A) They are the same in all languages.
    (B) They are often misinterpreted.
    (C) They are learned by imitation.
    (D) They are quite logical.

50. (A) They are too complicated.
    (B) She doesn't have time to talk about
        them today.
    (C) The class didn't have a chance to read
        about them.
    (D) She doesn't agree with them.

THIS IS THE END OF SECTION 1, LISTENING COMPREHENSION.

STOP WORK ON SECTION 1.

2 Structure and Written Expression

Time: 25 minutes

This section tests your ability to recognize grammar and usage suitable for standard written English. This section is divided into two parts, each with its own directions.

Structure

Directions: Items in this part are incomplete sentences. Following each of these sentences, there are four words or phrases. You should select the *one* word or phrase—(A), (B), (C), or (D)—that best completes the sentence. Then fill in the space on your answer sheet that matches the letter of the answer that you have selected.

Example I

Pepsin _____ an enzyme used
in digestion.

(A) that
(B) is
(C) of
(D) being

Sample Answer

(A) ● (C) (D)

This sentence should properly read "Pepsin is an enzyme used in digestion." You should fill in (B) on your answer sheet.

Example II

_____ large natural lakes are found
in the state of South Carolina.

(A) There are no
(B) Not the
(C) It is not
(D) No

Sample Answer

(A) (B) (C) ●

This sentence should properly read "No large natural lakes are found in the state of South Carolina." You should fill in (D) on your answer sheet.

As soon as you understand the directions, begin work on this part.

Go on to the next page

2 **2** **2** **2** **2** **2** **2** **2** **2** **2** **2** **2**

1. Ellen Swallow Richards became the first woman to enter, graduate from, and _____ at the Massachusetts Institute of Technology.
   (A) teach
   (B) a teacher
   (C) who taught
   (D) to teach

2. Coins last approximately twenty times _____ paper bills.
   (A) longer
   (B) as long
   (C) long
   (D) longer than

3. It has been estimated that _____ species of animals.
   (A) more than a million
   (B) it is a million or more
   (C) there are over a million
   (D) are over a million of

4. Dr. Seuss, _____ real name was Theodore Seuss Geisel, wrote and illustrated delightfully humorous books for children.
   (A) his
   (B) who had as his
   (C) with his
   (D) whose

5. _____ American landscape architects was Hideo Sasaki.
   (A) The most famous one of
   (B) One of the most famous
   (C) Of the one most famous
   (D) The one most famous of

6. Most young geese leave their nests at an early age, and young snow geese are _____ exception.
   (A) not
   (B) no
   (C) none
   (D) never

7. Vancouver, British Columbia, has a temperate climate for a city situated _____ far north.
   (A) as
   (B) so
   (C) very
   (D) by

2 2 2 2 2 2 2 2 2 2 2 2

8. _____ in 1849, Manuel A. Alonso recorded the customs, language, and songs of the people of Puerto Rico in his poetry and prose.
   (A) Beginning
   (B) He began
   (C) Having begun
   (D) The beginning was

9. _____ the sails of a distant ship are visible before the body of the ship.
   (A) The curve of the Earth makes
   (B) The Earth, in that it curves, makes
   (C) Because the curve of the Earth,
   (D) Because of the curve of the Earth,

10. Printing ink is made _____ of a paste, which is applied to the printing surface with rollers.
    (A) to form
    (B) the form
    (C) in the form
    (D) so that it forms

11. Although _____ cold climates, they can thrive in hot, dry climates as well.
    (A) sheep adapted well
    (B) well-adapted sheep
    (C) sheep, well adapted to
    (D) sheep are well adapted to

12. Not only _____ as a shade tree, but it also produces wood used for boxes and furniture.
    (A) the linden tree is of value
    (B) the value of the linden tree is
    (C) is the linden tree valuable
    (D) the valuable linden tree is used

13. _____ one of Laura Ingalls Wilder's many books about the American frontier are based on her own childhood experiences.
    (A) Except
    (B) All but
    (C) Without
    (D) Not any

14. One of the first industries to be affected by the Industrial Revolution _____.
    (A) was the textile industry
    (B) the textile industry
    (C) in the textile industry
    (D) the textile industry was

15. _____ the outer rings of a gyroscope are turned or twisted, the gyroscope itself continues to spin in exactly the same position.
    (A) However
    (B) Somehow
    (C) Otherwise
    (D) No matter

Go on to the next page

Written Expression

Directions: The items in this part have four underlined words or phrases—(A), (B), (C), and (D). You must identify the *one* underlined expression that must be changed for the sentence to be correct. Then find the number of the question on your answer sheet and fill in the space corresponding to the letter.

Example I   Sample Answer

                                                             (●) (B) (C) (D)

        Lenses may <u>to have</u> either <u>concave</u> <u>or</u>
                   A   B   C
        convex <u>shapes</u>.
                 D

This sentence should read "Lenses may have either concave or convex shapes." You should therefore select answer (A).

Example II   Sample Answer

                                                            (A) (●) (C) (D)

        <u>When</u> painting a fresco, an artist <u>is applied</u> paint
         A   B
        <u>directly</u> to the damp plaster <u>of a wall</u>.
         C   D

This sentence should read "When painting a fresco, an artist applies paint directly to the damp plaster of a wall." You should therefore select answer (B).

As soon as you understand the directions, begin work on this section.

② ② ② ② ② ② ② ② ② ② ② ②

16. The rock formations in the Valley of Fire in Nevada <u>has</u> been <u>worn</u> into many <u>strange</u> shapes
                                                 A   B   C

 by the <u>action</u> of wind and water.
         D

17. The <u>author</u> Susan Glaspell <u>won</u> a Pulitzer Prize in 1931 <u>for</u> <u>hers</u> play, *Alison's House*.
       A   B   C   D

18. Haywood Broun was a <u>read widely</u> <u>newspaper</u> columnist <u>who wrote</u> <u>during</u> the 1920's and
                                 A   B   C   D

 1930's.

19. <u>Researches</u> in <u>economics</u>, psychology, and <u>marketing</u> can <u>help</u> businesses.
     A   B   C   D

20. <u>Because of</u> their color and shape, seahorses blend <u>so well</u> with the seaweed <u>in which</u> they live
       A   B   C

 that it is almost impossible to see <u>themselves</u>.
                                        D

21. <u>Although</u> the social sciences <u>different</u> a great deal from <u>one another</u>, they share a common
       A   B   C

 <u>interest in</u> human relationships.
       D

22. Herman Melville's <u>novel</u> *Moby-Dick* describes the <u>dangers</u>, difficult, and often <u>violent</u> life
                   A   B   C

 <u>aboard</u> a whaling ship.
       D

23. Near <u>equator</u>, the slant of the sun's rays is never <u>great enough</u> to cause temperatures <u>to fall</u>
           A   B   C

 below <u>the freezing point</u>.
                D

24. Stephen Hopkins <u>was</u> a <u>cultural</u> and political <u>leadership</u> <u>in</u> colonial Rhode Island.
                     A   B   C   D

25. A mousebird's <u>tail</u> is <u>double</u> as <u>long</u> as <u>its body</u>.
              A   B   C   D

Go on to the next page ➡

② ② ② ② ② ② ② ② ② ② ② ②

26. The Uinta Mountains of northeastern Utah are <u>the only</u> range of mountains in North America

        A
<u>that runs</u> from east <u>and</u> west for its entire <u>length</u>.

   B   C   D

27. The <u>tools</u> used <u>most often</u> by <u>floral</u> designers are the <u>knives</u>, scissors, and glue gun.

     A   B   C   D

28. <u>Most</u> types of dolphins live <u>at less</u> 25 years, and <u>some</u> species may reach 50 years <u>of age</u>.

  A   B   C   D

29. Isle Royale National Park <u>in</u> Lake Superior <u>can</u> only <u>be reached</u> by <u>the boat</u>.

               A   B   C   D

30. The main <u>divisions</u> of geologic <u>time</u>, <u>called</u> eras, are subdivided <u>to</u> periods.

        A   B   C   D

31. All <u>root</u> vegetables <u>grow</u> underground, <u>and</u> not all vegetables <u>that</u> grow underground are

    A   B   C   D

roots.

32. The <u>process</u> of fermentation <u>takes place</u> <u>only in</u> the <u>absent</u> of oxygen.

    A   B   C   D

33. <u>In</u> about 1920, experimental <u>psychologists</u> have devoted more research <u>to learning</u> than to

  A   B   C

<u>any other</u> topic.

   D

34. Transfer taxes are <u>imposed on</u> the <u>sell</u> or <u>exchange</u> of stocks <u>and</u> bonds.

               A   B   C   D

35. One of the greatest of <u>mountains climbers</u>, Carl Blaurock was <u>the first</u> to climb <u>all of the</u>

                 A   B   C

mountains higher than 14,000 <u>feet</u> in the United States.

                        D

36. Biochemists <u>have solved</u> many of the <u>mysteries</u> about photosynthesis, the <u>process which</u>

           A   B   C

plants make <u>food</u>.

        D

37. Oceanic islands have been separated <u>from</u> the mainland for <u>too</u> long that <u>they have</u> evolved

distinctive animal <u>populations</u>.

        A   B   C

(A = from, B = too, C = they have, D = populations)

38. <u>Certain</u> species of penicillin mold <u>are used</u> to <u>ripe</u> <u>cheese</u>.

    A   B   C   D

(A = Certain, B = are used, C = ripe, D = cheese)

39. <u>Many of the</u> important products <u>obtained</u> from trees, one of <u>the most</u> important is wood pulp,

which is used in <u>paper-making</u>.

      A   B   C

(A = Many of the, B = obtained, C = the most, D = paper-making)

40. <u>Not longer</u> are contributions to the <u>advancement</u> of industry <u>made</u> primarily by individuals.

     A   B   C   D

(A = Not longer, B = contributions, C = advancement, D = made)

THIS IS THE END OF SECTION 2.

IF YOU FINISH BEFORE THE TIME LIMIT, CHECK YOUR WORK ON SECTION 2 ONLY.

DO NOT READ OR WORK ON ANY OTHER SECTION OF THE TEST.

3 Reading Comprehension

Time: 55 minutes

This section of the test measures your ability to comprehend written materials.

Directions: This section contains several passages, each followed by a number of questions. Read the passages and, for each question, choose the *one* best answer—(A), (B), (C), or (D)—based on what is stated in the passage or on what can be inferred from the passage. Then fill in the space on your answer sheet that matches the letter of the answer that you have selected.

▼ **Read the following passage:**

	Like mammals, birds claim their own territories. A bird's territory may be small or large. Some birds claim only their nest and the area right around it,
(line)	while others claim far larger territories that include
(5)	their feeding areas. Gulls, penguins, and other waterfowl nest in huge colonies, but even in the biggest colonies, each male and his mate have small territories of their own immediately around their nests.
	Male birds defend their territory chiefly against other
(10)	males of the same species. In some cases, a warning call or threatening pose may be all the defense needed, but in other cases, intruders may refuse to leave peacefully.

Example I   Sample Answer

What is the main topic of this passage?

(A) Birds that live in colonies
(B) Birds' mating habits
(C) The behavior of birds
(D) Territoriality in birds

The passage mainly concerns the territories of birds. You should fill in (D) on your answer sheet.

Example II   Sample Answer

According to the passage, male birds defend their territory primarily against

(A) female birds
(B) birds of other species
(C) males of their own species
(D) mammals

The passage states that "Male birds defend their territory chiefly ... ..."

Questions 1–11

> To date, Canada has produced only one classic children's tale to
> rank with *Alice's Adventures in Wonderland* and the works of Mark
> Twain; this was Lucy Maud Montgomery's *Anne of Green Gables*.
> (line) Lucy Maud Montgomery was born in Clinton, Prince Edward Island.
> (5) Her mother died soon after her birth, and when her father went to
> Saskatchewan to assume a business position, she moved in with her
> grandparents in Cavendish, Prince Edward Island. There she went
> to school, and later qualified to be a teacher.
>
> Montgomery wrote the *Anne* books while living in Cavendish and
> (10) helping her grandmother at the post office. The first of the
> books, *Anne of Green Gables*, was published in 1908, and in the
> next three years she wrote two sequels. Like Montgomery, the
> heroine of the book is taken in by an elderly couple who live in
> the fictional town of Avonlea, and Montgomery incorporated many
> (15) events from her life in Cavendish into the *Anne* books.
>
> In 1911, Montgomery married Ewan MacDonald, and the couple soon
> moved to Ontario, where she wrote many other books. However, it
> was her first efforts that secured her prominence, and the *Anne*
> books are still read all around the world. Her novels have
> (20) helped create a warm picture of Prince Edward Island's special
> character. Several movies, a television series, and a musical
> play have been based on her tales, and today visitors scour the
> island for locations described in the book.

1. The main purpose of this passage is to
   (A) introduce Montgomery and her *Anne* books
   (B) contrast Canadian children's literature with that of other countries
   (C) provide a brief introduction to Prince Edward Island
   (D) show the similarities between Montgomery's life and that of her fictional character Anne

2. The word "this" in line 3 refers to
   (A) Canada
   (B) a work of Mark Twain
   (C) *Alice's Adventures in Wonderland*
   (D) a Canadian children's classic

3. According to the passage, Montgomery was raised primarily
   (A) in an orphanage
   (B) by her grandparents
   (C) by her mother
   (D) by her father

Go on to the next page ➡

4. Approximately when did Lucy Maud Montgomery write the two sequels to her book *Anne of Green Gables*?
   (A) From 1874 to 1908
   (B) From 1908 to 1911
   (C) From 1911 to 1913
   (D) From 1913 to 1918

5. The word "elderly" in line 13 is closest in meaning to
   (A) kindly
   (B) old
   (C) friendly
   (D) sly

6. In the *Anne* books, the main character lives in
   (A) the town of Cavendish
   (B) Saskatchewan
   (C) the town of Avonlea
   (D) Ontario

7. Which of the following can be concluded from the passage about the *Anne* books?
   (A) They were at least partially autobiographical.
   (B) They were influenced by the works of Mark Twain.
   (C) They were not as successful as Montgomery's later works.
   (D) They were not popular until after Montgomery had died.

8. The word "prominence" in line 18 is closest in meaning to
   (A) reputation
   (B) excellence
   (C) effort
   (D) permanence

9. Which of the following is closest in meaning to the word "character" in line 21?
   (A) A person in a novel
   (B) Nature
   (C) A written symbol
   (D) Location

10. All of the following have been based on the *Anne* books EXCEPT
    (A) a television series
    (B) movies
    (C) a play
    (D) a ballet

11. In line 22, the word "scour" could be replaced by which of the following without changing the meaning of the sentence?
    (A) Cleanse
    (B) Admire
    (C) Search
    (D) Request

Questions 12–23

Certain animals have an intuitive awareness of quantities. They know without analysis the difference between a number of objects and a smaller number. In his book *The Natural History of Selbourne* (1786), the naturalist Gilbert White tells how he surreptitiously removed one egg a day from a plover's nest, and how the mother laid another egg each day to make up for the missing one. He noted that other species of birds ignore the absence of a single egg but abandon their nests if more than one egg has been removed. It has also been noted by naturalists that a certain type of wasp always provides five—never four, never six— caterpillars for each of their eggs so that their young have something to eat when the eggs hatch. Research has also shown that both mice and pigeons can be taught to distinguish between odd and even numbers of food pieces.

These and similar accounts have led some people to infer that creatures other than humans can actually count. They also point to dogs that have been taught to respond to numerical questions with the correct number of barks, or to horses that seem to solve arithmetic problems by stomping their hooves the proper number of times.

Animals respond to quantities only when they are connected to survival as a species—as in the case of the eggs—or survival as individuals—as in the case of food. There is no transfer to other situations or from concrete reality to the abstract notion of numbers. Animals can "count" only when the objects are present and only when the numbers involved are small—no more than seven or eight. In lab experiments, animals trained to "count" one kind of object were unable to count any other type. The objects, not the numbers, are what interest them. Animals' admittedly remarkable achievements simply do not amount to evidence of counting, nor do they reveal more than innate instincts, refined by the genes of successive generations, or the results of clever, careful conditioning by trainers.

(line)
(5)
(10)
(15)
(20)
(25)
(30)

12. What is the main idea of this passage?
    (A) Careful training is required to teach animals to perform tricks involving numbers.
    (B) Animals cannot "count" more than one kind of object.
    (C) Of all animals, dogs and horses can count best.
    (D) Although some animals may be aware of quantities, they cannot actually count.

Go on to the next page

13. Why does the author refer to Gilbert White's book in line 3?
    (A) To show how attitudes have changed since 1786
    (B) To contradict the idea that animals can count
    (C) To provide evidence that some birds are aware of quantities
    (D) To indicate that more research is needed in this field

14. The word "surreptitiously" in line 4 is closest in meaning to
    (A) quickly
    (B) secretly
    (C) occasionally
    (D) stubbornly

15. The word "abandon" in line 8 is closest in meaning to
    (A) vacate
    (B) rebuild
    (C) move
    (D) guard

16. The word "odd," as used in line 14, refers to which of the following?
    (A) Unusual numbers
    (B) Numbers such as 1, 3, 5, and so on
    (C) Lucky numbers
    (D) Numbers such as 2, 4, 6, and so on

17. The author mentions that all of the following are aware of quantities in some way EXCEPT
    (A) plovers
    (B) mice
    (C) caterpillars
    (D) wasps

18. The word "accounts" in line 15 is closest in meaning to
    (A) invoices
    (B) reasons
    (C) reports
    (D) deceptions

19. According to information in the passage, which of the following is LEAST likely to occur as a result of animals' intuitive awareness of quantities?
    (A) A pigeon is more attracted by a box containing two pieces of food than by a box containing one piece.
    (B) When asked by its trainer how old it is, a monkey holds up five fingers.
    (C) When one of its four kittens crawls away, a mother cat misses it and searches for the missing kitten.
    (D) A lion follows one antelope instead of a herd of antelopes because it is easier to hunt a single prey.

20. How would the author probably characterize the people who are mentioned in line 15?
    (A) As mistaken
    (B) As demanding
    (C) As clever
    (D) As foolish

21. The word "admittedly" in line 29 is closest in meaning to
    (A) improbably
    (B) arguably
    (C) apparently
    (D) undeniably

22. In line 31, the word "they" refers to
    (A) numbers
    (B) animals
    (C) achievements
    (D) genes

23. Where in the passage does the author mention research that supports his own view of animals' inability to count?
    (A) Lines 3-6
    (B) Lines 12-14
    (C) Lines 15-16
    (D) Lines 27-28

Questions 24–33

It would be hard to cite a development that has had more impact on American industry than the Bessemer process of making steel. It made possible the production of low-cost steel and
(line) established the foundation of the modern steel industry. In many
(5) ways it was responsible for the rapid industrialization of the United States that took place in the formative period of the late 1800's.

The first Bessemer plant in the United States was built in Wyandotte, Michigan, in 1864, near the end of the Civil War. It
(10) was capable of producing only 2 tons of steel ingots at a time. The ingots were rolled into rails—the first steel rails made in the United States. Acceptance of the process was initially slow. By 1870, the annual output of Bessemer steel was a mere 42 thousand tons. Production grew rapidly after about 1875, rising
(15) to 1.2 million tons in 1880, when it exceeded that of wrought iron for the first time.

Go on to the next page

The rise of the U.S. steel industry in the last quarter of the
19th century was brought about largely by the demand for Bessemer
steel rails for the nation's burgeoning rail network. Steel rails
(20)   were far more durable than those made of iron. Spurred by this
demand, the U.S. steel industry became the largest in the world
in 1886, when it surpassed that of Great Britain.
         The Bessemer Process was the chief method of making steel until
1907, when it was overtaken by the open-hearth process. By the
(25)   1950's, the Bessemer Process accounted for less than 3% of the
total U.S. production.

24. With what topic is this passage mainly concerned?
    (A) The history of metal-working
    (B) A comparison of the U.S. and British steel industries in the nineteenth century
    (C) The technical details of the Bessemer process
    (D) The effects of one method of making steel

25. According to the passage, the Bessemer process contributed to all of the following EXCEPT
    (A) the establishment of the modern steel industry in the United States
    (B) the manufacture of weapons during the Civil War
    (C) lowered costs for steel
    (D) industrial development in the United States during an important period

26. What can be inferred from the passage about wrought iron?
    (A) At one time, more of it was produced than Bessemer steel.
    (B) It is a by-product of the Bessemer process.
    (C) It was once primarily imported from Great Britain.
    (D) It later became a more important product than Bessemer steel.

27. The word "burgeoning" in line 19 is closest in meaning to
    (A) overpowering
    (B) planned
    (C) expanding
    (D) vital

28. According to the passage, why were Bessemer steel rails used in place of iron rails?
    (A) They lasted longer.
    (B) They did not have to be imported.
    (C) They could be installed faster.
    (D) They provided a smoother ride for passengers.

29. The word "Spurred" in line 20 is closest in meaning to which of the following?
    (A) Driven
    (B) Challenged
    (C) Dominated
    (D) Broken

Go on to the next page

30. According to the passage, in what year did the steel industry of the United States begin to produce more steel than that of Great Britain did?
(A) 1864
(B) 1875
(C) 1880
(D) 1886

31. What can be inferred about the steel industry in the United States during the 1950's?
(A) It had begun producing many new types of products.
(B) It was in a period of severe decline.
(C) It primarily involved methods of production other than the Bessemer Process.
(D) It was becoming more and more important.

32. The paragraph following this one probably concerns
(A) innovations in the railroad industry
(B) the open-hearth method of making steel
(C) industrialization in the twentieth century
(D) new methods of making wrought iron

33. The author first begins to discuss the growth of the Bessemer Process in
(A) lines 3-4
(B) lines 8-9
(C) lines 14-16
(D) lines 17-19

Questions 34–41

          Nearly 515 blocks of San Francisco, including almost all of Nob Hill, were destroyed by the 1906 earthquake and fires. Many of San Francisco's "painted ladies"—its gaudy, nineteenth century
(line)   Victorian houses—were lost in the disaster. Today, some 14,000
(5)   surviving houses have been preserved, particularly in the Cow Hollow, Mission, Pacific Heights, and Alamo Square districts.
          Distinguished by their design characteristics, three styles of San Franciscan Victorians can be found today. The Italianate, which flourished in the 1870's, is characterized by a flat roof,
(10)   slim pillars flanking the front door, and bays with windows that slant inward. The ornamentation of these narrow row houses was patterned after features of the Roman Classical styles. The Stick style, which peaked in popularity during the 1880s, added ornate woodwork outlines to the doors and windows. Other
(15)   additions included the French cap, gables, and three-sided bays. Designs changed dramatically when the Queen Anne style became the rage in the 1890's. Turrets, towers, steep gabled roofs, and glass art windows distinguished Queen Anne houses from their predecessors.

Go on to the next page

(20)   In the period after the earthquake, the Victorians came to be
regarded as impossibly old-fashioned, but beginning around 1960,
owners began peeling off stucco, tearing off false fronts,
reapplying custom woodwork, and commissioning multi-hued paint
jobs. Before long, many of these houses had been restored to
their former splendor.

34. Which of the following is NOT one of the author's purposes in writing the passage?
(A) To talk about the restoration of Victorian houses in San Francisco in the 1960's
(B) To discuss housing problems in San Francisco today
(C) To briefly trace the history of Victorian houses in San Francisco
(D) To categorize the three types of Victorian houses found in San Francisco

35. The word "gaudy" in line 3 is closest in meaning to
(A) showy
(B) enormous
(C) antiquated
(D) simple

36. According to the passage, in what district of San Francisco are authentic Victorian houses
LEAST likely to be found today?
(A) Cow Hollow
(B) Pacific Heights
(C) The Mission
(D) Nob Hill

37. According to the passage, which of the following styles of architecture was the last to become
fashionable in San Francisco?
(A) Roman Classical
(B) Italianate
(C) Stick
(D) Queen Anne

38. As used in the second paragraph, the word "bays" refers to
(A) bodies of water
(B) colors
(C) architectural features
(D) trees

39. Which of the following is most likely to be seen only on a Queen Anne style house?
(A) A flat roof
(B) A tower
(C) A French cap
(D) Gables

Go on to the next page ➡

40. During which of the following periods were San Francisco's Victorian houses generally thought of as old-fashioned?
    (A) From 1870 to 1890
    (B) During the 1890's
    (C) From 1907 to 1960
    (D) During the 1960's

41. What can be inferred from the passage about Victorian houses after they had been restored?
    (A) They were painted in many colors.
    (B) They looked exactly like modern houses.
    (C) They were covered with new fronts made of stucco.
    (D) They were more attractive than the original houses.

Questions 42–50

Sea otters dwell in the North Pacific. They are the largest of the mustelids, a group which also includes freshwater otters, weasels, and badgers. They are from four to five feet long, and most weigh from 60 to 85 pounds. Large males may weigh 100 pounds
(5) or more.

Unlike most marine mammals, such as seals or dolphins, sea otters lack a layer of blubber, and therefore have to eat up to 30% of their body weight a day in clams, crabs, fish, octopus, squids, and other delicacies to maintain body heat. Their
(10) voracious appetites do not create food shortages, though, because they are picky eaters, each animal preferring only a few food types. Thus no single type of food source is exhausted. Sea otters play an important environmental role by protecting forests of seaweed called kelp, which provide shelter and nutrients for
(15) many species. Certain sea otters feast on invertebrates like sea urchins and abalones that destroy kelp.

Sea otters eat and sleep while floating on their backs, often on masses of kelp. They seldom come on shore. Sea otters keep warm by means of their luxuriant double-layered fur, the densest
(20) among animals. The soft outer fur forms a protective cover that keeps the fine underfur dry. One square inch of underfur contains up to 1 million hairs. Unfortunately, this essential feature almost led to their extinction, as commercial fur hunters drastically reduced their numbers.

(25) Under government protection, the sea otter population has recovered. While elated by the otters return, scientists are concerned about the California sea otter population growth of 5% a year, lagging behind the 18% a year rate among Alaska otters. Sea otters are extremely sensitive to pollution. In 1989 up to
(30) 5,000 sea otters perished when the *Exxon Valdez* spilled oil in Prince William Sound, Alaska.

Go on to the next page ➤

42. According to the passage, what are mustelids?
    (A) A family of marine mammals that have blubber
    (B) A type of sea otter
    (C) A group of mammals that contains sea otters
    (D) A kind of sea animal that includes clams, crabs, and many other creatures

43. It can be inferred from that passage that, if a large male sea otter weighs 100 pounds, it must eat approximately how many pounds of food a day to maintain its body heat?
    (A) 5 pounds
    (B) 15 pounds
    (C) 30 pounds
    (D) 60 pounds

44. The author refers to sea otters as "picky eaters" (line 11) because
    (A) all sea otters eat many types of food
    (B) each sea otter eats only one type of food
    (C) all sea otters have voracious appetites
    (D) each sea otter eats only a few kinds of food

45. The word "exhausted" in line 12 is closest in meaning to
    (A) needed
    (B) used up
    (C) desired
    (D) tired out

46. According to the passage, which of the following best describes sea otters' relationship with kelp forests?
    (A) The kelp serves as food for the otters.
    (B) The otters protect the kelp by eating animals that destroy it.
    (C) The otters eliminate the kelp's source of nutrients.
    (D) The kelp is destroyed when the otters build shelters.

47. Which of the following could best replace the word "luxuriant" in line 19?
    (A) Expensive
    (B) Soft
    (C) Abundant
    (D) Attractive

48. According to the passage, the outer fur of sea otters
    (A) keeps the underfur from getting wet
    (B) seems finer than the underfur
    (C) is more desirable to hunters than the underfur
    (D) is not as soft as the underfur

49. The word "elated" in line 26 is closest in meaning to
    (A) disappointed
    (B) shocked
    (C) concerned
    (D) overjoyed

Go on to the next page

50. According to the passage, why are scientists concerned about the population of California sea otters?
(A) It has been growing at too fast a rate.
(B) Its growth rate has been steadily decreasing.
(C) Its growth rate is not as fast as that of the Alaska sea otters.
(D) It has been greatly reduced by oil spills and other forms of pollution.

THIS IS THE END OF THE SAMPLE READING COMPREHENSION SECTION.

IF YOU FINISH BEFORE THE TIME LIMIT,

GO BACK AND CHECK YOUR WORK IN THIS SECTION ONLY.

About the Author

Bruce Rogers has taught English as a second language and test-preparation courses at the Economics Institute in Boulder, Colorado, since 1979. He has also taught in programs in Indonesia, Vietnam, South Korea, and the Czech Republic. He is the author of *The Complete Guide to TOEIC* and *The Complete Guide to TOEFL: Practice Tests*.

SAMPLE LISTENING COMPREHENSION TEST
ANSWER SHEET

1. Ⓐ Ⓑ Ⓒ Ⓓ
2. Ⓐ Ⓑ Ⓒ Ⓓ
3. Ⓐ Ⓑ Ⓒ Ⓓ
4. Ⓐ Ⓑ Ⓒ Ⓓ
5. Ⓐ Ⓑ Ⓒ Ⓓ
6. Ⓐ Ⓑ Ⓒ Ⓓ
7. Ⓐ Ⓑ Ⓒ Ⓓ
8. Ⓐ Ⓑ Ⓒ Ⓓ
9. Ⓐ Ⓑ Ⓒ Ⓓ
10. Ⓐ Ⓑ Ⓒ Ⓓ
11. Ⓐ Ⓑ Ⓒ Ⓓ
12. Ⓐ Ⓑ Ⓒ Ⓓ
13. Ⓐ Ⓑ Ⓒ Ⓓ
14. Ⓐ Ⓑ Ⓒ Ⓓ
15. Ⓐ Ⓑ Ⓒ Ⓓ
16. Ⓐ Ⓑ Ⓒ Ⓓ
17. Ⓐ Ⓑ Ⓒ Ⓓ
18. Ⓐ Ⓑ Ⓒ Ⓓ
19. Ⓐ Ⓑ Ⓒ Ⓓ
20. Ⓐ Ⓑ Ⓒ Ⓓ
21. Ⓐ Ⓑ Ⓒ Ⓓ
22. Ⓐ Ⓑ Ⓒ Ⓓ
23. Ⓐ Ⓑ Ⓒ Ⓓ
24. Ⓐ Ⓑ Ⓒ Ⓓ
25. Ⓐ Ⓑ Ⓒ Ⓓ

26. Ⓐ Ⓑ Ⓒ Ⓓ
27. Ⓐ Ⓑ Ⓒ Ⓓ
28. Ⓐ Ⓑ Ⓒ Ⓓ
29. Ⓐ Ⓑ Ⓒ Ⓓ
30. Ⓐ Ⓑ Ⓒ Ⓓ
31. Ⓐ Ⓑ Ⓒ Ⓓ
32. Ⓐ Ⓑ Ⓒ Ⓓ
33. Ⓐ Ⓑ Ⓒ Ⓓ
34. Ⓐ Ⓑ Ⓒ Ⓓ
35. Ⓐ Ⓑ Ⓒ Ⓓ
36. Ⓐ Ⓑ Ⓒ Ⓓ
37. Ⓐ Ⓑ Ⓒ Ⓓ
38. Ⓐ Ⓑ Ⓒ Ⓓ
39. Ⓐ Ⓑ Ⓒ Ⓓ
40. Ⓐ Ⓑ Ⓒ Ⓓ
41. Ⓐ Ⓑ Ⓒ Ⓓ
42. Ⓐ Ⓑ Ⓒ Ⓓ
43. Ⓐ Ⓑ Ⓒ Ⓓ
44. Ⓐ Ⓑ Ⓒ Ⓓ
45. Ⓐ Ⓑ Ⓒ Ⓓ
46. Ⓐ Ⓑ Ⓒ Ⓓ
47. Ⓐ Ⓑ Ⓒ Ⓓ
48. Ⓐ Ⓑ Ⓒ Ⓓ
49. Ⓐ Ⓑ Ⓒ Ⓓ
50. Ⓐ Ⓑ Ⓒ Ⓓ

SAMPLE STRUCTURE AND WRITTEN EXPRESSION TEST
ANSWER SHEET

1. (A) (B) (C) (D)	21. (A) (B) (C) (D)
2. (A) (B) (C) (D)	22. (A) (B) (C) (D)
3. (A) (B) (C) (D)	23. (A) (B) (C) (D)
4. (A) (B) (C) (D)	24. (A) (B) (C) (D)
5. (A) (B) (C) (D)	25. (A) (B) (C) (D)
6. (A) (B) (C) (D)	26. (A) (B) (C) (D)
7. (A) (B) (C) (D)	27. (A) (B) (C) (D)
8. (A) (B) (C) (D)	28. (A) (B) (C) (D)
9. (A) (B) (C) (D)	29. (A) (B) (C) (D)
10. (A) (B) (C) (D)	30. (A) (B) (C) (D)
11. (A) (B) (C) (D)	31. (A) (B) (C) (D)
12. (A) (B) (C) (D)	32. (A) (B) (C) (D)
13. (A) (B) (C) (D)	33. (A) (B) (C) (D)
14. (A) (B) (C) (D)	34. (A) (B) (C) (D)
15. (A) (B) (C) (D)	35. (A) (B) (C) (D)
16. (A) (B) (C) (D)	36. (A) (B) (C) (D)
17. (A) (B) (C) (D)	37. (A) (B) (C) (D)
18. (A) (B) (C) (D)	38. (A) (B) (C) (D)
19. (A) (B) (C) (D)	39. (A) (B) (C) (D)
20. (A) (B) (C) (D)	40. (A) (B) (C) (D)

SAMPLE READING COMPREHENSION TEST
ANSWER SHEET

1. (A) (B) (C) (D)
2. (A) (B) (C) (D)
3. (A) (B) (C) (D)
4. (A) (B) (C) (D)
5. (A) (B) (C) (D)
6. (A) (B) (C) (D)
7. (A) (B) (C) (D)
8. (A) (B) (C) (D)
9. (A) (B) (C) (D)
10. (A) (B) (C) (D)
11. (A) (B) (C) (D)
12. (A) (B) (C) (D)
13. (A) (B) (C) (D)
14. (A) (B) (C) (D)
15. (A) (B) (C) (D)
16. (A) (B) (C) (D)
17. (A) (B) (C) (D)
18. (A) (B) (C) (D)
19. (A) (B) (C) (D)
20. (A) (B) (C) (D)
21. (A) (B) (C) (D)
22. (A) (B) (C) (D)
23. (A) (B) (C) (D)
24. (A) (B) (C) (D)
25. (A) (B) (C) (D)

26. (A) (B) (C) (D)
27. (A) (B) (C) (D)
28. (A) (B) (C) (D)
29. (A) (B) (C) (D)
30. (A) (B) (C) (D)
31. (A) (B) (C) (D)
32. (A) (B) (C) (D)
33. (A) (B) (C) (D)
34. (A) (B) (C) (D)
35. (A) (B) (C) (D)
36. (A) (B) (C) (D)
37. (A) (B) (C) (D)
38. (A) (B) (C) (D)
39. (A) (B) (C) (D)
40. (A) (B) (C) (D)
41. (A) (B) (C) (D)
42. (A) (B) (C) (D)
43. (A) (B) (C) (D)
44. (A) (B) (C) (D)
45. (A) (B) (C) (D)
46. (A) (B) (C) (D)
47. (A) (B) (C) (D)
48. (A) (B) (C) (D)
49. (A) (B) (C) (D)
50. (A) (B) (C) (D)

PRACTICE TEST 1
ANSWER SHEET

Name: _____

	Section 1		Section 2		Section 3

Section 1

1. (A) (B) (C) (D)
2. (A) (B) (C) (D)
3. (A) (B) (C) (D)
4. (A) (B) (C) (D)
5. (A) (B) (C) (D)
6. (A) (B) (C) (D)
7. (A) (B) (C) (D)
8. (A) (B) (C) (D)
9. (A) (B) (C) (D)
10. (A) (B) (C) (D)
11. (A) (B) (C) (D)
12. (A) (B) (C) (D)
13. (A) (B) (C) (D)
14. (A) (B) (C) (D)
15. (A) (B) (C) (D)
16. (A) (B) (C) (D)
17. (A) (B) (C) (D)
18. (A) (B) (C) (D)
19. (A) (B) (C) (D)
20. (A) (B) (C) (D)
21. (A) (B) (C) (D)
22. (A) (B) (C) (D)
23. (A) (B) (C) (D)
24. (A) (B) (C) (D)
25. (A) (B) (C) (D)
26. (A) (B) (C) (D)
27. (A) (B) (C) (D)
28. (A) (B) (C) (D)
29. (A) (B) (C) (D)
30. (A) (B) (C) (D)
31. (A) (B) (C) (D)
32. (A) (B) (C) (D)
33. (A) (B) (C) (D)
34. (A) (B) (C) (D)
35. (A) (B) (C) (D)
36. (A) (B) (C) (D)
37. (A) (B) (C) (D)
38. (A) (B) (C) (D)
39. (A) (B) (C) (D)
40. (A) (B) (C) (D)
41. (A) (B) (C) (D)
42. (A) (B) (C) (D)
43. (A) (B) (C) (D)
44. (A) (B) (C) (D)
45. (A) (B) (C) (D)
46. (A) (B) (C) (D)
47. (A) (B) (C) (D)
48. (A) (B) (C) (D)
49. (A) (B) (C) (D)
50. (A) (B) (C) (D)

Section 2

1. (A) (B) (C) (D)
2. (A) (B) (C) (D)
3. (A) (B) (C) (D)
4. (A) (B) (C) (D)
5. (A) (B) (C) (D)
6. (A) (B) (C) (D)
7. (A) (B) (C) (D)
8. (A) (B) (C) (D)
9. (A) (B) (C) (D)
10. (A) (B) (C) (D)
11. (A) (B) (C) (D)
12. (A) (B) (C) (D)
13. (A) (B) (C) (D)
14. (A) (B) (C) (D)
15. (A) (B) (C) (D)
16. (A) (B) (C) (D)
17. (A) (B) (C) (D)
18. (A) (B) (C) (D)
19. (A) (B) (C) (D)
20. (A) (B) (C) (D)
21. (A) (B) (C) (D)
22. (A) (B) (C) (D)
23. (A) (B) (C) (D)
24. (A) (B) (C) (D)
25. (A) (B) (C) (D)
26. (A) (B) (C) (D)
27. (A) (B) (C) (D)
28. (A) (B) (C) (D)
29. (A) (B) (C) (D)
30. (A) (B) (C) (D)
31. (A) (B) (C) (D)
32. (A) (B) (C) (D)
33. (A) (B) (C) (D)
34. (A) (B) (C) (D)
35. (A) (B) (C) (D)
36. (A) (B) (C) (D)
37. (A) (B) (C) (D)
38. (A) (B) (C) (D)
39. (A) (B) (C) (D)
40. (A) (B) (C) (D)

Section 3

1. (A) (B) (C) (D)
2. (A) (B) (C) (D)
3. (A) (B) (C) (D)
4. (A) (B) (C) (D)
5. (A) (B) (C) (D)
6. (A) (B) (C) (D)
7. (A) (B) (C) (D)
8. (A) (B) (C) (D)
9. (A) (B) (C) (D)
10. (A) (B) (C) (D)
11. (A) (B) (C) (D)
12. (A) (B) (C) (D)
13. (A) (B) (C) (D)
14. (A) (B) (C) (D)
15. (A) (B) (C) (D)
16. (A) (B) (C) (D)
17. (A) (B) (C) (D)
18. (A) (B) (C) (D)
19. (A) (B) (C) (D)
20. (A) (B) (C) (D)
21. (A) (B) (C) (D)
22. (A) (B) (C) (D)
23. (A) (B) (C) (D)
24. (A) (B) (C) (D)
25. (A) (B) (C) (D)
26. (A) (B) (C) (D)
27. (A) (B) (C) (D)
28. (A) (B) (C) (D)
29. (A) (B) (C) (D)
30. (A) (B) (C) (D)
31. (A) (B) (C) (D)
32. (A) (B) (C) (D)
33. (A) (B) (C) (D)
34. (A) (B) (C) (D)
35. (A) (B) (C) (D)
36. (A) (B) (C) (D)
37. (A) (B) (C) (D)
38. (A) (B) (C) (D)
39. (A) (B) (C) (D)
40. (A) (B) (C) (D)
41. (A) (B) (C) (D)
42. (A) (B) (C) (D)
43. (A) (B) (C) (D)
44. (A) (B) (C) (D)
45. (A) (B) (C) (D)
46. (A) (B) (C) (D)
47. (A) (B) (C) (D)
48. (A) (B) (C) (D)
49. (A) (B) (C) (D)
50. (A) (B) (C) (D)

PRACTICE TEST 2
ANSWER SHEET

Name:

Section 1	Section 2	Section 3

Section 1
1. A B C D
2. A B C D
3. A B C D
4. A B C D
5. A B C D
6. A B C D
7. A B C D
8. A B C D
9. A B C D
10. A B C D
11. A B C D
12. A B C D
13. A B C D
14. A B C D
15. A B C D
16. A B C D
17. A B C D
18. A B C D
19. A B C D
20. A B C D
21. A B C D
22. A B C D
23. A B C D
24. A B C D
25. A B C D
26. A B C D
27. A B C D
28. A B C D
29. A B C D
30. A B C D
31. A B C D
32. A B C D
33. A B C D
34. A B C D
35. A B C D
36. A B C D
37. A B C D
38. A B C D
39. A B C D
40. A B C D
41. A B C D
42. A B C D
43. A B C D
44. A B C D
45. A B C D
46. A B C D
47. A B C D
48. A B C D
49. A B C D
50. A B C D

Section 2
1. A B C D
2. A B C D
3. A B C D
4. A B C D
5. A B C D
6. A B C D
7. A B C D
8. A B C D
9. A B C D
10. A B C D
11. A B C D
12. A B C D
13. A B C D
14. A B C D
15. A B C D
16. A B C D
17. A B C D
18. A B C D
19. A B C D
20. A B C D
21. A B C D
22. A B C D
23. A B C D
24. A B C D
25. A B C D
26. A B C D
27. A B C D
28. A B C D
29. A B C D
30. A B C D
31. A B C D
32. A B C D
33. A B C D
34. A B C D
35. A B C D
36. A B C D
37. A B C D
38. A B C D
39. A B C D
40. A B C D

Section 3
1. A B C D
2. A B C D
3. A B C D
4. A B C D
5. A B C D
6. A B C D
7. A B C D
8. A B C D
9. A B C D
10. A B C D
11. A B C D
12. A B C D
13. A B C D
14. A B C D
15. A B C D
16. A B C D
17. A B C D
18. A B C D
19. A B C D
20. A B C D
21. A B C D
22. A B C D
23. A B C D
24. A B C D
25. A B C D
26. A B C D
27. A B C D
28. A B C D
29. A B C D
30. A B C D
31. A B C D
32. A B C D
33. A B C D
34. A B C D
35. A B C D
36. A B C D
37. A B C D
38. A B C D
39. A B C D
40. A B C D
41. A B C D
42. A B C D
43. A B C D
44. A B C D
45. A B C D
46. A B C D
47. A B C D
48. A B C D
49. A B C D
50. A B C D

PRACTICE TEST 3
ANSWER SHEET

Name: _____

Section 1	Section 2	Section 3

Section 1

1. A B C D
2. A B C D
3. A B C D
4. A B C D
5. A B C D
6. A B C D
7. A B C D
8. A B C D
9. A B C D
10. A B C D
11. A B C D
12. A B C D
13. A B C D
14. A B C D
15. A B C D
16. A B C D
17. A B C D
18. A B C D
19. A B C D
20. A B C D
21. A B C D
22. A B C D
23. A B C D
24. A B C D
25. A B C D
26. A B C D
27. A B C D
28. A B C D
29. A B C D
30. A B C D
31. A B C D
32. A B C D
33. A B C D
34. A B C D
35. A B C D
36. A B C D
37. A B C D
38. A B C D
39. A B C D
40. A B C D
41. A B C D
42. A B C D
43. A B C D
44. A B C D
45. A B C D
46. A B C D
47. A B C D
48. A B C D
49. A B C D
50. A B C D

Section 2

1. A B C D
2. A B C D
3. A B C D
4. A B C D
5. A B C D
6. A B C D
7. A B C D
8. A B C D
9. A B C D
10. A B C D
11. A B C D
12. A B C D
13. A B C D
14. A B C D
15. A B C D
16. A B C D
17. A B C D
18. A B C D
19. A B C D
20. A B C D
21. A B C D
22. A B C D
23. A B C D
24. A B C D
25. A B C D
26. A B C D
27. A B C D
28. A B C D
29. A B C D
30. A B C D
31. A B C D
32. A B C D
33. A B C D
34. A B C D
35. A B C D
36. A B C D
37. A B C D
38. A B C D
39. A B C D
40. A B C D

Section 3

1. A B C D
2. A B C D
3. A B C D
4. A B C D
5. A B C D
6. A B C D
7. A B C D
8. A B C D
9. A B C D
10. A B C D
11. A B C D
12. A B C D
13. A B C D
14. A B C D
15. A B C D
16. A B C D
17. A B C D
18. A B C D
19. A B C D
20. A B C D
21. A B C D
22. A B C D
23. A B C D
24. A B C D
25. A B C D
26. A B C D
27. A B C D
28. A B C D
29. A B C D
30. A B C D
31. A B C D
32. A B C D
33. A B C D
34. A B C D
35. A B C D
36. A B C D
37. A B C D
38. A B C D
39. A B C D
40. A B C D
41. A B C D
42. A B C D
43. A B C D
44. A B C D
45. A B C D
46. A B C D
47. A B C D
48. A B C D
49. A B C D
50. A B C D